KU-466-978

CONTENTS

Financial Stability and Business Sustainability

Solicitors' Fees

Solicitors' Outlays

Party Litigants

Stamp Taxes

List of Principal Statutory Instruments Included

Note: All fees are up to date to 30th June 2016

FINANCIAL STABILITY AND BUSINESS SUSTAINABILITY

Introduction

Most firms have had a tough time since the start of the recession and the finances of many are fragile. Several have gone into administration and many more across the UK are said to be in difficulty.

Profitability has reduced since 2008 and most firms have depleted reserves. The real issue is not profit, however, but cash and this is made more acute by a greater realisation on the part of most banks that solicitors are not necessarily the "safe bet" they were once presumed to be. They are often not as willing to lend as freely as they once did.

Indeed, part of the problem is that historically some banks lent too freely to law firms, often funding not just the overdraft and loans to the firm, but also Professional Practice Finance Loans to incoming partners. In effect, they were funding both sides of the balance sheet. Perhaps they were attracted by the sizeable client accounts law firms could bring, perhaps law firms were simply viewed as good quality clients, however the result is that now, if a firm gets into difficulty, the banks can be very exposed – more exposed than might initially be indicated by the firm's balance sheet.

Those banks, which were previously content to lend to solicitors without a proper assessment of all the factors looked at in other sectors, have now changed their parameters. Firms should expect banks to form a judgement of the lending risk informed by a critical review of up-to-date financial information and an assessment of management and leadership. Lenders will also be more likely to seek ongoing financial data to monitor performance, and for term lending they may introduce covenants based around financial performance. This is just 'business as usual' when lending to most SMEs, but for some law firms it may seem like a different regime.

There are many reasons firms need to improve their financial stability and make their businesses more sustainable. It is in the interest of:

- The partners who own the firms, who not only depend on the practice for an income but who are likely to be personally liable if things go wrong;

- Their staff, whose livelihoods depend on the firm's survival and success;

- Their clients, who shouldn't have to suffer in terms of service or financially as a result of avoidable firm failures;

- The profession as a whole as firm failures damage the solicitor brand and reputation of us all.

Life has been tough in recent years, and even if economic conditions improve, we will continue to see greater competition once alternative business structures become a reality and firms undertaking legal aid face yet more cuts, in particular those that offer criminal legal aid. Firms need greater financial resilience in order to withstand further blows.

These Guidance Notes are intended to be a valuable and confidential method of allowing partners to assess and improve their firm's financial standing. They replace earlier advice on capital adequacy published by the Law Society of Scotland several years ago which detailed two ratios, a partnership solvency test and a measure of profitability. The former compared partner capital with the firm's total gross assets, including property and other fixed assets. The latter expressed the firm's profits as a percentage of fees. Some accountants may well still use these ratios. If you use them in your firm and find them helpful, you should continue to do so, however the new ratios outlined below are considered to be more relevant in today's more challenging environment.

Structure

This toolkit has four parts:

- **A self-diagnostic** – to help you assess the financial process risks in your firm (available on Law Society of Scotland website)

- This guide, which starts with information on the key benchmarks to consider (available on Law Society of Scotland website)
- A Financial Stability Self Diagnosis tool, which allows you to assess your firm's financial stability – this requires your firm's latest annual or management accounts (available on Law Society of Scotland website)
- A worked example of the Financial Stability Self Diagnosis ((available on Law Society of Scotland website)

We have also included guidance on:

- Guidance on partner capital and drawings
- Ten Practical steps to improve financial stability
- Some tips on getting paid
- The characteristics of really well run firm- a banker's view

Acknowledgements:

We are grateful to Andrew Otterburn, of Otterburn Legal Consulting for his work developing these materials, and to the others who assisted him, notably:

James Oliver and Scott Foster of Royal Bank of Scotland

Alasdair Swan of Bank of Scotland

Shirley McIntosh and Steve Carter of Baker Tilly, Chartered Accountants

BENCHMARKS TO HELP YOU ASSESS YOUR FIRM'S FINANCIAL STABILITY

Over the years accountants have developed various measures to assess a firm's financial stability and these ratios are still used today. They consider:

- Whether a firm is solvent
- Whether its capital reserves are adequate
- Profitability

The various ratios used are applied across a range of business sectors and are not specific to law firms. Despite being difficult to apply to the legal sector, they are regularly used by banks when making lending decisions.

Due to the change in the lending environment since the start of the recession, the ratios of bank borrowing relative to money provided by the partners has become an important issue. Many firms have been, and still are, far too dependent on bank funding and have inadequate capital invested by their partners.

It is very useful, therefore, to understand the ratios developed by the banks to assess the credit worthiness of their customers because these are calculations a bank manager is likely use with respect to your firm. The ratios are a very good starting point when assessing a firm's financial health, and are in many ways more useful than traditional accounting measures. Generally most banks will be interested in three key areas:

- The firm's viability
- The quality of the management team
- The bank's security

Financial Stability Ratios

This section illustrates six important financial stability ratios that you should calculate at least once a year, more often if necessary. The trend of the business measured consistently and regularly can be a powerful management tool. It would be useful to calculate these ratios for the previous two years to establish any trends and they could also be calculated quarterly or half-yearly to measure the rate of improvement and decline – you will need to extract a balance sheet from your firm's management accounts and make sure it includes realistic values in areas like work in progress. A better judgement of the firm's financial health can be made when the following checks are carried out regularly:

1. **Borrowings (non-property): partner capital**
2. **Borrowings (non-property): unfunded capital**
3. **Cash flow available for debt servicing (CFAFDS)**
4. **Solvency – the "Quick" ratio**
5. **Ratio of profits: drawings – the "make & take" ratio**
6. **Profit per equity partner**

1. Borrowings (non-property): partner capital

This key ratio compares the capital the partners have invested in the firm with bank borrowings. The partners should have at least as much invested as the bank, and ideally they should have significantly more invested than the bank.

How do you calculate this?

You will need the year end accounts produced by your accountants. This will show bank borrowing and also the partner capital invested in the firm – which may be split into current accounts and capital accounts – you should take the total.

The following is an example of a **firm with two partners**:

Table 1 Borrowings: partner capital		
Office account		−50,000
Bank loans		−75,000
Total (non-property) borrowings		−125,000
Partner capital		
Partner 1	50,000	
Partner 2 (newly appointed)	50,000	
		100,000
Ratio		125%
What might a bank want?[1]		**100% or less**

The firm in this example has relatively little partner capital compared to the amount invested by the bank – over time the partners would need to either increase the amount of their capital in the firm, reduce their borrowings, or probably a combination of the two.

Action needed?

If you have less capital invested than the bank it is a cause for concern – you should always have more capital invested – so that in the event of a change in bank lending policy you are not exposed. It can take time to change this and will be achieved by a combination of capital injection, reduced drawings, higher profitability and better billing and cash collection.

---

[1] The indications in this section of what a bank might look for are based on one bank's opinion – other banks might take a different view. Also the ratios a bank might expect could be influenced by the size of the firm – a firm with a high proportion of equity partners might have different ratios to a larger firm.

2. Borrowings (non-property): unfunded capital

The first ratio looks at borrowings shown on the balance sheet. However, many firms (larger firms in particular) have "off balance sheet" borrowings in the form of Professional Practice Finance Loans, and in some cases, these loans are substantial. Most partners appointed in the last ten years are likely to have one of these loans.

Taking the example firm, whereas Partner 1 has been with the firm for many years and has built up his capital, the new partner was given a Professional Practice Finance Loan to fund her capital of £50,000. This loan is secured on the assets of the partnership and is interest only with the capital being re-payable when she leaves the firm.

How do you calculate this?

The calculation is the same as shown in Table 1 except you also need to take into account any Professional Practice Finance Loans the partners have. These are not included in the firm's balance sheet – you will have to ask each partner for the balance.

Your bank will be very interested in the firm's "unfunded" or "free" capital relative to borrowings as illustrated in Table 2:

Table 2 Borrowings: unfunded capital		
Office account		−50,000
Bank loans		−75,000
Total (non-property) borrowings		−125,000
Professional practice finance loan		−50,000
Total borrowings		−175,000
Partner capital		
Partner 1	50,000	
Partner 2 (newly appointed)	50,000	
	100,000	
Less Professional practice finance loan	50,000	
Unfunded capital		50,000
Ratio		350%
What might a Bank want?[1]		**175% or less**

The unfunded capital ratio will be difficult for most firms to change, at least in the short term, due to the scale of change needed and the fact that these are long term loans – however, your bank will be aware of it and it will influence their view of you.

Action needed?

Most new partners have been given these loans in recent years on an interest only basis. These will often be younger partners in their 20's or 30's who will be unlikely to be easily able to replace them with their own capital. The problem with such loans is that they assume there will be an easy way of repaying them on retirement, and that may not necessarily be the case. There could be much sense in partners repaying elements of the capital over time or at the very least making provision for its repayment and this may well require an adjustment in profit shares.

It is possible that the banks will move towards making loans for future partners on a repayment basis, thereby avoiding potential problems when a partner leaves or retires.

3. Cash flow available for debt servicing (CFAFDS)

Banks are obviously very keen to ensure their customers are generating sufficient cash to service any debts they have – and this is something with which the partners need to be concerned. CFAFDS will be new to most solicitors, but it is an expression well understood by bankers.

How do you calculate this?

From your firm's annual accounts simply take the overall profit before tax and add back interest paid and depreciation. The amount of loan repayments should be apparent from the balance sheet and the partner drawings will be in a note to the accounts. Partner drawings comprise monthly drawings and payment of income tax (if the firm is a sole practitioner or partnership).

This concept is illustrated in Table 3 which indicates that the example firm is not generating sufficient cash to service its debts. Crucially, the calculation depends not just on a firm's profitability but also the level of partner drawings. If drawings had been £20,000 less (or profits £20,000 more) there would not have been a problem. The firm will gradually start running out cash.

Table 3   Cash flow available for debt servicing

Fees		450,000
Staff salaries		157,500
Overheads	160,000	
Add back depreciation (not a cash item)	–2,500	
Add back interest	–10,000	147,500
Net profit before drawings, interest and depreciation		145,000
Partner drawings		140,000
Cash flow available for debt servicing		**5,000**
Interest (say)		10,000
Annual loan repayments (say)		15,000
Surplus / (deficit)		–20,000

Action needed?

This is an important ratio. Your firm has to generate sufficient cash to service its debts. This can be addressed by improving profits however that may not be easy and may take time, so initially the solution will be for the partners to reduce their drawings. There is further guidance on drawings at www.lawscot. org.uk/business-sustainability.

In the example, we have added back depreciation, as this is not a "cash item" but an accounting adjustment. The cash impact of any capital expenditure is felt at the time of purchase (if it is bought outright) or when monthly payments are made if it is bought on finance. Depreciation is merely an accounting device to adjust the firm's profits over the life of an asset.

It is not a cash item, so has been added back, however, depreciation has the effect of building a cash reserve towards an asset's replacement. If it is being utilised to fund drawings and loan repayments it will not be available when the asset is replaced. Ideally you need to generate sufficient cash **in addition** to any depreciation.

4. Solvency – the "Quick" ratio

The "Quick" ratio compares a firm's current assets with its current liabilities and assesses broadly whether it is able to meet its liabilities.

How do you calculate this?

All of the figures you will need are in the balance sheet in your firm's annual accounts. The calculation compares the firm's current assets (debtors, work in progress and cash) with its current liabilities (overdraft, short term loans, VAT, PAYE, trade creditors, etc).

Depending on the nature of your work, you will probably not include the full value of work in progress in this calculation because some work can take months to be paid.

The calculations below also include an allowance for partner income tax due within the next six months because that is also a liability the firm will need to fund. It is not technically a liability of the firm (it is a personal liability of each partner). However, in practice most firms will pay it on behalf of the partners, having previously retained part of partner profits for this purpose.

Table 4 illustrates the calculation and shows a healthy position, primarily because of the firm's work in progress:

Table 4   Current assets : Current liabilities (incl. WIP)

	£
Current assets	
Debtors	100,000
Work in progress/accrued income	150,000
Total	250,000
Current liabilities:	
Overdraft	50,000
VAT/PAYE	45,000
Partner income tax	25,000
Creditors	40,000
Total	160,000
Quick ratio	**1.6**

Accrued income

If your firm is an LLP, "work in progress" will be shown in your accounts under two headings – work in progress and accrued income:

- **Work in progress** is in respect of time where there is no contractual right to bill the matter at the balance sheet date. It is valued at cost and should be excluded from this calculation as it is unlikely to be paid any time soon;

- **Accrued income** is time where the matter has reached a point where there is a contractual right to the income. It is valued at selling price and is similar to a debtor. However, the fact that it is included as income for accounts purposes does not necessarily mean it is going to be paid in the next 3 or 4 months. If it was in respect of, say, an executry, it would be reasonable to include it in full, but if it was in respect of a litigation matter payment may be many months off. You should take a view on what proportion of the accrued income is going to be paid soon and include that.

If your firm is a partnership or if you are a sole principal your accounts may also include a line for accrued income, however many will simply show a single figure for work in progress. All firms are required to recognise accrued income for tax purposes although partnerships and sole principals are not required to include it in their annual accounts. The accounts of most smaller partnerships will simply include a single line for work in progress.

Table 5 repeats the calculation but includes just part of the WIP because the partners estimate 25% might be billed and paid reasonably quickly:

Table 5 Current assets : Current liabilities (reduced WIP)			
			£
Current assets			
Debtors			100,000
Work in progress/accrued income	150,000	25%	37,500
Total			137,500
Current liabilities:			
Overdraft			50,000
VAT/PAYE			45,000
Partner income tax			25,000
Creditors			40,000
Total			160,000
Quick ratio			**0.9**

This provides a more realistic assessment and indicates that the firm is (almost) able to cover its short-term liabilities. This calculation is prudent but is also a reasonable reflection of the firm's true position.

Action needed?

This is another important ratio. It needs to be at least 1.0 and something higher, like 1.3 would be even better. If it is below 1 it is an indication the firm is insolvent and that action is needed to strengthen its balance sheet – probably by the partners injecting more capital. You will need to obtain advice from your accountants and there may be legal implications if you are trading as a company.

---

5.   Ratio of profits: drawings – the "make & take" ratio

Most of the ratios discussed so far concern to the levels of borrowing relative to partner capital and the main way this can be improved is often to leave more profit within the firm by reducing partner drawings. This ratio compares drawings with profits and is illustrated in tables 6a and 6b, which relate to the small firm illustrated already and also show a larger firm with 20 partners:

How do you calculate this?

Simply take the profits available for the partners as shown in the accounts and compare this to total drawings in the accounts. This will comprise monthly drawings and payments of income tax.

Table 6a   "Make & Take" ratio – accounts basis – 2 partner firm

	£ Accounts basis
Fees	400,000
Opening work in progress/accrued income	−100,000
Closing work in progress/accrued income	150,000
Income	450,000
Staff salaries and overheads	317,500
Net profit per accounts	**132,500**
Monthly drawings	79,500
Partner income tax	53,000
Total drawings	**132,500**
"Make & Take" ratio	100%

Table 6b   "Make & Take" ratio – accounts basis – 20 partner firm

	£ Accounts basis
Fees	10,500,000
Opening work in progress/accrued income	−2,000,000
Closing work in progress/accrued income	2,500,000
Income	11,000,000
Staff salaries and overheads	8,000,000
Net profit per accounts	**3,000,000**
Monthly drawings	1,800,000
Partner income tax	1,200,000
Total drawings	**3,000,000**
"Make & Take" ratio	100%

The calculations for both firms appears to indicate all is well – drawings do not exceed the profits being generated.

The "Make & Take" ratio illustrated above is a useful starting point, however "profit" is not the same as cash. Because a firm's profits are affected by changes in debtors and work in progress, the profits shown in a firm's accounts may be very different to the cash in the bank.

In the 20 partner firm, the apparent profits shown in the accounts are £3m however part of these profits (£1/2m) are due to an increase in work in progress. The "cash profit" actually available for the partners to draw is £2.5m. The position of the two-partner firm is even worse – profits as shown in the accounts are £132,000, however £50,000 of this relates to an increase in work in progress and may take months to be translated into cash in the bank. Tables 7a and 7b show the cash position:

> **How do you calculate this?**
> To calculate the "cash" profit, take the profits figure as shown in the accounts and adjust it for any increase/decrease in work in progress. If debtors have changed significantly you could include that movement as well as that also affects the cash available, however you must avoid the calculations becoming over complicated.

Table 7a   "Make & Take" ratio – cash basis – 2 partner firm

	£	£
	Accounts basis	Cash basis
Fees	400,000	400,000
Opening work in progress /accrued income	-100,000	-100,000
Closing work in progress /accrued income	150,000	150,000
Income	450,000	450,000
Staff salaries and overheads	317,500	317,500
Net profit per accounts	132,500	132,500
Adjust for WIP movement (paper profit)		-50,000
Cash profit		82,500
Monthly drawings	79,500	79,500
Partner income tax	53,000	53,000
Total drawings	132,500	132,500
"Make & Take" ratio	100%	161%

Table 7b   "Make & Take" ratio – cash basis – 20 partner firm

	£	£
	Accounts basis	Cash basis
Fees	10,500,000	10,500,000
Opening work in progress /accrued income	–2,000,000	–2,000,000
Closing work in progress /accrued income	2,500,000	2,500,000
Income	11,000,000	11,000,000
Staff salaries and overheads	8,000,000	8,000,000
Net profit per accounts	3,000,000	3,000,000
Adjust for WIP movement (paper profit)		-500,000
Cash profit		2,500,000
Monthly drawings	1,800,000	1,800,000
Partner income tax	1,200,000	1,200,000
Total drawings	3,000,000	3,000,000
"Make & Take" ratio	100%	120%

Action needed?

Unless the firm has substantial cash balances, or bank agreement has been obtained, drawings should **not** exceed profits, so this ratio should always be less than 100%. If the firm has to fund any loan repayments the drawings need to take account of this.

Because the accounts profit takes account of changes in work in progress the apparent profit might not actually be available to take – it is a paper profit and may take several months to actually be translated into cash – so drawings should be constrained to the actual cash likely to be available. This is often a difficult figure to predict, but as a rule of thumb drawings might be restricted to 75% of profits. This also leaves some headroom for funding working capital.

6. Profit per equity partner

Each year the Law Society publishes the Cost of Time Survey which reports the profitability of firms across the country. It is very useful to compare the profitability of your firm with these published figures and consider whether your firm has performed as well as you might have expected? The profitability of firms in recent years is shown in the chart:

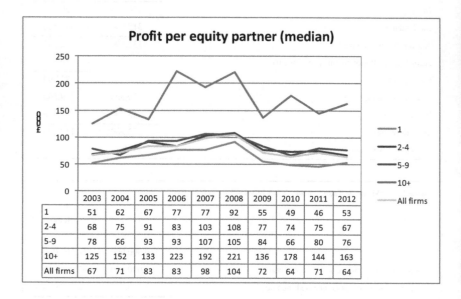

Profit per equity partner (median)

	2003	2004	2005	2006	2007	2008	2009	2010	2011	2012
1	51	62	67	77	77	92	55	49	46	53
2-4	68	75	91	83	103	108	77	74	75	67
5-9	78	66	93	93	107	105	84	66	80	76
10+	125	152	133	223	192	221	136	178	144	163
All firms	67	71	83	83	98	104	72	64	71	64

The chart of profit per equity partner is before any allowance for equity partner notional salaries.

How do you calculate this?

The figures you will need will be shown in the profit and loss account in your firm's annual accounts. Simply take the total profits and divide by the number of equity partners. If your firm is a limited company you will need to add back any directors' remuneration to the profit figure.

Table 8   Profit per equity partner

	£
Income (fees + change in work in progress)	450,000
Staff salaries	157,500
Overheads (including interest and depreciation)	160,000
Net profit	132,500
Profit per partner	66,250

This firm achieved profits very close to the median for firms of its size. This is the **average** profit per **equity** partner:

- the two partners may not share profits equally – the senior partner may take a higher share, so this is purely the average;

- it is after allowance for the salaries of any salaried partners, who will be included in staff salaries

In order to understand why your firm is doing well (or not so well) you will need to analyse the figures in more detail. The annual Cost of Time Report contains a range of key benchmarks you may want to look at together with a pro-forma for you to calculate these benchmarks for your own firm.

GUIDANCE ON PARTNER CAPITAL AND DRAWINGS

Partner capital

Partner capital is used to fund:

- Long-term assets such as offices and IT

- A firm's working capital – its work in progress and debtors

Broadly the partners might contribute 10-30% of the cost of long-term assets and should borrow **on a long-term basis** to fund the rest (i.e. it would not be funded out of the overdraft). They would normally contribute at least 50% of the firm's working capital with the balance being provided through the firm's overdraft.

It is very important that partners **do** invest sufficient in their firm. It is also very important that they **make provision for partner tax**, ideally by a monthly transfer to a separate deposit account. Many smaller firms do very little tax planning and the actual tax bill in January can come as a shock. To quote one tax partner, "Lawyers are amongst the worst at leaving their tax returns to the last minute and then complaining about their unexpected tax bill".

Firms should be wary of advice that they should not have too much money that has been taxed tied up in their firm as it is not an efficient use of money. Some accountants may also try to devise complex ways of minimising the tax their clients pay. Paying too much tax is not the number one problem for most firms. It is very important to have sufficient partner capital invested and remarkably easy for firms to get into difficulty if too little partner capital is retained in the firm.

It is quite easy (at least in theory) to set the working capital a firm needs. Let's take the example of a new firm with two partners, one fee earner and two secretaries:

Budget for year one	£
Partners @ £50,000 drawings and allowance for tax each	100,000
Employed solicitor	40,000
Secretaries @ £15,000 each	30,000
Cashier	20,000
	190,000
NIC and pension contributions (say 15%)	13,500
	203,500
Rent, and other overheads	156,500
	360,000
Per month	30,000
The firm has to bill £30,000 a month to break even	

Scenario 1

Assume the firm undertakes mainly residential conveyancing and matters are typically billed and paid on completion within (for simplicity) four weeks. Cash flow for the first six months is summarised below. It is assumed that:

- work is billed at the end of the month and paid immediately on completion
- that there is no opening bank balance
- that at this early stage the firm is just billing the £30,000 a month to break even

	Month 1	Month 2	Month 3	Month 4	Month 5	Month 6
Brought forward	0	−30,000	−30,000	−30,000	−30,000	−30,000
Payments	−30,000	−30,000	−30,000	−30,000	−30,000	−30,000
Income		30,000	30,000	30,000	30,000	30,000
Carried forward	−30,000	−30,000	−30,000	−30,000	−30,000	−30,000

The two partners need to provide working capital of £30,000 because at any one time one month's salaries and overheads have to be funded. Assuming there will be slippage they could assume a need to fund £50,000 of which half would come from the bank and half from themselves.

Scenario 2

The table below looks at the same firm but assumes a longer billing cycle, and that it takes three months to be paid. No cash comes in until month 4 and indicates funding is needed of at least £90,000. They might work on the basis that they were going to need to fund, say, £120,000, and once again half would come from the partners.

	Month 1	Month 2	Month 3	Month 4	Month 5	Month 6
Brought forward	0	−30,000	−60,000	−90,000	−90,000	−90,000
Payments	−30,000	−30,000	−30,000	−30,000	−30,000	−30,000
Income				30,000	30,000	30,000
Carried forward	−30,000	−60,000	−90,000	−90,000	−90,000	−90,000

These are **very** simple illustrations, however, the principle is that the partners need to ensure there is enough cash available to pay the firm's salaries and overheads, and that it should be broadly possible to predict the money that will be paid out and the income coming in. They need to fund the difference.

Tax on accrued income

It is important to understand that because the tax partners pay is based on a full valuation of accrued income that tax will have to be funded, even though the firm may not actually have been paid by the client. The work is taxable regardless of whether the firm has received the cash, so not only is it necessary to fund the actual monthly expenses such as salaries, overheads and drawings, but also make provision for the business tax that will become due.

Drawings

The general rule for determining drawings is that drawings should not exceed profits, however, as discussed earlier in this guide:

* allowance must be made for loan repayments;

* profit is not the same as **cash in the bank** because part of a firm's profits may have been created by a change in work in progress. They are paper profits – not cash that is available for drawings.

Table 9 (below) illustrates three options for the drawings of the 20 partner example firm discussed earlier.

The firm fully accounts for work in progress in its accounts as it is an LLP so its accounts are prepared strictly in accordance with UK GAAP. The budget for the coming year predicts an increase in WIP of £500k. It also assumes loan repayments of £500k. The table indicates three possible scenarios for the level of drawings the partners could take:

Column 1 indicates expected profits of £3m. After making allowance for partner tax at, say, 40% so long as partner drawings do not exceed £1.8m over the year or £150,000 a month, their capital accounts will be maintained as drawings will not exceed profits;

<u>Column 2</u> makes allowance for the £500k in loan repayments that will have to be paid during the year, and indicates that if the partners were to draw at that level they would exceed the cash available. The partners need to restrict their drawings to £1.3m or £108,000 a month in order to allow for these loan repayments;

<u>Column 3</u> makes allowance for the impact of the change in WIP on profits – of the £3m profit, part is due to the increase in WIP and is a paper profit. It may take months to be paid. Partner drawings will need to reflect this as well and the actual cash that is likely to be available for drawings is just £800,000 – and this is less than 1/3 the total that might have been taken.

Table 9 Drawings – Example – 20 partner firm			
	£	£	£
Fees	10,500,000	10,500,000	10,500,000
Opening work in progress	-2,000,000	-2,000,000	-2,000,000
Closing work in progress	2,500,000	2,500,000	2,500,000
Income	11,000,000	11,000,000	11,000,000
Staff salaries and overheads	8,000,000	8,000,000	8,000,000
Net profit per accounts	3,000,000	3,000,000	3,000,000
Allow for tax (say 40%)	1,200,000	1,200,000	1,200,000
Available after tax to draw	1,800,000	1,800,000	1,800,000
Loan repayments		500,000	500,000
Available after loan repayments			1,300,000
Adjust for WIP movement			500,000
Cash available			800,000
Available to draw	1,800,000	1,300,000	500,000
Per month	150,000	108,333	41,667
Per partner	7,500	5,417	2,083

So the issue of drawings is complex, and in many ways is not helped by the basis of preparing accounts, especially for an LLP, which, in an attempt to show a "true" position actually produce figures that are far removed from the real cash position.

Certainly the old maxim that drawings must not exceed profits no longer holds true. The new maxim is that they must not exceed **cash profits** and these need to be adjusted for any loan repayments. A rule of thumb might be that drawings should not exceed 75% of profits.

TEN PRACTICAL STEPS TO IMPROVE FINANCIAL STABILITY

1. Each firm should appoint one of its partners (or managers) to monitor its financial stability. This person could (but does not have to be) the Cash Room Manager. The person nominated should review the firm's overall financial position – both historically as shown in its annual and management accounts – but perhaps more importantly, projecting forwards, and should report to his/her fellow partners at least quarterly on the firm's financial stability. He/she should ensure the following;

2. A budget should be prepared at the start of each financial year, to include a monthly cash flow forecast. The partner capital required and levels of drawings should be reviewed as part of setting this budget;

3. Management accounts should be prepared at least every three months showing the firm's income, expenditure and profit to date, compared to this budget;

4. Key financial information such as the office account balance, cash collected and fees billed should be circulated to all partners or managers on a weekly (or even daily) basis. Certain information should be provided monthly such as cash collected, fees billed, numbers of new matters opened, amounts owing from clients (debtors), unbilled work in progress, and outlays paid but not yet billed;

5. The partners should ensure their drawings do not exceed the firm's <u>cash</u> profits – in other words be aware how much of your firm's profits are represented by changes in WIP or debtors and are paper profits as opposed to cash in the bank – and make allowance for loan repayments. In other words link your drawings to expected available cash;

6. The cash flow forecast should be updated on at least a quarterly basis. If you are close to your overdraft facility you may find it very useful to prepare a detailed cash plan:

   a. For the next 12 weeks on a weekly basis;

   b. Expenditure is easy to predict. Include salaries, drawings, rent, PAYE, VAT, income tax, etc;

   c. Make a best estimate of the money coming in each week, in particular any significant receipts;

   d. Update weekly for the actual payments and receipts and revise the forecasts.

   The advantage of a weekly forecast is that it helps you to manage the cash available, and is likely to improve cash flow (because you will be focused on it and are more likely to chase clients for payment). It also helps confidence with your bank.

7. At least once a year the key ratios outlined in this guide should be calculated and trends considered at a partners' meeting. Consider what can be done to improve them. In particular look at:

   a. Total (non property) borrowings : partner capital

   b. Total (non property) borrowings : unfunded capital

   c. Cash flow available for debt servicing (CFAFDS)

   d. The "Quick" ratio

   e. Profit per equity partner;

   f. The "make & take" ratio.

8. Each month an amount should be transferred to a separate deposit account in respect of VAT so that when this becomes due each quarter the firm already has funds available to pay it. Similarly transfer an amount each month into a deposit account in respect of partner income tax – it means that you have the funds to pay it in January and July;

9. Set up a "sinking fund" – and put money aside for future "knowns and unknowns" – to pay out partners, to pay for property dilapidations, to enable you to move quickly on a deal, to help the firm get through a crisis;

10. Make sure everyone is focussed on billing – that everything that can be billed is billed and that it is then chased and gets paid. Circulate appropriate financial reports to all fee earners and support staff so that everyone understands the importance not just of billing, but also of getting paid.

In April 2013 the Solicitors Regulation Authority[2] published guidance for firms in England & Wales which firms in Scotland may also find helpful. They published the following list of good behaviours to aim for and poor behaviours to avoid:

Poor behaviours

- Drawings exceeding net profits
- High borrowing to net asset ratios
- Increasing firm indebtedness by maintaining drawing levels
- Firms controlled by an "inner circle" of senior management
- Key financial information not shared with "rank and file" partners
- Payments made to partners irrespective of "cash at the bank"
- All net profits drawn, no "reserve capital pot" retained
- Short-term borrowings to fund partners' tax bills
- VAT receipts used as "cash received" resulting in further borrowings to fund VAT due to HMRC
- Partners out of touch with office account bank balances
- Heavy dependence on high overdraft borrowings

Good behaviours

- All partners regularly receive full financial information including office account bank balances
- Drawings are linked to cash collection targets and do not exceed net profits
- Provision is made to fund partners' tax from income received
- A capital element is retained from profit, and a capital reserve account built up
- Premises costs are contained
- Profitability levels are tested and unprofitable work is (properly) dropped

SOME TIPS ON GETTING PAID

Try to ensure you are paid as quickly as possible after the work has been done:

- Ensure you are clear in your initial engagement letter about likely fees; that you will issue interims; that you will issue your final bill promptly; that you will expect payment within x days;
- If it is a commercial client, check their credit rating. If it is a long standing client check it again as it may have changed from last month;
- Send regular interims – monthly if the matter is significant, quarterly for all other matters. Clients prefer to know where they are, and it avoids surprises at the end, and of course it helps your cash flow;
- Bill promptly at the end of the matter and let the client know it is coming. The fee earner should speak to the client and explain if the bill is different to what has been discussed previously;
- Let your cash room chase for payment. Don't interfere or hamper them;
- Do everything you can to avoid bad debts. Any increase in bad debts will come straight off your bottom line profits.

There is a particular danger that fee earners under pressure to maximise their fees will take on clients who may not be able to pay. Risk management is an area where many firms are weak – it is good practice:

---

[2] Reproduced from the website of the Solicitors Regulation Authority

- To identify a named supervisor for each area of work the firm undertakes;

- To maintain lists of work the firm will and will not undertake, together with the generic risks and causes of claims associated with each area, and make sure this is fully communicated to staff;

- For each fee earner to undertake an opening risk assessment for each new matter against these criteria. Experienced lawyers instinctively do this – and will know when a new client or matter doesn't feel quite right, but a new fee earner who lacks the equivalent experience may not. Require each fee earner to indicate on the file that they have undertaken an opening risk assessment, and that in particular they have considered whether the client will be able to pay.

THE CHARACTERISTICS OF REALLY WELL RUN FIRM- A BANKER'S VIEW

1. **Strategy /Vision** – Where do the firm/partners want to be in three years' time (position in market place, profitability, breadth of service offering)? What are opportunities for services provided and the best delivery channels? Will they withstand fluctuations in market demand? Willingness of Partners to re-invent historic models.

2. **Structure** – have they got this right? Partnership/LLP/Limited Company or formation of Service Company. Bank Funding – Capital structure appropriate?

3. **Governance Policy** – frequency of meetings – decision makers – Minutes of meetings. In larger firms – board rotation – sub committees for project work. Appointment of Non Exec Directors. Culture/Ethics and Reputation.

4. **Managing People** (morale and incentives) – Key Performance Measures, career progression, retaining trainees, and secondments.

5. **Finance function** – Is it helping us deliver our strategic direction? Role of FD or Cash Room Partner. Will they challenge Partners? – How we go about 'making (cash) versus take (accounting profits)' Audit provider input.

6. **Financial** – 'Keep it simple = easily understood' Management Information – monthly Profit and Loss/ Balance Sheet v Budgets (sensitised as to break even and downturn) and Cash Flow (on cash basis) Credit control – Fee collection and WIP management (Lock Up Days). WIP write off frequency. Bad and Doubtful Provisioning. Billing – Fixed Fee versus hourly rates?

7. **Cost Control** – Staffing levels (support: Fee Earners), Property Costs, Outsourcing of front end services (cash room?). Capital expenditure – Funding options (Asset Finance, Term Loans) and for e.g. Partner Pay Outs/Tax Funding/Technology. Legal Process Outsourcing (LPOs) In-House Counsel is likely to drive change in Panel work. Larger Firms better placed to commoditise. Creation of separate legal entities for volume work (e.g. PI work).

8. **Technology** – Is Technology being used to maximise cost benefits/streamline activities/enhance investment in different areas of the business? E.g.: Cloud Computing. E-billing. Web development. Full utilisation of existing Client Management systems.

9. **Profit Distribution** – Timing and Retention. Drawings v cash available. Funding of tax- by partners or firm tax reserve.

10. **Equity v fixed Salary** – Partner strategy for Lock Step. Fee earner retention, new arrivals, departures what issues this creates

11. **Client base** – Breadth and Depth of Customer base – do you know what they want you to deliver? Do you understand your 'Will bank'? Over reliance on particular Clients. Diversification and De-Risking strategies. How are clients affected by regulations and general economy (Understanding their Business)? Client inter-action = Customer face to face/Seminars/Podcast Marketing

12. **New business** - Who are the rain makers-Business Development strategy? How do we manage business we are not experts in?

13. **Succession** – merger options – Is merger the best option (not just to scale up Revenues) – may give Senior Partners exit option and future career progression for younger partners. Economies of scale. What plans does firm have for trainees/ recruitment/lateral hires? What formula will be used to ascertain value of lateral hires?

14. Risk management – People/Partners (leaving). Client Defection and ability to pay. Dependence on dominant clients. Letters of Engagement -Terms and Transparency. Client profitability. PI Claims-history. Complaints -handling. Relationship with Bank. ABS implications.

15. Credit card payment – Consider what transactions and clients credit card payment may be appropriate for.

SOLICITORS' FEES

Solicitors (Scotland) Act 1980 (c 46)

[Section 61A was inserted in the Solicitors (Scotland) Act 1980 (c 46) by s 36(3) of the Law Reform (Miscellaneous Provisions) (Scotland) Act 1990 (c 40) and took effect on 4th July 1992 (SI 1992 No 1599).]

Solicitors' fees

61A.—(1) Subject to the provisions of this section, and without prejudice to—

(a) section 32(1)(i) of the Sheriff Courts (Scotland) Act 1971; or

(b) section 5(h) of the Court of Session Act 1988,

where a solicitor and his client have reached an agreement in writing as to the solicitor's fees in respect of any work done or to be done by him for his client it shall not be competent, in any litigation arising out of any dispute as to the amount due to be paid under any such agreement, for the court to remit the solicitor's account for taxation.

(2) Subsection (1) is without prejudice to the court's power to remit a solicitor's account for taxation in a case where there has been no written agreement as to the fees to be charged.

(3) A solicitor and his client may agree, in relation to a litigation undertaken on a speculative basis, that, in the event of the litigation being successful, the solicitor's fee shall be increased by such a percentage as may, subject to subsection (4), be agreed.

(4) The percentage increase which may be agreed under subsection (3) shall not exceed such limit as the court may, after consultation with the Council, prescribe by act of sederunt.

Solicitors (Scotland) (Client Communication) Practice Rules 2005

Rules dated 24th March 2005, made by the Council of the Law Society of Scotland under section 34(1) of the Solicitors (Scotland) Act 1980 and approved by the Lord President of the Court of Session in terms of section 34(3) of the said Act.

Citation and Commencement

1. (1) These Rules may be cited as the Solicitors (Scotland) (Client Communication) Practice Rules 2005.
   (2) These Rules shall come into operation on 1st August 2005.

Definitions and Interpretation

2. (1) In these Rules, unless the context otherwise requires:–

"**the 1986 Act**" means the Legal Aid (Scotland) Act 1986;
"**the Act**" means the Solicitors (Scotland) Act 1980;
"**advice and assistance**" means advice and assistance as defined in section 6(1) of the 1986 Act to which Part II of the 1986 Act applies;
"**civil legal aid**" has the meaning given to it in section 13(2) of the 1986 Act;
"**client**" means a person who instructs a solicitor or to whom a solicitor tenders for business;
"**the Council**" means the Council of the Society;
"**legal aid**" has the meaning given to it in section 41 of the 1986 Act;
"**the Society**" means the Law Society of Scotland;
"**solicitor**" means a solicitor holding a practising certificate under the Act and includes a firm of solicitors and an incorporated practice; and
"**special urgency work**" has the meaning given to it in Regulation 18 of the Civil Legal Aid (Scotland) Regulations 2002.

(2) The Interpretation Act 1978 applies to the interpretation of these Rules as it applies to the interpretation of an Act of Parliament.

(3) The headings to these Rules do not form part of these Rules.

Provision of Information

3. A solicitor shall when tendering for business or at the earliest practical opportunity   upon   receiving instructions to undertake any work on behalf of a client, provide the following information to the client in writing:

    (a)   details of the work to be carried out on behalf of the client;

    (b)   save where the client is being provided with legal aid or advice and assistance, details of either–

        (i)   an estimate of the total fee to be charged for the work, including VAT and outlays which may be incurred in the course of the work; or

        (ii) the basis upon which a fee will be charged for the work, including VAT and outlays which may be incurred in the course of the work;

    (c)   if the client is being provided with advice and assistance or legal aid–

        (i)   where advice and assistance is being provided, details of the level of contribution required from the client, and

        (ii) where civil legal aid, special urgency work or advice and assistance is being provided, an indication of the factors which may affect any contribution which may be required from the client or any payment which may be required from property recovered or preserved;

    (d)   the identity of the person or persons who will principally carry out the work on behalf of the client; and

    (e)   the identity of the person whom the client should contact if the client becomes concerned in any way with the manner in which the work is being carried out.

Exceptions

4. (1) Where a client regularly instructs a solicitor in the same type of work, he need not be provided with the information set out in rule 3 in relation to a new instruction to do that type of work, provided that he has previously been supplied with that information in relation to a previous instruction to do that type of work and is informed of any differences between that information and the information which, if this paragraph (1) did not apply, would have been required to be provided to him in terms of rule 3.

(2) Where there is no practical opportunity for a solicitor to provide the   information set out in rule 3 to a client before the conclusion of the relevant work for that client then that information need not be provided to that client.

(3) Where a client is a child under the age of 12 years then the information set out in rule 3 need not be provided to that client.

Waiver

5. The Council shall have the power to waive any of the provisions of these Rules either generally or in any particular circumstances or case, provided that such waiver may be made subject to such conditions as the Council may in its discretion determine.

Professional Misconduct

6. Breach of these Rules may be treated as professional misconduct for the purposes of Part IV of the Act (Complaints and Disciplinary Proceedings).

Repeals

7. The Solicitors (Scotland) (Client Communication) (Residential Conveyancing) Practice Rules 2003 are hereby revoked.

Guidance Notes on the Solicitors (Scotland) (Client Communication) Practice Rules 2005

The above Practice Rules will come into force on 1st August 2005. They have been made under Section 34 of the Solicitors (Scotland) Act 1980. The Rules have been approved by the Lord President. They require solicitors to provide information in writing to clients about certain specific matters namely

(a) Details of the work to be done;

(b) An estimate of the total fee including VAT and outlays or the basis upon which the fee will be charged, including VAT and outlays;

(c) Details of any contribution towards Legal Advice & Assistance or Legal Aid and details of the effect of preservation or recovery of any property if relevant;

(d) Who will do the work;

(e) Who the client(s) should contact if they wish to express concern about the manner in which the work is being carried out.

With certain exceptions (see below) this information must be provided at the earliest practicable opportunity upon receiving instructions. It does not have to be contained in a single letter to comply with the Rule, but unless there is a particular reason why it cannot be done in a single letter, there is a risk of omitting certain of the information if it is done in different stages.

If a firm is tendering for new business, either from an established client or a new client, the information can be given when tendering. If it is, and the tender is accepted, there is no need to repeat the information subsequently.

It is quite in order to give the client more information than is necessary to comply with the Rule, but the Rule sets out the minimum requirement.

Exceptions

There are only 3 automatic exceptions to the Rule:

First where a client regularly instructs a solicitor in the same type of work, the information does not have to be provided repeatedly but it will have to be provided on at least the first occasion, and it will have to be updated if there is a change in the information previously provided. Client means any person who instructs a solicitor, which includes lenders as well as individual purchasers or borrowers. If the fee for the lenders work is included in the fee to be charged to the individual purchaser or borrower, that is all that need be said about fees in the information given to the lender.

The second exception is where there is no practical opportunity for the information to be provided before the conclusion of the work. That means where the work is completed at a single meeting. For example a client who may be about to go on holiday and wishes to make a will may have instructions implemented immediately and sign the will at the first meeting. It will not be necessary for solicitors receiving instructions on an agency basis to provide information to the principle solicitor acting, although it is prudent to have an agreed basis of charging for agency work.

The third exception is children under the age of 12. If the client is the child's parent or guardian (for example in a personal injury case) the information will still need to be provided.

Fees

With the withdrawal of the Society's Table of Fees, it will not be appropriate to refer to fees recommended by the Society. If, for example in executries, the file is to be feed by an external fee charger such as an Auditor or Law Accountant, the basis on which the external fee charger will be asked to fee up the file needs to be stated to the client needs to be included. If hourly rates are reviewed during the course of the work, the clients will need to be told about any increase or there is a risk that firms will be unable to charge the higher rate.

As well as the hourly rate any commission which will be charged on capital transactions or on the sale of a house would need to be included. In any matter where the account is being rendered on a detailed basis, the charges for letters, drafting papers, etc will need to be expressed as well as the hourly rate. They can be in a separate schedule referred to in the basic letter.

In terms of Section 61A of the Solicitors (Scotland) Act 1980, where a solicitor and client enter into a written fee charging agreement it is not competent for the Court to refer any dispute in the matter to the Auditor for taxation. Where an hourly rate is specified, and that is accepted in writing, the client would still be entitled to seek a taxation, but would not be able to challenge the agreed hourly rate at such a taxation.

It should be made clear at the outset whether the fee quoted is the fee to be charged or only an estimate. If it is not stated as an estimate and the client accepts it in writing, that could be regarded as a written fee charging agreement under Section 61A of the 1980 Act. If a client has been given an estimate, they should be advised in writing when it becomes known that the cost of work will materially exceed such an estimate. It is good practice to advise the client when the limit of the original estimate is being approached.

Information should be clear, and terms with which the client may not be familiar such as "outlays" may need to be briefly explained. If a payment to account is required, that should be clearly stated, as well as the consequences of failing to pay it on time. For example in a Court matter if the client is advised that failure to make a payment to account will lead to the solicitor withdrawing from acting, there is unlikely to be a professional difficulty about withdrawing from acting in compliance with that. However if the consequence is not stated, and the proof is approaching, solicitors could be vulnerable to a complaint if they withdraw at a late stage to the potential prejudice of the client.

If the clients costs are to be paid by a third party such as a Trade Union or Legal Expenses Insurer, specific details of the basis of charging do not need to be set out when writing to the individual client but any part of the fee which that client may be asked to pay should be included— such as a success fee in a speculative action.

While it is not strictly necessary to comply with the Practice Rule, it is also strongly recommended that any potential liability for other people's costs should be explained. This would include a tenant's liability to meet a landlord's fees as well as the potential liability for expenses in a Court action.

Executries and Trusts

In executries where the only executors are solicitors in the firm, the information should be provided to the residuary beneficiaries, as they will be meeting the fees out of their shares of the residue. In other executries the information should be provided to the non solicitor executors.

Legal Aid

It is not necessary to comply with the Rule for solicitors to explain the Statutory payment Scheme to Legal Aid clients in relation to Legal Advice & Assistance or Legal Aid. Solicitors may wish to forward copies of leaflets provided by SLAB to clients in receipt of Advice & Assistance or Legal Aid. If solicitors do wish to communicate detailed advice to clients about Advice & Assistance or Legal Aid, including for example the clients requirement to report changes in circumstances, that is optional and may be done in a separate letter.

Waivers

The Rules give the Council power to grant a waiver which may be subject to conditions. In practice this power will be delegated to the Professional Practice Committee, which meets monthly except in August. A specific reason should be given for seeking the waiver, and the request is likely to be continued for such information if it is not provided initially.

Failing to Comply with the Rules

The Rules state in terms that a breach may be treated as professional misconduct. For the avoidance of doubt, an occasional failure to send the information required, or sending information which does not fully comply with the Rule, is likely to be dealt with in the first instance as a matter for professional practice guidance. However regular failure to provide the information required may lead to a formal complaint about the solicitor's conduct, which may be categorised as professional misconduct.

Practice Guideline: Form of Accounts and Taxation

1. Accounts – preparation and presentation

(a) The form in which a solicitor presents an account is a matter for the solicitor's personal preference but if the person liable to pay requires details, the solicitor must give a narrative or summary sufficient to indicate the nature and the extent of the work done. If a breakdown is requested the solicitor should give such information as can readily be derived from the records, such as the total recorded time spent, the number and length of meetings, the number of letters and of telephone calls. No charge may be made for preparing the note of fee or for the provision of such information. However if having been given such information the party paying insists on a fully itemised account, the cost of preparing that may be charged to them.

(b) If the paying party is still dissatisfied the solicitor must inform them of the availability of taxation by an auditor and the procedure. If the payer requests a taxation without a fully itemised account, the solicitor may have such an account prepared at his own expense. That full account may be submitted for taxation even if it is for a greater amount than the original note of fee.

(c) A solicitor may submit the file to an auditor of court or a law accountant for assessment of the fee, but it is stressed that a unilateral reference of this kind does not constitute a taxation. Such an assessment of a fee must never be represented as a taxation or as having any official status. The fee for such a reference is not chargeable to the party paying unless that has been included in the terms of business intimated to the client at the outset. If the note of fee is disputed, the solicitor must advise of the right to taxation as above, although the fee note should be taxed by a different auditor from the one who prepared it.

2. Taxation

(a) Remit

The essence of taxation is that it proceeds upon either a remit by the court or a joint reference by both the solicitor and the party paying, including non-contentious cases in (c) below.

(b) Disputed accounts

When the party paying, whether client or third party, requires that the solicitor's account be taxed, the solicitor cannot refuse to concur in the reference unless the solicitor and client have entered into a written fee charging agreement in which the actual fee has been agreed, as opposed to the basis on which the fee is to be charged. The solicitor must forthwith submit the file and all relevant information including a note of fee or detailed account to the auditor. It is for the auditor to determine the procedure to be followed. In normal cases this will be a diet of taxation which should be intimated to the client by the solicitor. Evidence of: such intimation, which may be by ordinary first class post, may be required if the client does not appear at the diet. If either of the parties wishes to make written submissions, the auditor will ensure that each party is fully aware of the other's representations.

(c) Non-contentious cases

Taxation is necessary by law and in practice in certain circumstances. The accounts of a solicitor acting for:

an administrator of a company under the Insolvency Acts;

a liquidator appointed by the court;

a creditors' voluntary liquidator;

a trustee in bankruptcy;

a judicial factor;

curators of all kinds must be taxed.

A solicitor who acts:

as an administrator of a client's funds under a power of attorney where the granter is incapable;

in a representative capacity, e.g. a sole executor should have a fee note prepared or taxed by an auditor of court. A certificate by an auditor is appropriate in these cases.

A solicitor who is a co-executor with an unqualified person must not make a unilateral reference to the auditor for taxation. Such a reference needs the concurrence of the other executor. The auditor may require intimation of the taxation to any other party with an interest in the residue of the estate.

(d) Style of remit

A formal remit may be in the following form:

(place) (date). I, AB as Executor of the late CD and we, Messrs E & F, Solicitors to the Executor, hereby request the Auditor of the (Sheriff Court of /Court of Session) to tax the remuneration due and payable to the Solicitors for their whole work and responsibility in connection with (matter).

Signed: AB, E & F

This, however, is not essential; all the auditor requires is to be satisfied that the client is concurring in the request for taxation and accepting that it will be binding. It is often in practice a matter of agreement reached at an early meeting between solicitor and client. Any reasonable record of such an agreement having been reached will be sufficient for the auditor.

3. Expenses of taxation

The auditor will usually charge a fee for the taxation. It may be 3% or 4% of the amount of the account after taxation and may attract VAT. Any award of expenses of the taxation - not only the auditor's fee but also the time and expenses of parties attending - is wholly within the discretion of the auditor. If the matter is settled within the seven days preceding the diet of taxation the auditor may still charge a proportion of his fee, not exceeding 50%, at his discretion.

Solicitor and Client Accounts in the Sheriff Court

Act of Sederunt (Solicitor and Client Accounts in the Sheriff Court) 1992

(SI 1992 No 1434)

Remit of solicitor's account for taxation

2.—(1) Subject to section 61A(1) of the Solicitors (Scotland) Act 1980, the sheriff may remit the account of a solicitor to his client to the Auditor of Court for taxation.

(2) Where a remit is made under sub-paragraph (1)—

(a) the solicitor shall, within 21 days, lodge with the Auditor the account, which shall be in such form as shall enable the Auditor readily to establish the nature and extent of the work done to which the account relates and shall detail the outlays incurred by the solicitor, together with such supporting material as is necessary to vouch the items on the account;

(b) the Auditor shall assign a diet of taxation not earlier than fourteen days from the date he receives the account and intimate that diet forthwith to the solicitor;

(c) the solicitor shall then, forthwith, send by first class recorded delivery post a copy of the account lodged to the client (if such a copy has not already been sent to the client) and give notice in terms of Form A in the Schedule to this Act of Sederunt, of the date, time and place of the taxation to the client;

(d) the Auditor shall report his decision to the court and shall forthwith send a copy of his report to the solicitor and to the client; and

(e) the solicitor or the client may, provided that he or his representative has attended at the diet of taxation, lodge a note of reasoned objections to the report within seven days from the date of the report, and the sheriff shall dispose of such objections in a summary manner, with or without answers.

Taxation of litigation account

3.—(1) Where the Auditor taxes the account of a solicitor to his client in respect of the conduct of a litigation on behalf of the client, he—

(a) shall allow a sum in respect of such work and outlays as have been reasonably incurred;

(b) shall allow in respect of each item of work and outlay such sum as may be fair and reasonable having regard to all the circumstances of the case;

(c) shall, in determining whether a sum charged in respect of an item of work is fair and reasonable, take into account—

    (i) the complexity of the litigation and the number, difficulty or novelty of the questions raised;

    (ii) the skill, labour, specialised knowledge and responsibility involved;

    (iii) the time spent on the item of work and on the litigation as a whole;

    (iv) the number and importance of any documents or other papers prepared or perused without regard to length;

    (v) the place where and the circumstances (including the degree of expedition required) in which the solicitor's work or any part of it has been done;

    (vi) the amount or value of any money or property involved in the litigation; and

    (vii) the importance of the litigation or its subject matter to the client;

(d) shall presume (unless the contrary is demonstrated to his satisfaction) that—

    (i) an item of work or outlay was reasonably incurred if it was incurred with the express or implied approval of the client;

    (ii) the fee charged in respect of an item of work or outlay was reasonable if the amount of the fee or the outlay was expressly or impliedly approved by the client; and

(iii) an item of work or outlay was not reasonably incurred, or that the fee charged in respect of an item of work or outlay was not reasonable if the item of work, outlay or fee charged, was unusual in the circumstances of the case, unless the solicitor informed the client prior to carrying out the item of work or incurring the outlay that it might not be allowed (or that the fee charged might not be allowed in full) in a taxation in judicial proceedings between party and party; and

(e) may disallow any item of work or outlay which is not vouched to his satisfaction.

SCHEDULE Paragraph 2(2)(c)

Notice to Client Intimating Diet of Taxation of Solicitors' Account

FORM A

To: (*name and address*)

Date: (*date of posting*)

(*Name of solicitors*), Applicant v. [CD]. Respondent.

Case Number:

1. We enclose a copy of the solicitors' account in respect of which we seek payment.
2. The sheriff has remitted the account to the Auditor of Court for taxation (assessment).
3. The taxation hearing will take place at (*place*) Sheriff Court (*address*), in (*location*) on (*date and time*).
4. If you wish to object to any part of the account you must appear or be represented at the taxation hearing.
5. You will lose any right to object to the account if you do not appear or are not represented at the taxation hearing.

(*signed*)

Solicitors [for Pursuers]

(*address*)

IF YOU ARE UNCERTAIN ABOUT THE EFFECT OF THIS NOTICE CONSULT A SOLICITOR

Voluntary Pre-Action Protocols in Personal Injury, Diseases and Professional Negligence Claims

Voluntary pre-action protocols in respect of personal injury cases, disease cases, and professional negligence (except clinical negligence) cases are available for use in Scotland. Their terms have been agreed between the Law Society of Scotland and the Forum of Scottish Claims Managers representing most insurers. The protocols can be found on the Society's website www.lawscot.org.uk. The protocols are voluntary and not binding. Some insurance companies and self-insured bodies have not signed up to them at all.

There are related fees structures as set out below.

It is always open to a solicitor to offer to negotiate any claim in terms of one of the protocols and related fees structure e.g. where the value is higher or where the insurer is not in the Forum, but an insurer is not obliged to agree to that.

Personal Injury and Disease Claims settled after 1 January 2011

The fees for claims settled after 1 January 2011 and dealt with entirely under the Protocol are:

Instruction fee

On settlements up to and including £1,500-£370
On settlements over £1,500-£810

Completion fee

On settlements up to £2,500-25%
On the excess over £2,500 up to £5,000-15 %
On the excess over £5,000 up to £10,000-7.5 %
On the excess over £10,000 up to £20,000-5 %
On the excess over £20,000-2.5%

Personal Injury and Disease Claims settled after 1 July 2009 and before 1 January 2011

The fees for claims settled between 1 July 2009 and 31 December 2010 and dealt with entirely under the protocol are:

Instruction fee

On settlements up to and including £1,500-£358
On settlements over £1,500-£783

Completion fee

On settlements up to £2,500-25 %
On the excess over £2,500 up to £5,000-15 %
On the excess over £5,000 up to £10,000-7.5 %
On the excess over £10,000 up to £20,000-5 %
On the excess over £20,000-2.5%

Notes (irrespective of date)

(1) In addition, VAT (on all elements) and outlays will be payable.

NB Medical Agency Fees are not an agreed allowable outlay under the Protocol.

(2) In cases including payment to CRU the % fees will be calculated in accordance with the following examples:

  (a) Solatium £5,000

     Wage Loss £5,000

     CRU repayment £2,000

     Sum paid to Pursuer £8,000

     In these circumstances the scale fee will be based on £10,000 being the total value of the Pursuer's claim.

  (b) Settlement as above but repayment to the CRU is £6,000 and only £5,000 can be offset. Payment to the Pursuer is £5,000 and £6,000 to the CRU. The scale fee will be on £10,000 being the value of the pursuer's claim, as opposed to the total sum paid by the insurer – £11,000.

Professional Negligence Claims settled on or after 1st January 2011

In claims which are resolved without the need for litigation the claimant's agent will be entitled to recover fees from the professional or his insurers as follows:

Instruction fee

On all settlements: £1,041

Completion fee

(a)   On settlements up to £2,500 – 25%
(b)   On the excess over £2,500 up to £5,000-15%
(c)   On the excess over £5,000 up to £10,000-7.5%
(d)   On the excess over £10,000 up to £20,000-5%
(e)   On the excess over £20,000-2.5%

Professional Negligence Claims settled on or after 1st July 2009

Instruction fee

On all settlements: £ 1,006

Completion fee

(a)   On settlements up to £2,500-25%
(b)   On the excess over £2,500 up to £5,000-15%
(c)   On the excess over £5,000 up to £10,000-7.5%
(d)   On the excess over £10,000 up to £20,000- 5%
(e)   On the excess over £20,000-2.5%

Notes (irrespective of date)

(1) VAT will be payable in addition on all elements of the fee except where the claimant is VAT registered.

(2) Outlays reasonably incurred will be payable in addition.

Non-protocol claims

For claims which are not in one of the Protocols, there is no agreement which binds insurance companies to pay any particular fees to the claimant's solicitor. However most insurers will agree to pay fees based on what was Chapter 10 of the former Table of Fees recommended by the Society (which was withdrawn on 1 August 2005). Those fees were as follows:

Negotiation and completion fee

Settlements up to £2,500-25 %
On the excess over £2,500 up to £5,000-15 %
On the excess over £5,000 up to £10,000-7.5 %
On the excess over £10,000 up to £20,000-5 %
On the excess over £20,000-2.5%

Posts and Incidents up to a maximum of 5% of the fee may be added.

Outlays (Disbursements) and VAT on the fees and posts are payable in addition to the fees.

Table of Fees of Solicitors in the Court of Session

Practice Note No 3 of 1993

Office of the Auditor of the Court of Session

Consolidated Guidance Notes for Taxation of Accounts

General

1.1 These Guidance Notes are issued with a view to facilitating the conduct of taxations and minimising the necessity of holding continued diets.

1.2 These Guidance Notes will apply to judicial accounts lodged for taxation on or after 4th October 1993.

1.3 The Auditor will not delay consideration of an account to await subsequent production of documentation or information which is required **for the taxation of an account**.

Lodging of accounts of expenses

2.1 *[Revoked by Practice Note No. 1 of 2008 (effective 1st April 2008).]*

2.2 The account lodged for taxation shall have prefixed to it copies of every interlocutor which contains a remit to the Auditor, so far as relevant to any items contained in the account.

2.3 When an account of expenses is lodged for taxation it shall be accompanied by a note stating (1) the name and current address of the paying party, or his solicitor and the latter's file reference (2) the date on which a copy of the account was intimated to the paying party and (3) the estimated duration of the taxation when it is considered that more than half an hour will be required.

Fixing diet of taxation-contra-account

3.1 On receipt of the process and the account the Auditor will assign a diet of taxation for the earliest available date.

3.2 If the paying party has an outstanding award of expenses the account for these should be lodged forthwith to be dealt with at the same diet.

Points of objection

4.1 The paying party shall not later than three working days prior to the diet of taxation intimate to the Auditor, and the receiving party, specific points of objection, setting out the item objected to and stating concisely the nature and ground of objection in each case.

4.2 At the diet of taxation it will be expected that only those items so specified will be raised.

Papers and vouchers to be available at diet

5. There will be available at the diet of taxation the following:

    (a) all precognitions and reports charged for in the account, notes by counsel, documents showing adjustments, letters of instruction to counsel and experts, all solicitors' correspondence, attendance notes, and other papers necessary, to support the entries in the account;

    (b) fee notes detailing the work done by counsel; and

    (c) receipts and detailed vouchers (unless previously exhibited to, and agreed with each paying party) for all sums stated to have been paid giving full details of the services rendered and the time expended and unit rate of charge.

Numbering of vouchers

6. To facilitate the progress of the taxation the supporting documentation is to be arranged and presented in chronological order and appropriately numbered to correspond to the relevant item in the account.

Schedule of witnesses' expenses

7. The fees and expenses charged for witnesses are to be set out in a separate schedule to the account in the form prescribed by paragraph 2 of Chapter II of the Table of Fees of Solicitors in the Court of Session, and the total thereof stated in the body of the account in a lump sum.

Representation at diet

8.1 The Auditor from time to time receives intimation, frequently just prior to the diet of taxation, that the solicitors for the paying party are without instructions to appear at the diet.

8.2 As a cause in which expenses have been awarded is still before the court until the Auditor's report on the taxed account has been lodged, the solicitors who acted for the paying party have a responsibility to inform their client immediately on receiving notification of the diet of taxation, which is peremptory, of the date, time and place of it, so that the client can intimate timeously any points of objection and thereafter attend personally, or be represented, at the diet.

8.3 The Auditor will proceed with the taxation of an account on the basis that such notification has been given to the client timeously.

Taxation at an agreed amount

9 In the event of parties reaching agreement as to the amount of expenses for which the paying party is to be found liable and the receiving party wishing an Auditor's report thereon, the Auditor requires to have consent in writing of the paying party specifying (I) the agreed amount of expenses and (2) to what extent the fee fund dues, which are calculated on the amount of the account lodged for taxation, are to be added to the agreed amount.

Value added tax

10 Where applicable the certificate required by Practice Note dated 14 April 1973 is to be available at the diet of taxation.

30 September 1993

Table of Fees of Solicitors in the Court of Session

Act of Sederunt (Rules of the Court of Session) 1994

(SI 1994 No 1443)

[Chapter 42 is printed as amended by:

Act of Sederunt (Rules of the Court of Session 1994 Amendment No 2) (Fees of Solicitors) 1995 (SI 1995 No 1396);

Act of Sederunt (Rules of the Court of Session Amendment No 1) (Fees of Solicitors) 1996 (SI 1996 No 237);

Act of Sederunt (Rules of the Court of Session Amendment No 3) (Miscellaneous) 1996 (SI 1996 No 1756);

Act of Sederunt (Rules of the Court of Session Amendment) (Miscellaneous) 1998 (SI 1998 No 890);

Act of Sederunt (Rules of the Court of Session Amendment No 3) (Fees of Solicitors) 1998 (SI 1998 No 2674);

Act of Sederunt (Rules of the Court of Session Amendment No 7) (Miscellaneous) 1999 (SSI 1999 No 109) which came into force on 29th October 1999;

Act of Sederunt (Rules of the Court of Session Amendment No 4) (Miscellaneous) 2001 (SSI 2001 No 305) which came into force on 18th September 2001;

Act of Sederunt (Rules of the Court of Session Amendment No 5) (Fees of Solicitors) 2001 (SSI 2001 No 441) which came into force on 1st January 2002;

Act of Sederunt (Rules of the Court of Session Amendment) (Fees of Solicitors, Shorthand Writers and Witnesses) 2002 (SSI 2002 No 301) which came into force on 1st July 2002;

Act of Sederunt (Rules of the Court of Session Amendment) (Fees of Solicitors) 2003 (SSI 2003 No 194) which came into force on 1st April 2003;

Act of Sederunt (Rules of the Court of Session Amendment No 3) (Fees of Solicitors) 2004 (SSI 2004 No 151) which came into force on 4th May 2004;

Act of Sederunt (Rules of the Court of Session Amendment No 4) (Fees of Solicitors) 2006 (SSI 2006 No 294) which came into force on 15th July 2006;

Act of Sederunt (Rules of the Court of Session Amendment) (Fees of Solicitors) 2008 (SSI 2008 No 39) which came into force on 15th February 2008;

Act of Sederunt (Rules of the Court of Session Amendment) (Taxation of Accounts and Fees of Solicitors) 2011 (SSI 2011 No 87) which came into force on 1st April 2011;

Act of Sederunt (Rules of the Court of Session Amendment No 4) (Miscellaneous) 2011 (SSI 2011 No 288) which came into force on 21st July 2011;

Act of Sederunt (Rules of the Court of Session Amendment No 7) (Taxation of Accounts and Fees of Solicitors) 2011 (SSI 2011 No 402) which came into force on 1st January 2012;

Act of Sederunt (Rules of the Court of Session Amendment) (Fees of Solicitors) 2014 (SSI 2014 No 15) which came into force on 1st March 2014.]

CHAPTER 42

TAXATION OF ACCOUNTS AND FEES OF SOLICITORS

PART I — TAXATION OF ACCOUNTS

Remit to the Auditor

42.1.—(1) Where expenses are found due to a party in any cause, the court shall —

    (a) pronounce an interlocutor finding that party entitled to expenses and, subject to rule 42.6(1) (modification of expenses awarded against assisted persons), remitting to the Auditor for taxation; and

    (b) without prejudice to rule 42.4 (objections to report of the Auditor), unless satisfied that there is special cause shown for not doing so, pronounce an interlocutor decerning against the party found liable in expenses as taxed by the Auditor.

(2) Any party found entitled to expenses shall —

    (a) lodge an account of expenses in process not later than four months after the final interlocutor in which a finding in respect of expenses is made;

    (b) if he has failed to comply with sub-paragraph (a), lodge such account at any time with leave of the court but subject to such conditions (if any) as the court thinks fit to impose; and

    (c) on lodging an account under sub-paragraph (a) or (b), intimate a copy of it forthwith to the party found liable to pay those expenses.

(3) Rule 4.6(1) (intimation of steps of process) shall not apply to the lodging of an account of expenses.

Diet of taxation

42.2.—(1) Subject to paragraph (2), the Auditor shall fix a diet of taxation on receipt of—

    (a)   the process of the cause;

    (b)   vouchers in respect of all outlays, including counsel's fees; and

    (c)   a letter addressed to the Auditor confirming that the items referred to in subparagraph (b) have been intimated to the party found liable in expenses.

(2) The Auditor may fix a diet of taxation notwithstanding that paragraphs (1)(b) and (c) have not been complied with.

(3) The Auditor shall intimate the diet of taxation to—

    (a)   the party found entitled to expenses; and

    (b)   the party found liable in expenses.

(4) The party found liable in expenses shall, not later than 4.00pm on the fourth business day before the diet of taxation, intimate to the Auditor and to the party found entitled to expenses, particular points of objection, specifying each item objected to and stating concisely the nature and ground of objection.

(5) Subject to paragraph (6), if the party found liable in expenses fails to intimate points of objection under paragraph (4) within the time limit set out there, the Auditor shall not take account of them at the diet of taxation.

(6) The Auditor may relieve a party from the consequences of a failure to comply with the requirement contained in paragraph (5) because of mistake, oversight or other excusable cause on such conditions, if any, as the Auditor thinks fit.

(7) At the diet of taxation, the party found entitled to expenses shall make available to the Auditor all documents, drafts or copies of documents sought by the Auditor and relevant to the taxation.

(8) In this rule, a "business day" means any day other than a Saturday, Sunday, or public holiday as directed by the Lord President of the Court of Session.

Report of taxation

42.3.—(1) The Auditor shall —

    (a)   prepare a report of the taxation of the account of expenses, stating the amount of expenses as taxed;

    (b)   transmit the process of the cause, the taxed account and the report to the appropriate department of the Office of Court; and

    (c)   on the day on which he transmits the process, intimate that fact and the date of his report to each party to whom he intimated the diet of taxation.

(2) The party found entitled to expenses shall, within 7 days after the date of receipt of information under paragraph (1)(c), exhibit the taxed account, or send a copy of it, to the party found liable to pay the expenses.

Objections to report of the Auditor

42.4.—(1) Any party to a cause who has appeared or been represented at the diet of taxation may object to the report of the Auditor by lodging in process a note of objection within 14 days after the date of the report.

(2) A party lodging a note of objection shall—

    (a)   intimate a copy of the note and a motion under subparagraph (b) to the Auditor and to any party who appeared or was represented at the diet of taxation;

    (b)   apply by motion for an order allowing the note to be received; and

    (c)   intimate forthwith to the Auditor a copy of the interlocutor pronounced on a motion under subparagraph (b).

(2A) Within 14 days after the date of receipt of intimation under paragraph (2)(c), the Auditor shall lodge a minute stating the reasons for his or her decision in relation to the items to which objection is taken in the note.

(3) After the minute of the Auditor has been lodged in process, the party who lodged the note of objection shall, in consultation with any other party wishing to be heard, arrange with the Keeper of the Rolls for a diet of hearing before the appropriate court.

(4) At the hearing on the note of objection, the court may —

    (a)   sustain or repel any objection in the note or remit the account of expenses to the Auditor for further consideration; and

    (b)   find any party liable in the expenses of the procedure on the note.

(5) (Omitted by SSI 2011 No 402).

Modification or disallowance of expenses

42.5.—(1) —In any cause where the court finds a party entitled to expenses, the court may direct that expenses shall be subject to such modification as the court thinks fit.

(2) Where it appears to the Auditor that a party found entitled to expenses —

(a)   was unsuccessful, or

(b)   incurred expenses through his own fault,

in respect of a matter which would otherwise be included in those expenses, the Auditor may disallow the expenses in respect of that matter in whole or in part.

Modification of expenses awarded against assisted persons

42.6.—(1) In a cause in which the court finds an assisted person liable in expenses, the court may, on the motion of any party to the cause, instead of remitting the account of expenses of the party in whose favour the finding is made to the Auditor for taxation, determine to what extent the liability of the assisted person for such expenses shall be modified under —

(a)   section 2(6)(e) of the Legal Aid (Scotland) Act 1967; or

(b)   section 18(2) of the Legal Aid (Scotland) Act 1986.

(2) Where a remit is made to the Auditor for taxation in a cause in which an assisted person is found liable in expenses, an application for modification under a statutory provision mentioned in paragraph (1) may be made by motion within 14 days after the date of the report of the Auditor made under rule 42.3 (report of taxation).

Taxation of solicitors' own accounts

42.7.—(1) Subject to section 61A(1) of the Solicitors (Scotland) Act 1980, the court may remit to the Auditor the account of a solicitor to his client —

(a)   where the account is for work done in relation to a cause in the Court of Session, on the motion of the solicitor or the client; or

(b)   in an action in which the solicitor or his representative sues the client for payment of the account.

(2) A motion under paragraph (1)(a) may be enrolled notwithstanding that final decree in the cause has been extracted.

(3) The account referred to in paragraph (1) shall —

(a)   be in such form as will enable the Auditor to establish the nature and extent of the work done to which the account relates;

(b)   detail the outlays incurred by the solicitor; and

(c)   be accompanied by such supporting material as is necessary to vouch the items in the account.

(4) The Auditor shall —

(a)   fix a diet of taxation not earlier than 14 days after the date on which he receives the account; and

(b)   intimate the diet to the solicitor.

(5) On receipt of intimation of the diet of taxation from the Auditor, the solicitor shall forthwith send to his client by registered post or the first class recorded delivery service —

(a)   a copy of the account to be taxed;

(b)   a copy of the interlocutor remitting the account; and

(c)   a notice in Form 42.7 of the date, time and place of the diet of taxation.

(6) In taxing an account remitted to him under paragraph (1), the Auditor —

(a)   shall allow a sum in respect of such work and outlays as have been reasonably incurred;

(b)   shall allow, in respect of each item of work and outlay, such sum as may be fair and reasonable having regard to all the circumstances of the case;

(c)   shall, in determining whether a sum charged in respect of an item of work is fair and reasonable, take into account any of the following factors:–

(i)   the complexity of the cause and the number, difficulty or novelty of the questions raised;

(ii)   the skill, labour, and specialised knowledge and responsibility required, of the solicitor;(iii) the time spent on the item of work and on the cause as a whole;

    (iv) the number and importance of any documents prepared or perused.

    (v) the place and circumstances (including the degree of expedition required) in which the work of the solicitor or any part of it has been done;

    (vi) the importance of the cause or the subject-matter of it to the client;

    (vii) the amount or value of money or property involved in the cause; and

    (viii)any informal agreement relating to fees;

  (d) shall presume (unless the contrary is demonstrated to his satisfaction) that —

    (i) an item of work or outlay was reasonably incurred if it was incurred with the express or implied approval of the client;

    (ii) the fee charged in respect of an item of work or outlay was reasonable if the amount of the fee or the outlay was expressly or impliedly approved by the client; and

    (iii) an item of work or outlay was not reasonably incurred, or that the fee charged in respect of an item of work or outlay was not reasonable if the item of work, outlay or fee charged, was unusual in the circumstances of the case, unless the solicitor informed the client before carrying out the item of work or incurring the outlay that it might not be allowed (or that the fee charged might not be allowed in full) in a taxation in a cause between party and party; and

  (e) may disallow any item of work or outlay which is not vouched to his satisfaction.

(7) The Auditor shall —

  (a) prepare a report of the taxation of the account remitted to him under paragraph (1) stating the fees and outlays as taxed;

  (b) transmit his report to the appropriate department of the Office of Court; and

  (c) send a copy of his report to the solicitor and the client.

(7A) The solicitor shall, within 7 days after the date of receipt of the report under paragraph (7)(c), exhibit the taxed account, or send a copy of it, to his or her client.

(8) The solicitor or his client may, where he or a representative attended the diet of taxation, state any objection to the report of the Auditor; and rule 42.4 (objections to report of the Auditor) shall apply to such objection as it applies to an objection under that rule.

PART II — FEES OF SOLICITORS

Application and interpretation of this Part

42.8.—(1) This Part applies to fees of solicitors in a cause other than fees —

  (a) provided for by regulations made by the Secretary of State under section 14A of the Legal Aid (Scotland) Act 1967; or

  (b) for which the Secretary of State may make regulations under section 33 of the Legal Aid (Scotland) Act 1986.

(2) In this Part, "the Table of Fees" means the Table of Fees in rule 42.16.

Form of account of expenses

42.9.—An account of expenses presented to the Auditor in accordance with an order of the court shall set out in chronological order all items in respect of which fees are claimed.

Basis of charging

42.10.—(1) Only such expenses as are reasonable for conducting the cause in a proper manner shall be allowed.

(2) Where the work can properly be performed by a local solicitor, the Auditor in taxing an account shall allow such expenses as would have been incurred if the work had been done by the nearest local solicitor, including reasonable fees for instructing and corresponding with him, unless the Auditor is satisfied that it was in the interests of the client that the solicitor in charge of the cause should attend personally.

(3) Subject to paragraph (4), a solicitor may charge an account either on the basis of Chapter I or on the basis of Chapter III of the Table of Fees, but he may not charge partly on one basis and partly on the other.

(4) Where the inclusive fees set out in Chapter III of the Table of Fees are not conveniently applicable or do not properly cover the work involved, an account may be charged on the basis of Chapter I of that Table.

(5) The Auditor may increase or reduce an inclusive fee in Chapter III of the Table of Fees in appropriate circumstances whether or not those circumstances fall under Part IX of that Chapter.

42.11.—[Rule 42.11 revoked by SI 1998 No. 2674.]

Value added tax

42.12.—(1) Where work done by a solicitor constitutes a supply of services in respect of which value added tax is chargeable by him, there may be added to the amount of fees an amount equal to the amount of value added tax chargeable.

(2) An account of expenses or a minute of election to charge the inclusive fee in paragraph 1 of Chapter III of the Table of Fees shall contain a statement as to whether or not the party entitled to the expenses is registered for the purposes of value added tax.

Charges for witnesses

42.13.—Charges for the attendance at a proof or jury trial of a witness present but not called to give evidence may be allowed if the court has, at any time before the diet of taxation, granted a motion for the name of that witness to be noted in the minute of proceedings in the cause.

Charges for skilled persons

42.13A.—(1) If, at any time before the diet of taxation, the court has granted a motion for the certification of a person as skilled, charges shall be allowed for any work done or expenses reasonably incurred by that person which were reasonably required for a purpose in connection with the cause or in contemplation of the cause.

(2) A motion under paragraph (1) may be granted only if the court is satisfied that—

    (a)the person was a skilled person; and

    (b)it was reasonable to employ the person.

(3) Where a motion under paragraph (1) is enrolled after the court has awarded expenses, the expenses of the motion shall be borne by the party enrolling it.

(4) The charges which shall be allowed under paragraph (1) shall be such as the Auditor determines are reasonable.

(5) Where the court grants a motion under paragraph (1), it shall record the name of the skilled person in its interlocutor.

Additional fee

42.14.—(1) An application for the allowance of an additional fee shall be made by motion to the court.

(2) The court may, on such an application to it —

    (a)   determine the application itself; or

    (b)   remit the application to the Auditor for him to determine whether an additional fee should be allowed.

(3) In determining whether to allow an additional fee under paragraph (2), the court or the Auditor, as the case may be, shall take into account any of the following factors:–

    (a)   the complexity of the cause and the number, difficulty or novelty of the questions raised;

    (b)   the skill, time and labour, and specialised knowledge required, of the solicitor or the exceptional urgency of the steps taken by him;

    (c)   the number or importance of any documents prepared or perused;

    (d)   the place and circumstances of the cause or in which the work of the solicitor in preparation for, and conduct of, the cause has been carried out;

    (e)   the importance of the cause or the subject-matter of it to the client;

    (f)   the amount or value of money or property involved in the cause;

    (g)   the steps taken with a view to settling the cause, limiting the matters in dispute or limiting the scope of any hearing.

(4) In fixing an additional fee, the Auditor shall take into account any of the factors mentioned in paragraph (3).

Fees of a reporter

42.15. Subject to any other provision in these Rules, any order of the court or agreement between a party and his solicitor, where any matter in a cause is remitted by the court, at its own instance or on the motion of a party, to a reporter or other person to report to the court —

    (a)   the solicitors for the parties shall be personally liable, in the first instance, to the reporter or other person for his fee and outlays unless the court otherwise orders; and

    (b)   where —

(i)   the court makes the remit at its own instance, the party ordained by the court, or

(ii) the court makes the remit on the motion of a party, that party, shall be liable to the reporter or other person for his fee and outlays.

Table of fees

42.16.—(1) —The Table of Fees shall regulate the fees of a solicitor charged in an account in any cause between party and party.

(1A) In addition to the matters set out in the Table of Fees, travel time at a rate of £35 per quarter hour may be claimed on cause shown at the discretion of the Auditor.

(2) In the Table of Fees, "sheet" means a page of 250 or more words or numbers.

(3) The Table of Fees is as follows.

TABLE OF FEES
CHAPTER I — TABLE OF DETAILED CHARGES

[Chapter I is printed as amended by:

Act of Sederunt (Rules of the Court of Session 1994 Amendment No 2) (Fees of Solicitors) 1995 (SI 1995 No 1396) which came into force on 22nd June 1995;

Act of Sederunt (Rules of the Court of Session Amendment No 1) (Fees of Solicitors) 1996 (SI 1996 No 237) which came into force on 1st April 1996;

Act of Sederunt (Rules of the Court of Session 1994 Amendment No 3) (Fees of Solicitors) 1998 (SI 1998 No 2674) which came into force on 1st December 1998;

Act of Sederunt (Rules of the Court of Session Amendment No 8) (Fees of Solicitors) 1999 (SSI 1999 No 166) which came into force on 1st January 2000;

Act of Sederunt (Rules of the Court of Session Amendment No 8) (Fees of Solicitors) 2000 (SSI 2000 No 450) which came into force on 1st January 2001;

Act of Sederunt (Rules of the Court of Session Amendment No 5) (Fees of Solicitors) 2001 (SSI 2001 No 441) which came into force on 1st January 2002;

Act of Sederunt (Rules of the Court of Session Amendment) (Fees of Solicitors, Shorthand Writers and Witnesses) 2002 (SSI 2002 No 301) which came into force on 1st July 2002;

Act of Sederunt (Rules of the Court of Session Amendment) (Fees of Solicitors) 2003 (SSI 2003 No 194) which came into force on 1st April 2003;

Act of Sederunt (Rules of the Court of Session Amendment No 3) (Fees of Solicitors) 2004 (SSI 2004 No 151) which came into force on 4th May 2004;

Act of Sederunt (Rules of the Court of Session Amendment No 2) (Fees of Solicitors) 2005 (SSI 2005 No 147) which came into force on 25th April 2005;

Act of Sederunt (Rules of the Court of Session Amendment No 4) (Fees of Solicitors) 2006 (SSI 2006 No 294) which came into force on 1st July 2006;

Act of Sederunt (Rules of the Court of Session Amendment No 2) (Fees of Solicitors) 2007 (SSI 2007 No 86) which came into force on 1st April 2007;

Act of Sederunt (Rules of the Court of Session Amendment) (Fees of Solicitors) 2008 (SSI 2008 No 39) which came into force on 1st April 2008;

Act of Sederunt (Rules of the Court of Session Amendment No 2) (Fees of Solicitors) 2009 (SSI 2009 No 82) which came into force on 27th April 2009;

Act of Sederunt (Rules of the Court of Session Amendment No 4) (Fees of Solicitors) 2012 (SSI 2012 No 270) which came into force on 5th November 2012;

Act of Sederunt (Rules of the Court of Session Amendment) (Fees of Solicitors) 2014 (SSI 2014 No 15) which came into force on 1st March 2014.]

1.   Framing documents   £

(a) Framing precognitions and other papers (but not including affidavits, witness summaries and witness statements), per sheet 19.50

(b) Framing formal documents such as inventories and title pages, etc., per sheet 9.75

(c) Framing affidavits and (where ordered by the court) witness summaries and witness statements, per sheet 39.00

(d) Framing accounts of expenses, per sheet 19.50

Note: Where a skilled witness prepares his or her own precognition or report, the solicitor shall be allowed for perusing it (whether or not in the course of so doing he or she revises or adjusts it), half of the framing fee per sheet.

2. Copying

For the copying of papers by whatever means—

    (a)   where a copy is required to be lodged, or sent, in pursuance of any of rules 4.7, 22.1 and 22.3, such charge as the Auditor may from time to time determine (and the Auditor may make different provision for different classes of case); and

    (b)   in any other case, if the Auditor determines (either or both) that—

        (i)   the copying had to be done in circumstances which were in some way exceptional;

        (ii)   the papers which required to be copied were unusually numerous having regard to the nature of the cause,

    such charge, if any, as the Auditor considers reasonable (but a charge based on time expended by any person in copying shall not be allowed)

Notes:

    1. Where a determination is required under subparagraph (b), the purpose of copying, the number of copies made and the charge claimed shall be shown in the account.

    2. Copying done other than in the place of business of the solicitor shall be shown as an outlay.

		£
3. Revising		
Papers drawn by counsel or other person having a right of audience, open and closed records, etc., for each five sheets or part of a sheet		9.75

4. Citation of parties, witnesses, havers and instructions to messenger-at-arms

(a)	Each party	19.50
(b)	Each witness or haver	19.50
(c)	Instructing messenger-at-arms including examining, execution and settling fee	19.50

5. Time charge

(a)	Preparation for proof, jury trial or any other hearing at court, per quarter hour (or such other sum as in the opinion of the Auditor is justified)	39.00
(b)	Attendance at meetings, proof, jury trial or any other hearing at court including waiting time, or consultation with counsel or other person having a right of audience, per quarter hour (or such other sum as in the opinion of the Auditor is justified)	39.00
(c)	Perusal of documents per quarter hour (or such other sum as in the opinion of the Auditor is justified)	39.00
(d)	Allowance for time of clerk, one-half of the above	
(e)	Attendance at Office of Court—	
	(i) for making up and lodging process	19.50
	(ii) for lodging all first steps of process	19.50
	(iii) for performance of formal work (other than work under head (ii))	9.75

Note: In the event of a party in a proof or jury trial being represented by one counsel or other person having a right of audience only, allowance may be made to the solicitor should the case warrant it, for the attendance of a clerk at one-half the rate chargeable for the attendance of the solicitor.

6. Correspondence

(a)	Letters including instruction to counsel or other person having a right of audience (whether sent by hand, post, telex or facsimile transmission), each page of 125 words	19.50
(b)	Formal letters	4.88
(c)	Telephone calls (except under subparagraph (d))	9.75
(d)	Telephone calls (lengthy), to be charged at attendance rate	

Note: In relation to subparagraph (d), whether a telephone call is "lengthy" will be determined by the Auditor.

CHAPTER II — SKILLED PERSONS AND WITNESSES' FEES

[Chapter II is printed as amended by:

Act of Sederunt (Rules of the Court of Session Amendment) (Witnesses' Fees) 1999 (SI 1999 No 187) which came into force on 1st March 1999;

Act of Sederunt (Rules of the Court of Session Amendment) (Fees of Solicitors, Shorthand Writers and Witnesses) 2002 (SI 2002 No 301) which came into force on 1st July 2002;

Act of Sederunt (Rules of the Court of Session Amendment No 2) (Fees of Solicitors) 2005 (SSI 2005 No 147) which came into force on 25th April 2005;

Act of Sederunt (Rules of the Court of Session Amendment) (Miscellaneous) 2007 (SSI 2007 No 7) which came into force on 29th January 2007;

Act of Sederunt (Rules of the Court of Session Amendment No 4) (Miscellaneous) 2011 (SSI No 288) which came into force on 21st July 2011.]

1. Skilled persons

Where it was reasonable to employ a skilled person to carry out work for any purpose, any charges for such work and for any attendance at any proof or jury trial shall be allowed at such a rate which the Auditor of Court shall determine is fair and reasonable.

2. Witnesses

A person who is cited to give evidence and in consequence incurs financial loss shall be allowed reimbursement, being such reasonable sum as the Auditor may determine to have been reasonably and necessarily incurred by the witness, but not exceeding £400 per day.

3. Travelling allowance

In respect of any witness there shall be allowed a travelling allowance, being such sum as the Auditor may determine to have been reasonably and necessarily incurred by the witness in the travelling from and to the witnesses' residence or place of business and the Court.

4. Subsistence allowance

In respect of any witness there shall be allowed a subsistence allowance, being such sum as the Auditor may determine to have been reasonably incurred by the witness for the extra cost of subsistence during the witnesses' absence from the witnesses' home or place of business for the purpose of giving evidence, and where the witness reasonably requires to stay overnight, for the reasonable cost of board and lodging.

5. Value Added Tax

Where any witness is a taxable person in terms of the Value Added Tax Act 1983, the amount of value added tax may be added by the witness to the witnesses' note of fee, and may be paid to the witness by the Solicitor.

6. Receipts and vouchers

Receipts and detailed vouchers for all payments claimed in respect of a witness shall be produced to the party found liable in expenses, prior to the taxation of the Account of Expenses, and to the Auditor, if the Auditor requires.

7. Account of fees of witnesses

The fees charged for any witness shall be stated in the Account of Expenses in a lump sum and the details of the charges shall be entered in a separate schedule appended to the Account as follows:

Name and designation	Where from	Days charged	Rate per day	Travelling and subsistence allowance	Total	Taxed off

CHAPTER III

[Chapter III is printed as amended by:

Act of Sederunt (Rules of the Court of Session 1994 Amendment No 2) (Fees of Solicitors) 1995 (SI 1995 No 1396) which came into force on 22nd June 1995;

Act of Sederunt (Rules of the Court of Session Amendment No 1) (Fees of Solicitors) 1996 (SI 1996 No 237) which came into force on 1st April 1996;

Act of Sederunt (Rules of the Court of Session Amendment No 3) (Fees of Solicitors) 1998 (SI 1998 No 2674) which came into force on 1st December 1998;

Act of Sederunt (Rules of the Court of Session Amendment No 8) (Fees of Solicitors) 1999 (SSI 1999 No 166) which came into force on 1st January 2000;

Act of Sederunt (Rules of the Court of Session Amendment No 8) (Fees of Solicitors) 2000 (SSI 2000 No 450) which came into force on 1st January 2001;

Act of Sederunt (Rules of the Court of Session Amendment No 5) (Fees of Solicitors) 2001 (SSI 2001 No 441) which came into force on 1st January 2002;

Act of Sederunt (Rules of the Court of Session Amendment) (Fees of Solicitors, Shorthand Writers and Witnesses) 2002 (SSI 2002 No 301) which came into force on 1st July 2002;

Act of Sederunt (Rules of the Court of Session Amendment) (Fees of Solicitors) 2003 (SSI 2003 No 194) which came into force on 1st April 2003;

Act of Sederunt (Rules of the Court of Session Amendment No 3) (Fees of Solicitors) 2004 (SSI 2004 No 151) which came into force on 4th May 2004;

Act of Sederunt (Rules of the Court of Session Amendment No 2) (Fees of Solicitors) 2005 (SSI 2005 No 147) which came into force on 25th April 2005;

Act of Sederunt (Rules of the Court of Session Amendment No 4) (Fees of Solicitors) 2005 (SSI 2006 No 294) which came into force on 1st July 2006;

Act of Sederunt (Rules of the Court of Session Amendment No 2) (Fees of Solicitors) 2007 (SSI 2007 No 86) which came into force on 1st April 2007;

Act of Sederunt (Rules of the Court of Session Amendment) (Fees of Solicitors) 2008 (SSI 2008 No 39) which came into force on 1st April 2008;

Act of Sederunt (Rules of the Court of Session Amendment No 2) (Fees of Solicitors) 2009 (SSI 2009 No 82) which came into force on 27th April 2009;

Act of Sederunt (Rules of the Court of Session Amendment) (Taxation of Accounts and Fees of Solicitors) 2011 (SSI 2011 No 87) which came into force on 1st April 2011;

Act of Sederunt (Rules of the Court of Session Amendment No 4) (Miscellaneous) 2011 (SSI 2011 No 288) which came into force on 21st July 2011;

Act of Sederunt (Rules of the Court of Session Amendment No 7) (Taxation of Accounts and Fees of Solicitors) 2011 (SSI 2011 No 402) which came into force on 1st January 2012;

Act of Sederunt (Rules of the Court of Session Amendment No 4) (Fees of Solicitors) 2012 (SSI 2012 No 270) which came into force on 5th November 2012;

Act of Sederunt (Rules of the Court of Session Amendment) (Fees of Solicitors) 2014 (SSI 2014 No 15) which came into force on 1st March 2014;

Act of Sederunt (Rules of the Court of Session 1994 and Fees of Solicitors in the Sheriff Court Amendment) (Courts Reform (Scotland) Act 2014) 2015 (SSI 2015 No 246) which came into force on 22nd September 2015.]

PART I — UNDEFENDED CAUSES

(other than consistorial actions)

1. Inclusive fee

In all undefended causes where no proof is led, the pursuer's solicitor may at his or her option elect to charge an inclusive fee to cover all work from taking instructions up to and including obtaining extract decree. The option shall be exercised by the solicitor for the pursuer endorsing a minute of election to the above effect on the principal summons or petition before decree is taken.

		£
(a)	All work up to and obtaining extract decree	351.00
(b)	Outlays to an amount not exceeding £448.50 (exclusive of value added tax) shall also be allowed.	

PART II — UNDEFENDED CONSISTORIAL ACTIONS

(other than by affidavit procedure in Part III of this Chapter)

1. All work (other than precognitions) up to and including the calling of the summons in court   468.00

Note: Precognitions to be charged as in paragraph 10 of Part V of this Chapter of this Table.

2. Incidental procedure

Fixing diet, enrolling action, preparing for proof, citing witnesses, etc.   273.00

3. Amendment

(a)	Where summons amended, re-service is not ordered and motion is not starred	78.00
(b)	Where summons amended, re-service is not ordered and motion is starred	97.50
(c)	Where summons amended and re-service is ordered	117.00

4. Commission to take evidence on interrogatories

(a)	All work up to and including lodging of completed interrogatories, but excluding attendance at execution of commission	117.00
(b)	Attendance at execution of commission (if required), per quarter hour	39.00
(c)	In addition a fee per sheet for completed interrogatories, including all copies, of	19.50

5. Commission to take evidence on open commission

(a)	All work up to and including lodging of report of commission, but excluding attendance at execution of commission	117.00
(b)	Attendance at execution of commission, per quarter hour	39.00

6. **Other matters**

Where applicable, charges under paragraphs 11, 12, 15, 20 and 22 of Part V of this Chapter of this Table.

7. **Proof and completion fee**

All work to and including sending extract decree, but excluding account of expenses 351.00

8. **Accounts**

Framing and lodging account and attending taxation 117.00

PART III — UNDEFENDED CONSISTORIAL ACTIONS

(affidavit procedure)

1.—(1) This paragraph applies to any undefended action of divorce or separation where —

    (a)   the facts set out in section 1(2)(a) (adultery) or 1(2)(b) (unreasonable behaviour) of the Divorce (Scotland) Act 1976 ("the 1976 Act") are relied on;

    (b)   there are no conclusions relating to any ancillary matters; and

    (c)   the pursuer seeks to prove those facts by means of affidavits.

(2) The solicitor for the pursuer may, in respect of the work specified in column 1 of Table A below, charge the inclusive fee specified in respect of that work in column 2 of that Table.

(3) Where the pursuer has been represented in respect of work specified in column 1 of Table A below by an Edinburgh solicitor and a solicitor outside Edinburgh, the Auditor may, where he is satisfied that it was appropriate for the pursuer to be so represented, allow the inclusive fee specified in column 3 instead of the inclusive fee specified in column 2 of that Table.

TABLE A

Column 1 *Work done*	Column 2 *Inclusive fee* £	Column 3 *Discretionary inclusive* *fee Edinburgh solicitor* *and solicitor* *outside Edinburgh* £
1. All work to and including calling of the summons	780.00	897.00
2. All work from calling to and including swearing affidavits	546.00	663.00
3. All work from swearing affidavits to and including sending extract decree	156.00	273.00
4. All work to and including sending extract decree	1,482.00	1,833.00

2.—(1) This paragraph applies to any undefended action of divorce or separation where —

    (a)   the facts set out in section 1(2)(c) (desertion), 1(2)(d) (two years' non-cohabitation and consent) or 1(2)(e) (five years' non-cohabitation) of the 1976 Act are relied on;

    (b)   there are no conclusions relating to any ancillary matters; and

    (c)   the pursuer seeks to prove those facts by affidavit.

(2) The solicitor for the pursuer may, in respect of the work specified in column 1 of Table B below, charge the inclusive fee specified in respect of that work in column 2 of that Table.

(3) Where the pursuer has been represented in respect of work specified in column 1 of Table B below by an Edinburgh solicitor and a solicitor outside Edinburgh, the Auditor may, where he is satisfied that it was appropriate for the pursuer to be so represented, allow the inclusive fee specified in respect of that work in column 3 instead of the inclusive fee specified in column 2 of that Table.

TABLE B

Column 1 *Work done*	Column 2 *Inclusive fee* £	Column 3 *Discretionary inclusive fee Edinburgh solicitor and solicitor outside Edinburgh* £
1. All work to and including calling of the summons	624.00	741.00
2. All work from calling to and including swearing affidavits	312.00	429.00
3. All work from swearing affidavits to and including sending extract decree	156.00	273.00
4. All work to and including sending extract decree	1,092.00	1,443.00

3. If —

    (a) the solicitor for the pursuer charges an inclusive fee under either paragraph 1 or 2 of this Part, and

    (b) the action to which the charge relates includes a conclusion relating to an ancillary matter, in addition to that fee he may charge in respect of the work specified in column 1 of Table C below the inclusive fee specified in respect of that work in column 2 of that Table.

TABLE C

Column 1 *Work done*	Column 2 *Discretionary inclusive fee Edinburgh solicitor and solicitor outside Edinburgh*
1. All work to and including calling of the summons	156.00
2. All work from calling to and including swearing affidavits	156.00
3. All work under items 1 and 2	312.00

PART IV — OUTER HOUSE PETITIONS

1. Unopposed petition   £

    (a) All work including precognitions and all copyings, up to and obtaining extract decree   702.00

    (b) Where the party has been represented by an Edinburgh solicitor and a solicitor outside Edinburgh, the Auditor may, where he is satisfied that it was necessary for the party to be so represented, allow a fee of 936.00

    (c) Outlays including duplicating charges to be allowed in addition.

2. Opposed petition

    (a) All work (other than precognitions) up to and including lodging petition, obtaining and executing warrant for service 546.00

    (b) Outlays including duplicating charges to be allowed in addition.

    (c) Where applicable, charges under paragraphs 2, 3, 4, 6(a) to (e), 7 and 10 to 26 of Part V of this Chapter of this table

3. Reports in opposed petitions

    (a) For each report by the Accountant of Court 78.00

    (b) For any other report, as under paragraph 11 of Part V of this Chapter of this Table.

4. Obtaining bond of caution   78.00

PART V — DEFENDED ACTIONS

1. Instruction   £

   (a) All work (apart from precognitions) from commencement until lodgement of open record 702.00

   (b) Instructing re-service where necessary 78.00

   (c) If counterclaim lodged, additional fee for each party 156.00

2. Work before action commences

All work which the Auditor is satisfied has reasonably been undertaken in contemplation of, or preparatory to, the commencement of proceedings (or such other sum as in the opinion of the Auditor is justified) 702.00

3. Lodging productions

   (a) For lodging productions – each inventory 78.00

   (b) For considering opponent's productions – each inventory 39.00

4. Record

   (a) All work in connection with adjustment and closing of record (including subsequent work in connection with By Order (Adjustment) Roll, except in actions proceeding under Chapter 42A) 780.00

   (b) All work as above, so far as applicable, where cause settled or disposed of before record closed 468.00

   (c) If consultation held before record closed, additional fees may be allowed as follows—

      (i) arranging consultation 78.00

      (ii) attendance at consultation, per quarter hour 39.00

   (d) Additional fee to subparagraph (a) or (b) (to include necessary amendments) to be allowed to every existing party for each pursuer, defender or third party brought in before the record is closed 234.00

   (e) Additional fee to every existing party if an additional pursuer, defender or third party is brought in after the record is closed 351.00

   (f) Fee allowable to a new pursuer who requires to be brought in as a result of the death of an existing pursuer 234.00

5. By Order (Adjustment) Roll in actions proceeding under Chapter 42A

   (a) Fee to cover preparing and instruction of counsel or other person having a right of audience to include attendance not exceeding half an hour 117.00

   (b) Thereafter attendance fee, per quarter hour 39.00

6. Notes of Argument, Statements of Facts or Issues and Notes of Proposals for Further Procedure

   (a) Instructing, perusing and lodging first Note of Arguments (either party) 156.00

   (b) Perusing opponent's Note of Arguments 78.00

   (c) Instructing, perusing and lodging any further Note of Arguments (either party) 78.00

   (d) Instructing, perusing and lodging (each) Statement of Facts or Issues 117.00

   (e) Perusing opponent's Statement of Facts or Issues (each) 78.00

   (f) Instructing, revising and lodging (each) Note of Proposals for Further Procedure 117.00

   (g) Perusing opponent's Note of Proposals for Further Procedure (each) 78.00

7. Procedure Roll, preliminary, procedural or other hearing

   (a) Preparing for hearing including all work, incidental work and instruction of counsel or other person having a right of audience 156.00

   (b) Attendance fee, per quarter hour 39.00

   (c) Advising and work incidental to it 117.00

8.   Valuation of claim in actions proceeding under Chapter 42A   £

    (a)   Fee to cover note on quantum/valuation of claim 468.00

    (b)   Opponent's fee for inspection of valuation of claim 234.00

    (c)   Inspection of documents, per quarter hour 39.00

9.   Adjustment of issues and counter issues

    (a)   All work in connection with and incidental to the lodging of an issue and adjustment and approval of it 156.00

    (b)   If one counter-issue, additional fee to pursuer 39.00

    (c)   Where more than one counter-issue, an additional fee to pursuer for each additional counter-issue 19.50

    (d)   All work in connection with and incidental to the lodging of a counter-issue and adjustment and approval of it 156.00

    (e)   Fee to defender or third party for considering issue where no counter-issue lodged 39.00

    (f)   Fee to defender or third party for considering each additional counter-issue 19.50

10.   Precognitions, affidavits and (where ordered by the court) witness summaries and witness statements

    (a)   Taking and drawing precognitions, per sheet 78.00

    (b)   All work in connection with preparation and lodging of affidavits and (where ordered by the court) witness summaries and witness statements, per sheet 78.00

    (c)   Perusing opponent's witness summaries, witness statements and affidavits, per sheet.... 39.00

Note: Where a skilled person prepares his or her own precognition or report, the solicitor shall be allowed, for perusing it (whether or not in the course of doing so he or she revises or adjusts it), half of the taking and drawing fee per sheet.

11.   Reports obtained under order of court excluding Auditor's report

    (a)   All work incidental to it 156.00

    (b)   Additional, fee for perusal of report, per quarter hour (or such other sum as in the opinion of the Auditor is justified) 35.00

12.   Specification of documents

    (a)   Instructing counsel or other person having a right of audience, revising and lodging and all incidental procedure to obtain a diligence up to and including obtaining interlocutor 156.00

    (b)   Fee to opponent 78.00

    (c)   Arranging commission to recover documents, citing havers, instructing commissioner and shorthand writer and preparation for commission 156.00

    (d)   Fee to opponent 78.00

    (e)   Attendance at execution of commission, per quarter hour 39.00

    (f)   If alternative procedure adopted, a fee per person on whom order served 58.50

    (g)   Fee for perusal of documents recovered under a specification of documents (or by informal means) where not otherwise provided for in the Table of Fees, per quarter hour   39.00

13.   Commission to take evidence on interrogatories

    (a)   Applying for commission to cover all work up to and including lodging report of commission with completed interrogatories and cross-interrogatories 312.00

    (b)   Fee to opponent if cross-interrogatories lodged 234.00

    (c)   Fee to opponent if no cross-interrogatories lodged 97.50

    (d)   In addition to above, fee per sheet to each party for completed interrogatories or cross-interrogatories, including all copies 19.50

14.   Commission to take evidence on open commissions

    (a)   Applying for commission up to and including lodging report of commission, but excluding subparagraph (c) 351.00

£

(b) Fee to opponent.. 156.00

(c) Fee for attendance at execution of commission, per quarter hour 39.00

15. Miscellaneous motions and minutes where not otherwise covered by this Part

(a) Where attendance of counsel or other person having a right of audience and/or solicitor not required 39.00

(b) Where attendance of counsel or other person having a right of audience and/or solicitor required, inclusive of instruction of counsel or other person having a right of audience, not exceeding half an hour.. 117.00

(c) Thereafter attendance fee, per additional quarter hour.................................... 39.00

(d) Instructing counsel or other person having a right of audience for a minute (other than a minute ordered by the court), revising and lodging as a separate step in process including any necessary action 117.00

(e) Perusing a minute of admission or abandonment... 39.00

16. Incidental Procedure (not chargeable prior to the approval of issue of allowance of proof)

Fixing diet, obtaining note on the line of evidence etc., borrowing and returning process and all other work prior to the consultation on the sufficiency of evidence..................... 351.00

17. Amendment of record

(a) Amendment of conclusions only, fee to proposer 117.00

(b) Amendment of conclusions only, fee to opponent 39.00

(c) Amendment of pleadings after record closed, where no answers to the amendment are lodged, fee to proposer 156.00

(d) In same circumstances, fee to opponent... 78.00

(e) Amendment of pleadings after record closed, where answers are lodged, fee for proposer and each party lodging answers.. 390.00

(f) Additional fee for adjustment of minute and answers, where applicable, to be allowed to each party... 234.00

18. Preparation for proof or jury trial

To include fixing consultation on the sufficiency of evidence, fee-funding precept, citing witnesses, all work checking and writing up process and preparing for proof or jury trial—

(a) if action settled before proof or jury trial, or lasts only one day, to include, where applicable, instruction of counsel or other person having a right of audience 1,014.00

(b) for each day or part of day after the first, including instruction of counsel or other person having a right of audience 97.50

(c) preparing for adjourned diets and all work incidental to it as in subparagraph (a), if adjourned for more than five days... 234.00

(d) if consultation held before proof or jury trial, attendance at it, per quarter hour 39.00

(e) all work in connection with making up and pagination of joint bundle of medical records in actions proceeding under Chapter 42A.. 156.00

19. Pre-trial meeting

(a) Fee arranging pre-trial meeting (each occasion) 78.00

(b) Fee preparing for pre-trial meeting.. 429.00

(c) Fee for preparing for continued pre-trial meeting (each occasion)................................. 156.00

(d) Fee attending pre-trial meeting, per quarter hour.. 39.00

(e) Joint minute of pre-trial meeting 39.00

20. Copying

For the copying of papers by whatever means—

(a) where a copy is required to be lodged, or sent, in pursuance of any of rules 4.7, 22.1 and 22.3, such charge as the Auditor may from time to time determine (and the Auditor may make different provision for different classes of case); and

(b) in any other case, if the Auditor determines (either or both) that —

    (i) the copying had to be done in circumstances which were in some way exceptional;

    (ii) the papers which required to be copied were unusually numerous having regard to the nature of the cause,

such charge, if any, as the Auditor considers reasonable (but a charge based on time expended by any person in copying shall not be allowed).

Notes:

1. Where a determination is required under subparagraph (b), the purpose of copying, the number of copies and the charge claimed shall be shown in the account.

2. Copying done other than in the place of business of the solicitor shall be shown as an outlay.

21. Settlement £

(a) Judicial tender—

    (i) lodging or considering first tender 234.00

    (ii) lodging or considering each further tender 156.00

    (iii) if tender accepted, an additional fee to each accepting party 156.00

(b) Extrajudicial settlement – advising on, negotiating and agreeing extrajudicial settlement (not based on judicial tender) to include preparation and lodging of joint minute........... 390.00

(c) The Auditor may allow a fee in respect of work undertaken with a view to settlement (whether or not settlement is in fact agreed), including offering settlement 624.00

(d) If consultation held to consider tender, extrajudicial settlement (not based on judicial tender) or with a view to settlement (whether or not settlement is in fact agreed), attendance at it, per quarter hour 39.00

22. Hearing limitation fee

To include all work undertaken with a view to limiting the matters in dispute or limiting the scope of any hearing, and including exchanging documents, precognitions and expert reports, agreeing any fact, statement or document, and preparing and lodging any joint minute 780.00

23. Proof or jury trial

Attendance fee, per quarter hour... 39.00

24. Accounts

(a) To include framing, adjusting and lodging account 234.00

(b) To include considering Notes of Objections, and generally preparing for taxation.......... 234.00

(c) Attendance at taxation, per quarter hour 39.00

25. Ordering and obtaining extract 58.50

26. Final procedure

(a) If case goes to proof or jury trial, or is settled within 14 days before the diet of proof or jury trial, to include all work to close of cause so far as not otherwise provided for....... 312.00

(b) In any other case 97.50

PART VA — DEFENDED PERSONAL INJURIES ACTIONS COMMENCED ON OR AFTER
1 APRIL 2003

1. Precognitions/Expert Reports/Factual Reports £

Taking and drawing precognitions, per sheet 78.00

Note: Where a skilled person prepares his or her own precognition or report, the solicitor shall be allowed, for perusing it (whether or not in the course of doing so he or she revises or adjusts it), half of the taking and drawing fee per sheet.

2. Pre-litigation fee

£

All work which the Auditor is satisfied has reasonably been undertaken in contemplation of, or preparatory to the commencement of proceedings particularly to include communications between parties in relation to areas of medical/quantum/discussion re settlement (or such other sum as in the opinion of the Auditor is justified) 702.00

3. Lodging productions

    (a) For lodging productions, each inventory 78.00

    (b) For considering opponent's productions, each inventory 39.00

4. Instruction

    (a) To cover all work (except as otherwise specially provided for in this Part) from commencement to lodging of defences 702.00

    (b) Specification of documents per Form 43.2-B.. 117.00

    (c) Fee to opponent for considering specification of documents.. 78.00

    (d) In the event of the summons being drafted without the assistance of counsel or other person having a right of audience such further fee will be allowed as the Auditor considers appropriate, up to 234.00

    (e) Instructing re-service where necessary 78.00

    (f) If counterclaim lodged, additional fee for each party to include Answers 234.00

    (g) Arranging commission to recover documents, citing havers, instructing commissioner and shorthand writer and preparation for commission 156.00

    (h) Fee to opponent where commission arranged 78.00

    (i) Attendance at execution of commission, per quarter hour.. 39.00

    (j) If alternative procedure adopted, a fee per person on whom order served 58.50

    (k) Fee for perusal of documents recovered under a specification of documents (or by informal means) where not otherwise provided for in the Table of Fees, per quarter hour 39.00

5. Record

    (a) All work in connection with adjustment and closing of record 780.00

    (b) All work as above, so far as applicable, where cause settled or disposed of before record closed 468.00

    (c) If consultation held before record closed, additional fees may be allowed as follows—

        (i)   arranging consultation 78.00

        (ii) attendance at consultation, per quarter hour.. 39.00

    (d) Additional fee to subparagraph (a) or (b), to include necessary amendments, to be allowed to every existing party for each pursuer, defender or third party brought in before the record is closed 234.00

    (e) Additional fee to every existing party if an additional pursuer, defender or third party is brought in after the record is closed 351.00

    (f) Fee allowable to a new pursuer who requires to be brought in as a result of the death of an existing pursuer 234.00

6. Notes of arguments

    (a) Instructing, perusing and lodging first Note of Arguments, where ordained by the Court (either party).. 156.00

    (b) Perusing opponent's Note of Arguments 78.00

    (c) Instructing, perusing and lodging any further Note of Arguments, where ordained by the Court (either party) 78.00

7. Valuation of claim £

    (a)   Fee to cover note on quantum/valuation of claim 468.00

    (b)   Opponent's fee for inspection of valuation of claim 234.00

    (c)   Inspection of documents, per quarter hour 39.00

8. Adjustment of issues and counter-issues

    (a)   All work in connection with and incidental to the lodging of an issue, and adjustment and approval of it 156.00

    (b)   If one counter-issue, additional fee to pursuer 39.00

9. By Order Roll/variation of timetable order/adjustment on final decree/interim payment of damages

    (a)   Fee to cover preparing and instruction of counsel or other person having a right of audience to include attendance not exceeding half an hour 117.00

    (b)   Thereafter attendance fee, per additional quarter hour 39.00

    (c)   In the event of a separate Advising/Opinion and all work incidental thereto 117.00

10. Reports obtained under order of court excluding Auditor's Report

    (a)   All work incidental to it 156.00

    (b)   Additional fee for perusal of report, per quarter hour (or such other sum as in the opinion of the Auditor is justified) 35.00

11. Incidental procedure (not chargeable prior to the approval of issue or allowance of proof)

Fixing diet, obtaining note on the line of evidence etc., borrowing and returning process, and all other work prior to the consultation on the sufficiency of evidence 351.00

12. Specification of documents (if further specification considered necessary)

    (a)   Instructing counsel or other person having a right of audience, revising and lodging and all incidental procedure to obtain a diligence up to and including obtaining interlocutor   156.00

    (b)   Fee to opponent 78.00

    (c)   Arranging commission to recover documents, citing havers, instructing commissioner and shorthand writer and preparation for commission 156.00

    (d)   Fee to opponent 78.00

    (e)   Attendance at execution of commission, per quarter hour 39.00

    (f)   If alternative procedure adopted, a fee per person on whom order served 58.50

    (g)   Fee for perusal of documents recovered under a specification of documents (or by informal means) where not otherwise provided for in the Table of Fees, per quarter hour   39.00

13. Commission to take evidence on interrogatories

    (a)   Applying for commission to cover all work up to and including lodging report of commission with completed interrogatories and cross-interrogatories 312.00

    (b)   Fee to opponent if cross-interrogatories lodged 234.00

    (c)   Fee to opponent if no cross-interrogatories lodged 97.50

    (d)   In addition to above, fee per sheet to each party for completed interrogatories or cross-interrogatories, including all copies 19.50

14. Commission to take evidence on open commission

    (a)   Applying for commission up to and including lodging report of commission, but excluding subparagraph (c) 351.00

£

(b) Fee to opponent.. 156.00

(c) Fee for attendance at execution of commission, per quarter hour 39.00

15. Miscellaneous motions and minutes where not otherwise covered by this Part

(a) Where attendance of counsel or other person having a right of audience and/or solicitor not required 39.00

(b) Where attendance of counsel or other person having a right of audience and/or solicitor required inclusive of instruction of counsel or other person having a right of audience, not exceeding half an hour... 117.00

(c) Thereafter attendance fee, per quarter hour... 39.00

(d) Instructing counsel or other person having a right of audience for a minute/note on further procedure (if applicable), revising and lodging as a separate step in process including any necessary action 117.00

(e) Perusing a minute of admission or abandonment, a note ordered by the court, or a notice of grounds 39.00

16. Amendment of record

(a) Amendment of conclusions only, fee to proposer... 17.00

(b) Amendment of conclusions only, fee to opponent.. 39.00

(c) Amendment of pleadings after record closed, where no answers to the amendment are lodged, fee to proposer 156.00

(d) In same circumstances, fee to opponent... 78.00

(e) Amendment of pleadings after record closed, where answers are lodged, fee for proposer and each party lodging answers.. 390.00

(f) Additional fee for adjustment of minute and answers, where applicable, to be allowed to each party... 234.00

17. Copying

(a) Where a copy is required to be lodged, or sent, in pursuance of rules 4.7 or 43.6(4), such charge as the Auditor may from time to time determine (and the Auditor may make different provision for different classes of case); and

(b) In any other case, if the Auditor determines (either or both) that—

   (i) the copying had to be done in circumstances which were in some way exceptional;

   (ii) the papers which required to be copied were unusually numerous having regard to the nature of the cause,

   such charge, if any, as the Auditor considers reasonable (but a charge based on time expended by any person in copying shall not be allowed).

Notes:

1. Where a determination is required under subparagraph (b), the purpose of copying, the number of copies made and the charge claimed shall be shown in the account.

2. Copying done other than in the place of business of the solicitor shall be shown as an outlay.

18. Preparation for proof or jury trial

To include fixing consultation on the sufficiency of evidence, fee-funding precept, citing witnesses, all work checking and writing up process and preparing for proof or jury trial—..

(a) if action settled before proof or jury trial, or lasts only one day, to include where applicable, instruction of counsel or other person having a right of audience 1,014.00

(b) for each day or part of day after the first, including instruction of counsel or other person having a right of audience 97.50

£

(c) preparing for adjourned diets and all work incidental to it as in subparagraph (a), if adjourned for more than five days 234.00

(d) if consultation held before proof or jury trial, attendance at it, per quarter hour 39.00

19. Pre-trial meeting

(a) Fee arranging pre-trial meeting (each occasion) 78.00

(b) Fee preparing for pre-trial meeting 429.00

(c) Fee for preparing for continued pre-trial meeting (each occasion) 156.00

(d) Fee attending pre-trial meeting, per quarter hour 39.00

(e) Joint Minute of pre-trial meeting 39.00

20. Hearing limitation fee

For any work undertaken to limit matters in dispute not otherwise provided for — subject to details being provided 312.00

21. Settlement

(a) Judicial tender—

    (i) lodging or considering first tender 234.00

    (ii) lodging or considering each further tender 156.00

    (iii) if tender accepted, an additional fee to each accepting party 156.00

(b) Extrajudicial settlement — advising on, negotiating and agreeing extrajudicial settlement (not based on judicial tender) to include preparation and lodging of joint minute 390.00

(c) The Auditor may allow a fee in respect of work undertaken with a view to settlement (whether or not settlement is in fact agreed), including offering settlement 624.00

(d) If consultation held to consider tender, extrajudicial settlement (not based on judicial tender) or with a view to settlement (whether or not settlement is in fact agreed), attendance at it, per quarter hour 39.00

22. Proof or jury trial

Attendance fee, per quarter hour 39.00

23. Accounts

(a) Preparation of judicial account, to include production of vouchers and adjustment of expenses 312.00

(b) Perusal of points of objections, per quarter hour 39.00

(c) Attendance at taxation, per quarter hour 39.00

24. Ordering and obtaining extract 58.50

25. Final procedure

(a) If case goes to proof or jury trial, or is settled within 14 days before the diet of proof or jury trial, to include all work to close of cause so far as not otherwise provided for 312.00

(b) In any other case 97.50

PART VI — INNER HOUSE BUSINESS

1. Reclaiming motions   £

(a) Fee for reclaimer for all work (except as otherwise provided for in this Part) up to interlocutor sending cause to roll 234.00

£

(b)   Fee for respondent 117.00

(c)   Additional fee for each party for preparing or revising every 50 pages of Appendix 97.50

2. Appeals from inferior courts

(a)   Fee for appellant 273.00

(b)   Fee for respondent 136.50

(c)   Additional fee for each party for preparing or revising every 50 pages of Appendix 97.50

3. Special cases, Inner House petitions and appeals other than under paragraph 2 of this Part

According to circumstances of the case.

4. Note of objection

(a)   Instructing, perusing and lodging note of objection 156.00

(b)   Perusing opponent's note of objection 78.00

(c)   Where attendance of counsel or other person having a right of audience and/or solicitor required inclusive of instruction of counsel or other person having a right of audience, not exceeding half an hour 117.00

(d)   Thereafter attendance fee, per additional quarter hour 39.00

5. Grounds of appeal or cross appeal

(a)   Instructing, perusing and lodging grounds of appeal or cross appeal 156.00

(b)   Perusing opponent's note of appeal or cross appeal 78.00

6. Incidental procedure

All work in connection with noting remittance of cause to Summar Roll and fixing of Summar Roll hearing 156.00

7. Summar Roll

(a)   Preparing for hearing and instructing counsel or other person having a right of audience including instructing and lodging lists of authorities and notes of arguments 234.00

(b) Attendance fee, per quarter hour 39.00

8. Obtaining a bond of caution 97.50

9. Other matters

Where applicable, charges under Part V of this Chapter of this Table

PART VII — ADMIRALTY, MERCANTILE SEQUESTRATIONS AND
APPLICATIONS FOR SUMMARY TRIAL UNDER SECTION 26 OF THE ACT OF 1988 AND
CAUSES REMITTED FROM THE SHERIFF COURT

Charges under this Part shall be based on this Table according to the circumstances.

PART VIII — SOLICITORS EXERCISING RIGHTS OF AUDIENCE UNDER SECTION 25 OF THE
SOLICITORS (SCOTLAND) ACT 1980

1.   The Auditor shall allow to a solicitor who exercises a right of audience by virtue of section 25A of the Solicitors (Scotland) Act 1980 such fee for each item of work done by the solicitor in the exercise of such right as he would allow to counsel for an equivalent item of work.

2.   Where a solicitor exercises a right of audience by virtue of section 25A of the Solicitors (Scotland) Act 1980, and is assisted by another solicitor or a clerk, the Auditor may also allow attendance fees in accordance with Parts IV and V of this Chapter of this Table.

PART IX — GENERAL

The Auditor shall have the power to apportion the foregoing fees in this chapter between parties' solicitors in appropriate circumstances or to modify them in the case of a solicitor acting for more than one party in the same cause or in the case of the same solicitor acting in more than one cause arising out of the same circumstances or in the event of a cause being settled or disposed of at a stage when the work covered by an inclusive fee has not been completed.

CHAPTER IV — TRANSCRIPTS OF EVIDENCE ETC.

[Chapter IV is printed as amended by:

Act of Sederunt (Rules of the Court of Session 1994 Amendment) (Shorthand Writers' Fees) 1995 (SI 1995 No 1023) which came into force on 1st May 1995;

Act of Sederunt (Rules of the Court of Session Amendment No 2) (Fees of Shorthand Writers) 1996 (SI 1996 No 754) which came into force on 1st May 1996;

Act of Sederunt (Rules of the Court of Session Amendment No 5) (Transcripts of Evidence and Attendance Fees for Shorthand Writers etc.) 1997 (SI 1997 No 1260) which came into force on 1st May 1997;

Act of Sederunt (Rules of the Court of Session Amendment No 2) (Fees of Shorthand Writers) 1998 (SI 1996 No 993) which came into force on 1st May 1998;

Act of Sederunt (Rules of the Court of Session Amendment No 2) (Fees of Shorthand Writers) 1999 (SI 1999 No 615) which came into force on 1st May 1999;

Act of Sederunt (Rules of the Court of Session Amendment No 2) (Fees of Shorthand Writers) 2000 (SSI 2000 No 143) which came into force on 1st June 2000;

Act of Sederunt (Rules of the Court of Session Amendment No 2) (Fees of Shorthand Writers) 2001 (SSI 2000 No 135) which came into force on 1st May 2001;

Act of Sederunt (Rules of the Court of Session Amendment) (Fees of Solicitors, Shorthand Writers and Witnesses) 2002 (SSI 2002 No 301) which came into force on 1st July 2002;

Act of Sederunt (Rules of the Court of Session Amendment No 4) (Fees of Shorthand Writers) 2003 (SSI 2003 No 247) which came into force on 1st June 2003;

Act of Sederunt (Rules of the Court of Session Amendment No 2) (Fees of Shorthand Writers) 2004 (SSI 2004 No 150) which came into force on 4th May 2004;

Act of Sederunt (Rules of the Court of Session Amendment No 3) (Fees of Shorthand Writers) 2005 (SSI 2005 No 148) which came into force on 25th April 2005;

Act of Sederunt (Rules of the Court of Session Amendment No 2) (Fees of Shorthand Writers) 2006 (SSI 2006 No 87) which came into force on 1st May 2006;

Act of Sederunt (Rules of the Court of Session Amendment No 3) (Fees of Shorthand Writers) 2007 (SSI 2007 No 234) which came into force on 1st May 2007;

Act of Sederunt (Rules of the Court of Session Amendment No 2) (Fees of Shorthand Writers) 2008 (SSI 2008 No 120) which came into force on 5th May 2008;

Act of Sederunt (Rules of the Court of Session Amendment No 4) (Fees of Shorthand Writers) 2009 (SSI 2009 No 105) which came into force on 4th March 2009;

Act of Sederunt (Rules of the Court of Session Amendment No 2) (Fees of Shorthand Writers) 2011 (SSI 2011 No 165) which came into force on 2nd May 2011;

Act of Sederunt (Rules of the Court of Session Amendment) (Fees of Shorthand Writers) 2012 (SSI 2012 No 100) which came into force on 21st May 2012;

Act of Sederunt (Rules of the Court of Session Amendment No 4) (Fees of Solicitors) 2012 (SSI 2012 No 270) which came into force on 5th November 2012;

Act of Sederunt (Rules of the Court of Session Amendment No 2) (Fees of Shorthand Writers) 2013 (SSI 2013 No 111) which came into force on 21st May 2013.]

1. **Attendance of shorthand writer** .... £

    Attendance by shorthand writer at proof, jury trial or commission, per hour, with a minimum fee of £166.80 per day 41.75

2. **Notes of evidence: extension by shorthand writer or transcriber**

    (a)   Except where these are transcribed daily, per sheet 6.80

    (b)   Where these are transcribed daily, per shee 8.36

    (c)   Where notes of evidence have been directed to be supplied for the use of the court, copies may be made available to parties, payable to the shorthand writer or transcriber by the solicitor for the parties obtaining the copies, per sheet 0.57

PART III — FEES IN SPECULATIVE CAUSES

Fees of solicitors in speculative causes

42.17.—(1) Where —

(a) any work is undertaken by a solicitor in the conduct of a cause for a client,

(b) the solicitor and client agree that the solicitor shall be entitled to a fee for the work only if the client is successful in the cause, and

(c) the agreement is that the fee of the solicitor for all work in connection with the cause is to be based on an account prepared as between party and party,

the solicitor and client may agree that the fees element in that account shall be increased by a figure not exceeding 100 per cent.

(2) The client of the solicitor shall be deemed to be successful in the cause where —

(a) the cause has been concluded by a decree which, on the merits, is to any extent in his favour;

(b) the client has accepted a sum of money in settlement of the cause; or

(c) the client has entered into a settlement of any other kind by which his claim in the cause has been resolved to any extent in his favour.

(3) In paragraph (1), "the fees element" means all the fees in the account of expenses of the solicitor —

(a) for which any other party in the cause other than the client of the solicitor has been found liable as taxed or agreed between party and party;

(b) before the deduction of any award of expenses against the client; and

(c) excluding the sums payable to the solicitor in respect of —

(i) any fees payable for copying documents and the proportion of any session fee in the Table of Fees and posts and incidental expenses under rule 42.11;

(ii) any additional fee allowed under rule 42.14 to cover the responsibility undertaken by the solicitor in the conduct of the cause; and

(iii) any charges by the solicitor for his outlays.

Table of Fees of Solicitors in the Sheriff Appeal Court

Act of Sederunt (Fees of Solicitors in the Sheriff Appeal Court) 2015

(SSI 2015 No 387)

Interpretation

3.—(1) In this Act of Sederunt—

"advocate" means a practising member of the Faculty of Advocates;

"the Court" means the Sheriff Appeal Court;

"solicitor" means a person qualified to practise as a solicitor under section 4 of the Solicitors (Scotland) Act 1980;

"solicitor advocate" means a solicitor having a right of audience before the Court of Session by virtue of section 25A of the Solicitors (Scotland) Act 1980.

(2) In this Act of Sederunt—

    (a)   a sheet consists of 250 words or numbers;

    (b)   a page consists of 125 words.

(3) Where there is a reference in this Act of Sederunt to a rule, it is a reference to that rule in the Act of Sederunt (Sheriff Appeal Court Rules) 2015.

Basis of charging

4.—(1) A solicitor may prepare an account of expenses on the basis of—

    (a)   Schedule 1 (detailed fees); or

    (b)   Schedule 2 (inclusive fees).

(2) A solicitor may not prepare an account of expenses partly on the basis of Schedule 1 and partly on the basis of Schedule 2.

(3) Only the proper expenses of process may be included in an account of expenses.

Outlays

5.   Any outlays reasonably incurred by a solicitor in relation to an appeal may be included in an account of expenses.

Value added tax

6.—(1) This paragraph applies where work done by a solicitor constitutes a supply of services in respect of which value added tax is chargeable.

(2) The amount of value added tax chargeable may be included in an account of expenses.

Copying of documents

7.—(1) This paragraph applies where a solicitor proposes to include a charge for copying of documents in an account of expenses.

(2) Where the copying was done other than in the place of business of the solicitor, it is to be shown as an outlay.

(3) The account of expenses must specify—

    (a)   the purpose of the copying;

    (b)   the number of copies made;

    (c)   the amount of the charge or outlay that the solicitor proposes should be allowed.

(4) The auditor of court is only to allow a charge or outlay if the auditor determines that—

    (a)   the copying had to be done in circumstances which were in some way exceptional;

    (b)   the documents which required to be copied were unusually numerous having regard to the nature of the appeal.

(5) Where the auditor allows a charge or outlay, the auditor is to allow an amount that the auditor considers reasonable in the circumstances.

Travel time

8. Where a charge for travel time is included in an account of expenses, the auditor is only to allow it on cause shown.

Employment of advocate or solicitor advocate

9.—(1) This paragraph applies where the Court has sanctioned work in an appeal as suitable for the employment of counsel.

(2) Where an advocate or a solicitor advocate is instructed, the auditor is to allow—

    (a)   the reasonable fees of an advocate or a solicitor advocate for doing that work; and

    (b)   the applicable fees for instructing an advocate or a solicitor advocate.

(3) Where a consultation is reasonably required in relation to that work, the auditor may allow—

    (a)   the reasonable fees of an advocate or a solicitor advocate for the consultation;

    (b)   the applicable fees for attending a consultation.

(4) Except on cause shown, the auditor may only allow fees under paragraph (3) in respect of one consultation in the course of the appeal.

(5) Where a solicitor advocate is not instructed by another solicitor, the auditor is not to allow the fees mentioned in subparagraphs (2)(b) and (3)(b).

Disallowance of expenses

10.—(1) At taxation, the auditor may only allow expenses if they are reasonable for conducting the appeal in a proper manner.

(2) The auditor is to disallow any expenses—

    (a)   that the auditor considers to be unnecessary;

    (b)   in relation to any part of the appeal where the party entitled to expenses was unsuccessful;

    (c)   where any part of the expenses have been incurred through the fault of the party entitled to them.

Inclusive fees: modification by auditor

11. Where an account of expenses is prepared on the basis of Schedule 2 (inclusive fees), the auditor may increase or reduce any fee if the auditor thinks it appropriate to do so.

SCHEDULE 1

DETAILED FEES

(Payable from 1st January 2016)

                  £

Time charges

		£
1.	Attendance at court conducting any hearing, per quarter hour	39.00
2.	Any other attendances with clients and others and at court except as otherwise provided—	
	(a) by solicitor, per quarter hour	39.00
	(b) by clerk, per quarter hour	19.50
3.	Travel time, per quarter hour	35.00
4.	Considering any document, per quarter hour	39.00

Documents

5.	Preparation of all necessary documents (except affidavits), per sheet	19.50

£

6. Preparation of affidavits, per sheet	39.00
7. Certifying or signing a document	9.75
8. Revising documents (where revisal ordered), per five sheets	9.75

Lodging in and borrowing from process

9. Making up and lodging the process	19.50
10. Lodging each necessary document in process	9.75
11. Borrowing from process, where necessary	9.75
12. Uplifting from process, where necessary	9.75

Note: The fee in paragraph 11 includes returning the borrowed item to the process.

Correspondence

13. Letters (except formal letters), per page	19.50
14. Formal letters	4.88
15. Telephone calls (except lengthy telephone calls)	9.75
16. Lengthy telephone calls, per quarter hour	39.00

Note: For the purposes of paragraph 16, the auditor is to determine whether a telephone call is lengthy.

Sheriff officers and extracts

17. Accepting intimation of any appeal or application	19.50
18. Instructing sheriff officer to give intimation or to execute diligence	9.75
19. For each additional party on whom intimation is simultaneously made	9.75
20. Ordering, procuring and examining any extract	39.00

Note: The fee in paragraph 18 includes examining the execution of intimation or diligence.

SCHEDULE 2

INCLUSIVE FEES

(Payable from 1st January 2016)

PART 1 — APPEALS UNDER THE STANDARD APPEAL PROCEDURE OR THE ACCELERATED APPEAL PROCEDURE

£

Initiation of appeal

1. All work (except appearances) up to appointment of appeal to standard appeal procedure or accelerated appeal procedure—

(a) fee for appellant	390.00
(b) fee for respondent	195.00

Cross appeals

2. Preparing and lodging—

(a) grounds of appeal	156.00
(b) answers to grounds of appeal	156.00
3. Considering opponent's grounds of appeal or answers to grounds of appeal	78.00

Referral of questions about competency of appeal

4. Preparing and lodging reference	156.00

£

5. Considering opponent's reference 78.00

6. Preparing and lodging note of argument 156.00

Lodging documents prior to procedural hearing

7. Lodging all necessary documents (except appendix) as required by the timetable 156.00

8. Preparing or revising appendix, per 50 pages 97.50

Conduct of and attendance at hearings

9. Conducting any hearing, per quarter hour 39.00

10. Attending any hearing (where advocate or solicitor advocate is instructed to conduct hearing), per quarter hour 35.00

Note: Paragraphs 9 and 10 do not apply where any other paragraph in this Part specifies that it includes initial attendance at court, unless that hearing is continued.

Preparation for appeal hearing

11. Preparing for appeal hearing (including instruction of advocate or a solicitor advocate to conduct the hearing).. 156.00

Motions and minutes

12. Preparing and lodging any written motion or minute, including initial attendance at court to conduct hearing—

    (a) where opposed 195.00

    (b) where unopposed 78.00

13. Considering opponent's written motion or minute, including initial attendance at court to conduct hearing—

    (a) where opposed 195.00

    (b) where uopposed 78.00

Amendment of pleadings

14. Preparing and lodging motion to amend 156.00

15. Considering opponent's motion to amend 117.00

16. Preparing and lodging opposition to motion 78.00

17. Considering opponent's opposition to motion 78.00

Withdrawal of solicitors

18. All work preparing for a peremptory hearing fixed under rule 17.3(1), including initial attendance at court to conduct peremptory hearing.. 156.00

Expenses

19. Preparing and lodging account of expenses 234.00

20. Conducting taxation hearing, per quarter hour 39.00

Extracts

21. Ordering and obtaining an extract 58.50

Instruction of advocate or solicitor advocate

22. Instructing advocate or solicitor advocate to revise pleadings 58.50

23. Instructing advocate or solicitor advocate to attend court to conduct a hearing 195.00

24. Attending consultation with advocate or solicitor advocate.......................................

    (a) where total time engaged does not exceed one hour 195.00

    (b) for each additional quarter hour.. 39.00

PART 2 — APPLICATIONS FOR NEW TRIAL OR TO ENTER JURY VERDICT

£

Initiation of application

1. All work (except appearances) up to issue of timetable—

    (a)   fee for applicant 390.00

    (b)   fee for respondent 195.00

Referral of questions about competency of application

2. Preparing and lodging reference.. 156.00

3. Considering opponent's reference 78.00

4. Preparing and lodging note of argument... 156.00

Lodging documents prior to procedural hearing

5. Lodging all necessary documents (except appendix) as required by the timetable.................. 156.00

6. Preparing or revising appendix, per 50 pages 97.50

Conduct of and attendance at hearings

7. Conducting any hearing, per quarter hour... 39.00

8. Attending any hearing (where advocate or solicitor advocate is instructed to conduct hearing), per quarter hour.. 35.00

Note: Paragraphs 7 and 8 do not apply where any other paragraph in this Part specifies that it includes initial attendance at court, unless that hearing is continued.

Preparation for hearing required to dispose of application

9. Preparing for hearing required to dispose of application (including instruction of advocate or a solicitor advocate to conduct the hearing).. 156.00

Motions and minutes

10. Preparing and lodging any written motion or minute, including initial attendance at court to conduct hearing—

    (a)   where opposed 195.00

    (b)   where unopposed 78.00

11. Considering opponent's written motion or minute, including initial attendance at court to conduct hearing—

    (a)   where opposed 195.00

    (b)   where unopposed 78.00

Amendment of pleadings

12. Preparing and lodging motion to amend 156.00

13. Considering opponent's motion to amend.. 117.00

14. Preparing and lodging opposition to motion 78.00

15. Considering opponent's opposition to motion... 78.00

Withdrawal of solicitors

16. All work preparing for a peremptory hearing fixed under rule 17.3(1), including initial attendance at court to conduct peremptory hearing... 156.00

Expenses

17. Preparing and lodging account of expenses 234.00

18. Conducting taxation hearing, per quarter hour.. 39.00

£

Extracts

19. Ordering and obtaining an extract 58.50

Instruction of advocate or solicitor advocate

20. Instructing advocate or solicitor advocate to revise pleadings............................... 58.50

21. Instructing advocate or solicitor advocate to attend court to conduct a hearing...... 195.00

22. Attending consultation with advocate or solicitor advocate

    (a) where total time engaged does not exceed one hour.. 195.00

    (b) for each additional quarter hour.. 39.00

PART 3 — APPEALS FROM SUMMARY CAUSES AND SMALL CLAIMS

£

Preparation for hearing required to dispose of appeal

1. Preparing for hearing under rule 29.4 (including instruction of advocate or a solicitor advocate to conduct the hearing).. 156.00

Conduct of and attendance at hearings

2. Conducting any hearing, per quarter hour... 39.00

3. Attending any hearing (where advocate or solicitor advocate is instructed to conduct hearing), per quarter hour... 35.00

Note: Paragraphs 2 and 3 do not apply where any other paragraph in this Part specifies that it includes initial attendance at court, unless that hearing is continued.

Motions and minutes

4. Preparing and lodging any written motion or minute, including initial attendance at court to conduct hearing—

    (a) where opposed 195.00

    (b) where unopposed 78.00

5. Considering opponent's written motion or minute, including initial attendance at court to conduct hearing—

    (a) where opposed 195.00

    (b) where unopposed 78.00

Withdrawal of solicitors

6. All work preparing for a peremptory hearing fixed under rule 17.3(1), including initial attendance at court to conduct peremptory hearing.. 156.00

Expenses

7. Preparing and lodging account of expenses 234.00

8. Conducting taxation hearing, per quarter hour... 39.00

Extracts

9. Ordering and obtaining an extract 58.50

Instruction of advocate or solicitor advocate

10. Instructing advocate or solicitor advocate to attend court to conduct a hearing..... 195.00

11. Attending consultation with advocate or solicitor advocate

    (a) where total time engaged does not exceed one hour.. 195.00

    (b) for each additional quarter hour.. 39.00

Table of Fees of Solicitors in the Sheriff Court

Act of Sederunt (Fees of Solicitors in the Sheriff Court) (Amendment and Further Provisions) 1993 (SI 1993 No 3080)

[This Schedule is printed as amended by:

Act of Sederunt (Fees of Solicitors in the Sheriff Court) (Amendment) 1998 (SI 1998 No 2675) which came into force on 1st December 1998;

Act of Sederunt (Fees of Solicitors in the Sheriff Court) (Amendment) 2002 (SSI 2002 No 235) which came into force on 10th June 2002;

Act of Sederunt (Fees of Solicitors in the Sheriff Court) (Amendment No 2) 2002 (SSI 2002 No 274) which came into force on 1st July 2002;

Act of Sederunt (Fees of Solicitors in the Sheriff Court) (Amendment No 4) 2002 (SSI 2002 No 568) which came into force on 1st January 2003;

Act of Sederunt (Fees of Solicitors and Witnesses in the Sheriff Court) (Amendment) 2004 (SSI 2004 No 152) which came into force on 4th May 2004;

Act of Sederunt (Fees of Solicitors in the Sheriff Court) (Amendment) 2008 (SSI 2008 No 40) which came into force on 1st April 2008;

Act of Sederunt (Fees of Solicitors in the Sheriff Court) (Amendment No. 2) 2008 (SSI 2008 No 72) which came into force on 31st March 2008;

Act of Sederunt (Fees of Solicitors and Witnesses in the Sheriff Court) (Amendment) 2011 (SSI 2011 No 403) which came into force on 1st January 2012;

Act of Sederunt (Fees of Solicitors in the Sheriff Court) (Amendment) 2014 (SSI 2014 No 14) which came into force on 1st March 2014.]

SCHEDULE

GENERAL REGULATIONS

1. The Tables of Fees in this Schedule shall regulate the taxation of accounts between party and party; and shall be subject to the aftermentioned powers of the court to increase or modify such fees.

2. The pursuer's solicitor's account shall be taxed by reference to the sum decerned for unless the court otherwise directs.

3. Where an action has been brought under summary cause procedure, only expenses under Chapter IV of the Table of Fees shall be allowed unless the court otherwise directs.

4. Fees for work done in terms of the Social Work (Scotland) Act 1968 and summary applications shall be chargeable under Chapter III of the Table of Fees.

5. The court shall have the following discretionary powers in relation to the Table of Fees:

    (a) In any case the court may direct that expenses shall be subject to modification.

    (b) The court may, on a motion on or after the date of any interlocutor disposing of expenses, pronounce a further interlocutor regarding those expenses allowing a percentage increase in the fees authorised by the Table of Fees to cover the responsibility undertaken by the solicitor in the conduct of the cause. In fixing the amount of the percentage increase the following factors shall be taken into account:

        (i) the complexity of the cause and the number, difficulty or novelty of the questions raised;

        (ii) the skill, time and labour and specialised knowledge required, of the solicitor;

        (iii) the number and importance of any documents prepared or perused;

        (iv) the place and circumstances of the cause or in which the work of the solicitor in preparation for, and conduct of, the cause has been carried out;

        (v) the importance of the cause or the subject matter of it to the client;

        (vi) the amount or value of money or property involved in the cause;

        (vii) the steps taken with a view to settling the cause, limiting the matters in dispute or limiting the scope of any hearing.

(c) Where a party or his solicitor abandons, fails to attend or is not prepared to proceed with any diet of proof, debate, appeal or meeting ordered by the court, the court shall have power to decern against that party for payment of such expenses as it considers reasonable.

6. The expenses to be charged against an opposite party shall be limited to proper expenses of process, subject to this proviso that precognitions, plans, analyses, reports, and the like (so far as relevant and necessary for proof of the matters in the record between the parties), although taken or made before the bringing of an action or the preparation of defences, or before proof is allowed, and although the case may not proceed to trial or proof, may be allowed.

7. Except as otherwise provided in the Table of Fees, a solicitor may charge an account either on the basis of the inclusive fees of Chapters I and II or on the basis of the detailed fees of Chapter III of the Table of Fees, but he may not charge partly on the one basis and partly on the other.

8. In order that the expenses of litigation may be kept within proper and reasonable limits only such expenses shall be allowed in the taxation of accounts as are reasonable for conducting it in a proper manner. It shall be competent to the auditor to disallow all charges for papers, parts of papers or particular procedure or agency which he shall judge irregular or unnecessary.

9. Notwithstanding that a party shall be found entitled to expenses generally yet if on the taxation of the account it appears that there is any particular part of the cause in which such party has proved unsuccessful or that any part of the expenses has been occasioned through his own fault he shall not be allowed the expense of such part of the proceedings.

10. When a remit is made by the court regarding matters in the record between the parties to an accountant, engineer, or other reporter the solicitors shall not, without special agreement, be personally responsible to the reporter for his remuneration, the parties alone being liable therefor.

11. Subject to paragraph 14 of these General Regulations, in all cases, the solicitor's outlays reasonably incurred in the furtherance of the cause shall be allowed.

12. Where the court has sanctioned work in a cause as suitable for the employment of counsel, the Auditor is to allow—

(a) where counsel is instructed, the reasonable fees of counsel for doing that work and the applicable fees for instructing counsel in Chapter II, Chapter III or Chapter IV of the Table of Fees; or

(b) where a solicitor advocate is instructed, the reasonable fees of a solicitor advocate for doing that work and, where the solicitor advocate is appearing on the instructions of another solicitor rather than on his or her own, the applicable fees for instructing counsel in Chapter II, Chapter III or Chapter IV of the Table of Fees.

12A. The Auditor may also allow fees of counsel or a solicitor advocate and of the instructing solicitor for consultations reasonably required in relation to the work for which sanction is granted, but except on cause shown, fees for only two consultations in the course of the cause are to be allowed.

12B. Otherwise, no fees are to be allowed for the work of counsel and no special account is to be taken of the work of a solicitor advocate.

12C. In paragraphs 12 to 12B of these general regulations and in the Table of Fees, "solicitor advocate" means a solicitor who possesses a right of audience in the Court of Session by virtue of section 25A of the Solicitors (Scotland) Act 1980 (rights of audience in the Court of Session etc.)(1).

13. Where work done by a solicitor constitutes a supply of services in respect of which value added tax is chargeable by him, there may be added to the amount of fees an amount equal to the amount of value added tax chargeable.

14. In Chapter IV, of the Table of Fees —

(a) necessary outlays, including fees for witnesses, are allowable in addition to the fees allowable under that Chapter;

(b) in Parts I, II, III, and IIIA and IIIB, sheriff officers' fees and costs of advertising are allowable as outlays;

(c) No fee is allowable under the following provisions for attendance at a continuation of the first calling, unless specially authorised by the court—

   (i) in Part I, paragraph 3 (attendance at court);

   (ii) in Part II, paragraph 3 (attendance at court);

   (iii) in Part III, paragraph 5 (attendance at court);

   (iv) in Part IIIA, paragraph 5 (attendance at court);

   (v) in Part IIIB, paragraph 18 (attendance at court);

(d) in Part II, in respect of paragraph 7 (precognitions), in a case where a skilled witness prepares his own precognition or report, half of the drawing fee is allowable to the solicitor for perusing it (whether or not in the course of doing so he revises or adjusts it);

(e) in Part II, in respect of paragraph 15 (appeals), in Part III, in respect of paragraph 18 (appeals), in Part IIIA, in respect of paragraph 18 (appeals) and Part IIIB, in respect of paragraph 22 (appeals) no fees shall be allowed in respect of accounts of expenses when the hearing on the claim for expenses takes place immediately on the sheriff or sheriff principal announcing his decision;

(f) except in personal injury claims falling within paragraph I (actions of a value from £1,000 to £2,500) of the following table all fees chargeable under that Chapter in respect of the actions mentioned in the left-hand column of the following table shall unless the sheriff, on a motion in that behalf, otherwise directs, be reduced by the amount of the percentage specified opposite those actions in the right-hand column of the following table:

15. In addition to the matters set out in the Table of Fees, travel time at a rate of £35 per quarter hour may be claimed on cause shown at the discretion of the Auditor.

TABLE

Actions	Percentage reduction
1. of a value* from £1,000 to £2,500	25%
2. of a value* of less than £1,000	50%

* "value" in relation to any action in which a counterclaim has been lodged, is the total of the sums craved in the writ and the sum claimed in the counterclaim.

(g) in Part I, in respect of paragraph 1 (instruction fees), in relation to actions for reparation there are allowable such additional fees for precognitions and reports as are necessary to permit the framing of the writ and necessary outlays in connection therewith; and

(h) in Part II, the fee allowable in respect of paragraph 14 (supplementary note of defence) is a fixed fee allowable only when a supplementary note of defence is ordered by the court.

TABLE OF FEES

[This Table of Fees is printed as amended by:
Act of Sederunt (Fees of Solicitors in the Sheriff Court) (Amendment) 1994 (SI 1994 No 1142) which came into force on 24th May 1994;
Act of Sederunt (Fees of Solicitors in the Sheriff Court) (Amendment) 1995 (SI 1995 No 1395) which came into force on 22nd June 1995;
Act of Sederunt (Fees of Solicitors in the Sheriff Court) (Amendment) 1996 (SI 1996 No 236) which came into force on 1st April 1996;
Act of Sederunt (Fees of Solicitors in the Sheriff Court) (Amendment) 1998 (SI 1998 No 2675) which came into force on 1st December 1998;
Act of Sederunt (Fees of Solicitors in the Sheriff Court) (Amendment) 1999 (SSI 1999 No 149) which came into force on 1st January 2000;
Act of Sederunt (Fees of Solicitors in the Sheriff Court) (Amendment) 2000 (SSI 2000 No 420) which came into force on 1st January 2001;
Act of Sederunt (Fees of Solicitors in the Sheriff Court) (Amendment) 2001 (SSI 2001 No 438) which came into force on 1st January 2002;
Act of Sederunt (Fees of Solicitors in the Sheriff Court) (Amendment) 2002 (SSI 2002 No 235) which came into force on 10th June 2002;
Act of Sederunt (Fees of Solicitors in the Sheriff Court) (Amendment No 4) 2002 (SSI 2002 No 568) which came into force on 1st January 2002;
Act of Sederunt (Fees of Solicitors in the Sheriff Court) (Amendment) 2003 (SSI 2003 No 162) which came into force on 1st April 2003;
Act of Sederunt (Fees of Solicitors and Witnesses in the Sheriff Court) (Amendment) 2004 (SSI 2004 No 152) which came into force on 4th May 2004;
Act of Sederunt (Fees of Solicitors and Witnesses in the Sheriff Court) (Amendment No 2) 2004 (SSI 2004 No 196) which came into force on 3rd May 2004;
Act of Sederunt (Fees of Solicitors and Witnesses in the Sheriff Court) (Amendment) 2005 (SSI 2005 No 149) which came into force on 25th April 2005;

Act of Sederunt (Fees of Solicitors in the Sheriff Court) (Amendment) 2006 (SSI 2006 No 295) which came into force on 1st July 2006;

Act of Sederunt (Fees of Solicitors in the Sheriff Court) (Amendment) 2007 (SSI 2007 No 87) which came into force on 1st April 2007;

Act of Sederunt (Fees of Solicitors in the Sheriff Court) (Amendment) 2008 (SSI 2008 No 40) which came into force on 1st April 2008;

Act of Sederunt (Fees of Solicitors in the Sheriff Court) (Amendment) 2009 (SSI 2009 No 81) which came into force on 27th April 2009;

Act of Sederunt (Fees of Solicitors in the Sheriff Court) (Amendment No 2) 2009 (SSI 2009 No 321) which came into force on 2nd November 2009;

Act of Sederunt (Fees of Solicitors in the Sheriff Court) (Amendment) 2011 (SSI 2011 No 86) which came into force on 1st April 2011;

Act of Sederunt (Fees of Solicitors and Witnesses in the Sheriff Court) (Amendment) 2011 (SSI 2011 No 403) which came into force on 1st January 2012;

Act of Sederunt (Fees of Solicitors in the Sheriff Court) (Amendment) 2014 (SSI 2014 No 14) which came into force on 1st March 2014;

Act of Sederunt (Rules of the Court of Session 1994 and Fees of Solicitors in the Sheriff Court Amendment) (Courts Reform (Scotland) Act 2014) 2015 (SSI 2015 No 246) which came into force on 22nd September 2015.]

CHAPTER I

PART I. — UNDEFENDED ACTIONS (OTHER THAN ACTIONS OF DIVORCE OR SEPARATION AND ALIMENT (AFFIDAVIT PROCEDURE)

£

1. Actions (other than those specified in Part II of this Chapter) in which decree is granted without proof£

   (a) Inclusive fee to cover all work from taking instructions up to and including obtaining extract decree 273.00

   (b) In cases where settlement is effected after service of a writ but before the expiry of the induciae 234.00

   (c) In cases where a court appearance is necessary because of a time to pay direction an additional fee of 58.50

Note:

1. If the pursuer's solicitor elects to charge this inclusive fee he or she shall endorse a minute to that effect on the initial writ before ordering extract of decree.

2. Outlays such as court fees shall be chargeable in addition and taxation shall be unnecessary.

2. Actions of separation and aliment, adherence and aliment and custody and aliment where proof (other than by way of affidavit evidence) takes place

Inclusive fee to cover all work from taking instructions up to and including obtaining extract decree 1,014.00

Note:

1. If the pursuer's solicitor elects to charge this inclusive fee he or she shall endorse a minute to that effect on the initial writ after the close of the proof and before extract of decree is ordered.

2. When the option is so exercised, decree for expenses shall be granted against the defender for the said sum together with the court fee, any shorthand writer's fee actually charged as provided by Act of Sederunt and also any other necessary outlays without the necessity for taxation.

3. Petition for appointment of discharge of a curator bonis

Inclusive fee to cover all work enquiring into estate and taking instructions up to and including obtaining extract decree 936.00

Note:

1. If the solicitor elects to charge the inclusive fee and to recover only the normal outlays as set out in note 2, he or she shall endorse on the petition before ordering extract of the decree a minute setting out the said fee and the outlays. Taxation of charges so specified shall be unnecessary.

2. The normal outlays referred to in note 1 are—
reasonable fees for medical reports;
court dues for deliverance;
sheriff officers' fees for service;
advertising costs incurred;
value added tax chargeable on solicitors' fees.

PART II. — UNDEFENDED ACTIONS OF DIVORCE AND OF SEPARATION AND ALIMENT (AFFIDAVIT PROCEDURE)

1. In any undefended action of divorce or separation and aliment where —

   (a) the facts set out in section 1(2)(b) (unreasonable behaviour) of the Divorce (Scotland) Act 1976 ("the 1976 Act") are relied on;

   (b) there is no crave relating to any ancillary matters; and

   (c) the pursuer seeks to prove those facts by means of affidavits,

the pursuer's solicitor may, in respect of the work specified in column 1 of Table A, charge the inclusive fee specified in respect of that work in column 2 of that Table.

TABLE A

	Column 1 *Work done*	Column 2 *Inclusive fee* £
1.	All work to and including the period of notice	702.00
2.	All work from the period of notice to and including swearing affidavits	507.00
3.	All work from swearing affidavits to and including sending extract decree	156.00
4.	All work to and including sending extract decree	1,365.00
	Add process fee of	10%

2. In any undefended action of divorce or separation and aliment where —

   (a) the facts set out in sections 1(2)(a) (adultery), 1(2)(c) (desertion), 1(2)(d) (two years' non-cohabitation and consent) and 1(2)(e) (five years' non-cohabitation) of the 1976 Act are relied on;

   (b) there is no crave relating to any ancillary matters; and

   (c) the pursuer seeks to prove those facts by means of affidavits,

the pursuer's solicitor may, in respect of work specified in column 1 of Table B, charge the inclusive fee specified in respect of that work in column 2 of that Table.

TABLE B

	Column 1 *Work done*	Column 2 *Inclusive fee* £
1.	All work to and including the period of notice	585.00
2.	All work from the period of notice to and including swearing affidavits	273.00
3.	All work from swearing affidavits to and including sending extract decree	156.00
4.	All work to and including sending extract decree	1,014.00
	Add process fee of	10%

3. If —

   (a) the pursuer's solicitor charges an inclusive fee under either paragraph 1 or paragraph 2 of this Part; and

   (b) the action to which the charge relates includes a crave relating to an ancillary matter,

in addition to that fee he may charge, in respect of the work specified in column 1 of Table C, the inclusive fee specified in respect of that work in column 2 of that Table.

TABLE C

Column 1 *Work done*	Column 2 *Inclusive fee* £
1. All work to and including the period of notice	273.00
2. All work from the period of notice to and including swearing affidavits	156.00
4. All work under items 1 and 2	429.00
Add process fee of	10%

4. If the pursuer's solicitor elects to charge an inclusive fee under this Part he shall endorse a minute to that effect on the initial writ before extract of the decree is ordered; and when the option is so exercised decree for expenses shall be granted against the defender for said sum together with necessary outlays; and taxation shall be unnecessary.

CHAPTER II

[PART I WAS REVOKED BY ACT OF SEDERUNT (FEES OF SOLICITORS IN THE SHERIFF COURT) (AMENDMENT) 2000 (SSI 2000 No 420) WITH EFFECT FROM 1ST JANUARY 2001.]

PART II. — DEFENDED ORDINARY ACTIONS (OTHER THAN PERSONAL INJURIES ACTIONS TO WHICH PART IIA APPLIES), COMMERCIAL ACTIONS AND FAMILY ACTIONS COMMENCED AFTER 1ST JANUARY 1994

£

1. Work before action commences – Ordinary Action and Family Action

To cover all work which the Auditor is satisfied has reasonably been undertaken in contemplation of, or preparatory to, the commencement of proceedings (or such lesser sum as in the opinion of the Auditor is justified) 624.00

2. Work before action commences – Commercial Action

To cover all work which the Auditor is satisfied has reasonably been undertaken in contemplation of, or preparatory to, the commencement of proceedings in a commercial action or such other sum as in the opinion of the Auditor is justified.................................... 702.00

3. Instruction

(a) To cover all work (except as otherwise specifically provided for in this Part) from commencement to the lodging of defences including copying 780.00

(b) Additional fee where separate statement of facts and counterclaim and answers lodged 273.00

4. Precognitions and reports

Taking and drawing precognitions, per sheet 78.00

Note: Where a skilled witness prepares his or her own precognition or report, the solicitor shall be allowed, for perusing it (whether or not in the course of doing so he or she revises or adjusts it), half of the taking and drawing fee per sheet.

5. Productions

(a) For lodging productions, each inventory 78.00

(b) For considering opponent's productions, each inventory 39.00

6. Adjustment

To cover all work (except as otherwise specifically provided for in this Part) in connection with the adjustment of the record including making up and lodging certified copy record—.

		£
(a)	Solicitor for any party	351.00
(b)	If action settled before expiry of adjustment period, each original party's solicitor	195.00
(c)	If additional defender brought in before Options Hearing, additional fee to each original party's solicitor..	156.00
(d)	If additional defender brought in after Options Hearing, additional fee to each original party's solicitor	234.00

7. Affidavits

To framing affidavits, per sheet 39.00

7A. Valuation of claim in actions proceeding under Chapter 36A

(a) Fee to cover preparation of statement of valuation of claim

    (i) where counsel or solicitor advocate not employed 234.00

    (ii) where valuation of claim prepared by counsel or solicitor advocate 117.00

(b) Fee to cover consideration of opponent's valuation of claim............................. 117.00

(c) Inspection of documents, per quarter hour 39.00

8. Options Hearing or Child Welfare Hearing

To include preparation for and conduct of (each of) an Options Hearing or a Child Welfare Hearing and noting interlocutor— ....

(a) where initial hearing does not exceed half an hour.. 273.00

(b) where initial hearing exceeds half an hour, per additional quarter hour.......................... 39.00

(c) where hearing continued, for each continued hearing that does not exceed half an hour . 156.00

(d) where continued hearing exceeds half an hour, per additional quarter hour..................... 39.00

(e) for lodging and intimating or for considering note of the basis of preliminary plea, for each note lodged 78.00

9. Additional Procedure

For all work subsequent to Options Hearing including preparation for and attendance at procedural hearing—

(a) where initial hearing does not exceed half an hour.. 273.00

(b) where initial hearing exceeds half an hour, per additional quarter hour.......................... 39.00

10. Case Management Conference – Commercial Action

(a) To include preparation for and all work incidental thereto prior to the first case management conference.. 234.00

(b) To include preparation and all work incidental thereto prior to each subsequent conference;.. 117.00

(c) For every quarter hour engaged at conference 39.00

(d) Waiting time, per quarter hour 35.00

Note: Where case management conference takes place by way of telephone or other remote means the foregoing charges shall apply.

10A. Procedural Hearing in actions proceeding under Chapter 36A

To include preparation for and conduct of Procedural Hearing—

(a) where Procedural Hearing does not exceed half an hour................................ 273.00

(b) where Procedural Hearing exceeds half an hour, per additional quarter hour.................. 39.00

10B. Adjustment of issues and counter-issues

(a) All work in connection with and incidental to the lodging of an issue and adjustment and approval of it.. 156.00

£

(b) If one counter-issue, additional fee to pursuer 39.00

(c) Where more than one counter-issue, an additional fee to pursuer for each additional counter-issue 19.50

(d) All work in connection with and incidental to the lodging of a counter-issue and adjustment and approval of it 156.00

(e) Fee to defender or third party for considering issue where no counter-issue lodged 39.00

(f) Fee to defender or third party for considering each additional counter-issue 19.50

11. Note of Arguments – Commercial Action

(a) Fee for lodging and intimating or for considering first Note of Arguments 195.00

(b) For each Note lodged thereafter 78.00

12. Debate (other than on evidence)

(a) Where counsel or solicitor advocate not employed—

    (i) to include preparation for and all work in connection with any hearing or debate other than on evidence.. 312.00

    (ii) for every quarter hour engaged 39.00

(b) Where counsel or solicitor advocate employed, fee to solicitor appearing with counsel, per quarter hour... 35.00

(c) Waiting time, per quarter hour... 35.00

13. Interim Interdict Hearings and other Interim Hearings

(a) Preparation for each hearing, each party 156.00

(b) Fee to conduct hearing, per quarter hour 39.00

(c) Where counsel or solicitor advocate employed, fee to solicitor appearing with counsel, per quarter hour 35.00

(d) Waiting time, per quarter hour.. 35.00

14. Reports obtained under order of court

(a) Fee for all work incidental thereto 156.00

(b) Additional fee for perusal of report, per quarter hour 35.00

15. Commissions to take evidence

(a) On interrogatories—

    (i) fee to solicitor applying for commission to include drawing, intimating and lodging motion, drawing and lodging interrogatories, instructing commissioner and all incidental work (except as otherwise specially provided for in this Chapter) but excluding attendance at execution of commission... 429.00

    (ii) fee to opposing solicitor if cross-interrogatories prepared and lodged 273.00

    (iii) if no cross-interrogatories lodged 78.00

(b) Open commissions—

    (i) fee to solicitor applying for commission to include all work (except as otherwise specially provided for in this Chapter) up to lodging report of commission but excluding attendance at execution of commission 273.00

    (ii) fee to opposing solicitor 156.00

    (iii) fee for attendance at execution of commission, per quarter hour............................ 39.00

    (iv) if counsel or solicitor advocate employed, fee for attendance of solicitor, per quarter hour.. 35.00

£

16. Specification of documents

(a) Fee to cover drawing, intimating and lodging specification and relative motion—

    (i)   where motion unopposed.. 156.00

    (ii) where motion opposed, additional fee per quarter hour 39.00

(b) Fee to opposing solicitor—

    (i)   where motion not opposed.. 78.00

    (ii) where motion opposed, additional fee per quarter hour 39.00

(c) Fee for citation of havers, preparation for and attendance before commissioner at execution of commission—

    (i)   where a ttendance before commissioner does not exceed one hour 156.00

    (ii) for each additional quarter hour after the first hour 39.00

(d) If optional procedure adopted, fee per person upon whom order is served 39.00

(e) Fee for perusal of documents recovered, per quarter hour.. 39.00

17. Amendment of Record

(a) Fee to proposer—

    (i)   to cover drawing, intimating and lodging minute of amendment and relative motion 156.00

    (ii) fee for perusal of answers 78.00

    (iii) fee for any court appearance necessary, per quarter hour 39.00

£

(b) Fee to opponent—

    (i)   for perusing minute of amendment 117.00

    (ii) fee for preparation of answers... 78.00

    (iii) fee for any court appearance necessary per quarter hour........................... 39.00

(c) Additional fee for adjustment of minute and answers, where applicable, to be allowed to each party 156.00

18. Motions and minutes

(a) Fee to cover drawing, intimating and lodging any written motion or minute, including a reponing note, and initial attendance at court (except as otherwise specially provided for in this Chapter)—

    (i)   where opposed.. 195.00

    (ii) where unopposed (including for each party a joint minute other than under paragraph 26(b)) 78.00

(b) Fee to cover considering opponent's written motion, minute or reponing note, and attendance at court—

    (i)   where opposed.. 195.00

    (ii) where unopposed 78.00

19. Withdrawal of solicitors

(a) Fee to cover all work in preparation for any diet (or any diets) fixed under rule 24.2(1) and attendance at first such diet 156.00

(b) Fee for attendance at each additional such diet, per quarter hour................................ 39.00

20. Attendance not otherwise provided for

(a) Where hearing does not exceed half an hour 78.00

(b) Where hearing exceeds half an hour, per additional quarter hour 39.00

£

21. Hearing limitation fee

Fee to include work (except as otherwise specifically provided for in this Chapter) undertaken with a view to limiting the scope of any hearing, and including the exchange of documents, precognitions and expert reports, agreeing any fact, statement or document not in dispute, preparing and intimating any notice to admit or notice of non-admission (and consideration thereof) and preparing and lodging any joint minute, not exceeding 702.00

22. Preparation for proof or jury trial

(a) Fee to cover all work preparing for proof or jury trial (except as otherwise specially provided for in this Chapter)—

    (i) if action settled or abandoned not later than 14 days before the diet of proof or jury trial 468.00

    (ii) in any other case 780.00

(b) For each day or part day after the first, including instruction of counsel or solicitor advocate 117.00

(c) Fee to cover preparing for adjourned diet and all incidental work as in (a) if diet postponed for more than 6 days, for each additional diet 195.00

22A. Pre trial meeting in actions proceeding under Chapter 36A

(a) Fee arranging pre-trial meeting (each occasion) 78.00

(b) Fee preparing for pre-trial meeting—

    (i) where counsel or solicitor advocate not employed 429.00

    (ii) where counsel or solicitor advocate employed 214.50

(c) Fee for attending pre-trial meeting per quarter hour—

    (i) where counsel or solicitor advocate not employed 39.00

    (ii) where counsel or solicitor advocate employed 35.00

(d) Joint minute of pre-trial meeting 78.00

Note: Where pre-trial meeting takes place by way of video conference, the foregoing charges are to apply

23. Conduct of proof or jury trial

(a) Conduct of proof or jury trial, and debate on evidence if taken at close of proof or jury trial, per quarter hour 39.00

(b) If counsel or solicitor advocate employed, fee to solicitor appearing with counsel or solicitor advocate, per quarter hour 35.00

(c) Waiting time, per quarter hour 35.00

24. Debate on evidence

(a) Where debate on evidence not taken at conclusion of proof or jury trial, preparing for debate 156.00

(b) Fee for conduct of debate, per quarter hour 39.00

(c) If counsel or solicitor advocate employed, fee to solicitor appearing with counsel or solicitor advocate, per quarter hour 35.00

(d) Waiting time, per quarter hour 35.00

25. Appeals

(a) To sheriff principal—

    (i) fee to cover instructions, marking of appeal or noting that appeal marked, noting diet of hearing thereof and preparation for hearing

        (aa) no counsel or solicitor advocate employed 429.00

        (bb) if counsel or solicitor advocate employed, fee to solicitor 234.00

£

    (ii) fee to cover conduct of hearing, per quarter hour 39.00

    (iii) if counsel or solicitor advocate employed, fee to solicitor appearing with counsel or solicitor advocate, per quarter hour 35.00

    (iv) waiting time, per quarter hour 35.00

  (b) To Court of Session— ....
Fee to cover instructions, marking appeal or noting that appeal marked and instructing Edinburgh correspondents 156.00

26. Settlements

  (a) Judicial tender—

    (i) fee for preparation and lodging or for consideration of each minute of tender 156.00

    (ii) fee on acceptance of tender, to include preparation and lodging or consideration of minute of acceptance and attendance at court when decree granted in terms thereof.. 117.00

  (b) Extra-judicial settlement, to include negotiations resulting in settlement, framing or revising joint minute and attendance at court when authority interponed thereto (not to include drawing, intimating and lodging any written motion) 292.50

  (c) Whether or not fees are payable under (a) or (b) above, where additional work has been undertaken with a view to effecting settlement, including offering settlement, although settlement is not agreed, a fee not exceeding 292.50

  (d) If consultation held to consider tender, extrajudicial settlement (not based on judicial tender) or with a view to settlement (whether or not settlement is in fact agreed), attendance at it, per quarter hour 39.00

27. Final procedure

  (a) Fee to cover settling with witnesses, enquiring for cause at avizandum and noting final interlocutor 214.50

  (b) Fee to cover drawing account of expenses, arranging, intimating and attending diet of taxation and obtaining approval of auditor's report and where necessary, ordering, procuring and examining extract decree or adjusting account with opponent 195.00

28. Copying

For the copying of papers by whatever means, if the Auditor determines (either or both) that—

  (a) the copying had to be done in circumstances which were in some way exceptional;

  (b) the papers which required to be copied were unusually numerous having regard to the nature of the case,

such charge, if any, as the Auditor considers reasonable (but a charge based on time expended by any person shall not be allowed).

Note:

    1. Where a determination is required under this paragraph, the purpose of copying, the number of copies made and the charge claimed shall be shown in the account.

    2. Copying done other than in the place of business of the solicitor shall be shown as an outlay

29. Process fee

Fee to cover all consultations between solicitor and client during the progress of the cause and all communications, written or oral, passing between them – 10 per cent on total fees and copyings allowed on taxation.

30. Instruction of counsel or solicitor advocate

  (a) Fee for instructing counsel or solicitor advocate to revise pleadings 78.00

  (b) Fee for instructing counsel or solicitor advocate to attend court 195.00

£

(c) Fee for attending consultation with counsel or solicitor advocate—

    (i) where total time engaged does not exceed one hour 195.00

    (ii) for each additional quarter hour 39.00

PART IIA – DEFENDED PERSONAL INJURIES ACTIONS PROCEEDING UNDER PART AI OF CHAPTER 36 OF THE ORDINARY CAUSE RULE

1. Precognitions and reports £

Taking and drawing, per sheet 78.00

Note: Where a skilled witness prepares his or her own precognition or report, the solicitor shall be allowed, for perusing it (whether or not in the course of doing so he or she revises or adjusts it), half of the taking and drawing fee per sheet.

2. Pre-litigation fee

All work which the Auditor is satisfied has reasonably been undertaken in contemplation of, or preparatory to the commencement of proceedings (or such lesser sum as in the opinion of the Auditor is justified) 624.00

3. Instruction

(a) To cover all work (except as otherwise specifically provided for in this Part) from commencement to the lodging of defences 780.00

(b) Instructing re-service by sheriff officers where necessary 78.00

(c) Specification of documents as per Form PI2.. 78.00

(d) Fee to opponent for considering specification of documents.. 78.00

(e) Arranging commission to recover documents, citing havers, instructing commissioner and shorthand writer and preparation for commission.. 156.00

(f) Fee to opponent where a commission arranged 78.00

(g) Attendance at execution of commission, per quarter hour 39.00

(h) If optional procedure adopted, a fee per person on whom order is served........................ 39.00

(i) Fee for perusal of documents recovered under a specification of documents (or by informal means) where not otherwise provided for in the Table of Fees, per quarter hour 39.00

(j) Attendance in chambers for appointment of cause to Chapter 36A, per quarter hour 39.00

(k) Additional fee where separate counterclaim and answers lodged 273.00

4. Productions £

(a) For lodging productions, each inventory... 78.00

(b) For considering opponent's productions, each inventory... 39.00

5. Adjustment

To cover all work (except as otherwise specifically provided for in this Part) in connection with adjustment of the record including making up and lodging certified copy record—

(a) Solicitor for any party... 351.00

(b) If action settled before expiry of adjustment period, each original party's solicitor 195.00

(c) Additional fee to sub-paragraph (a) or (b), to include amendment to the pursuer and existing defender, to be allowed for each pursuer, defender or third party brought in before the record is lodged under the timetable issued under rule 36.G1(1)(b) 156.00

(d) Additional fee if an additional pursuer, defender or third party is brought in after the record is lodged under the timetable issued under rule 36.G1(1)(b) to the existing pursuer and existing defender or defenders.. 234.00

5A. Adjustment of issues and counter issues

   (a) All work in connection with and incidental to the lodging of an issue and adjustment and approval of it 156.00

   (b) If one counter-issue, additional fee to pursuer 39.00

6. Affidavits

Framing affidavits, per sheet.. 39.00

7. Valuation of Claim

   (a) Fee to cover preparation of statement of valuation of claim—

      (i) where counsel or solicitor advocate not employed 234.00

      (ii) where valuation of claim prepared by counsel or solicitor advocate 117.00

   (b) Fee to cover consideration of opponent's valuation of claim 117.00

   (c) Inspection of documents, per quarter hour 39.00

8. Incidental hearings/variation of timetable order

   (a) Fee to cover preparing for and attendance at hearing not exceeding half an hour 117.00

   (b) Thereafter attendance fee, per additional quarter hour 39.00

   (c) In event of separate advising/opinion and all work incidental thereto 117.00

9. Reports obtained under order of court excluding Auditor's Report

   (a) All work incidental thereto 156.00

   (b) Additional fee for perusal of report, per quarter hour 35.00

10. Specification of documents (if further specification deemed necessary)

   (a) Fee to cover drawing, intimating and lodging specification and relevant motion—

      (i) where motion unopposed.. 156.00

      (ii) where motion opposed, additional fee per quarter hour.......................... 39.00

   (b) Fee to opponent—

      (i) where motion not opposed.. 78.00

      (ii) where motion opposed, additional fee per quarter hour.......................... 39.00

   (c) Fee for arranging commission to recover documents, citing havers, instructing commissioner and shorthand writer and preparation for commission 156.00

   (d) Fee to opponent... 78.00

   (e) Attendance at execution of commission, per quarter hour... 39.00

   (f) If optional procedure adopted, fee per person upon whom order is served..................... 39.00

   (g) Fee for perusal of documents recovered under a specification of documents (or by informal means) where not otherwise provided for in the Table of Fees, per quarter hour 39.00

11. Commission to take evidence   £

   (a) On interrogatories—

      (i) fee to solicitor applying for commission to include drawing, intimating and lodging interrogatories, instructing commissioner and all incidental work (except as otherwise specifically provided for in this Chapter) but excluding attendance at execution of commission... 429.00

      (ii) fee to opposing solicitor if cross-interrogatories prepared and lodged.................... 273.00

   (b) Open commission—

      (i) fee to solicitor applying for commission to include all work (except as otherwise specifically provided for in this Chapter) up to and lodging report of commission but excluding attendance at execution of commission... 273.00

(ii)   fee to opposing solicitor 156.00

(iii)   fee for attendance at execution of commission, per quarter hour 39.00

(iv)   if counsel or solicitor advocate employed, fee to solicitor appearing with counsel or solicitor advocate, per quarter hour 35.00

12. Motions and minutes

(a)   Fee to cover drawing, intimating and lodging any written motion or minute, including a reponing note, and relative attendance at court (except as otherwise specifically provided for in this Chapter)—

    (i)   where opposed 195.00

    (ii)   where unopposed (including for each party a joint minute other than under paragraph 24(b)) 78.00

    (iii)   attendance at continued motion, per quarter hour 39.00

(b)   Fee to cover considering opponent's written motion, minute or reponing note and attendance at court—

    (i)   where opposed 195.00

    (ii)   where unopposed 78.00

    (iii)   attendance at continued motion, per quarter hour 39.00

13. Debate (other than on evidence)

(a)   Where counsel or solicitor advocate not employed—

    (i)   to include preparation for all work incidental to any hearing or debate other than on evidence 312.00

    (ii)   fee for conduct of hearing or debate other than on evidence, per quarter hour 39.00

(b)   Where counsel or solicitor advocate employed—

    (i)   to include preparation for and all work incidental to any hearing or debate other than on evidence 156.00

    (ii)   fee to solicitor appearing with counsel or solicitor advocate, per quarter hour 35.00

(c)   Waiting time, per quarter hour 35.00

(d)   Fee for lodging and intimating or for considering first note of arguments 78.00

(e)   For each note lodged thereafter 78.00

14. Incidental Procedure (not chargeable prior to allowance of proof or jury trial)

To cover all work, where applicable, in connection with noting diet of proof or jury trial and—

(a)   preparing note on line of evidence; or 273.00

(b)   instructing counsel or solicitor advocate to prepare a note on line of evidence 195.00

15. Amendment of Record

(a)   Fee to proposer—

    (i)   to cover drawing, intimating and lodging minute of amendment and relevant motion 156.00

    (ii)   Fee for perusal of answers 78.00

    (iii)   Fee for any court appearance necessary, per quarter hour 39.00

(b)   Fee to opponent—

    (i)   for perusal of minute of amendment 117.00

    (ii)   Fee for preparation of answers 78.00

    (iii)   Fee for any court appearance necessary, per quarter hour 39.00

(c)   Additional fee for adjustment of minute of amendment and answers, where applicable, to be allowed to each party 156.00

£

16. Withdrawal of solicitors

   (a)   Fee to cover all work in preparation for any diet (or diets) fixed under rule 24.2(1) and attendance at first such diet 156.00

   (b)   Fee for attendance at each additional such diet, per quarter hour................................... 39.00

17. Attendance not otherwise provided for

   (a)   Where hearing does not exceed half an hour 78.00

   (b)   Where hearing exceeds half an hour, per additional quarter hour..................................... 39.00

18. Hearing limitation fee

Fee to include work (except as otherwise specifically provided for in this Chapter) undertaken with a view to limiting the scope of any hearing, and including the exchange of documents, precognitions and expert reports, agreeing any fact, statement or document not in dispute, preparing and intimating any notice to admit or notice of non-admission (and consideration thereof) and preparing and lodging any joint minute, not exceeding..................................... 273.00

19. Preparation for proof or jury trial

   (a)   Fee to cover all work preparing for proof or jury trial (except as otherwise specifically provided for in this Chapter)—

      (i)   if action settled or abandoned not later than 14 days before diet of proof or jury trial... 468.00

      (ii)   in any other case 858.00

      (iii)   additional fee chargeable over and above foregoing fees upon the Auditor being satisfied as to additional work undertaken as evidenced by production of a detailed breakdown of the work undertaken

   (b)   For each day or part day after the first, including instruction of counsel or solicitor advocate 117.00

   (c)   Fee to cover preparing for adjourned diet and all incidental work as in (a) if diet postponed for more than 6 days, each additional diet... 195.00

20. Pre-trial meeting

   (a)   Fee arranging pre-trial meeting (each occasion) 78.00

   (b)   Fee preparing for pre-trial meeting—

      (i)   where counsel or solicitor advocate not employed 429.00

      (ii)   where counsel or solicitor advocate employed 214.50

   (c)   Fee for attending pre-trial meeting per quarter hour—

      (i)   where counsel or solicitor advocate not employed 39.00

      (ii)   where counsel or solicitor advocate employed 35.00

Note: where pre-trial meeting takes place by way of video conference, the foregoing charges are to apply.

21. Joint minute of pre-trial meeting... 78.00

22. Conduct of proof or jury trial

   (a)   Conduct of proof or jury trial, and debate on evidence if taken at close of proof or jury trial, per quarter hour 39.00

   (b)   If counsel or solicitor advocate employed, fee to solicitor appearing with counsel or solicitor advocate, per quarter hour... 35.00

   (c)   Waiting time, per quarter hour... 35.00

23. Debate on evidence

   (a)   Where debate on evidence not taken at conclusion of proof or jury trial, preparing for debate 156.00

£

(b) Fee for conduct of debate, per quarter hour 39.00

(c) If counsel or solicitor advocate employed, fee to solicitor appearing with counsel or solicitor advocate, per quarter hour 35.00

(d) Waiting time, per quarter hour 35.00

24. Settlements

(a) Settlement by judicial tender—

    (i) fee for preparation and lodging or for consideration of each minute of tender 156.00

    (ii) additional fee on acceptance of tender, to include preparation and lodging or consideration of minute of acceptance of tender and attendance at court when decree granted in terms thereof (not to include drawing, intimating and lodging any written motion) 117.00

(b) Extra-judicial settlement, to include negotiations resulting in settlement, framing or revising joint minute and attendance at court when authority interponed thereto (not to include drawing, intimating and lodging any written motion) 292.50

(c) Whether or not fees payable under (a) or (b) above, where additional work has been undertaken with a view to effecting settlement, including offering settlement, although settlement is not agreed, not exceeding 292.50

25. Final procedure

(a) If case goes to proof or jury trial, or is settled within 14 days before the diet of proof or jury trial, fee to cover settling with witnesses and enquiring for cause at avizandum and noting final interlocutor 214.50

(b) In any other case 97.50

26. Copying

For the copying of papers by whatever means, if the Auditor determines (either or both) that—

(a) the copying had to be done in circumstances which were in some way exceptional;

(b) the papers which required to be copied were unusually numerous having regard to the nature of the case,

such charge, if any, as the Auditor considers reasonable (but a charge based on the time expended by any person shall not be allowed).

Note:

1. Where a determination is required under this paragraph, the purpose of copying, the number of copies made and the charge claimed shall be shown in the account.

2. Copying done other than in the place of business of the solicitor shall be shown as an outlay.

27. Process fee

Fee to cover all consultations between solicitor and client during the progress of the cause and all communications, written or oral, passing between them — 10 per cent on total fees and copyings allowed on taxation.

28. Instruction of counsel or solicitor advocate

 £

(a) Fee for instructing counsel or solicitor advocate to revise the pleadings 78.00

(b) Fee for instructing counsel or solicitor advocate to attend court 195.00

(c) Fee for attending consultation with counsel or solicitor advocate—

    (i) where total time engaged does not exceed one hour 195.00

    (ii) for each additional quarter hour 39.00

£

29. Appeals

(a) To sheriff principal—

   (i) fee to cover instructions, marking of appeal or noting that appeal marked, noting diet of hearing thereof and preparation for hearing

      (aa) no counsel or solicitor advocate employed... 429.00

      (bb) if counsel or solicitor advocate employed, fee to solicitor............................... 234.00

   (ii) fee to cover conduct of hearing, per quarter hour... 39.00

   (iii) if counsel or solicitor advocate employed, fee to solicitor appearing with counsel or solicitor advocate, per quarter hour 35.00

   (iv) waiting time, per quarter hour... 35.00

(b) To Court of Session—

Fee to cover instructions, marking appeal or noting that appeal marked and instructing Edinburgh correspondents... 156.00

30. Accounts

Fee to cover drawing account of expenses, arranging, intimating and attending diet of taxation and obtaining approval of auditor's report and where necessary, ordering, procuring and examining extract decree or adjusting account with opponent... 195.00

31. Ordering and procuring extract 39.00

CHAPTER III
CHARGES FOR TIME, DRAWING OF PAPERS, CORRESPONDENCE ETC

1. Attendance at court

Conduct of trial, proof or formal debate or hearing, per quarter hour 39.00

2. Time occupied in the performance of all other work

To include attendances with clients and others and attendances at court in all circumstances, except as otherwise specially provided—

(a) solicitor, per quarter hour 39.00

(b) allowance for time of clerk, one-half of above

3. Drawing papers

Drawing all necessary papers (other than affidavits), per sheet 19.50

Note: The sheets throughout this Chapter are to consist of 250 words or numbers.

4. Framing affidavits, per sheet   39.00

5. Revising papers where revisal ordered, for each five sheets 9.75

6. Copying

For the copying of papers by whatever means, if the Auditor determines (either or both) that—

(a) the copying has to be done in circumstances which were in some way exceptional;

(b) the papers which required to be copied were unusually numerous having regard to the nature of the case,

such charge, if any, as the Auditor considers reasonable (but a charge based on time expended by any person shall not be allowed).

Note:

    1. Where a determination is required under this paragraph, the purpose of copying, the number of copies made and the charge claimed shall be shown in the account.

    2. Copying done other than in the place of business of the solicitor shall be shown as an outlay.

	£
7. Certifying or signing a document	9.75
8. Perusing any document, per quarter hour	39.00

9. Lodging in process

Each necessary lodging in or uplifting from process; also for each necessary enquiry for documents due to be lodged 9.75

10. Borrowing process

Each necessary borrowing of process to include return of same 9.75

11. Extracts

Ordering, procuring and examining extracts, interim or otherwise 39.00

12. Correspondence, intimation, etc.

    (a) Formal letters and intimation 4.88

    (b) Letters other than above — per page of 125 words 19.50

    (c) Telephone calls except under (d) 9.75

    (d) Telephone calls (lengthy) to be treated as attendances or long letters

13. Citations

Each citation of party or witness including execution thereof 19.50

14. Instructions to officers

    (a) Instructing officer to serve, execute or intimate various kinds of writs or diligence including the examination of executions 9.75

    (b) For each party after the first on whom service or intimation is simultaneously made 9.75

    (c) Agency accepting service of any writ 19.50

    (d) Reporting diligence 19.50

15. Personal diligence

    (a) Recording execution of charge 19.50

    (b) Procuring fiat 19.50

    (c) Instructing apprehension 19.50

    (d) Framing state of debt and attendance at settlement 19.50

16. Sales

    (a) Obtaining warrant to sell 19.50

    (b) Instructing auctioneer or officer to conduct sale 19.50

    (c) Perusing report of sale 19.50

    (d) Reporting sale under poindings or sequestrations or any other judicial sales 19.50

    (e) Noting approval of roup roll 19.50

    (f) Obtaining warrant to pay 19.50

CHAPTER IV — SUMMARY CAUSES

PART I — UNDEFENDED ACTIONS

£

1. Inclusive fee

To include taking instructions, framing summons and statement of claim, obtaining warrant for service, instructing service as necessary by sheriff officer (where appropriate), attendance endorsing minute for and obtaining decree in absence and extract decree 213.00

2. Service

    (a) Citation by post wheresoever after the first citation, for each party 17.75

    (b) Framing and instructing service by advertisement, for each party 35.50

3 Attendance at court 35.50

PART II — DEFENDED ACTIONS (COMMENCED BEFORE 10TH JUNE 2002)

1. Instructions fee, to include taking instructions (including instructions for a counterclaim), framing summons and statement of claim, obtaining warrant for service, instructing service as necessary by sheriff officer (where appropriate), attendance endorsing minute for and obtaining decree in absence and extract decree 174.65

2. Service —

    (a) Citation by post within the United Kingdom, Isle of Man, Channel Islands, or the Republic of Ireland — for each party 14.45

          Citation by post elsewhere — for each party 31.85

    (b) Instructing service or reservice by sheriff officer including perusing execution of citation and settling sheriff officer's fee — for each party 14.45

    (c) Framing and instructing service by advertisement — for each party 46.10

3. Attendance at court —

    Attendance at any diet except otherwise specially provided. 46.10

4. Preparing for proof, to include all work in connection with proof not otherwise provided for 158.95

5. Fee to cover preparing for adjourned diet and all incidental work if diet for more than six days – for each adjourned diet 76.35

6. (a) Drawing and lodging inventory of productions, lodging the productions specified therein and considering opponent's productions (to be charged only once in each process) 69.75

    (b) Where only one party lodges productions, opponent's charges for considering same 31.95

7. Precognitions —

    (a) Drawing precognitions, including instructions, attendances with witnesses and all relative meetings and correspondence — per witness.. 69.75

    (b) Where precognitions exceed 2 sheets — for each additional sheet 31.95

8. Motions and minutes —

    Fee to cover drawing, intimating and lodging of any written motion or minute, excluding a minute or motion to recall decree, and relative attendance at court (except as otherwise provided in this Chapter) —

    (a) Where opposed.. 94.90

    (b) Where unopposed (including for each party a joint minute or joint motion) 58.50

9. Fee to cover considering opponent's written motion or minute excluding minute or motion to recall decree and relative attendance at court —

    (a) Where motion or minute opposed 76.35

    (b) Where motion or minute unopposed 46.10

£

10. Conduct of proof —

    (a)   Fee to cover conduct of proof or trial and debate on evidence taken at close of proof — per half hour.. 46.10

    (b)   Waiting time — per half hour... 24.05

11. Settlements —

    (a)   Judicial tender, fee for consideration of, preparing and lodging of tender 94.90

        (i)   Fee for consideration and rejection tenders... 69.75

        (ii) Fee on acceptance of tender — to include preparing and lodging, or consideration of minute of acceptance and attendance at court when decree granted in terms thereof.. 69.75

    (b)   Extra-judicial settlement — fee to cover negotiations resulting in settlement, framing or revising joint minute and attendance at court when authority interponed thereto............ 158.95

12. Specification of documents —

    (a)   Fee to cover drawing, intimating and lodging specification of documents and relative motion and attendance at court... 79.35

    (b)   Inclusive fee to opposing Solicitor... 71.20

    (c)   Fee to citation of havers, preparation for and attendance before commissioner, to each party — for each half hour 46.10

    (d)   If alternative procedure adopted, a fee per person upon whom order served.................. 31.95

13. Commissions to take evidence —

    (a)   Fee to cover drawing, lodging and intimating motion and attendance at court

        (i)   Where opposed 94.90

        (ii) Where unopposed 58.50

    (b)   Fee to cover considering such motion and attendance at court

        (i)   Where opposed 76.35

        (ii) Where unopposed 46.10

    (c)   Fee to cover instructing commissioner and citing witnesses 46.10

    (d)   Fee to cover drawing and lodging interrogatories and cross-interrogatories — per sheet 31.95

    (e)   Attendance before commissioner — per hour.. 44.40

    (f)   Travelling time — per hour 31.95

14. Supplementary note of defence (when ordered).. 31.95

15. Appeals

    (a)   Fee to cover instructions, marking of appeal or noting that appeal marked, noting of diet of hearing thereof and preparation for hearing... 214.45

    (b)   Fee to cover conduct of hearing — per half hour 46.10

16. Final procedure —

    (a)   Fee to cover settling with witnesses, enquiring for cause at avizandum, noting final interlocutor.. 94.90

    (b)   Fee to cover drawing account of expenses, arranging, intimating and attending hearing on expenses, and obtaining approval of sheriff clerk's report.. 94.90

    (c)   Fee to cover considering opponents' account of expenses and attendance at hearing on expenses 46.10

PART III — DEFENDED ACTIONS (COMMENCED ON OR AFTER 10TH JUNE 2002)

1.   Work before action commences

To cover all work of a pre-litigation basis, to include discussions/correspondence with opposing party, exchange of documentation, etc. (not exceeding 1 hour)............................... 142.00

£

2. Instruction

(a) To include taking instructions, framing summons and statement of claim, statement of valuation, obtaining warrant for service, enquiring for and consideration of Response Form (1½ hours) 213.00

(b) Where counterclaim and answers lodged, additional fee (1½ hours) 213.00

(c) If additional defender/third party brought in, additional fee to each original party's solicitor (1 hour) 142.00

3. Service

(a) Citation by post for each party—

(i) within the United Kingdom, Isle of Man, Channel Islands, or the Republic of Ireland 17.75

(ii) elsewhere 35.50

(b) Instructing service or re-service by sheriff officer including perusing execution of citation and settling sheriff officer's fee, for each party 17.75

(c) Framing and instructing service by advertisement, for each party 53.25

4. Attendance at first calling

(a) To include necessary preparation for and conduct of (each of) such hearings and noting interlocutor (1½ hours) 213.00

(b) Where waiting/hearing exceeds half an hour, per additional quarter hour 35.50

5. Attendance at court

Attendance at any hearing except as otherwise specially provided, per half hour 35.50

6. Precognitions

Taking and drawing precognitions, per sheet 71.00

Note: Where a skilled witness prepares his or her own precognition or report, the solicitor shall be allowed for perusing it (whether or not in the course of doing so he or she revises or adjusts it), half of the taking and drawing fee per sheet.

7. Reports obtained under order of court

(a) All work incidental to report 142.00

(b) Additional fee for perusal of report, per quarter hour 32.00

8. Productions

(a) For lodging productions, each inventory 71.00

(b) For considering opponent's productions, each inventory 35.50

9. Affidavits

To framing affidavits (where ordered), per sheet 35.50

10. Incidental applications and minutes

(a) Fee to cover drawing, intimating and lodging of any written incidental applications or minute, excluding a minute to recall decree, and initial attendance at court (except as otherwise provided in this Chapter)

(i) where opposed 142.00

(ii) where unopposed — including for each party a joint minute or joint incidental application (other than under paragraph 15(b)) 71.00

(iii) where incidental application exceeds half an hour, additional fee per quarter hour 35.50

£

(b) Fee to cover considering opponent's written incidental application or minute, excluding minute to recall decree, and relative attendance at court—

    (i) where opposed 142.00

    (ii) where unopposed 71.00

    (iii) where incidental application exceeds half an hour, additional fee per quarter hour 35.50

11. Hearing limitation fee

Fee to include work done (except as otherwise specially provided in this Chapter) undertaken with a view to limiting the scope of any hearing, and including the agreement of evidence generally including the exchange of documents, precognitions and expert reports, agreeing any fact, statement or document not in dispute, preparation and lodging of witness list, preparing Schedule of Damages and preparing and lodging joint minute (not exceeding 1 hour) 142.00

12. Procedure preliminary to proof

(a) Fee to cover all work preparing proof (except as otherwise specially provided for in this Chapter)

    (i) if action settled or abandoned not later than 7 days before the diet of proof 390.50

    (ii) in any other case 461.50

(b) Fee to cover preparing for adjourned diet and all incidental work as in (a) if diet postponed for more than 6 days, for each additional diet 142.00

(c) Fee for attendance inspecting opponent's documents, per quarter hour 35.50

13. Conduct of proof

(a) Fee to cover conduct of proof or trial and debate on evidence taken at close of proof, per quarter hour 35.50

(b) Waiting time, per quarter hour 32.00

14. Debate on evidence

(a) Where debate on evidence not taken at conclusion of proof, preparing for debate 106.50

(b) Fee for conduct of debate, per quarter hour 35.50

(c) Waiting time, per quarter hour 32.00

15. Settlements

(a) Judicial tender—

    (i) fee for preparation and lodging or for consideration of each minute of tender 142.00

    (ii) fee on acceptance of tender, to include preparation and lodging or consideration of minute of acceptance and attendance at court when decree granted in terms thereof 106.50

(b) Extra judicial settlement, to include negotiations resulting in settlement, framing or revising joint minute and attendance at court when authority interponed thereto 248.50

(c) Whether or not fees are payable under (a) or (b) above, where additional work has been undertaken with a view to effecting settlement, including offering settlement, although settlement is not agreed, not exceeding 248.50

16. Specification of documents

(a) Fee to cover drawing, intimating and lodging specification and relative incidental application—

    (i) where incidental application unopposed 142.00

    (ii) where incidental application opposed, additional fee per quarter hour 35.50

(b) Fee to opponent—

    (i) where incidental application unopposed 71.00

    (ii) where incidental application opposed, additional fee per quarter hour 35.50

£

(c) Fee for citation of havers, preparation for and attendance before commissioner at execution of commission—

    (i) where attendance before commissioner does not exceed one hour 142.00

    (ii) for each additional quarter hour after the first hour 35.50

(d) If optional procedure adopted, fee per person upon whom order is served 35.50

(e) Fee for perusal of documents recovered, per quarter hour 35.50

17. Commissions to take evidence – open commissions

(a) Fee to solicitor applying for commission to include all work (except as otherwise specially provided for in this Chapter) up to lodging report of commission but excluding attendance at execution of commission 213.00

(b) Fee to opponent 106.50

(c) Fee for attendance at execution of commission, per quarter hour 35.50

18. Appeals

(a) Fee to cover instructions, marking of appeal or noting that appeal marked, noting of diet of hearing thereof, perusing Stated Case, framing questions in law and adjustment thereof, including preparation for hearing 319.50

(b) Fee to cover conduct of hearing on adjustments, per quarter hour 35.50

(c) Conduct of appeal, per quarter hour 35.50

19. Final procedure

(a) Fee to cover settling with witnesses and noting final interlocutor 159.75

(b) Fee to cover drawing of expenses, arranging, intimating and attending diet of taxation and obtaining approval of auditor's report and where necessary, ordering, procuring and examining extract decree or adjusting account with opponent 142.00

(c) Fee to cover considering opponent's account of expenses, objections and attendance at hearing on expenses, per quarter hour 35.50

PART IIIA – DEFENDED ACTIONS: PERSONAL INJURY CLAIMS ONLY (COMMENCED ON OR AFTER 10TH JUNE 2002)

1. Work before action commences

To cover all work of a pre-litigation basis, to include discussions/correspondence with opposing party, exchange of documentation, etc. (not exceeding 3 hours) 426.00

2. Instruction

(a) To include taking instructions, framing summons and statement of claim, statement of valuation, obtaining warrant for service, enquiring for and consideration of Response Form (not exceeding 3⅛ hours) 443.75

(b) Where counterclaim and answers lodged, additional fee (not exceeding 1½ hours) 213.00

(c) If additional defender/third party brought in, additional fee to each original party's solicitor (not exceeding 1½ hours) 213.00

3. Service

(a) Citation by post for each party—

    (i) within the United Kingdom, Isle of Man, Channel Islands, or the Republic of Ireland 17.75

    (ii) elsewhere 35.50

£

(b) Instructing service or re-service by sheriff officer including perusing execution of
      citation and settling sheriff officer's fee, for each party 17.75

(c) Framing and instructing service by advertisement, for each party 53.25

4. Attendance at first calling

(a) To include necessary preparation for and conduct of (each of) such hearings and noting
      interlocutor (2 hours) 284.00

(b) Where waiting/hearing exceeds half an hour, for every extra quarter hour 35.50

5. Attendance at court

Attendance at any hearing except, as otherwise specially provided, per half hour 71.00

6. Precognitions

Taking and drawing, per sheet 71.00

Note: Where a skilled witness prepares his or her own precognition or report, the solicitor shall be allowed
for perusing it (whether or not in the course of doing so he or she revises or adjusts it), half of the taking
and drawing fee per sheet.

7. Reports obtained under order of court

(a) All work incidental to it 142.00

(b) Additional fee for perusal of report, per quarter hour 32.00

8. Productions

(a) For lodging productions, each inventory 71.00

(b) For considering opponent's productions, each inventory 35.50

9. Affidavits

To framing affidavits (where ordered), per sheet 35.50

10. Incidental applications and minutes

(a) Fee to cover drawing, intimating and lodging of any written incidental applications or
      minute, excluding a minute to recall decree, and initial attendance at court (except as
      otherwise provided in this Chapter)—

      (i)   where opposed 177.50

      (ii) where unopposed — including for each party a joint minute or joint incidental
            application (other than under paragraph 15(b)) 71.00

      (iii) where incidental application exceeds half an hour, additional fee per quarter hour   35.50

(b) Fee to cover considering opponent's written incidental application or minute, excluding
      minute to recall decree, and relative attendance at court—

      (i)   where opposed 177.50

      (ii) where unopposed 71.00

      (iii) where incidental application exceeds half an hour, additional fee per quarter hour   35.50

11. Procedure preliminary to proof

(a) Fee to cover all work preparing proof — as follows – exchanging of witness list,
      documents list, skilled witnesses, reports, consideration of defender's schedule of
      damages, citation of witnesses, general preparation for proof (except as otherwise
      specifically provided for in this Chapter) (not exceeding 3 hours)—

      (i)   if action settled or abandoned not later than 7 days before the diet of proof 585.75

      (ii) in any other case 781.00

£

(b) Fee to cover preparing for adjourned diet and all incidental work as in (a) if diet postponed for more than 6 days, for each additional diet 177.50

12. Hearing limitation fee

Fee to include work done (except as otherwise specially provided in this Chapter) undertaken with a view to limiting the scope of any hearing and including the agreement of evidence generally, including the agreement of photographs, sketch plans, documents, precognitions and expert reports, agreeing any fact, statement or documents, agreeing Schedule of Damages and preparing and lodging joint minute of admissions (not exceeding 4 hours) 585.75

13. Conduct of proof

(a) Fee to cover conduct of proof or trial and debate on evidence taken at close of proof, per quarter hour 35.50

(b) Waiting time, per quarter hour 32.00

14. Debate on evidence

(a) Where debate on evidence not taken at conclusion of proof, preparing for debate 142.00

(b) Fee for conduct of debate, per quarter hour 35.50

(c) Waiting time, per quarter hour 32.00

15. Settlements

(a) Judicial tender—
    (i) fee for preparation and lodging or for consideration of each minute of tender 142.00
    (ii) fee on acceptance of tender, to include preparation and lodging or consideration of minute of acceptance and attendance at court when decree granted in terms thereof 106.50

(b) Extra judicial settlement, to include negotiations resulting in settlement, framing or revising joint minute and attendance at court when authority interponed thereto 248.50

(c) Whether or not fees are payable under (a) or (b) above, where additional work has been undertaken with a view to effecting settlement, including offering settlement, although settlement is not agreed, not exceeding 248.50

16. Specification of documents

(a) Fee to cover drawing, intimating and lodging specification and relative incidental application—
    (i) where incidental application unopposed 142.00
    (ii) where incidental application opposed, additional fee per quarter hour 35.50

(b) Fee to opponent—
    (i) where incidental application unopposed 142.00
    (ii) where incidental application opposed, additional fee per quarter hour 35.50

(c) Fee for citation of havers, preparation for and attendance before commissioner at execution of commission—
    (i) where attendance before commissioner does not exceed one hour 142.00
    (ii) for each additional quarter hour after the first hour 35.50

(d) If optional procedure adopted, fee per person upon whom order is served 35.50

(e) Fee for perusal of documents recovered, per quarter hour 35.50

17. Commissions to take evidence – open commissions

(a) Fee to solicitor applying for commission to include all work (except as otherwise specially provided for in this Chapter) up to lodging report of commission but excluding attendance at execution of commission 248.00

(b) Fee to opponent 142.00

(c) Fee for attendance at execution of commission, per quarter hour 35.50

£

18. Appeals

(a) Fee to cover instructions, marking of appeal or noting that appeal marked, noting of diet of hearing thereof, perusing Stated Case, framing questions in law and adjustment thereof, including preparation for hearing 390.50

(b) If Counsel [or solicitor advocate] employed 213.00

(c) Fee to cover conduct of hearing on adjustments, per quarter hour 35.50

(d) Conduct of appeal, per quarter hour 35.50

19. Final procedure

(a) Fee to cover settling with witnesses and noting final interlocutor 213.00

(b) Fee to cover drawing of expenses, arranging, intimating and attending diet of taxation and obtaining approval of auditor's report and where necessary, ordering, procuring and examining extract decree or adjusting account with opponent 177.50

(c) Fee to cover considering opponent's account of expenses, objections and attendance at hearing on expenses, per quarter hour 35.50

20. Instruction of Counsel or solicitor advocate

(a) Fee for instructing counsel or solicitor advocate to attend court 177.50

(b) Fee for attending consultation with counsel or solicitor advocate—

    (i) where total time engaged does not exceed one hour 177.50

    (ii) fee for each additional quarter hour 35.50

Note: Excludes Adjustment, Debate, Amendment, Interrogatories, Process Fee.

PART IIIB – DEFENDED ACTIONS: PERSONAL INJURY CLAIMS COMMENCED ON OR AFTER 1ST MARCH 2014

1. Precognition and reports

£

Taking and drawing precognitions, per sheet 71.00

Note: Where a skilled witness prepares his or her own precognition or report, the solicitor shall be allowed, for perusing it (whether or not in the course of doing so he or she revises or adjusts it), half of the taking and drawing fee per sheet.

2. Work before action commences

All work which the Auditor is satisfied has reasonably been undertaken in contemplation of, or preparatory to the commencement of proceedings (or such lesser sum as in the opinion of the Auditor is justified). 426.00

3. Instruction fee

(a) To cover all work (except as otherwise specifically provided for in this Chapter) from commencement to the lodging of the form of response, including effecting service of summons by post 284.00

(b) Fee for consideration of each additional form of response lodged 71.00

(c) Specification of documents as per Form 10e 71.00

(d) Fee to opponent for considering specification of documents 71.00

(e) Instructing service or re-service by way of sheriff officer including perusing execution of citation and settling sheriff officers' charges 71.00

(f) If counterclaim lodged, additional fee to each party to include answers 213.00

(g) Arranging commission for recovery of documents including citing havers, instructing commissioner and shorthand writer and preparation for commission 106.50

(h) Fee to opponent where a commission arranged 71.00

£

(i) Attendance at execution of commission, per quarter hour 35.50

(j) If optional procedure adopted, fee per person on whom order is served 35.50

(k) Fee for perusal of documents recovered, per quarter hour 35.50

4. Adjustment fee

(a) All work (except as otherwise specifically provided for in this Chapter) in connection with adjustment of statement of claim and/or response thereto including preparing and lodging certified adjusted statement of claim or response 266.25

(b) All work as above, so far as applicable, where cause settled or disposed of before expiry of adjustment period 159.75

5. Introduction of additional parties

Fee (to include necessary amendments) to the pursuer and existing defender to be allowed for each pursuer, defender or third party brought in 213.00

6. Valuation of claim

(a) Fee for preparation and lodging of statement of valuation of claim 213.00

(b) Fee for consideration of opponent's statement of valuation of claim 106.50

(c) Fee for inspection of documents, per quarter hour 35.50

7. Productions

(a) Fee for lodging productions, each inventory 71.00

(b) Fee for consideration of opponent's productions, each inventory 35.50

8. Affidavits

Framing affidavits, per sheet 35.50

9. Incidental applications and minutes

(a) Fee to cover drawing, intimating and lodging any written incidental application and minute including a minute for recall of decree, and relative attendance at court (except as otherwise provided for in this Chapter)—

   (i) where opposed 177.50

   (ii) where unopposed – including for each party a joint minute or joint incidental application (other than under paragraph 19(b)) 71.00

   (iii) where incidental application exceeds half an hour, additional fee per quarter hour 35.50

   (iv) attendance at continued incidental application, per quarter hour 35.50

(b) Fee for consideration of opponent's written incidental application or minute and relative attendance at court—

   (i) where opposed 177.50

   (ii) where unopposed 71.00

   (iii) where incidental application exceeds half an hour, additional fee per quarter hour 35.50

   (iv) attendance at continued incidental application, per quarter hour 35.50

10. Reports obtained under order of court excluding Auditor's Report

(a) All work incidental to report 142.00

(b) Additional fee for perusal of report, per quarter hour 32.00

11. Specification of documents (if further specification deemed necessary)

(a) Fee to cover drawing, intimating and lodging specification of documents and relevant incidental application—

   (i) where incidental application unopposed 142.00

   (ii) where incidental application opposed, additional fee per quarter hour 35.50

£

(b) Fee to opponent—

    (i) where incidental application not opposed 71.00

    (ii) where incidental application opposed, additional fee per quarter hour 35.50

(c) Fee for arranging commission to recover documents, citing havers, instructing commissioner and shorthand writer and preparation for commission 142.00

(d) Fee to opponent 71.00

(e) Attendance at execution of commission, per quarter hour 35.50

(f) If optional procedure adopted, fee per person upon whom order is served..................... 35.50

(g) Fee for perusal of documents recovered under a specification of documents (or by informal means) not otherwise provided for in this Chapter, per quarter hour................ 35.50

12. Commissions to take evidence – open commissions

(a) Fee to solicitor applying for commission to include all work (except as otherwise specially provided for in this Chapter) up to lodging report of commission but excluding attendance at execution of commission 248.50

(b) Fee to opponent 142.00

(c) Fee for attendance at execution of commission, per quarter hour 35.50

13. Hearing limitation fee

Fee to include work done (except as otherwise specifically provided for in this Chapter) with a view to limiting the scope of any hearing and including the exchange of documents, precognitions and expert reports, agreeing in fact, statement or document not in dispute and preparing and lodging or considering any joint minute, not exceeding 248.50

14. Preparation for proof

(a) Fee to cover all work preparing for proof (except as otherwise specially provided for in this Chapter)—

    (i) if action settled or abandoned within 7 days of diet of proof 781.00

    (ii) in any other case 568.00

(b) Fee to cover preparing for any adjourned diet and all incidental work as in (a) if diet postponed for more than 6 days, each additional diet 177.50

15. Pre-proof conference

(a) Fee for arranging pre-proof conference (each occasion) 71.00

(b) Fee preparing for pre-proof conference—

    (i) where counsel or solicitor advocate not employed 390.50

    (ii) where counsel or solicitor advocate employed 195.25

(c) Fee for attending pre-proof conference, per quarter hour—

    (i) where counsel or solicitor advocate not employed 35.50

    (ii) where counsel or solicitor advocate employed 32.00

(d) Joint minute of pre-proof conference 71.00

Note: Where pre-proof conference takes place by telephone or other remote means, the foregoing charges shall apply.

16. Conduct of proof

(a) Fee to cover conduct of proof or trial, and debate on evidence taken at close of proof, per quarter hour 35.50

(b) If counsel or solicitor advocate employed, fee to solicitor appearing with counsel or solicitor advocate, per quarter hour 32.00

	£
(c) Waiting time, per quarter hour	32.00

17. Debate on evidence

		£
(a)	Where debate on evidence not taken at conclusion of proof, fee preparing for debate ...	142.00
(b)	Fee for conduct of debate, per quarter hour	35.50
(c)	If counsel or solicitor advocate employed, fee to solicitor appearing with counsel or solicitor advocate, per quarter hour	32.00
(d)	Waiting time, per quarter hour	32.00

18. Attendance at court

	£
Attendance at any hearing except as otherwise specially provided	71.00

19. Settlements

		£
(a)	Settlement by judicial tender—	
(i)	fee for preparation and lodging or for consideration of each minute of tender	142.00
(ii)	fee on acceptance of tender to include preparation and lodging or consideration of minute of acceptance of tender and attendance at court when decree granted in terms thereof	106.50
(b)	Extra-judicial settlement, to include negotiations resulting in settlement, framing or revising joint minute and attendance at court when authority interponed thereto	248.50
(c)	Whether or not fees payable under (a) or (b) above, where additional work has been undertaken with a view to effecting settlement, including offering settlement, although settlement not agreed, not exceeding	248.50

20. Final procedure

		£
(a)	If case proceeds to proof or is settled within 14 days before the diet of proof, fee to cover settling with witnesses and enquiring for cause at avizandum and noting final interlocutor	195.25
(b)	In any other case	88.75

21. Copying

For the copying of papers by whatever means, if the Auditor determines (either or both) that—

(a) the copying had to be done in circumstances which were in some way exceptional;

(b) the papers which required to be copied were unusually numerous having regard to the nature of the case,

such charge, if any, as the Auditor considers reasonable (but a charge based on the time expended by any person shall not be allowed).

Notes:

1. Where a determination is required under this paragraph, the purpose of the copying, the number of copies made and the charge claimed shall be shown in the account.

2. Copying done other than in the place of business of the solicitor shall be shown as an outlay.

22. Appeals

		£
(a)	Fee to cover instructions, marking of appeal or noting that appeal marked, noting of diet of hearing thereof, perusing Stated Case and all work re adjustment thereof, including preparation for hearing	390.50
(b)	Conduct of appeal, per quarter hour	35.50
(c)	If counsel or solicitor advocate employed, fee to solicitor appearing with counsel or solicitor advocate, per quarter hour	32.00
(d)	Waiting time, per quarter hour	32.00

23. Instruction of counsel or solicitor advocate

    (a) Fee for instructing counsel or solicitor advocate to attend court 177.50

    (b) Fee for attending consultation with counsel or solicitor advocate—

        (i)   Where total time engaged does not exceed one hour 177.50

        (ii) Fee for each additional quarter hour 35.50

24. Accounts of Expenses

Preparation of judicial account of expenses to include production of vouchers and adjustment thereof 177.50

25. Ordering and procuring extract 35.50

Act of Sederunt (Fees of Solicitors in Speculative Actions) 1992
(SI 1992 No 1879)

[This Act of Sederunt came into force on 24th August 1992.]

Speculative fee charging agreement

2. (1) Where —

   (a) Any work is undertaken by a solicitor in the conduct of litigation for a client; and

   (b) the solicitor and the client agree that the solicitor shall be entitled to a fee for the work only if the client is successful in the litigation; and

   (c) the agreement is that the solicitor's fee for all work in connection with the litigation is to be based on an account prepared as between party and party,

   the solicitor and client may agree that the fees element in that account, as hereinafter defined, shall be increased by a figure not exceeding 100%.

   (2) The client shall be deemed to be successful in the litigation where —

   (a) the litigation has been concluded by the pronouncing of a decree by the court which, on the merits, is to any extent in his favour;

   (b) the client has accepted a sum of money in settlement of his claim in the litigation; or

   (c) the client has entered into a settlement of any other kind by which his claim in the litigation has been resolved to any extent in his favour.

   (3) The fees element referred to in sub-paragraph (1) above shall, subject to sub-paragraph (4) below, comprise all the fees in the solicitor's account of expenses for which any other party to the litigation has been found liable, taxed as between party and party or agreed, before the deduction of any award of expenses against the client.

   (4) The fees element referred to in sub-paragraph (3) shall not include the sums payable to the solicitor in respect of —

   (a) any fees payable for copying papers and the proportion of any process fee and posts and incidents exigible thereon;

   (b) any discretionary fee allowed under Regulation 5 of the General Regulations set out in the Schedule to the Act of Sederunt (Fees of Solicitors in the Sheriff Court) 1989; and

   (c) any charges by the solicitor for his outlays.

Act of Sederunt (Fees of Witnesses and Shorthand Writers in the Sheriff Court) 1992 (SI 1992 No 1878)

SCHEDULE 1

WITNESSES' FEES

[Schedule 1 is substituted by:

Act of Sederunt (Fees of Witnesses and Shorthand Writers in the Sheriff Court) (Amendment) 2000 (SSI 2002 No 280) which came into force on 1st July 2002.

Amended by:

Act of Sederunt (Fees of Solicitors and Witnesses in the Sheriff Court) (Amendment) 2004 (SSI 2004 No 152) which came into force on 4th May 2004;

Act of Sederunt (Fees of Solicitors and Witnesses in the Sheriff Court) (Amendment) 2011 (SSI 2004 No 403) which came into force on 1st January 2012.]

1. Skilled Persons

1.—(1) If, at any time before the diet of taxation, the sheriff has granted a motion for the certification of a person as skilled, charges shall be allowed for any work done or expenses reasonably incurred by that person which were reasonably required for a purpose in connection with the cause or in contemplation of the cause.

(2) A motion under paragraph (1) may be granted only if the sheriff is satisfied that—

    (a) the person was a skilled person; and

    (b) it was reasonable to employ the person.

(3) Where a motion under paragraph (1) is enrolled after the sheriff has awarded expenses, the expenses of the motion shall be borne by the party enrolling it.

(4) The charges which shall be allowed under paragraph (1) shall be such as the Auditor of Court determines are fair and reasonable.

(5) Where a sheriff grants a motion under paragraph (1), the name of the person shall be recorded in the interlocutor..

2. Witnesses

2.—(1) Charges for the attendance at a proof or jury trial of a witness present but not called to give evidence may be allowed if the sheriff has, at any time before the diet of taxation, granted a motion for the name of that witness to be noted in the minute of proceedings in the cause.

(2) A person who is cited to give evidence and in consequence incurs financial loss shall be allowed reimbursement, being such sum as the Auditor of Court may determine to have been reasonably and necessarily incurred by the witness, but not exceeding £400 per day.

3. Travelling Allowance

In respect of any witness there shall be allowed a travelling allowance, being such sum as the Auditor may determine to have been reasonably and necessarily incurred by the witness in the travelling from and to the witnesses' residence or place of business and the Court.

4. Subsistence Allowance

In respect of any witness there shall be allowed a subsistence allowance, being such sum as the Auditor may determine to have been reasonably incurred by the witness for the extra cost of subsistence during the witnesses' absence from the witnesses' home or place of business for the purpose of giving evidence, and where the witness reasonably requires to stay overnight, for the reasonable cost of board and lodging.

5. Value Added Tax

Where any witness is a taxable person in terms of the Value Added Tax Act 1983, the amount of value added tax may be added by the witness to the witnesses' note of fee, and may be paid to the witness by the Solicitor.

6. Receipts and Vouchers

Receipts and detailed vouchers for all payments claimed in respect of a witness shall be produced to the party found liable in expenses, prior to the taxation of the Account of Expenses, and to the Auditor, if the Auditor requires.

7. Account of fees of Witnesses

The fees charged for any witness shall be stated in the Account of Expenses in a lump sum and the details of the charges shall be entered in a separate schedule appended to the Account as follows:

Name and designation	Where from	Days charged	Rate per day	Travelling and allowance	Total subsistence	Taxed off

SCHEDULE 2
SHORTHAND WRITERS' FEES

[Schedule 2 is printed as amended by:

Act of Sederunt (Fees of Shorthand Writers in the Sheriff Court) (Amendment) 1995 (SI 1995 No 1024) which came into force on 1st May 1995;

Act of Sederunt (Fees of Shorthand Writers in the Sheriff Court) (Amendment) 1996 (SI 1996 No 767) which came into force on 1st May 1996;

Act of Sederunt (Fees of Shorthand Writers in the Sheriff Court) (Amendment) 1997 (SI 1997 No 1118) which came into force on 1st May 1997;

Act of Sederunt (Fees of Shorthand Writers in the Sheriff Court) (Amendment No 2) 1997 (SI 1997 No 1265) which came into force on 1st May 1997;

Act of Sederunt (Fees of Shorthand Writers in the Sheriff Court) (Amendment) 1998 (SI 1998 No 999) which came into force on 1st May 1998;

Act of Sederunt (Fees of Shorthand Writers in the Sheriff Court) (Amendment) 1999 (SI 1999 No 613) which came into force on 1st May 1999;

Act of Sederunt (Fees of Shorthand Writers in the Sheriff Court) (Amendment) 2000 (SSI 2000 No 145) which came into force on 1st June 2000;

Act of Sederunt (Fees of Shorthand Writers in the Sheriff Court) (Amendment) 2001 (SSI 2001 No 136) which came into force on 1st May 2001;

Act of Sederunt (Fees of Witnesses and Shorthand Writers in the Sheriff Court) (Amendment) 2002 (SSI 2002 No 280) which came into force on 1st July 2002;

Act of Sederunt (Fees of Shorthand Writers in the Sheriff Court) (Amendment) 2003 (SSI 2003 No 246) which came into force on 1st June 2003;

Act of Sederunt (Fees of Shorthand Writers in the Sheriff Court) (Amendment) 2004 (SSI 2004 No 149) which came into force on 4th May 2004;

Act of Sederunt (Fees of Shorthand Writers in the Sheriff Court) (Amendment) 2005 (SSI 2005 No 150) which came into force on 25th April 2004;

Act of Sederunt (Fees of Shorthand Writers in the Sheriff Court) (Amendment) 2006 (SSI 2006 No 86) which came into force on 1st May 2006;

Act of Sederunt (Fees of Shorthand Writers in the Sheriff Court) (Amendment) 2007 (SSI 2007 No 211) which came into force on 1st May 2007;

Act of Sederunt (Fees of Shorthand Writers in the Sheriff Court) (Amendment) 2008 (SSI 2008 No 118) which came into force on 5th May 2008;

Act of Sederunt (Fees of Shorthand Writers in the Sheriff Court) (Amendment) 2009 (SSI 2009 No 166) which came into force on 4th May 2009;

Act of Sederunt (Fees of Shorthand Writers in the Sheriff Court) (Amendment) 2011 (SSI 2011 No 103) which came into force on 2nd May 2011;

Act of Sederunt (Fees of Shorthand Writers in the Sheriff Court) (Amendment) 2012 (SSI 2012 No 101) which came into force on 21st May 2012;

Act of Sederunt (Fees of Shorthand Writers in the Sheriff Court) (Amendment) 2013 (SSI 2013 No 112) which came into force on 21st May 2013.]

1. *Attendance*   £

     Attending at proofs or commissions —

     (a) per hour 41.75

(b)   minimum per day... 166.80

2. *Cancellation*

Where intimation of cancellation of attendance is made to the shorthand writer —

(a)   more than 21 days prior to the date of attendance no fee shall be charged;

(b)   21 days or less prior to, and before 4 pm on the day prior to the date of attendance 75% of the minimum daily fee in paragraph 1(b) shall be charged;

(c)   on or after 4 pm on the day prior to the date of attendance the minimum daily fee in paragraph 1(b) shall be charged.

3. *Subsistence Allowance*

A shorthand writer shall be allowed a subsistence allowance appropriate to civil servants entitled to class 2 rates.

4. *Transcripts*

Extending notes of evidence —

(a)   subject to (b) below, per sheet of 250 words.. 6.80

(b)   overnight, per sheet of 250 words 8.35

5. *Copies*

Copies of notes of evidence by carbon or any other means —

per sheet.. 0.57

Rules as to Retaining Fees for Advocates

I. Special Retainers

1. A special retainer may be given with reference to any particular cause, and may be given in name and on behalf of one party, or of several parties having the same interest in the particular cause.

2. If the cause be not in dependence, the name and designation of the party, or (if more than one) of all the parties for whom the counsel is intended to be retained, should be distinctly specified in the letter of retainer. A retainer for A B and others, in any action between them and C D, or a retainer for A B in any action between him and C D and others, relative to a particular contract, or the like, is a good retainer for A B against C D, but not for or against others unnamed, who, when action is raised, may come to have a common interest with A B or C D as pursuers or defenders. But if the particular process or action is so described in the retainer as to be identified, and the counsel is expressly retained for or against the whole pursuers or defenders in that particular action, it is not necessary to specify all the names.

3. Counsel may be retained by special retainer for a corporation or public company, or for a common trading company, by its company name, without specifying the names of the partners, but this will not operate as a retainer for any individual partner for his separate or individual interest even in the same matter.

4. A special retainer endures for a year, but must be renewed before the expiry of every year, except in the case of a depending process, as explained in next rule.

5. A special retainer gives to the client a right to the services of the counsel retained throughout the whole progress of the cause, without the necessity of annual renewal. But if the counsel retained is not employed in any step of the cause in which, according to ordinary practice, such counsel — junior or senior as the case may be — would be employed, the retainer falls. The professional duty of counsel in matters of confidentiality will preclude his further involvement in the case for any other party.

II. Implied Retainer

1. When a counsel is employed to draw or revise a summons, defences, or other pleading, or is instructed to appear for a party to a cause in court, that is equivalent to a special retainer in the cause for the party by whom he is so employed or instructed.

2. But when a counsel is merely consulted as to the merits of a case, or gives advice, verbal or written, as to the raising or defending of an action intended or threatened, he is not thereby retained in the cause, but may be precluded by reason of confidentiality from acting for another party in the same cause.

III. General Retainers

1. A general retainer secures the services of a counsel for the party in all cases in which he may be engaged as a party on the record.

2. A general retainer may be expressed in general terms, provided the name and designation of the party may be distinctly stated.

3. If a special retainer be offered to a counsel, such instructions or employment in a cause as imply a special retainer, it is the duty of his clerk forthwith to intimate this to the agent of the party for whom he is retained in general, who may then send a special retainer applicable to the particular case, and is in that event entitled to a preference over the prior special retainer, or implied special retainer, on the other side. But if the agent of the party who has given the general retainer fails upon such notice to send a special retainer, it is the duty of the counsel to accept the special retainer, or instructions or employment offered on the other side.

4. A general retainer endures for the lifetime of the client and counsel, subject, however, to this condition, that if the client becomes a party to any action to process after the general retainer is given and does not employ the counsel who holds his general retainer, the retainer falls *eo ipso*, not merely as regards the particular case, but absolutely and to all effects.

5. General retainers are preferable according to their dates. If a counsel holds a general retainer for the pursuer, and also a general retainer for the defender of an action, he will be found to act for that party whose general retainer is earliest in date, provided that party avails himself of his preference by sending a special retainer applicable to the case. If the first special retainer comes from the party whose general retainer is the latest in date, notice must be given to the party having the right of preference, in the manner already explained, and that party must forthwith send his special retainer, otherwise the counsel will be bound to accept the special retainer of the party whose general retainer is latest in date.

12th June 1878

The Dean of Faculty determined that a general retainer binds counsel who accepts it to appear for person sending it in every Court of Law in Scotland, civil or criminal, in which his client is interested, and specially it binds counsel to appear for any client who is indicated before Court of Justiciary.

Only exceptions to rule are — (1) appeals to House of Lords; (2) Courts in which counsel are not expected to attend, eg Police Courts and Licensing Courts of Justices.

2008 Scheme

REVISED 2008 SCHEME
for the
ACCOUNTING FOR AND RECOVERY
OF COUNSEL'S FEES

Issued by the authority of
THE FACULTY OF ADVOCATES

Status of counsel's fees

1.—(1) Except in legal aid cases, or as otherwise provided for, every solicitor who instructs counsel has a professional obligation so far as reasonably practicable to ensure payment of counsel's fees, either as agreed or, failing agreement, as taxed by the Auditor of the Court of Session or the auditor of the appropriate sheriff court, as the case may be, on the basis of agent and client, client paying.

It will be good practice, where there is any room for doubt about the ability of the client to reimburse him for payment of counsel's fees, for the instructing solicitor to take an adequate deposit against costs to be incurred. Payment of counsel's fees shall be made in accordance with the provisions of paragraph 7.

Except as provided hereafter "the instructing solicitor" means the solicitor who instructs counsel. Where, however, the letter of instruction in terms of paragraph 2 (d) includes the name of the correspondent firm in Scotland from whom the instruction originates "the instructing solicitor" in this paragraph and in paragraphs 7(3), 7(7) and 7(8) means the correspondent firm in Scotland from whom the instruction originates.

(2) As standard practice, each item of work will be the subject of a proposed fee as it is undertaken. Where it is intended that payment of fees should be deferred, whether for a particular case or otherwise, agreement to such a process must be concluded with counsel's clerk prior to or at the time of issue of instructions. Where such agreement has been concluded, it will be assumed, provided all relevant letters of instruction note the basis of deferment and unless the counsel's clerk has specifically re-negotiated the matter with the solicitor concerned, that any other counsel whom the solicitor instructs in the same case, including other counsel to whom the instructions are passed on, will accept instructions on the same basis.

(3) A note of proposed fee will normally be issued within 30 days of completion of the item of work concerned. If counsel fails to issue a note of a proposed fee within 30 days of completion of an item of work, the instructing solicitor may make a request in writing to the counsel for a proposed note of fee to be issued in relation to that item. Unless otherwise agreed, if counsel fails without good reason to issue a proposed note of fee within 6 weeks of such a request, the instructing solicitor shall have no obligation to ensure payment thereof. Any dispute regarding the failure by counsel to issue a proposed note of fee and the obligation of the solicitor in that event shall be referred to the Committee referred to in paragraph 9. The Committee shall consider the matter having regard to any representations made by counsel and the solicitor and shall make recommendations to the Dean of Faculty. The decision of the Dean of Faculty shall be final.

(4) Whilst responsibility for meeting counsel's fees in a legally aided case is assumed by the Scottish Legal Aid Board, it remains incumbent upon the instructing solicitor to take reasonable care to comply with his obligations under the legal aid legislation. Where it becomes necessary to instruct counsel before the issue of a legal aid certificate, or after its expiry or suspension, the instructing solicitor must be prepared to accept the obligation so far as reasonably practicable of meeting counsel's fees, or issue instructions on a speculative basis. In each case the letter of instruction must be clear on the point.

Letters of instruction

2. The letter of instruction shall contain the following information:-

    (a)   the name of the counsel instructed;

    (b)   the name of the case or an identifying description of the matter to which the letter relates; (it is essential that such description should be consistent in succeeding instructions so that case records may be correctly integrated);

    (c)   where appropriate, the party for whom counsel is instructed to appear, or whom counsel is instructed to advise or represent;

    (d)   where appropriate, the name of the correspondent firm in Scotland from whom the instruction originates;

    (e)   any reference which the solicitor wishes Faculty Services Limited to quote on counsel's account;

(f)   the Faculty Services Limited case reference (except in the instance of the first instructions in a case or where the first fee note has yet to be issued);

(g)   where appropriate, the legal aid reference; and

(h)   where fees are to be paid otherwise than when rendered, a note to that effect.

Fee with instructions and retainers

3. If a solicitor wishes to tender a fee with his instructions, he should do so by means of a cheque for the fee together with the appropriate VAT drawn in favour of Faculty Services Limited, or in favour of counsel if counsel is not a subscriber. The same applies to fees sent as retainers. A VAT receipt will then be issued by Faculty Services Limited, or by counsel's clerk where counsel is not a subscriber.

Special arrangements as to fees

4.—(1) Solicitors are at liberty to negotiate in advance with counsel's clerk the fees to be paid in any particular case or matter including speculative cases and deferment of fees. Likewise the basis on which fees are to be settled may be agreed by prior negotiation with counsel's clerk. Where agreement of this kind has been made, and in so doing the right to proceed to taxation has not been expressly reserved, it cannot thereafter be altered or taken to the Auditor for adjudication except by subsequent agreement between counsel and solicitor. It should be noted that the only proper channel of communication regarding counsel's fees is through counsel's clerk or , following the issue of a proposed fee note, through Faculty Services Limited. This does not mean that when a case is marked speculative, the only fees liable to be paid to counsel are those which are judicially recoverable by the solicitor. Counsel can insist on a taxation in any event to protect and preserve his fees.

(2)   Counsel may accept instructions on a speculative basis but are not bound to do so. A solicitor may only instruct counsel to act on a speculative basis in any case where the solicitor is acting on such a basis. (For the avoidance of doubt a speculative case is one where the solicitor is only to be paid a fee if the client is successful in the litigation). If a solicitor wishes to instruct counsel on this basis, he must state the fact explicitly in every letter of instruction in the case. It may not be assumed that because one counsel agrees to accept such instructions another will also agree to do so. During the course of a speculative action counsel shall raise notes of proposed fee in the ordinary way.

N.B. Counsel are not permitted to accept instructions on a contingency basis i.e. that fees will be based on any quantum measurement of the outcome.

Rendering of notes of proposed fees

5.—(1) In normal circumstances, Faculty Services Limited shall send to the instructing solicitor a note of proposed fee in respect of each item of work within a case as it is undertaken.

(2)   In respect of criminal legal aid cases, notes of proposed fee may be sent direct to the Scottish Legal Aid Board; but in that event a copy of the note of proposed fee will be sent to the solicitor endorsed to the effect that the fee note has been rendered direct. Notes of proposed fee rendered under this rule and received prior to the solicitor rendering his own account will be included in the solicitor's account and will be dealt with by the Scottish Legal Aid Board in accordance with the relevant arrangements.

(3)   If the instructing solicitor wishes to question the fee proposed by counsel he should inform Faculty Services Limited in writing as soon as possible and in any event within 6 weeks of the issue of the note of proposed fee. Where the instructing solicitor feels that a particular fee is grossly excessive, he may refer the matter to the Dean of Faculty.

(4)   Where, following notification to Faculty Services Limited as set out in sub-paragraph (3), the appropriate fee cannot be agreed, the Auditor of the Court of Session or the Auditor of the appropriate sheriff court, as the case may be, shall adjudicate as to what is a reasonable fee. Unless otherwise agreed in advance, this will be on an agent and client, client paying basis. In the event that there is at that time a final taxation disposing of expenses on an agent and client basis, such adjudication shall take place as part of that final taxation. Where there is no such taxation there may be a separate taxation if either the solicitor or counsel so wish. Where the amount of counsel's fee on the basis of agent and client is challenged at taxation, counsel or his representative shall be entitled to appear before the Auditor and make representations, and the diet of taxation may, if necessary, be adjourned for this purpose. In general, the expenses incurred in taxing counsel's fees shall form part of the general expenses of taxation, but if the Auditor considers the fee proposed by counsel to be excessive, and if counsel has exercised the right to appear before the Auditor and make representations, the Auditor may, at his discretion, order that such part of the expenses of taxation as are attributable to the intervention of counsel be borne by counsel.

(5) It should be noted that, unless otherwise agreed in advance, counsel's fees are to be paid on an agent and client, client-paying basis and are not restricted to what may be recoverable on a party and party basis. Counsel may accept instructions for pursuers in personal injury actions on the basis that he will only receive such fees as are recovered in judicial expenses but is not bound to do so. If a solicitor wishes to instruct counsel on this basis he must state the fact explicitly in every letter of instruction in the case. It may not be assumed that because one counsel agrees to adopt such instructions another will also agree to do so. If such a request is not specified in any letter of instruction counsel who accepts those instructions will be entitled payment of his fee for the work undertaken in terms of said letter of instruction even if the fee is not ultimately recovered from another party to the action.

Completion

6.—(1) This paragraph refers to cases where payment of fees has been deferred by prior agreement, speculative cases and civil legal aid cases.

(2) "Completion" in this paragraph means practical completion of the litigation up to the point to which it has been agreed that payment of fees should be deferred. The fact of completion shall be notified by the instructing solicitor to Faculty Services Limited as soon as practicable but in any event within one calendar month of that completion. In speculative and legal aid cases, and cases under the deferred guidelines in the Appendix hereto, Faculty Services Limited will make enquiry regarding completion one year after the last note of proposed fee is rendered. If no reply is received within one month, the case will be deemed to be completed. Where counsel has reason to believe that completion has been achieved, he may instruct Faculty Services Limited to initiate the process described at subparagraph (3). If completion has not in fact been achieved, the instructing solicitor should so inform Faculty Services Limited as soon as possible and preferably within 14 days of receipt of the statement.

(3) When completion is notified to Faculty Services Limited by the instructing solicitor, he shall indicate the date of the latest item of work undertaken by counsel. Where such date is more than 30 days prior to the receipt of notification of completion, Faculty Services Limited shall normally issue a statement forthwith. If the date of the latest item of work is less than 30 days prior to receipt of notification, issue of the statement may be deferred for a reasonable period having regard to paragraph 1 (3) hereof to allow Faculty Services Limited to obtain the appropriate information from counsel. In legal aid cases only notification of the fee by Faculty Services Limited will take place within 60 days of the instructing solicitor advising them of completion, failing which the solicitor will be entitled to render his account from the Board and, for the avoidance of any doubt will have no further liability to counsel in relation to any fees not yet rendered (unless recovered from the Board) The statement to be sent to the instructing solicitor shall take the form of a computer printout showing all appropriate details of the case including all fees indicating which items, if any, have been paid and shall be accompanied by all notes of proposed fee not already issued.

Payment of fees

7.—(1) Payment of fees in all cases where counsel is a subscriber should be made to Faculty Services Limited and NOT to counsel. Where counsel is not a subscriber payment should be to counsel and remittance should be to counsel's clerk.

(2) Payment will be expected when the note of proposed fee has been issued or on the issue of a statement in terms of paragraph 6(3) except as otherwise provided or agreed. For the purpose of this scheme the fees shall be regarded as "due" as from this point.

(3) In criminal legal aid cases, the instructing solicitor shall be responsible for furnishing counsel with such documentation as is required by the Scottish Legal Aid Board. It shall be the further responsibility of both the instructing solicitor and counsel to submit his account to the Scottish Legal Aid Board within three calendar months of conclusion of the trial or appeal as the case may be. Where such prompt submission of the solicitor's account cannot be made, Faculty Services Limited should be advised of the delay and the reasons for this in writing within the three month period outlined above. Where such prompt submission of the solicitor's account is made, Faculty Services Limited may be so advised. Otherwise, fees in this category shall be regarded as "due" six months from the conclusion of a criminal case to allow for submission of accounts by the instructing solicitor to the Scottish Legal Aid Board and for processing by the Board.

(4) Fees shall be placed in the "due" category by Faculty Services Limited at the end of the calendar month in which they become "due".

(5) Where fees have remained unpaid in the "due" category for one full calendar month and there has been no advice of good reason for delay in payment or non-payment, Faculty Services Limited shall place the case in the "overdue" category.

(6) Where fees have remained unpaid in the "overdue" category for a full calendar month and there has been no advice of good reason for delay in payment or non-payment, Faculty Services Limited shall intimate to the instructing solicitor an intention to refer the matter to the Committee referred to in paragraph 9.

(7) If the instructing solicitor has a reason for the non-payment of counsel's fees, he shall, within 21 days of receipt of intimation of the intention to refer the matter to the Committee, provide for the use of the Committee a brief report explaining that reason and a proposed timescale for payment or an explanation as to why he believes the proposed fee should be withdrawn. This report shall be considered by the Committee along with any representations from the counsel concerned. Thereafter the Committee shall make a recommendation to the Dean of Faculty as to whether in the Committee's view there is a good reason for non-payment. The recommendation of the Committee shall be intimated to the instructing solicitor.

(8) If no such report is received from the instructing solicitor the matter will be referred by Faculty Services Limited to the Dean of Faculty.

(9) If the Dean of Faculty does not accept there is good reason for non-payment, he shall write to the instructing solicitor, with a copy where appropriate to the senior partner and to the correspondent Edinburgh firm, in the following terms:—

"I am advised by Faculty Services Limited that the fees listed in the attached schedule have been overdue for payment for 3 full calendar months and the Committee and I / I have determined that no good reason has been intimated for non-payment. Under mandate from the Faculty I am obliged to advise you that unless settlement is received within one full calendar month from service of this notice, the name of your firm and its partners will be advertised within the practising membership of Faculty as defaulting in payment of fees, whereafter members will be permitted to accept instructions which come from you only in legal aid cases or if accompanied by payment of the appropriate fee."

(10) At the end of one full calendar month after the notice set out in subparagraph (9) has been served and in the event that the overdue fees in question remain unpaid, the Dean of Faculty, except where there is good reason to the contrary, shall advise practising members of Faculty in the following terms:-

"Non-payment of counsel's fees

Heading (Name of firm)
Heading (Partners)

I am advised by Faculty Services Limited that counsel's fees issued to the above firm remain overdue and unpaid without good reason having been given. Having myself applied for payment to the firm in writing in the terms authorised by the Faculty, and having been informed by Faculty Services Limited that payment has not been received despite my application, I now give notice that instructions which come directly or indirectly from this firm or its partners may be accepted only in legal aid cases or if accompanied by payment of an appropriate fee."

A copy of this notice shall be sent to the firm concerned and, where appropriate, to the correspondent Edinburgh firm.

(11) At the time that the Dean of Faculty advises the Faculty as set out in sub-paragraph (10), he shall also write to the Law Society of Scotland as follows:-

"Non-payment of counsel's fees

Heading (Name of firm)
Heading (Partners)

I have to advise you that the above firm has failed to meet its professional obligation to ensure payment of counsel's fees. The Committee has intimated to me that no good reason has been advanced for such failure [or – Notwithstanding the view of the Committee that a good reason has been advanced for non payment I have concluded that I do not accept there is a good reason for such failure]. Having served due notice of my intention to do so, I have today instructed members of Faculty that instructions which come directly or indirectly from this firm or its partners may be accepted only in legal aid cases or if accompanied by payment of an appropriate fee. Please treat this letter as a formal complaint."

A copy of this letter shall be sent to the firm in question and, where appropriate, to the correspondent Edinburgh firm.

(12) In normal circumstances payment of the fees in question will result in immediate revocation by the Dean of Faculty of his advice to practising members of Faculty in terms of paragraph 7(10), but in exceptional circumstances such revocation may, in the discretion of the Dean of Faculty, be delayed or

otherwise withheld. Notice of the decision of the Dean of Faculty will be sent to the Law Society, to the firm concerned and, where appropriate, to the correspondent Edinburgh firm.

(13) Where a case is legally aided and has been placed in the "due" category in accordance with subparagraph (3), Faculty Services Limited may apply for payment direct to the Scottish Legal Aid Board.

Monitoring outstanding fees

8. At the beginning of each month Faculty Services Limited shall provide to each firm of solicitors a statement in the form of a computer printout (analysed by partner where requested) of all cases where fees of subscribers are regarded as due for payment. The statement will highlight fees that are currently under dispute. There will be no such listing of those cases where by prior agreement payment of fees is deferred and remains deferred. Likewise, uncompleted legal aid cases will not be listed. It is open to a solicitor to seek a full listing of all cases at any time or on a regular basis. Correspondent firms of solicitors will receive a statement of all cases where fees have been issued and remain outstanding

Committee

9. There will be a Committee comprising 3 members of the Faculty of Advocates appointed by the Dean. The remit of the Committee will be:

    (a) To consider the Scheme for Accounting for and Recovery of counsel's Fees and make recommendations to the Faculty on amendments thereto.

    (b) To carry out regular review of the financial limits for payment of counsel's fees in terms of Guidelines 3 and 4 to the Scheme's Appendix and make recommendations on an annual basis.

    (c) To consider cases where a report is made in terms of paragraph 7(7) in connection with a dispute between the instructing solicitor and Faculty Services Limited as to whether "good reason" exists for non payment of counsel's fees and make recommendations to the Dean of Faculty.

Speculative and civil legal aid cases

10. In speculative cases, and in civil legal aid cases where a solicitor proposes to accept judicial expenses in lieu of a claim against the legal aid fund, before those judicial expenses are agreed or determined the solicitor shall confer with counsel's clerk in order to agree (i) what part of any proposed agreed global sum for judicial expenses represents counsel's fees; (ii) the sums for counsel's fees to be included in any account of judicial expenses to be submitted to the Auditor for taxation.

Non-subscribers

11. Where counsel are not subscribers to Faculty Services Limited this Scheme applies with such modifications as are necessary to take account of that fact: in particular (without prejudice to the generality of this paragraph) all references to Faculty Services Limited (except those in this paragraph and in paragraphs 3 and 7(1), and in the Appendix) shall be read as being references instead to "counsel's clerk".

Scope

12. This Scheme applies to the instruction by solicitors of counsel. For the avoidance of doubt it does not apply to (i) fees rendered by counsel for work done other than in their capacity as advocates (e.g. as a Commissioner, Reporter or Curator) (ii) direct access instructions.

APPENDIX

GUIDELINES TO COUNSEL IN RESPECT OF DEFERMENT OF FEES
UNDER THE NEW SCHEME FOR
THE ACCOUNTING FOR AND RECOVERY OF FEES IN CIVIL CASES

In terms of paragraphs 1(2) and 4(1) of the Scheme, deferment of payment of fees is permitted under an agreement reached by the solicitor with counsel's clerk. In order to preserve the main aims of the Scheme as a whole, however, deferment will be permitted, except in cases of the kind mentioned in the Note annexed hereto, only in one or other of the following circumstances: -

1. Upon an agreement between the solicitor and counsel's clerk in relation to a particular case or in relation to cases in a particular category or for a particular client or in relation to all cases, whereby it is agreed that fees should be rendered and payable at each of the following stages in the case, viz., at the closing of the

Record, after completion of a Procedure Roll Debate, Proof or Jury Trial and after completion of a Hearing in the Inner House.

2. Upon an agreement between the solicitor and counsel's clerk in relation to a particular case or in relation to cases in a particular category or for a particular client or in relation to all cases, whereby it is agreed that fees should be rendered and payable at certain prearranged periods in time, subject to a maximum of six months in relation to any such period.

3. Upon an agreement between the solicitor and counsel's clerk in relation to a particular case or in relation to cases in a particular category or for a particular client or in relation to all cases, whereby it is agreed that fees should be rendered and payable at every point when a prearranged total of rendered and unpaid fees net of VAT has been reached in that case, subject to a maximum total sum at any one time net of VAT of £5,000 in relation to senior counsel and £3,500 in relation to junior counsel.

4. Upon an agreement between the solicitor and counsel's clerk in relation to a particular case or in relation to cases in a particular category or for a particular client or in relation to all cases, whereby it is agreed that fees should be rendered and payable at every point when a prearranged global total of counsel's fees rendered and unpaid net of VAT has been reached in that case subject to a maximum total sum at any one time of £1,000.

It is emphasised that except in cases of the kind mentioned in the note annexed hereto, the Scheme and these Guidelines do not permit any agreement to be reached between counsel or his clerk and a solicitor whereby all fees for work in any case are to be deferred until its completion. If an advocate wishes to achieve deferment in circumstances other than those covered by these Guidelines he should consult first with the Chairman of Faculty Services Limited whom failing any other Faculty officer.

As aids to interpretation:-

1. Examples of "completion" as defined in paragraph 6(2) of the Scheme are: -
   (a) In relation to paragraph 1 above – the date of the Interlocutor closing the Record OR the date of the Interlocutor making avizandum at the end of a Procedure Roll Debate, Proof or Jury Trial or Hearing in the Inner House.
   (b) In relation to paragraph 2 above – the expiry of the agreed period in time.
   (c) In relation to paragraph 3 above – the issue of the proposed fee note which results in the agreed total being reached.
   (d) In relation to a case of the kind mentioned in the Note annexed hereto – the date of the final Interlocutor.
   (e) In relation to cases settled extra judicially – the date of authority being interposed to the Joint Minute.

2. "good reason" in terms of paragraph 7 of the Scheme will depend on the particular circumstances of the case but may, for example, include a situation where a solicitor has had to instruct counsel in an emergency situation and has been assured at the time that adequate funds would be forthcoming to meet counsel's fees, but in the event this proves not to be so. On the other hand mere unwillingness on the part of the solicitor to obtain funds to meet counsel's fees would not be likely to amount to "good reason"

3. "exceptional circumstances" in terms of paragraph 7(12) of the Scheme will depend on the particular circumstances of the case but may, for example, include a situation where a firm has persistently been the subject of action in terms of paragraph 7(10) and (11).

4. "subscriber" means counsel who is a subscriber to Faculty Services Limited.

NOTE ANNEXED

1. Petitions for the appointment of and work instructed on behalf of liquidators, trustees in bankruptcy, curators bonis, judicial factors, curators ad litem and the like.

2. Multiple poindings.

3. Speculative cases.

Tables of Fees under the Legal Aid Acts

Part A — Legal aid under the Legal Aid (Scotland) Act 1967 and advice and assistance under the Legal Advice and Assistance Act 1972

Paragraph 3 (1) of Schedule 4 to the Legal Aid (Scotland) Act 1986 provides that nothing in the 1986 Act shall affect any legal aid under the 1967 Act or advice and assistance under the 1972 Act in respect of which an application was determined before 1 April 1987; and, notwithstanding the repeal by the 1986 Act of the 1967 Act and the 1972 Act, they and any schemes, regulations, orders or rules of court made under them are to continue to have effect for the purposes of such legal aid or advice and assistance.

Part B — Legal aid and advice and assistance under the Legal Aid (Scotland) Act 1986

1. Advice and assistance (including assistance by way of representation)

Advice and Assistance (Scotland) (Consolidation and Amendment) Regulations 1996 (SI 1996 No 2447)

[This Statutory Instrument is printed as amended by:
Advice and Assistance (Scotland) Amendment Regulations 1997 (SI 1997 No 726) which came into force on 1st April 1997;
Advice and Assistance (Scotland) Amendment Regulations 2000 (SSI 2000 No 181) which came into force on 7th July 2000;
The Advice and Assistance (Scotland) Amendment (No 2) Regulations 2004 (SSI 2004 No 262) which came into force on 23rd June 2004;
The Advice and Assistance (Scotland) Amendment (No 2) Regulations 2005 (SSI 2005 No 171) which came into force on 30th April 2005;
The Advice and Assistance (Scotland) Amendment (No 2) Regulations 2006 (SSI 2006 No 233) which came into force on 12th June 2006;
The Advice and Assistance (Scotland) Amendment Regulations 2007 (SSI 2007 No 60) which came into force on 1st May 2007;
The Criminal Legal Assistance (Fees and Information etc.) (Scotland) Regulations 2008 (SSI 2008 No 240) which came into force on 30th June 2008;
The Criminal Legal Assistance (Fees) (No 2) (Scotland) Regulations 2010 (SSI 2010 No 312) which came into force on 30th September 2010;
The Legal Aid and Advice and Assistance (Solicitors' Travel Fees) (Scotland) Regulations 2011 (SSI 2011 No 41) which came into force on 28th February 2011;
The Children's Legal Assistance (Fees) (Miscellaneous Amendments) (Scotland) Regulations 2013 (SSI 2013 No 144) which came into force on 24 June 2013;
The Legal Aid and Advice and Assistance (Photocopying Fees and Welfare Reform) (Miscellaneous Amendments) (Scotland) Regulations 2013 (SSI 2013 No 250) which came into force on 31st October 2013.]

Fees and outlays of solicitors

17.—(1) Subject to paragraph (2) below, fees and outlays allowable to the solicitor upon any assessment or taxation mentioned in regulations 18 and 19 in respect of advice or assistance shall, and shall only, be —

    (a) fees for work actually, necessarily and reasonably done in connection with the matter upon which advice and assistance was given, due regard being had to economy, calculated, in the case of assistance by way of representation, in accordance with the table of fees in Part I of Schedule 3 and, in any other case, in accordance with the table of fees in Part II of Schedule 3; and

    (b) outlays actually, necessarily and reasonably incurred in connection with that matter, due regard being had to economy, provided that, without prejudice to any other claims for outlays, there shall not be allowed to a solicitor outlays representing posts and incidents.

(2) The fees and outlays allowable to the solicitor under paragraph (1) above shall not exceed the limit applicable under section 10 of the Act as read with regulation 12.

(3) In the application of paragraph (1) above so far as concerning assistance by way of representation in relation to a summary criminal matter, there is to be taken into account time necessarily spent in travelling to and from the relevant court (other than one in the town or other place where the solicitor has a place of business) or any other place visited for the purpose of preparing or conducting the defence.

(4) Paragraph (3) above does not apply if it would have been more economical to use a local solicitor (where that would have been reasonable in the interests of the client).

(5) This regulation (so far as concerning criminal matters) is subject to the Criminal Legal Aid (Fixed Payments) (Scotland) Regulations 1999.

Assessment and taxation of fees and outlays

18.—(1) Where the solicitor considers that the fees and outlays properly chargeable for the advice or assistance exceed any contribution payable by the client under the provisions of section 11 of the Act together with any expenses or property recovered or preserved under the provisions of section 12 of the Act as read with regulation 16, he shall, within one year of the date when the giving of advice and assistance was completed, submit an account to the Board:

Provided that, where civil legal aid has been made available to an applicant to whom in connection with the same matter advice or assistance has been given, the account for such advice and assistance shall be submitted to the Board at the same time as that for civil legal aid; and any work which is charged under civil legal aid shall not be charged in the advice and assistance account.

(2) The Board may accept an account for advice and assistance submitted outwith the period referred to in paragraph (1) above if it considers that there is a special reason for late submission.

(3) Where the Board receives an account in accordance with paragraph (1) above, it shall assess the fees and outlays allowable to the solicitor for the advice or assistance in accordance with regulation 17 and shall determine accordingly any sum payable out of the Fund and pay it to the solicitor.

(3A) Where the solicitor has given advice and assistance by way of a diagnostic interview then he shall, within 3 months of the date when the giving of the advice and assistance was completed, submit an account to the Board separate from any account or accounts submitted under paragraph (1). No account supplementary to that provided for in this paragraph may be submitted.

(4) If the solicitor is dissatisfied with any assessment of fees and outlays by the Board under paragraph (3) above, he may require taxation of his account by the auditor; the auditor shall tax the fees and outlays allowable to the solicitor for the advice or assistance in accordance with regulation 17, and such taxation shall be conclusive of the fees and outlays so allowable.

SCHEDULE 3

TABLE OF FEES ALLOWABLE TO SOLICITORS

PART I — TABLE OF FEES ALLOWABLE TO SOLICITORS FOR ASSISTANCE BY WAY OF REPRESENTATION

1.   Subject to paragraph 3 of this Part, the fees allowable to a solicitor for providing assistance by way of representation shall be for criminal matters and civil matters and children's matters arising out of hearings or proceedings under the Children's Hearings (Scotland) Act 2011 as follows—

   (a)   Omitted by SSI 2008 No 240.

   (b)   fees, as undernoted, for work other than or subsequent to that described in Schedule 1B to the Criminal Legal Aid (Fixed Payments) (Scotland) Regulations 1999.

		Criminal	*Civil*	*Children*
1.	The fee for —			
(i)	any time up to the first half hour spent by a solicitor appearing in court or conducting another hearing;.....................................	£27.40	£33.15	£33.15
(ii)	each quarter hour (or part thereof) subsequent to the first half hour spent in court or conducting another hearing.	£13.70	£16.60	£16.60
2.	The fee for —			
(i)	each quarter hour (or part thereof) spent by a solicitor in carrying out work other than that prescribed in paragraphs 1 and 3 to 5 hereof, provided that any time is additional to the total time charged for under paragraph 1 above;...............................	£10.55	£12.75	12.75

(ii) for each quarter hour (or part thereof) spent by a solicitor's clerk in carrying out work other than that prescribed in paragraphs 3 to 5 hereof shall be..	£5.25	£6.35	£6.26

3. The fee for —
  (i) each citation of a witness including execution thereof;
  (ii) framing and drawing precognitions and other necessary papers, subject to paragraph 4 (iii) below — per sheet (or part thereof);
  (iii) instructing messengers-at-arms and sheriff officers, including examining execution and settling fee;
  (iv) lengthy telephone calls (of over 4 and up to 10 minutes duration); and
  (v) letters, including instructions to counsel, subject to paragraph 4 (ii) below — per page (or part thereof). £6.00   £7.25   £7.25

4. The fee for —
  (i) attendance at court offices for performance of formal work including each necessary lodging in or uplifting from court or each necessary enquiry for documents due to be lodged;
  (ii) short letters of a formal nature, intimations and letters confirming telephone calls;
  (iii) framing formal papers, including inventories and title pages — per sheet (or part thereof);
  (iv) revising papers drawn by counsel or where revisal ordered by court — per 5 sheets (or part thereof); and
  (v) short telephone calls (of up to 4 minutes duration), ... £2.40   £2.90   £2.90

4A. The fee for each quarter of an hour (or part thereof) spent travelling—
  (a) by a solicitor £5.28   £6.38   £6.38
  (b) by a solicitor's clerk.. £2.63   £3.18   £3.18

5. (a) There is no fee for photocopying—
    (i) where fewer than 20 sheets are copied at one time;
    (ii) in relation to the first 20 sheets copied at any one time.
  (b) Subject to sub-paragraph (a), the fee for all photocopying in the matter in relation to which assistance by way of representation was given is—
    (i) 5 pence for each sheet copied for up to 10,000 sheets; and
    (ii) 1 penny per sheet for each sheet copied in addition to the first 10,000 sheets.

Interpretation

2. In this table —
  a "sheet" shall consist of 250 words or numbers;
  a "page" shall consist of 125 words or numbers.

Petition by debtor for sequestration

3. The fees allowable to a solicitor for providing assistance by way of representation in relation to a petition by a debtor for the sequestration of his estate under section 5(2)(a) of the Bankruptcy (Scotland) Act 1985 shall be —
  (a) £33.15 for any time spent by a solicitor appearing in court in connection with the petition; and
  (b) £54.45 for all other work in connection with the petition.

1. The fees allowable to a solicitor shall be calculated for criminal matters and for civil matters and for children's matters arising out of Part II of the Children (Scotland) Act 1995 or in connection with any hearings or proceedings under the Children's Hearings (Scotland) Act 2011 as follows:

	Criminal	*Civil*	*Children*
A. Time occupied in carrying out work for the client other than work described in paragraphs B to G below —			
(i) solicitor — per quarter hour (or part thereof)	£11.60	£12.75	£12.75
(ii) solicitor's clerk — per quarter hour (or part thereof)	£5.77	£6.35	£6.35
B. For short letters of a formal nature, short telephone calls (of up to 4 minutes duration), framing formal documents such as inventories and engrossing formal documents for signature — per sheet (or part thereof)	£2.64	£2.90	£2.90
C. For letters other than in B above — per page (or part thereof), framing non-formal documents other than precognitions — per sheet of 250 words (or part thereof) and lengthy telephone calls (of over 4 and up to 10 minutes duration)	£6.60	£7.25	£7.25
D. For taking and drawing precognitions			
for the first sheet of 250 words or less	£23.15	£25.50	£25.50
for each subsequent sheet of 250 words	£23.15	£25.50	£25.50
for each subsequent sheet of less than 250 words	£11.60	£12.75	£12.75
DA. The fee for each quarter of an hour (or part thereof) spent travelling—			
(a) by a solicitor	£5.80	£6.38	£6.38
(b) by a solicitor's clerk	£2.89	£3.18	£3.18

E. (a) There is no fee for photocopying—

    (i) where fewer than 20 sheets are copied at any one time;

    (ii) in relation to the first 20 sheets copied at any one time.

  (b) Subject to sub-paragraph (a), the fee for all photocopying in the matter is—

    (i) 5 pence for each sheet copied for up to 10,000 sheets; and

    (ii) 1 penny per sheet for each sheet copied in addition to the first 10,000

F. For the first half hour (or part thereof) providing advice and assistance to the client if—			
(a) the client is being detained under section 14(1) of the Criminal Procedure (Scotland) Act 1995(2) or is otherwise at a police station for the purposes of questioning; and	£30.94	—	—

  (b) the period—

    (i) concludes after 2200 hours; or

    (ii) begins before 0700 hours.

G. For each quarter hour (or part thereof), subsequent to the first half hour, providing advice and assistance to the client in the circumstance mentioned in paragraph F(a), if the quarter hour period—	£15.47	—	—

  (a) concludes after 2200 hours; or

  (b) begins before 0700 hours.

2. Omitted by SSI 2008 No 240.

Interpretation

3. In this Table —

a "sheet" shall consist of 250 words or numbers; and

a "page" shall consist of 125 words or numbers.

2. Criminal legal aid

NOTE: THE UNDERNOTED REGULATIONS APPLY SUBJECT TO THE PROVISIONS OF THE CRIMINAL LEGAL AID (FIXED PAYMENTS) (SCOTLAND) REGULATIONS 1999 (SI 1999 NO 491) — SEE PP 131–145

Criminal Legal Aid (Scotland) (Fees) Regulations 1989 (SI 1989 No 1491)

[This Statutory Instrument is printed as amended by:
Criminal Legal Aid (Scotland) (Fees) Amendment Regulations 1990 (SI 1990 No 474) (counsel's fees);
Criminal Legal Aid (Scotland) (Fees) Amendment (No 2) Regulations 1990 (SI 1990 No 1035) (solicitors' fees);
Criminal Legal Aid (Scotland) (Fees) Amendment Regulations 1991 (SI 1991 No 566) (solicitors' fees) which came into force on 1st April 1991;
Criminal Legal Aid (Scotland) (Fees) Amendment Regulations 1992 (SI 1992 No 374) (solicitors' fees) which came into force on 1st April 1992;
Criminal Legal Aid (Scotland) (Fees) Amendment Regulations 1997 (SI 1997 No 719) which came into force on 1st April 1997;
The Scotland Act 1998 (Consequential Modifications) No 1 Order 1999 (SI 1999 No 1042) which came into force on 6th May 1999;
Criminal Legal Aid (Scotland) (Fees) Amendment Regulations 2002 (SSI 2002 No 246) which came into force on 17th June 2002;
Criminal Legal Aid (Youth Courts) (Scotland) Regulations 2003 (SSI 2003 No 249) which came into force on 2nd June 2003;
Criminal Legal Aid (Scotland) (Fees) Amendment Regulations 2004 (SSI 2004 No 264) which came into force on 28th June 2004;
Criminal Legal Aid (Scotland) (Fees) Amendment (No 2) Regulations 2004 (SSI 2004 No 316) which came into force on 2nd July 2004;
Criminal Legal Aid (Scotland) (Fees) Amendment Regulations 2005 (SSI 2005 No 113) which came into force on 25th March 2005;
Criminal Legal Aid (Scotland) (Fees) Amendment (No 2) Regulations 2005 (SSI 2005 No 584) which came into force on 10th December 2005;
Criminal Legal Aid (Scotland) (Fees) Amendment (No 3) Regulations 2005 (SSI 2005 No 656) which came into force on 29th January 2006;
Criminal Legal Aid (Summary Justice Pilot Courts and Bail Conditions) (Scotland) Regulations 2006 (SSI 2006 No 234) which came into force on 2nd June 2006;
Criminal Legal Aid (Scotland) (Fees) Amendment Regulations 2006 (SSI 2006 No 515) whcih came into force on 16th November 2006;
Criminal Legal Aid (Scotland) (Fees) Amendment Regulations 2007 (SSI 2007 No 180) which came into force on 29th March 2007;
Criminal Legal Assistance (Fees and Information etc.) (Scotland) Regulations 2008 (SSI 2008 No 240) which came into force on 30th June 2008;
Legal Aid (Supreme Court) (Scotland) Regulations 2009 (SSI 2009 No 312) which came into force on 1st October 2009;
Criminal Legal Aid (Scotland) (Fees) Amendment Regulations 2010 (SSI 2010 No 63) which came into force on 23rd March 2010;
Criminal Legal Aid (Scotland) (Fees) Amendment (No 2) Regulations 2010 (SSI 2010 No 212) which came into force on 5th July 2010;
Legal Aid and Advice and Assistance (Solicitors' Travel Fees) (Scotland) Regulations 2011 (SSI 2011 No 41) which came into force on 28th February 2011;
Criminal Legal Aid (Scotland) (Fees) Amendment Regulations 2011 (SSI 2011 No 135) which came into force 17th March 2011;
Criminal Legal Aid (Scotland) (Fees) Amendment Regulations 2012 (SSI 2012 No 276) which came into force on 3rd December 2012;
Scotland Act 2012 (Transitional and Consequential Provisions) Order 2013 (SSI 2013 No 7) which came into force on 22nd April 2013;
Legal Aid and Advice and Assistance (Photocopying Fees and Welfare Reform) (Miscellaneous Amendments) (Scotland) Regulations 2013 (SSI 2013 No 250) which came into force on 31st October 2013;
Criminal Legal Aid (Scotland) (Fees) Amendment Regulations 2013 (SSI 2013 No 320) which came into force on 8th January 2014;
Legal Aid (Miscellaneous Amendments) (Scotland) Regulations 2015 (SSI 2015 No 337) which came into force on 22nd September 2015]

Fees allowance to solicitors: general provisions

4.—(1) Subject to the following provisions of this regulation and to regulations 5, 6 and 9, the fees allowable to solicitors shall be those specified in Schedule 1.

(2) Where a nominated solicitor represents two or more persons charged in the same indictment or complaint, or appealing against conviction or sentence in respect of the same indictment or complaint he shall submit one account in respect of all those persons.

(3) Where a nominated solicitor requires another solicitor, whether an Edinburgh solicitor in connection with an appeal or on a remit for sentence, or a solicitor at the place of the prison or the court, or a local solicitor for the purpose of local precognitions or inquiry, nevertheless only one account shall be submitted by the nominated solicitor (payment of the other solicitor being a matter for adjustment between the nominated solicitor and the other solicitor out of the fees payable hereunder), but in determining the sum to be allowed to the nominated solicitor account shall be taken also of the work carried out by that other solicitor.

(4) Where the work done by a solicitor constitutes a supply of services in respect of which value-added tax is chargeable, there may be added to the amount of fees allowed to the solicitor an amount equal to the amount of value-added tax chargeable.

Solicitors' fees for identification parades and judicial examinations

5.—(1) For attending an identification parade to which section 21(4)(b) of the 1986 Act applies, a solicitor shall be allowed a fee at the following rates:—

    (a) where paragraph (2) applies—
        (i) £114.00 for the first hour; and
        (ii) £12.67 for each subsequent quarter of an hour; or
    (b) where paragraph (2) does not apply—
        (i) £93.80 for the first hour; and
        (ii) £11.82 for each subsequent quarter of an hour.

(2) This paragraph applies where a solicitor represents an accused person at an identification parade in connection with or in contemplation of solemn criminal proceedings if—

    (a) when the identification parade is held, criminal legal aid has been made available in respect of those proceedings and the solicitor is the nominated solicitor; or
    (b) after the identification parade has been held, criminal legal aid is made available in respect of those proceedings and the solicitor becomes the nominated solicitor.

(3) In paragraphs (1) and (2) "a solicitor" means the duty solicitor or, where criminal legal aid may be provided by a solicitor other than the duty solicitor, the nominated solicitor.

(4) For the purposes of paragraph (1), where attendance at an identification parade is required on more than one occasion each occasion is a separate identification parade.

(5) Subject to paragraph (6), the duty solicitor shall be allowed in respect of representing an accused person at a judicial examination (whether a first examination or a further examination) to which sections 35 to 39 of the Criminal Procedure (Scotland) Act 1995 apply—

    (a) fees in accordance with the rates specified in regulation 6(1); and
    (b) fees in respect of any necessary waiting time or any other necessary work relating to the judicial examination, determined in accordance with regulation 7.

(6) No fee shall be allowed under paragraph (5) if the duty solicitor goes on to become the accused person's nominated solicitor in respect of the same proceedings and entitled to a fee in accordance with paragraph 1 of Part 2 of the Table of Fees set out in Schedule 1.

Duty solicitors' fees

6.—(1) There shall be allowed to the duty solicitor representing accused persons in the sheriff or district court fees on the following scales:

    (a) for attendance at the first session of a court for the day, a sessional fee of £63 for the first case in which the accused pleads not guilty or which is adjourned under section 145 of the 1995 Act and £9 for each additional such case, subject to a maximum total fee of £140 for the session until its termination on completion of business for the day or on adjournment by the court, whichever is the earlier;
    (aa) for attendance a that session, a fee of £70 for each case in which the accused pleads guilty;
    (b) for attendance at any other session of that court on the same day, a sessional fee of £63 for the first case in which the accused pleads not guilty or which is adjourned under section 145 of the 1995 Act and £9 for each additional such case, subject to a maximum total fee of £93 for each such other session;
    (c) for attendance at any other such session, a fee of £70 for each case in which the accused pleads guilty:

Provided that the fee according to the foregoing scale shall cover the appearance in court of the duty solicitor on behalf of the accused as well as any interview or interviews with the accused or others whether such interview or interviews take place during the same or another session.

(2) Where, following a plea of guilty or in circumstances where the accused has not been called on to plead, one or more adjournments are ordered by the court, and the duty solicitor requires to appear again, then an additional fee shall be payable to the duty solicitor in respect of —

(a)   additional interviews with the accused or others; and

(b)   attendances at court other than during the course of the duty solicitor's period of duty.

The amount of such additional fee calculated on the basis of the fees set out in Schedule 1 shall be such sum not exceeding £150 (of which the relevant fee of £70 under paragraph (1) is to form part) as shall form reasonable remuneration having regard to the additional work and time involved.

(3) There shall be allowed to the duty solicitor making, for an accused person in the sheriff or district court, a preliminary plea to the competency or relevancy of the petition or complaint, or conducting any plea in bar of trial or any mental health proof, or any proof in mitigation or any proof of a victim statement an additional fee to be calculated on the basis of the fees set out in Schedule 1, the amount of such additional fee to be such sum not exceeding £150 as shall form reasonable remuneration having regard to the additional work and time involved.

(3A) In an exceptional case, the Board may pay to the duty solicitor such fees other than those specified in paragraph (2) or (3) (and to a higher limit) as it considers appropriate in the circumstances of the case.

(3B) Where fees are payable under this regulation, the duty solicitor is not entitled to separate payment in respect of any expenses incurred in travelling to and from the court (despite any entitlement to such payment that would arise but for this paragraph).

(3C) But paragraph (3B) does not prevent the Board paying such fees as are reasonably required for the purpose of securing the availability of a duty solicitor at a remote court.

(4) Where the duty solicitor represents an accused person before a court which has been designated by the sheriff principal as a youth court, domestic abuse court or summary justice pilot court, the maximum fees prescribed in paragraph (2) shall not apply.

Fees allowable to solicitors

7.—(1) Subject to the provisions of regulations 4, 5, 6 and 9, a solicitor shall be allowed such amount of fees as shall be determined to be reasonable remuneration for work actually and reasonably done, and travel and waiting time actually and reasonably undertaken or incurred, due regard being had to economy. The fees allowed shall be calculated in accordance with Schedule 1.

Solemn proceedings (exceptional) fees

7A. (1) A solicitor who provides criminal legal aid in relation to solemn criminal proceedings—

(a)   where the circumstances prescribed in paragraph (3) exist; and

(b)   subject to the conditions prescribed in paragraph (5),

is to be paid for all work only in accordance with Part 1 of the Table of Fees (detailed fees) in Schedule 1.

(2) It is for the Board to determine whether the circumstances prescribed at paragraph (3) exist, and whether the conditions prescribed at paragraphs (5) and (10) are met.

(3) The circumstances referred to in paragraph (1)(a) are where an assisted person would be deprived of the right to a fair trial in a case because of the amount of fees payable to the solicitor in accordance with these Regulations (other than paragraph (1)).

(4) Factors to be taken into account by the Board in considering whether the circumstances prescribed at paragraph (3) exist include whether the case involves legal or factual complexity (including procedural complexity).

(5) The conditions referred to in paragraph (1)(b) are as follows—

(a)   the solicitor providing the criminal legal aid is to make an application to the Board in such a manner and form (which may include an online form) and containing such information as the Board may specify at as early a stage in the provision of the criminal legal aid as is reasonably practicable;

(b)   that solicitor is, if required by the Board to do so, to supply such further information or such documents as the Board may require to enable it to determine the application; and

(c)   that solicitor is to keep proper records of all professional services provided by way of, and outlays incurred in the provision of, that criminal legal aid, whether before or after the Board determines whether the conditions prescribed in this paragraph are met.

(6) A solicitor may apply for review where the Board has determined that the circumstances prescribed in paragraph (3) do not exist.

(7) An application for review must—

    (a)   subject to paragraph (8), be lodged with the Board within 15 days, beginning on the day notice of the Board's determination was given to the applicant;

    (b)   include a statement of any matters which the applicant wishes the Board to take into account in reviewing the application; and

    (c)   be accompanied by such additional precognitions and other documents as the applicant considers to be relevant to the review.

(8) Paragraph (7)(a) does not apply where the Board considers there is a special reason for it to consider a late application for review.

(9) Where the Board has granted an application for a change of solicitor under regulation 17(3) of the Criminal Legal Aid (Scotland) Regulations 1996 (changes of solicitor), any solicitor who provided criminal legal aid prior to that grant is to be paid, where the Board has determined that the circumstances prescribed in paragraph (3) exist, for all work only in accordance with Part 1 of the Table of Fees (detailed fees) in Schedule 1.

(10) A solicitor to whom paragraph (9) applies is only to be paid in accordance with paragraph (9) where that solicitor has kept proper records of all professional services provided by way of, and outlays incurred in the provision of, that criminal legal aid.

Outlays allowable to solicitors

8.—(1)   A solicitor shall be allowed the following outlays, due regard being had to economy —

    (a)   travelling expenses actually and reasonably incurred by himself or his clerk in connection with travel for which a fee for travelling time is chargeable and, in calculating the travelling expenses due, paragraph 5(4) of the notes on the operation of Schedule 1 applies to those expenses as it applies to the fee for travelling time;

    (b)   fees paid to witnesses who are not on the Crown list, which fees shall not exceed such sums as are considered by the Board to be reasonable having regard to the sums payable from time to time by the Crown to witnesses of the same categories; and

    (c)   any out of pocket expenses actually and reasonably incurred, provided that without prejudice to any other claims for outlays there shall not be allowed to a solicitor outlays representing posts and incidents.

(2) Where a witness is a person giving evidence of fact or expert evidence and value-added tax is chargeable in respect of giving that evidence, and the witness adds an amount equal to the tax chargeable to his note of fee, the amount so added may be allowed to the solicitor as an outlay.

Submission of accounts

9.—(1)   Subject to paragraph (2) accounts prepared in respect of fees and outlays allowable to solicitors and fees allowable to counsel shall be submitted to the Board not later than 4 months after the date of conclusion of the proceedings in respect of which that legal aid was granted.

(2) The Board may accept accounts submitted in respect of fees and outlays allowable to solicitors and fees allowable to counsel later than the 4 months referred to in paragraph (1) if it considers that there is a special reason for late submission.

Fees allowable to counsel

10.—(1)   Counsel shall be allowed such fee as appears to the Board, or at taxation the auditor to represent reasonable remu neration, calculated in accordance with Schedule 2 or 3, for work actually and reasonably done, due regard being had to economy.

(2) Where work done by counsel constitutes a supply of services in respect of which value-added tax is chargeable, there may be added to the amount of fees allowable to counsel an amount equal to the amount of value-added tax chargeable thereon.

10A. In determining whether work has been actually and reasonably done for the purposes of these Regulations the Board, or as the case may be the auditor, is to deem solicitors and counsel to be as up to date with the substantive and procedural law of the field in which they practise as a competent solicitor or counsel practising in that field.

Taxation of fees and outlays

11.—(1)   If any question or dispute arises between the Board and a solicitor or counsel as to the amount of fees or outlays allowable to the solicitor, or as to the amount of fees allowable to counsel, from the Fund in respect of legal aid in criminal proceedings in–

(a)   the High Court, including appeals or the Sheriff Appeal Court, the matter shall be referred for taxation to the Auditor of the Court of Session;

(b)   the Supreme Court, the matter shall be referred for taxation to the Registrar of the Supreme Court; or

(c)   the sheriff or district court, the matter shall be referred for taxation to the auditor of the sheriff court for the district in which those proceedings took place.

(2) A reference to an auditor under this regulation may be made at the instance of the solicitor concerned or, where the question in dispute affects the fees allowable to counsel, of the counsel concerned, or of the Board and the auditor concerned shall give reasonable notice of the diet of taxation to the solicitor or counsel as appropriate and the Board.

(3) The Board and any other party to a reference under paragraph (1)(a) or (c) shall have the right to state written objections to the High Court or, as the case may be, the sheriff in relation to the report of the auditor within 14 days of issue of such report and the Board and any such other party may be heard thereon.

11A. —(1) In relation to proceedings in the Supreme Court, the Board on a reference to the auditor who is dissatisfied with all or part of a taxation shall have the right to lodge a petition to the Supreme Court within 14 days of the taxation setting out the items objected to and the nature and grounds of the objections.

(2) The petition shall be served on the Board, any such other party who attended the taxation and any other party to whom the auditor directs that a copy should be delivered.

(3) Any party upon whom such a petition is delivered may within 14 days after such delivery lodge a response to the petition which shall be served on the Board, any such other party who attended the taxation and any other party to whom the auditor directs that a copy should be delivered.

(4) The petition and responses, if any, shall be considered by a panel of Justices, as defined by rule 3(2) of the Supreme Court Rules 2009, which may allow or dismiss the petition without a hearing, invite any or all of the parties to lodge submissions or further submissions in writing or direct that an oral hearing be held.

SCHEDULE 1   Regulation 7
FEES OF SOLICITORS

Notes on the operation of Schedule 1

1.—(1) In relation to solemn criminal proceedings, other than proceedings to which regulation 7A(1) (solemn proceedings (exceptional) fees) applies, the fees payable to a solicitor are to be calculated as follows:—

(a)   for all work falling within a block of work prescribed in Part 2 of the Table of Fees (inclusive fees), the fee specified for that block of work in that Part;

(b)   for all other work, unless no fee is chargeable by virtue of paragraph 3, the fees specified in Part 1 of the Table of Fees (detailed fees).

(2) In a case in which an indictment has been served, the relevant column of Part 2 of the Table of Fees for the purposes of sub-paragraph (1)(a)—

(a)   for proceedings in the High Court of Justiciary which relate to an offence listed in Schedule 2, Part I, Chapter 1—

  (i)   paragraph 3(a) is column A;

  (ii)   paragraph 3(b) or (c) is column B;

(b)   for proceedings in the sheriff court is column C.

(3) In a case in which an indictment has not been served, the relevant column of Part 2 of the Table of Fees for the purposes of sub-paragraph (1)(a)—

(a)   is column A if the proceedings relate to any of the following offences:—

  (i)   murder;

  (ii)   multiple attempted murder;

  (iii)   culpable homicide;

  (iv)   rape;

  (v)   assault and robbery involving commercial premises;

  (vi)   importation of controlled drugs;

  (vii)   an offence under section 1 of the 1988 Act (causing death by dangerous driving);

  (viii) an offence under the Explosive Substances Act 1883;

  (ix)   a firearms offence;

  (x)   incest;

  (xi)   sodomy;

    (xii) sedition;

    (xiii) treason;

    (xiv) torture; and

    (xv) war crimes;

  (b) is column C if the proceedings do not relate to any of offences specified in sub-paragraph (a).

(3A) Where the Table of Fees does not prescribe a fee for any item of work, and unless no fee is chargeable by virtue of paragraph 3, the Board or the auditor, as the case may be, is to allow such fees as appear appropriate to provide reasonable remuneration for the work with regard to all the circumstances, including the general levels of fees in the Table of Fees.

(4) For the purposes of sub-paragraph (2)(a), where the proceedings relate to an offence which is not listed in paragraph 3(a), (b) or (c) of Chapter 1 of Part I of Schedule 2 the offence is deemed to be listed in whichever of those sub-paragraphs the Board, or as the case may be the auditor, considers appropriate having regard to all the circumstances.

(5) The following items of work do not fall within any block of work prescribed in Part 2 of the Table of Fees and the fees for these items are payable in accordance with Part 1 of the Table of Fees (detailed fees)—

  (a) travel;

  (b) attending locus visits;

  (c) work in connection with the taking of a witness precognition;

  (d) perusing, for the first time, the indictment, witness lists, statements, productions and labels received from the Crown and defence precognitions;

  (e) instructing expert witnesses;

  (f) conducting, or attending court when counsel is conducting, a hearing;

  (g) time spent waiting;

  (h) post conviction work, except for the work described in paragraph 5 of Part 2 of the Table of Fees; and

  (i) the work described in paragraph 3 of Part 2 of the Table of Fees, where the Board is satisfied that the case raised unusually complex issues of fact.

2. In relation to summary criminal proceedings, including appeals, the fee for any item of work is to be calculated in accordance with Part 1 of the Table of Fees.

3. Without prejudice to the discretion of the Board or auditor in relation to summary proceedings, in solemn proceedings no fee is chargeable for—

  (a) making a telephone call that is not answered;

  (b) making a telephone call that is answered only by an automated device or system that allows the caller to record a message, except on cause shown;

  (c) framing a file note;

  (d) framing a precognition following a meeting where a file note would suffice;

  (e) perusing correspondence;

  (f) a letter of acknowledgement, unless expressly requested or required;

  (g) more than two consultations, except on cause shown;

  (h) a meeting with the client, unless it is clear from a brief narrative in the account that information was received from or imparted to the client at the meeting advancing the case;

  (i) more than one solicitor attending a meeting with the client, without the prior sanction of the Board;

  (j) preparing for a hearing, other than where the fee for preparation is as provided for within a block of work prescribed in Part 2 of the Table of Fees (inclusive fees);

  (k) preparing for a hearing to which paragraph 4(a) of Part 2 of the Table of Fees relates unless—

    (i) the indictment, containing a libel against the client, proceeds to trial; or

    (ii) on or after the day fixed for trial, the Crown withdraws any libel against the client;

  (l) preparing for a hearing to which paragraph 4(a) of Part 2 of the Table of Fees relates if a fee under that paragraph has already been charged in respect of the case;

  (m) preparing for a subsequent day of trial if more than two fees have already been charged under paragraph 4(b) of Part 2 of the Table of Fees;

  (n) more than one solicitor attending a hearing, without the prior sanction of the Board;

  (o) during the court's lunch break, time spent at court for a hearing or travelling to or from court, except on cause shown;

(p) settling with witnesses in respect of a trial where a fee is charged in terms of paragraph 4(a) of Part 2 of the Table of Fees.

3A. (1) In solemn proceedings, where fees would otherwise be chargeable under both paragraph 4A(c) and paragraph 6(a) or (ab) of Part 2 of the Table of Fees (inclusive fees), only one fee is chargeable, being the higher amount of the two.

(2) Under paragraph 4A a fee is chargeable for preparing lines of enquiry and preparing submissions, but is not chargeable for consultations which concern preparation.

Research

3B. The fee prescribed in paragraph 6 of Part 1 of the Table of Fees (detailed fees) may be payable for time spent in researching a novel, developing or unusual point of law where the following conditions are met:—

    (a) the Board considers that the circumstances of the case are exceptional, whether or not the Board has made a determination under regulation 7A (solemn proceedings (exceptional) fees); and

    (b) the research required in the case, in the opinion of the Board, goes beyond the understanding of the substantive and procedural law expected of solicitors in accordance with regulation 10A.

Time spent waiting and travelling

4. A fee for time spent waiting is chargeable only for time necessarily spent waiting at court for a hearing, provided that time has not been occupied in connection with another case (legally aided or not).

5.—(1) Subject to sub-paragraph (2), a fee for travelling time is chargeable only for time necessarily spent travelling to and from—

    (a) court, provided that—

        (i) a fee is chargeable for the work undertaken at the court; and

        (ii) the court is not in a town or place where the solicitor has a place of business;

    (b) a meeting with the client—

        (i) in prison; or

        (ii) elsewhere, if the client is unable to travel on medical grounds;

    (c) a meeting with the Procurator Fiscal or Advocate Depute at their office;

    (d) a consultation with counsel or an expert witness;

    (e) a locus inspection;

    (f) an examination of productions.

(2) A fee for travelling time is chargeable in circumstances other than those listed in sub-paragraph (1) only if the Board, or as the case may be the auditor, is satisfied that it was necessary for the advancement of the case that the solicitor be physically present at the place travelled to.

(3) A fee for travelling time is not chargeable if it would have been more economical to use a local solicitor, unless it was reasonable in the interests of the client that the nominated solicitor, or a solicitor assisting the nominated solicitor in terms of regulation 4(3), attended personally.

(4) The fee chargeable for travelling time is the fee for time necessarily spent travelling divided by the number of cases (legally aided or not) in connection with which the travel was undertaken.

Transfer of agency

6. Where agency is transferred from one solicitor to another—

    (a) the fee for a block of work commenced and completed by the same solicitor is payable to that solicitor;

    (b) the fee for a block of work commenced by one solicitor but completed by another is to be apportioned equally between the solicitors who undertook work falling within that block.

Uplifts

7.—(1) The fee for time spent by a solicitor travelling and taking a statement in connection with a precognition to which this paragraph applies is £12.67 for each quarter of an hour.

(2) This paragraph applies to a precognition in relation to solemn proceedings if—

    (a) it is the first precognition of the client; or

    (b) cause is shown that the statement had to be taken by a solicitor.

Interpretation

8. In this Schedule—

"court" means the Supreme Court, the High Court of Justiciary, the Sheriff Appeal Court, the sheriff court, the justice of the peace court or any remaining district court as the case may be;

"hearing" includes diet;

"quarter of an hour" will be read as if immediately followed by the words "(or part thereof)";

a "sheet" shall consist of 250 words or numbers; and

a "page" shall consist of 125 words or numbers.

TABLE OF FEES
PART 1 DETAILED FEES

	Summary Procedure	Solemn Procedure
1. In connection with the conduct of a hearing–		
(a) in summary proceedings, the fee for–		
(i) any time up to the first half hour spent by a solicitor conducting the hearing	£27.40	—
(ii) each quarter hour spent, subsequent to the first half hour, conducting the hearing	£13.70	—
(b) in solemn proceedings, the fee for each quarter of an hour spent by a solicitor conducting the hearing		£18.30
2. The fee for any of the following:–	£6.00	£6.95
(a) each citation of a witness, including execution;		
(b) framing and drawing necessary papers other than those referred to in paragraph 3(c);		
(c) instructing messengers at arms and sheriff officers, including examining execution and settling fee;		
(d) lengthy telephone calls (of over 4 and up to 10 minutes' duration), subject to paragraph 4(e); and		
(e) letters, including instructions to counsel, per page (or part thereof), subject to paragraph 3(b)		
3. The fee for any of the following:–	£2.40	£2.75
(a) attendance at court offices for performance of formal work including each necessary lodging in or uplifting from court or each necessary inquiry for documents due to be lodged;		
(b) short formal letters, letters of acknowledgement, letters each having a similar nature, intimations and letters confirming telephone calls;		
(c) framing formal papers, including inventories and title pages, per sheet (or part thereof);		
(d) revising papers drawn by counsel or where revisal ordered by court, per 5 sheets (or part thereof); and		
(e) subject to paragraph 4(e), short telephone calls (of up to 4 minutes' duration) and telephone calls (of any duration) where the intended recipient is not reached or insufficient narrative is provided in the account to ascertain the duration of the call.		
4. In connection with taking a precognition in relation to solemn proceedings–		
(a) subject to paragraph 7 of the notes on the operation of Schedule 1, the fee for each hour (or part thereof) spent–		
(i) travelling	—	£11.55
(ii) taking a statement	—	£11.55
(b) the fee for–		
(i) framing the precognition, per sheet	—	£2.40
(ii) each letter making arrangements for taking a statement	—	£1.45
(iii) a telephone call, of any duration	—	£0.95

5. (a) There is no fee for photocopying—
    (i) where fewer than 20 sheets are copied at any one time;.........................
    (ii) in relation to the first 20 sheets copied at any one time.........................

  (b) Subject to sub-paragraph (a), the fee for all photocopying in relation to proceedings is—

(i) for each sheet copied for up to 10,000 sheets	£0.05	£0.05
(ii) for each sheet copied in addition to the first 10,000 sheets	£0.01	£0.01

5A. The fee for each quarter of an hour spent travelling—

(a) by a solicitor..	£5.28	£6.10
(b) by a solicitor's clerk..	£2.63	£3.05

6. The fee for each quarter of an hour spent carrying out work other than that prescribed in the preceding paragraphs–

(a) by a solicitor, provided the time is additional to the total time charged for under paragraph 1	£10.55	£12.20
(b) by a solicitor's clerk...	£5.25	£6.10

PART 2
INCLUSIVE FEES FOR SOLEMN FIRST INSTANCE PROCEEDINGS

	Column A	Column B	Column C
1. The fee for all work from the taking of initial instructions up until the client is admitted to bail or committed until liberated in due course of law, where–			
(a) at the first examination the client is either–			
(i) not committed for further examination; or..............................	£152.00	£133.00	£571.00
(ii) committed for further examination and admitted to bail.			
(b) at the first examination the client is committed for further examination and not admitted to bail.	£228.00	£209.00	£133.00
2. The fee for all work preparing for a bail appeal hearing including any continued diet and, where necessary, instructing Edinburgh agents	£57.00	£57.00	£57.00
3. The fee for arranging and attending all meetings, including consultations, in prison with the client after full committal for trial up to the conclusion of the case	£437.00	£304.00	£152.00
4. The fee for preparation, including citing and settling with witnesses, perusing evidence and preparing lines of enquiry and submissions but excluding relative consultations, in respect of–			
(a) the first day of trial	£399.00	£285.00	£152.00
(b) a subsequent day of trial	£152.00	£114.00	£38.00
4A. The fee for preparation for—...	£38.00	£38.00	£38.00
(a) a hearing under section 76 of the 1995 Act (procedure where accused decides to plead guilty);			
(b) a hearing on a plea in bar of trial;			
(c) a hearing raising a preliminary issue, where the preliminary issue would have the effect of excusing the accused person from trial and no other fee is prescribed for this preparation.			
5. The fee for all work in connection with post conviction discussions, advice and representation, including advising and giving an opinion on the prospects of any appeal...	£177.00	£177.00	£101.00
6. Unless dealt with in the course of the preliminary hearing or a first diet, the fee for all work in connection with any of the following:–	£152.00	£152.00	£152.00
(a) a devolution or compatibility issue, in terms of Schedule 6 to the Scotland Act 1998;			
(ab) a compatibility issue in terms of section 288ZA of the 1995 Act(1);			
(b) a vulnerable witnesses application, in terms of section 271A, B, C or D of the 1995 Act;			

    (c)   a specification of documents;

    (d)   a precognition on oath;

    (e)   an evidence on commission;

    (f)   an application to lead evidence relating to sexual offences under section 275(1) of the 1995 Act;

    (g)   a proof in mitigation; and

    (h)   an examination of facts.

SCHEDULE 2

Regulation 10

FEES OF COUNSEL

Notes on the operation of Schedule 2

1. Subject to the following provisions of this Schedule fees including those within a range of fees, shall be determined or calculated by the Board, and in the event of a question or dispute by the auditor, in accordance with the Table of Fees in this Schedule.

2. Where the Table of Fees does not prescribe a fee for any item of work or category of proceedings the Board, or as the case may be the auditor, shall allow such fee as appears appropriate to provide reasonable remuneration for the work with regard to all the circumstances, including the general levels of fees in the Table of Fees.

3. In the assessment and taxation of counsel's fees–

    (a)   counsel's fees are allowed only where the Board has sanctioned the employment of counsel or counsel is automatically available;

    (b)   junior counsel's fees shall be allowable as prescribed in Chapter 1 of Parts I to III of the Table of Fees even where sanction has been granted for the employment of senior counsel in the case, except in any case to which sub-paragraph (c) below applies;

    (c)   where a senior junior is representing an accused person in a multiple accused case at first instance and where any co-accused is represented by senior counsel, the fees payable to senior junior shall be those prescribed in the Table of Fees for junior as leader, and the fees payable to any junior counsel assisting senior junior shall be those of junior with leader;

    (d)   except on cause shown, fees for only two consultations in the case shall be allowed;

    (e)   except on cause shown (and subject to sub-paragraphs (ea) and (eb)), fees for senior counsel or, as the case may be, for both senior and junior counsel or for more than one junior counsel shall not be payable for attendance at hearings which do not require the attendance of senior or, as the case may be, both senior and junior counsel or more than one junior counsel;

    (ea) a fee is to be allowed to one counsel only in respect of a hearing of the type described in paragraph 6A of Chapters 1 and 2 of Part 2 of the Table of Fees that did not involve a debate, motion for re-trial or further procedure;

    (eb) a fee, under Part 1 or 3 of the Table of Fees, is to be allowed to one counsel only in respect of—

        (i)   a diet of deferred sentence, except where there is in contemplation the imposition of any of the following—

            (a)   a mandatory or discretionary life sentence;

            (b)   an order for lifelong restriction;

            (c)   any disposal under Part 6 of the 1995 Act (mental disorder),

           or where there is a hearing of evidence in mitigation; and

        (ii) a continued preliminary hearing, except where designated as a hearing at which any of the following matters is intended to be heard—

            (a)   a preliminary minute;

            (b)   a preliminary issue;

            (c)   a devolution or compatibility minute;

            (d)   an application under section 275 of the 1995 Act;

            (e)   a petition to recover documents under a specification of documents where the petition is opposed or likely to involve substantive legal argument,

           or an evidential hearing or any other hearing involving substantive legal argument;

    (f)   except on cause shown, the auditor shall not have regard to any information produced by counsel at taxation which was not made available to the Board at the time the Board made the offer to counsel which is subject to taxation;

    (g)   although counsel may keep records of professional services based on the number of hours expended on the work, counsel shall not be entitled to fees at an hourly rate in addition to the fees prescribed in the Table of Fees; and

    (h)   correspondence, telephone calls, written work (other than work for which fees are prescribed in the Table of Fees) and meetings between counsel acting for the same assisted person are not allowable as separate items and shall be subsumed within the fees set out for the conduct of a hearing.

Appeals

4. In a hearing as specified in paragraph 1(c) or (d) or 2(b) of Chapter 1 or 2 of Part 2 of the Table of Fees which is set down for half a day or longer or where the appellant has been sentenced to a period of imprisonment of 10 years or more, to life imprisonment or where an order for lifelong restriction has been made, the fee payable shall be that in the range specified in paragraph 3(d) of Chapter 1 or 2 of Part 2 respectively.

4A. Where a hearing on a bill of advocation is set down for half a day or longer, counsel is to be paid (in addition to the fees payable under paragraph 2 of the applicable Chapter of Part 2 of the Tables of Fees) a fee for relative written work in the range specified in paragraph 3(b) of the applicable Chapter of Part 2 of the Table of Fees.

5. Subject to paragraphs 9 to 11B below, the fees including those within a range of fees, as prescribed in Part II of the Table of Fees, shall include all preparation.

6. Where counsel is seeking a higher fee within the range under paragraph 3(d), or (da) or 6(a), (b), (c), (ca) or (cb) (hearings) of Chapter 1 or 2 of Part 2 he or she will need to justify this by establishing that due to the nature of the case an unusually high level of preparation was required or that any of the factors below exist and that they have had a significant effect on the conduct of the case:–

  (a) novelty of the issues of law;

  (b) unusually complex issues of fact;

  (c) issues of considerable legal significance.

7. Where the Auditor determines the appropriate fee he or she shall specify which of the factors in paragraph 6 justify such a fee and the extent to which each of those factors contribute to that fee.

8. Where counsel is seeking a higher fee within the range under paragraph 2(a), 3(a), (b), (e) 6(d) or 11 (written work) of Chapter 1 or 2 of Part 2 he or she will need to justify this by reference to either or both of the following factors:–

  (a) the content rather than the length of the document; and

  (b) the amount of documentation necessarily referred to.

9. Where a hearing has been fixed in an appeal under paragraph 3, 4 or 6 of Chapter 1 or 2 of Part 2 of the Table of Fees counsel may claim an additional fee for preparation for the hearing only where:–

  (a) it is set down for a day or more and counsel has spent more than 2 hours per day on preparation; or

  (b) the case is abnormal in magnitude, or difficulty, or in any other material respect.

10. Where an additional fee for preparation is claimed counsel must provide the Board with details of the nature of the preparation including:–

  (a) where a higher fee has been claimed or received within a range of fees, identification of the part or parts of that fee which relate to those factors mentioned in subparagraphs (a) to (c) of paragraph 6 above or to the factor of an unusually high level of preparation;

  (b) records providing a detailed summary of the nature of the work or, if applicable, the nature of the documentation perused at each stage of the process, the time taken and when and where the work was undertaken and the details of authorities referred to in the course of preparation; and

  (c) any contemporaneous record or notes made in the course of preparation.

11. Except on cause shown, an additional fee for preparation shall only be allowable once to both junior and senior counsel notwithstanding that the assisted person may be represented by more than one junior or senior counsel or both during the course of the case.

11A. In assessing the amount of time for which an additional fee for preparation is payable the Board, or the Auditor as the case may be, will consider the amount of time that is reasonable having regard to the following factors:–

  (a) the facts and circumstances of the case; and

  (b) the extent to which payment for preparation is already covered by the prescribed fee or the fee deemed appropriate within the range of fees, taking into account that in cases set down for a day or more 2 hours preparation is covered by that fee by virtue of paragraph 9(a).

11B. The additional fee shall be calculated by dividing the time allowed for additional preparation in terms of paragraph 11A above into units of 8 hours, each unit payable at the rate of two thirds of the prescribed fee or the fee deemed appropriate within the range of fees in Chapter 1 or 2 of Part 2 of the Table of Fees.

11C.—(1) This paragraph applies in relation to a hearing on appeal against conviction or conviction and sentence if rule 15.15A (requirement for case and argument) of the Act of Adjournal (Criminal Procedure Rules) 1996(3) applies to all aspects of the appeal.

(2) For the purposes of sub-paragraph (1), rule 15.15A is to be deemed to apply to an appeal if the court has ordered under rule 19.18A (presentation of summary conviction appeals in writing) of the Act of Adjournal (Criminal Procedure Rules) 1996(4) that rules 15.15A and 15.15B of those Rules are to apply to the appeal as if it were an appeal to which those rules apply.

(3) In respect of a hearing in the course of an appeal against conviction or against conviction and sentence to which this paragraph applies, a fee is to be paid under paragraph 3(da) of Chapter 1, or as the case may be Chapter 2, of Part 2 of the Table of Fees.

(4) In respect of a hearing in the course of an appeal against conviction or against conviction and sentence to which this paragraph does not apply, a fee is to be paid under paragraph 3(d) of Chapter 1, or as the case may be Chapter 2, of Part 2 of the Table of Fees.

11D. In Chapters 1 and 2 of Part 2 of the Table of Fees, the fees prescribed in paragraphs 1 to 6 do not apply to a hearing of the type described in paragraph 6A in each of those Chapters.

11E. This paragraph applies to a hearing of the type described in paragraph 6A of Chapters 1 and 2 of Part 2 of the Table of Fees if the Board is satisfied that a fee in accordance with paragraph 6A(a) of the relevant Chapter is justified on the grounds that the hearing involved a debate, motion for re-trial or further procedure.

11F. A fee is to be allowed to counsel for an opinion concluding that there is no stateable appeal case only if—

- (a) the counsel who prepared the opinion did not represent the assisted person at the trial; and
- (b) the Board, or as the case may be the auditor, is satisfied that it would not have been possible, or would not have been reasonable, in the circumstances for the counsel who represented the assisted person at the trial to have prepared the opinion.

Proceedings in the High Court of Justiciary (other than appeals) and the Sheriff Court

12. Subject to paragraphs 13 to 15 below, the fees prescribed in Parts I and III of the Table of Fees in this Schedule shall include all preparation.

13. A fee for separate preparation shall be allowed only on the following conditions:–

- (a) such a fee is allowable only once in any case to junior or senior, junior and senior or junior and junior, counsel representing an applicant or assisted person, notwithstanding that the applicant or assisted person is represented by more than one junior or senior counsel during the course of the case;
- (b) in allowing such a fee the Board, or as the case may be the auditor, must be satisfied that the level of preparation was necessary, reasonable and proportionate in all the circumstances of the case;
- (c) counsel shall produce records providing a detailed summary of the nature of the work or, if applicable, the nature of the documentation perused, at each stage of the process, the time taken and when and where the work was undertaken and shall retain and produce, if requested, any contemporaneous record or notes made in the course of preparation; and
- (d) such a fee is not payable until the case to which it relates has concluded.

14. A fee for separate preparation shall be allowed only in any case—

- (a) where–
  - (i) the case is disposed of at a hearing under section 76 of the 1995 Act; or
  - (ii) the case proceeds to trial or for a hearing where a fee is payable at the full rate for a trial under paragraphs 4(q) to (t) of Chapters 1 and 2 of Part 1 or paragraphs 3(p) to (t) of Chapters 1 and 2 of Part 3 of the Table of Fees,

  and the level of preparation is that to which paragraph 15 (d) below applies; or
- (b) where a plea of guilty is tendered, or a plea of not guilty is accepted or where a case is deserted simpliciter or deserted and the Crown does not intend to re-raise proceedings, up to and including the first day of trial and the case does not proceed to trial, and the level of preparation is that to which paragraph 15 (c) below applies.

15. A fee for separate preparation allowed under paragraphs 13 and 14 above shall be calculated by reference to the total number of actual sheets of documentation considered by counsel as follows:–

- (a) no fee for separate preparation for the first 1,000 sheets shall be allowed under any circumstances;
- (b) each range set out in sub-paragraphs (c) and (d) below specifies a total number of days which may be allowed per total number of sheets within the range, and each day shall be paid at the rate of two-thirds of the fee prescribed for the conduct of a trial at paragraph 3 of Chapters 1 and 2 of Part I, or as the case may be, paragraph 2 of Chapters 1 and 2 of Part III of the Table of Fees in this Schedule depending on the nature of the charges and the status of counsel;
- (c) the ranges are–
  - (i) 3 days are allowable for 1,001 3,500 sheets;
  - (ii) 5.5 days are allowable for 1,001 7,000 sheets;
  - (iii) 7.5 days are allowable for 1,001 10,000 sheets;
  - (iv) 2.5 days are allowable for each additional 2,500 sheets;
- (d) where the total number of sheets exceeds 7,500, 2.5 days are allowable for each additional 2,500 sheets;
- (e) omitted by SSI 2012 No 276;
- (f) a fee for separate preparation allowed under–

    (i)   paragraph 14(a) above shall be calculated on the basis of sub-paragraph (d); or

    (ii)   paragraph 14(b) above shall be calculated on the basis of sub-paragraph (c) above.

15A.—(1) Where a case has more than one preliminary hearing, the fee payable for any further preliminary hearings as prescribed in paragraphs 1B(a) of Chapters 1 and 2 of Part 1 of the Table of Fees is reduced as specified in sub-paragraphs (2) and (3).

(2) Where charges in a case have been split into more than one indictment, the fee payable for any further preliminary hearings is half that prescribed.

(3) Where in a case an indictment is deserted and subsequently re-raised, the fee for any further preliminary hearings is two thirds that prescribed.

15B. For the purposes of the fees prescribed in paragraphs 1A and 6 of Chapters 1 and 2 of Part 1 and paragraphs 1A and 5 of Chapters 1 and 2 of Part 3 of the Table of Fees—

    (a)   the fee for drafting defence statements is payable only once in any case, regardless of how many statements are drafted in that case;

    (b)   a fee is only payable for a second necessary note in a case on cause shown and where counsel establishes there were exceptional circumstances in the case, and in any case fees for no more than two necessary notes are payable; and

    (c)   where written work, for which there is a prescribed fee, or a necessary note is drafted and revised, the fee payable for the written work or necessary note is, if there is more than one counsel, shared equally between counsel who made the revisals.

16. Where a fee is claimed in respect of paragraph 1B(c) of Chapter 1 or 2 of Part I of the Table of Fees or adjournment of any other hearing including trial–

    (a)   information shall be provided by or on behalf of counsel as to the reason for the adjournment; and

    (b)   no fee shall be allowed by the Board or the auditor where satisfied that an adjournment was caused because the defence was not prepared to proceed, or where the preliminary hearing could have been altered in advance under section 75A(5) of the 1995 Act.

16A.—(1) A consultation fee is payable under paragraph 5 of Chapter 1 or 2 of Part 1 and paragraph 4 of Chapter 1 or 2 of Part 3 of the Table of Fees only once a day for a case, regardless of how many consultations in relation to that case are held that day. This applies where any of the following parties attend more than one consultation in one day—

    (a)   the same counsel and solicitor;

    (b)   the same counsel and accused;

    (c)   the same counsel and Crown counsel or Procurator Fiscal; or

    (d)   the same counsel and expert.

(2) A fee for an abortive consultation is payable under paragraph 5A of Chapter 1 or 2 of Part 1 and paragraph 4A of Chapter 1 or 2 of Part 3 of the Table of Fees where counsel attended for a consultation but the consultation did not proceed due to no fault of counsel.

17. For the purposes of the fees prescribed in Parts I and III of the Table of Fees in this Schedule–

    (a)   a trial shall be taken to commence when the jury is empanelled;

   (aa) where a trial, or other hearing where a prescribed fee is payable at the full rate for a trial, exceeds 30 days in total, the fee payable is reduced by 10% for every day in excess of 30 days;

   (ab) where counsel attends in one day more than one trial, or other hearing where a prescribed fee is payable at the full rate for trial, the fee payable to counsel for the first trial or other hearing of that day is as prescribed and the fee payable for any subsequent trial or other hearing is half that prescribed in those Parts;

    (b)   where the trial of an accused person proceeds in respect of more than one offence, the fee payable in terms of paragraphs 3 of Chapters 1 and 2 of Part I and paragraphs 2 of Chapters 1 and 2 of Part III shall be that for the offence for which the highest fee is prescribed;

   (ba) where at a trial diet there is more than one accused and counsel represents an accused who pled guilty at an earlier diet, the fee under paragraph 3 of Chapter 1 or 2 of Part 1 or under paragraph 2 of Chapter 1 or 2 of Part 3 is not payable, but a fee may be payable on cause shown under paragraph 4(pa) of Chapter 1 or 2 of Part 1 or paragraph 3(oa) of Chapter 1 or 2 of Part 3;

    (c)   where counsel conducts a number of deferred sentences on the same day the prescribed fee shall be reduced by half for a second deferred sentence, and by a further half for a third and any subsequent deferred sentence;

    (d)   the fees allowed under Part III shall be no more than four fifths of the fees prescribed in Part I of the Table of Fees in this Schedule, and except on cause shown, fees for counsel in the Sheriff Court shall not be allowable for attendance at hearings which are routine or procedural only or which do not materially advance the case;

    (e)   subject to paragraph (ee), the prescribed fees for a trial or any hearing shall include all work undertaken in the case that day;

   (ee) a fee for a consultation with an expert, in addition to the prescribed fees for a trial or a hearing under paragraph (e), may be payable where counsel establishes that—

       (i)   previous attempts had been made to consult with the expert which were unsuccessful;

       (ii)   the need to hold the consultation was urgent; and

    (iii) the consultation took place on the same day as the trial or hearing before 0800 hours or after 1800 hours due to the limited availability of the expert;

(f)   fees for a waiting day shall be allowed on the basis of paragraph 18 below;

(g)   the fees prescribed in Parts I and III cannot be increased or reduced in terms of paragraphs 4 to 11 above.

(h)   where the trial of an accused person proceeds in respect of the offence of attempting to pervert the course of justice, the fee payable in terms of paragraph 3 of Chapter 1 or 2 of Part I and paragraph 2 of Chapter 1 or 2 of Part III shall be that for the offence to which the charge of attempting to pervert the course of justice relates. Where the offence to which the charge relates is not prescribed in Schedule 2, the fee payable shall be in terms of paragraph 3(b) of Chapter 1 or 2 of Part I and paragraph 2(b) of Chapter 1 or 2 of Part III;

(ha)   where a trial of an accused person proceeds in respect of the offence of conspiracy to commit an offence, the fee payable in terms of paragraph 3 of Chapter 1 or 2 of Part 1 and paragraph 2 of Chapter 1 or 2 of Part 3 of the Table of Fees, is that for the offence to which the charge of conspiracy relates. Where the offence to which the charge of conspiracy relates is not prescribed in Schedule 2, the fee payable is in terms of paragraph 3(b) of Chapter 1 or 2 of Part 1 and paragraph 2(b) of Chapter 1 or 2 of Part 3 of the Table of Fees;

(i)   where an accused person pleads guilty at a hearing fixed for trial before the jury is empanelled, or where the case is brought to an end by the Crown's acceptance of a plea of not guilty, or where, following the court deserting the trial *simpliciter* or *pro loco et tempore*, the indictment falls or, for any other reason, is not brought to trial and where no order is made by the court to postpone or appoint a further trial diet, the fee payable shall be two-thirds of the fee payable in terms of paragraph 3(a) or (b) of Chapter 1 or 2 of Part I and paragraph 2 of Chapter 1 or 2 of Part III; and

(j)   in the same circumstances as those described at paragraph (i) above but where the category of charge falls under paragraph 3(c) of Chapter 1 or 2 of Part I, the fee payable shall be that prescribed in paragraph 4(a) of Chapter 1 or 2 of Part I.

17A. Where counsel claims a fee in respect of the first diet under paragraph 3(t) of Chapter 1 or 2 of Part III of the Table of Fees, the fee shall only be payable where a plea of guilty is tendered at that hearing or where the case is brought to an end by the Crown's acceptance of a plea of not guilty, withdrawal of the libel, desertion of the diet or by other means.

18. Where counsel claims a fee for a waiting day—

(a)   the fee payable to junior counsel, depending on the status of counsel in the case, for such a day shall be–

    (i)   half of the fee prescribed at paragraph 4(a) of Chapter 1 of Part I of the Table of Fees or at paragraph 3(a) of Chapter 1 of Part III depending on the applicable court, where no travel for the purposes of paragraph 7 of Chapter 2 of Part I or paragraph 6 of Chapter 2 of Part III is incurred; or

    (ii)   two-thirds of the fee prescribed at either paragraph referred to in sub paragraph (a)(i) above, depending on the applicable court, where such travel is incurred;

(b)   the fee payable to senior counsel for such a day shall be—

    (i)   half the fee prescribed at paragraph 4(a) of Chapter 2 of Part I of the Table of Fees or at paragraph 3(a) of Chapter 2 of Part III depending on the applicable court, where no travel for the purposes of paragraph 7 of those Chapters is incurred; or

    (ii) two-thirds of the fee prescribed at either paragraph referred to in sub paragraph (b)(i) above, depending on the applicable court, where such travel is incurred;

(c)   no other chargeable work shall be undertaken in the case that day; and

(d)   provided that counsel remains available at court in case the trial proceeds that day, chargeable work in respect of other cases may be undertaken on that day, other than conducting a hearing or trial.

19. Where counsel claims a fee in respect of paragraph 2 of Chapter 1 or 2 of Part I, or paragraph 1B of Chapter 1 or 2 of Part III, of the Table of Fees—

(a)   subject to sub-paragraphs (b) or (c) below, no fee shall be payable under paragraph 1B, 3 or 4 of each Chapter of Part I, or paragraph 2 or 3 of each Chapter of Part III, of the Table of Fees;

(b)   a fee shall be payable for all post conviction hearings including hearings for which a prescribed fee is set out in paragraphs 4(j), (k), (l) and (m) of each Chapter of Part I, and paragraphs 3(j), (k), (l) and (m) of each Chapter of Part III, of the Table of Fees and

(c)   where a case proceeded by indictment, was deserted, and proceedings were re- raised and disposed of by way of a hearing under section 76 of the 1995 Act, the following fees are chargeable by counsel in the Tables of Fees:

    (i)   a fee for the section 76 hearing under the re-raised indictment, as prescribed in paragraph 2 of Chapters 1 and 2 of Part 1 and paragraph 1B of Chapters 1 and 2 of Part 3, and fees for any court hearings which took place under the initial indictment, as prescribed in paragraph 4 of Chapters 1 and 2 of Part 1 and paragraph 3 of Chapters 1 and 2 of Part 3; or

(ii) fees prescribed in Parts 1 and 3 of the Table of Fees for any hearings, including trial, which took place under the initial indictment, and fees for any hearings under the re-raised indictment, as prescribed in paragraph 4 of Chapters 1 and 2 of Part 1 and paragraph 3 of Chapters 1 and 2 of Part 3, but not the fee for the section 76 hearing under the re-raised indictment, as prescribed in paragraph 2 of Chapters 1 and 2 of Part 1 and paragraph 1B of Chapters 1 and 2 of Part 3.

20.—(1) The supplementary fee for travel prescribed in paragraph 7 of Chapters 1 and 2 of Part 1, paragraph 9 of Chapters 1 and 2 of Part 2 and paragraph 6 of Chapters 1 and 2 of Part 3 of the Table of Fees is chargeable only as provided for in this regulation.

(2) The fee is only chargeable where the travel involves a round trip exceeding 60 miles in each direction.

(3) The fee is not chargeable for travel to courts in any of the following locations for the purposes of a trial or any other hearing—

(a) Edinburgh;

(b) Glasgow;

(c) Airdrie;

(d) Alloa;

(e) Dunfermline;

(f) Falkirk;

(g) Hamilton;

(h) Kirkcaldy;

(i) Lanark;

(j) Livingston;

(k) Paisley;

(l) Stirling.

(4) Where counsel travels to a court in any of the locations listed in paragraph (3) for the purposes of a trial or any other hearing and also attends to business relating to any case on the same day, (subject to paragraph 5) the fee is not chargeable.

(5) The fee may be chargeable in the circumstances set out in paragraph (4) where the Board is satisfied that the trip relating to business in any case is separate and additional to the trip relating to the court.

(6) Counsel must, if required, produce vouching of the travel undertaken.

(7) The fee is chargeable once only in respect of each round trip, irrespective of the number of cases for which the trip is undertaken.

(8) The fee chargeable excludes any travel costs.

20A. Travel costs are chargeable as an outlay only in circumstances where a supplementary fee for travel is chargeable under paragraph 20.

21. Necessary accommodation and subsistence is chargeable only—

(a) as an outlay up to the amount specified in specified in paragraph 8 of Chapters 1 and 2 of Part 1, paragraph 10 of Chapters 1 and 2 of Part 2 or paragraph 7 of Chapters 1 and 2 of Part 3 of the Table of Fees;

(b) where a supplementary fee for travel is chargeable in accordance with paragraph 20; and

(c) on cause shown.

Interpretation

22. In this Schedule–

"the 2010 Act" means the Criminal Justice and Licensing (Scotland) Act 2010;

"commercial premises" means a bank, building society, post office, security vehicle, currency exchange or licensed gambling premises;

"consultation" means a formal meeting, including meeting by means of a conference call, with counsel on the instructions of the solicitor concerning a significant issue which advances the cause taking place usually, but not always, in the presence of the accused or an expert witness, including formal meetings with Crown Counsel taking place following the first preliminary hearing;

"documentation" means Crown statements, precognitions, productions including defence productions and labels;

"retail premises" means any premises, other than commercial premises;

"waiting day" means a day where counsel is required to attend court and does so but the trial does not proceed; and

"sheet" shall consist of 250 words and numbers, or each minute of an un-transcribed tape.

TABLE OF FEES

PART I

FEES OF COUNSEL FOR PROCEEDINGS IN THE HIGH COURT OF JUSTICIARY

CHAPTER 1 –

JUNIOR COUNSEL

1A. *Written work*

(a) petition to Nobile Officium	£225.00
(b) drafting devolution or compatibility minute	£150.00
(c) drafting section 275 application under the 1995 Act	£150.00
(d) drafting specification of documents	£125.00
(e) drafting interrogatories	£125.00
(f) drafting defence statement under section 70A of the 1995 Act or section 125 of the 2010 Act	£125.00

1B. *Preliminary hearing*

(a) Preliminary hearing including all managed meetings or equivalent communication with Crown Counsel or the Procurator Fiscal by whatever means and including any note on the line of evidence

Payable at one and a half times the full rate for a trial (paragraph 3 below) depending on category of case and status of counsel.

(aa) preliminary hearing adjourned or continued in which witnesses called to give evidence

Payable at the full rate for a trial (paragraph 3 below) depending on category of case and status of counsel.

(b) further diet which involves substantive debate or the resolution of outstanding issues, preliminary pleas, objections to the admissibility of evidence by minute, devolution minutes or applications under section 275 of the 1995 Act

Payable at two thirds of the full rate for a trial (paragraph 3 below) depending on category of case and status of counsel.

(c) adjourned diet under section 75A of the 1995 Act, or continued diet

Payable at one-half of the full rate for a trial (paragraph 3 below) depending on category of case and status of counsel.

(d) attendance at managed meeting or work in connection with equivalent communication with the Crown by whatever means and including any note on the line of evidence where counsel does not attend preliminary hearing

Payable at one-half of the fee prescribed at paragraph 1B(a) above.

(e) conduct of preliminary hearing on receipt of detailed instructions not having been involved in pre hearing communication with the Crown

Payable at one-half of the fee prescribed at paragraph 1B(a) above.;

	Junior as leader	*Junior Alone*	*Junior with leader*
2. *Early Plea* Hearing under section 76 of the 1995 Act	£1,250.00	£1,250.00	£625.00

3. *Trial per day*

Category Charges Prosecuted in the High Court

(a) Murder, Multiple attempted murder, Culpable homicide, Rape, Assault and Robbery (involving commercial premises), Importation of controlled drugs, Fraud and related offences, Section 1 of the 1988 Act (causing death by dangerous driving), Section 3A of the 1988 Act (causing death by careless driving when under the influence of drink or drugs), Sedition, Treason, Offences under the 2000 Act, Torture, War crimes, Offences under the Explosive Substances Act 1883, sections 327 to 333 and 339(1A) of the Proceeds of Crime	£750.00	£650.00	£450.00

Act 2002 (Money Laundering), Firearms offences, Incest, Sodomy, Embezzlement, Lewd and Libidinous behaviour against children under the age of 12, Section 2B of the 1988 Act, Section 3ZB of the 1988 Act, Sections 1, 2, 3(2)(a) and 18 to 27 of the 2009 Act.

(b) Attempted Murder, Assault to severe injury (with aggravations), Indecent Assault, Assault and Robbery (involving retail premises), Possession with intent to supply or being concerned in the supply of a Class A drug, Attempted Rape, Lewd and libidinous behaviour (other than under category (a) above), Offences under the Sexual Offences Act, Offences against Children under the 1995 Consolidation Act, Offences under section 16A of the 1995 Consolidation Act, Abduction and/or unlawful imprisonment, Extortion, Counterfeiting, Bribery and Corruption, Mobbing and rioting, Indecent or Obscene Publications, Environmental Protection prosecutions, Health and Safety offences, Intellectual Property offences, Offences under the Immigration Act 1971, Offences under section 52 or 52A of the Civic Government (Scotland) Act 1982, Offences under section 12(1) of the Children and Young Persons (Scotland) Act 1937, All offences under the 2009 Act not otherwise prescribed in this Table of Fees   £617.50   £535.00   £375.00

(c) Possession with intent to supply or being concerned in the supply of a Class B or Class C drug, Assault to severe injury, Assault and robbery, Mobbing, Wilful fire raising, Housebreaking, Opening lockfast places, Bigamy, Contempt of Court, Perjury, Theft, Forgery, Uttering, Reset, Concealing a pregnancy, Deforcement of Sheriff's Officers, Malicious Mischief, Brothel keeping, Public Order Offences (stirring of racial hatred, wearing of uniforms, disrupting lawful meetings), Harassment, Road traffic offences (other than section 1 or 3A of the 1988 Act), Possession of offensive weapons, Violation of sepulchres, Robbery, Breach of the peace   £495.00   £430.00   £305.00

4. *Miscellaneous Hearings*

(a)	fee for a day in court for miscellaneous hearings other than those for which a fee is prescribed	£360.00 £315.00 £225.00	
(aa)	judicial examination	£360.00	£315.00 £225.00
(b)	preliminary diet	£360.00	£315.00 £225.00
(c)	hearing under section 275 of the 1995 Act	£360.00	£315.00 £225.00
(d)	hearing on specification of documents	£360.00	£315.00 £225.00
(e)	hearing on a devolution or compatibility minute	£360.00	£315.00 £225.00
(f)	hearing on an application by the Crown for an extension of time	£360.00	£315.00 £225.00
(g)	hearing under section 72 of the 1995 Act	£180.00	£157.50 £112.50
(h)	hearing on a motion to adjourn	£180.00	£157.50 £112.50
(i)	hearing on an application for special measures	£180.00	£157.50 £112.50
(j)	confiscation diet in which substantial evidence is led or where full settlement is agreed where the confiscation proceedings follow acceptance of a guilty plea to the charge or charges categorised as below or follow a trial as specified in this Chapter in—		
	(i) paragraph 3(a)	£750.00	£650.00 £450.00
	(ii) paragraph 3(b)	£617.50	£535.00 £375.00
	(iii) paragraph 3(c)	£495.00	£430.00 £305.00
(k)	confiscation diet where no substantial evidence is led	£360.00	£315.00 £225.00
(l)	deferred sentence where mitigation is led	£360.00	£315.00 £225.00
(m)	deferred sentence where no mitigation is led	£180.00	£157.50 £112.50
(n)	remit for sentence	£360.00	£315.00 £225.00

(na)	drug treatment and testing order review	£180.00	£157.50	£112.50
(nb)	drug treatment and testing order review where mitigation led and order revoked	£360.00	£315.00	£225.00
(o)	adjourned trial diet	£180.00	£157.00	£112.00
(p)	adjourned trial diet (trial having commenced)	£360.00	£315.00	£225.00
(pa)	trial diet where there is more than one accused and counsel represents an accused who pled guilty at an earlier diet	£360.00	£315.00	£225.00
(q)	trial within a trial	Payable at the full rate for a trial (paragraph 3 above) depending on category of case and status of counsel.		
(qa)	commission on evidence and any other hearing other than one at which evidence is adduced for which a fee is prescribed	Payable at the full rate for a trial (paragraph 3 above) depending on the category of case and status of counsel.		
(r)	examination of the facts in a case of insanity or diminished responsibility	Payable at the full rate for a trial (paragraph 3 above) depending on category of case and status of counsel.		
(s)	proof in mitigation	Payable at the full rate for a trial (paragraph 3 above) depending on category of case and status of counsel.		
(t)	deferred sentence in which evidence is taken from an expert witness	Payable at the full rate for a trial (paragraph 3 above) depending on category of case and status of counsel.;		

5. *Fee for consultations, accused and counsel meetings and locus visits*

	£210.00	£184.00	£135.00

5A. *Fee for abortive consultation*

	£105.00	£92.00	£67.50

6. *Fee for a necessary Note*

	£50.00	£50.00	£50.00

7. *Travel*

Supplementary fee chargeable in addition to any of the above fees where necessary travel is undertaken within Scotland, including travel to a Procurator Fiscal's office or elsewhere to view productions	£100.00	£100.00	£100.00
Supplementary fee chargeable in addition to any of the above fees where necessary travel is undertaken furth of Scotland; and	£200.00	£200.00	£200.00

8. *Accommodation and associated subsistence*

Payment of necessary accommodation and associated subsistence per day	£100.00	£100.00	£100.00

CHAPTER 2 –

SENIOR COUNSEL

1. *Preliminary Hearing*

(a)	preliminary hearing including managed meeting or equivalent communication with the Crown by whatever means and including any note on the line of evidence	Payable at the full rate for a trial (paragraph 3 below) depending on category of case and status of counsel.

1A. *Written work*

(a)	petition to Nobile Officium	£225.00
(b)	drafting devolution or compatibility minute	£150.00
(c)	drafting section 275 application under the 1995 Act(a)	£150.00
(d)	drafting specification of documents	£125.00

(f)   drafting defence statement under section 70A of the 1995   £125.00
Act or section 125 of the 2010 Act

(e)   drafting interrogatories   £125.00

1B. *Preliminary hearing*

(a) Preliminary hearing including all managed meetings or equivalent communication with Crown Counsel or the Procurator Fiscal by whatever means and including any note on the line of evidence	Payable at one and a half times the full rate for a trial (paragraph 3 below) depending on category of case and status of counsel.
(aa) preliminary hearing, adjourned or continued in which witnesses called to give evidence	Payable at the full rate for a trial (paragraph 3 below) depending on category of case and status of counsel.
(b) further diet which involves substantive debate or the resolution of outstanding issues, preliminary pleas, objections to the admissibility of evidence by minute, devolution minutes or applications under section 275 of the 1995 Act	Payable at two thirds of the full rate for a trial (paragraph 3 below) depending on category of case and status of counsel.
(c) adjourned diet under section 75A of the 1995 Act, or continued diet	Payable at one-half of the full rate for a trial (paragraph 3 below) depending on category of case and status of counsel.
(d) attendance at managed meeting or work in connection with equivalent communication with the Crown by whatever means and including any note on the line of evidence where counsel does not attend preliminary hearing	Payable at one-half of the fee prescribed at paragraph 1B(a) above.
(e) conduct of preliminary hearing on receipt of detailed instructions not having been involved in pre hearing communication with the Crown	Payable at one-half of the fee prescribed at paragraph 1B(a) above.

2.   *Early Plea*

Hearing under section 76 of the 1995 Act   £1,250.00

3.   *Trial (per day)*

Category Charges Prosecuted in the High Court

(a)   Murder, Multiple attempted murder, Culpable homicide,   £900.00
Rape, Assault and Robbery (involving commercial premises),
Importation of controlled drugs, Fraud and related offences,
Section 1 of the 1988 Act (causing death by dangerous
driving), Section 3A of the 1988 Act (causing death by
careless driving when under the influence of drink or
drugs), Sedition, Treason, Offences under the 2000
Act, Torture, War crimes, Offences under the Explosive
Substances Act 1883, sections 327 to 333 and 339(1A) of
the Proceeds of Crime Act 2002 (Money Laundering),
Firearms offences, Incest, Sodomy, Embezzlement, Lewd
and Libidinous behaviour against children under the age of
12, Section 2B of the 1988 Act, Section 3ZB of the 1988 Act,
Sections 1, 2, 3(2)(a) and 18 to 27 of the 2009 Act.

(b)   Attempted Murder, Assault to severe injury (with   £700.00
aggravations), Indecent Assault, Assault and Robbery
(involving retail premises), Possession with intent to supply
or being concerned in the supply of a Class A drug,
Attempted Rape, Lewd and libidinous behaviour (other than
under category (a) above), Offfences under the Sexual Offences
Act, Offences against Children under the 1995 Consolidation
Act, Offences under section 16A of the 1995 Consolidation
Act, Abduction and/or unlawful imprisonment, Extortion,
Counterfeiting, Bribery and Corruption, Mobbing and rioting,
Indecent or Obscene Publications, Environmental Protection
prosecutions, Health and Safety offences, Intellectual
Property offences, Offences under the Immigration Act 1971,

offences under section 52 or 52A of the Civic Government
(Scotland) Act 1982, Offences under section 12(1) of the
Children and Young Persons (Scotland) Act 1937, All
offences under the 2009 Act not otherwise prescribed in this
Table of Fees

(c) Possession with intent to supply or being concerned in the £560.00
supply of a Class B or Class C drug, Assault to severe injury,
Assault and robbery, Mobbing, Wilful fire raising,
Housebreaking, Opening lockfast places, Bigamy, Contempt
of Court, Perjury, Theft, Shameless Indecency, Offences under
the SexualOffences Act 2003, Forgery, Concealing a pregnancy,
Deforcement of Sheriff's Officers, Malicious mischief,
Brothel keeping, Public order offences (stirring up racial hatred,
wearing of uniforms, disrupting lawful meetings), Harassment,
Road traffic offences (other than section 1 or 3A of the 1988
Act), Possession of offensive weapons, Violation of sepulchres,
Robbery, Breach of the peace

4. *Miscellaneous Hearings*

(a)	fee for a day in court for miscellaneous hearings other than those for which a fee is prescribed	£410.00
(aa)	judicial examination	£410.00
(b)	preliminary diet	£410.00
(c)	hearing under section 275 of the 1995 Act	£410.00
(d)	hearing on specification of documents	£410.00
(e)	hearing on a devolution or compatibility minute	£410.00
(f)	hearing on an application by the Crown for an extension of time	£410.00
(g)	hearing under section 72 of the 1995 Act	£205.00
(h)	hearing on a Motion to adjourn	£205.00
(i)	hearing on an application for special measures	£205.00
(j)	confiscation diet in which substantial evidence is led or where full settlement is agreed where the confiscation proceedings follow acceptance of a guilty plea to the charge or charges categorised as below or follow a trial as specified in this Chapter in–	
	(i) paragraph 3(a)	£900.00
	(ii) paragraph 3(b)	£700.00
	(iii) paragraph 3(c)	£560.00
(k)	confiscation diet where no substantial evidence is led	£410.00
(l)	deferred sentence where mitigation is led	£410.00
(m)	deferred sentence where no mitigation is led	£205.00
(n)	remit for sentence	£410.00
(na)	drug treatment and testing order review	£205.00
(nb)	drug treatment and testing order review where mitigation led and order revoked	£410.00
(o)	adjourned trial diet	£205.00
(p)	adjourned trial diet (trial having commenced)	£410.00
(pa)	trial diet where there is more than one accused and counsel represents an accused who pled guilty at an earlier diet	£410.00
(q)	trial within a trial	Payable at the full rate for a trial (paragraph 3 above) depending on category of case.
(qa)	commission on evidence and any other hearing, other than one for which a fee is prescribed, at which evidence is adduced	Payable at the full rate for a trial (paragraph 3 above) depending on the category of case and status of counsel.
(r)	examination of the facts in a case of insanity or diminished responsibility	Payable at the full rate for a trial (paragraph 3 above) depending on category of case.
(s)	proof in mitigation	Payable at the full rate for a trial (paragraph 3 above) depending on category of case.

(t) deferred sentence in which evidence is taken from an expert witness

Payable at the full rate for a trial (paragraph 3 above) depending on category of case.

5. *Fee for consultations, accused and counsel meetings and locus visits*

£250.00

5A. *Fee for abortive consultation*

£125.00

6. *Fee for a necessary Note*

£50.00

7. *Travel*

Supplementary fee chargeable in addition to any of the above fees where necessary travel is undertaken within Scotland, including travel to a Procurator Fiscal's office or elsewhere to view productions

£100.00

Supplementary fee chargeable in addition to any of the above fees where necessary travel is undertaken furth of Scotland

£200.00

8. *Accommodation and associated subsistence*

Payment of necessary accommodation and associated subsistence per day

£100.00

PART 2

FEES OF COUNSEL IN APPEAL PROCEEDINGS

CHAPTER 1 –

JUNIOR COUNSEL

		Junior as leader	*Junior alone*	*Junior with leader*
1.	*Appeal against Sentence*			
	(a) drafting Grounds or Note of Appeal against sentence	£82	£82	£82
	(b) written Submissions in Appeal against Sentence	£125	£100	£75
	(c) any hearing under sections 107 and 187 of the Criminal Procedure (Scotland) Act 1995, including any consultation on the day of the appeal	£201	£150	£112
	(d) any hearing on appeal against sentence, including any consultation on the day of the appeal	£201	£150	£112
	(e) opinion (or note) on appeal against sentence (where not otherwise prescribed)	£75	£75	£75
2.	*Appeal by way of Bill of Suspension, Bill of Advocation or Stated Case*			
	(a) drafting Bill of Suspension or Bill of Advocation or adjustment of Stated Case	£85-£266	£82-£200	£75-£150
	(b) appearance at any hearing on Stated Case, Bill of Suspension or Advocation	£335	£250	£187
	(c) opinion	£125	£125	£125
3.	*Appeal against Conviction or Conviction and Sentence*			
	(a) drafting Grounds of Appeal against conviction or conviction and sentence	£250-£420	£200-£350	£140-£300
	(b) written Submissions in Appeal against conviction or conviction and sentence	£250-£420	£200-£350	£140-£300
	(c) Omitted SSI 2011 No 135			
	(d) Hearing on Appeal against conviction or conviction and sentence (to which paragraph 11C of the notes on the operation of Schedule 2 does not apply)	£700-£1,089	£500-£825	£400-£625

(da) Hearing on Appeal against conviction or conviction and sentence (to which paragraph 11C of the notes on the operation of Schedule 2 applies)—			
(i) where the hearing lasts fewer than 3 hours	£395	£350	£250
(ii) where the hearing lasts more than 3 hours, but fewer than 6 hours	£467–£726	£334–£550	£267–£417
(iii) where the hearing lasts 6 hours or more—			
(aa) for each 6 hour period	£700–£1,089	£500–£825	£400–£625
(ab) for any remaining period of fewer than 3 hours	£395	£350	£250
(ac) for any remaining period of more than 3 hours	£467–£726	£334–£550	£267–£417
(e) opinion	£250–£400	£200–£350	£140–£300
4. *Appeal Hearing before a Full Bench (5 or more Judges)*	£1,300	£1000	£750
5. *Appeals in relation to Bail or Interim Liberation*			
(a) all work in connection with an appeal relating to granting of bail or interim liberation, except (ab) or (b)	£30	£30	£30
(ab) all work in connection with a continued diet in relation to such an appeal	£30	£30	£30
(b) all work in connection with an application for interim liberation before 3 judges	£140	£100	£75
6. *Appeals conduct other*			
(a) hearing on petition to the Nobile Officium	£700–£1,089	£500–£825	£305–£625
(b) reference to the High Court (devolution issue)	£700–1,089	£500–825	£400–£625
(c) appeal arising from pre-trial or continuing trial hearing	£700–£1,089	£500–£825	£400–£625
(ca) appeal from the Sheriff Appeal Court to the High Court under section 194ZB of the 1995 Act	£700–£1,089	£500–£825	£400–£625
(cb) referral from the Sheriff Appeal Court to the High Court under section 175A of the 1995 Act	£700–£1,089	£500–£825	£400–£625
(d) opinion	£250–£400	£200–£350	£140–£300
6A. *Advising hearing*			
Any hearing relative to proceedings of a type described in the preceding paragraphs held subsequent to the court making avizandum, if paragraph 11E of the notes on the operation of Schedule 2—			
(a) applies	£360	£315	£225
(b) does not apply	£150	£150	£150
7. *Appeals written work other*			
(a) drafting devolution or compatibiilty minute	£150	£150	£150
(b) drafting Petition to the Nobile Officium	£225	£225	£225
(c) opinion in connection with an application under section 94(2A) of the Criminal Procedure (Scotland) Act 1995 (transcripts of record and documentary productions)	£50	£50	£50
8. *Consultations*	£210	£184	£135
9. *Travel*			
Supplementary fee chargeable in addition to any of the above fees where necessary travel is undertaken within Scotland, including travel to a Procurator Fiscal's office or elsewhere to view productions	£100	£100	£100
Supplementary fee chargeable in addition to any of the above fees where necessary travel is undertaken furth of Scotland	£200	£200	£200
10. *Accommodation and associated subsistence*			
Payment of necessary accommodation and associated subsistence per day	£100.00	£100.00	£100.00
11. Opinion where, in the circumstance mentioned in paragraph 11F of the notes on the operation of Schedule 2, counsel concludes that there is no stateable case	£250–£800	£200–£700	£140–£600

CHAPTER 2 –

SENIOR COUNSEL
Senior

1. *Appeal against Sentence*
   (a) drafting Grounds or Note of Appeal against sentence   £124
   (b) written Submissions in Appeal against Sentence   £152
   (c) any hearing under sections 107 and 187 of the Criminal Procedure (Scotland) Act
        1995, including any consultation on the day of the appeal   £228
   (d) any hearing on appeal against sentence, including any consultation on the day of the
        appeal   £228
   (e) opinion (or note) on appeal against sentence (where not otherwise prescribed)   £114

2. *Appeal by way of Bill of Suspension, Bill of Advocation or Stated Case*
   (a) drafting Bill of Suspension or Bill of Advocation or adjustment of Stated Case   £124-£300
   (b) appearance at any hearing on Stated Case, Bill of Suspension or Advocation   £393
   (c) opinion   £187.50

3. *Appeal against Conviction or Conviction and Sentence*
   (a) drafting Grounds of Appeal against conviction or conviction and sentence   £250-£506
   (b) written Submissions in Appeal against conviction or conviction and sentence   £250-£506
   (c) Omitted SSI 2011 No 135
   (d) Hearing on Appeal against conviction or conviction and sentence (to which
        paragraph 11C of the notes on the operation of Schedule 2 does not apply   £900-£1,250
   (da) Hearing on Appeal against conviction or conviction and sentence (to which
        paragraph 11C of the notes on the operation of Schedule 2 applies)—
        (i)ii   where the hearing lasts fewer than 3 hours   £450
        (ii)i   where the hearing lasts more than 3 hours, but fewer than 6 hours   £600 - £834
        (iii)   where the hearing lasts 6 hours or more—
        (iii) (aa) for each 6 hour period   £900 - £1,250
        (iii) (ab) for any remaining period of fewer than 3 hours   £450
        (iii) (ac) for any remaining period of more than 3 hours   £600 - £834
   (e) opinion   £350-£700

4. *Appeal Hearing before a Full Bench (5 or more Judges)*

5. *Appeals in relation to Bail or Interim Liberation*   £1,500
   (a) all work in connection with an appeal relating to granting of bail or interim
        liberation, except (ab) or (b)   £50
   (ab) all work in connection with a continued diet in relation to such an appeal   £50
   (b) all work in connection with an application for interim liberation before 3 judges   £150

6. *Appeals conduct other*
   (a) hearing on petition to the Nobile Officium   £900-£1,250
   (b) reference to the High Court (devolution issue)   £900-£1,250
   (c) any appeal arising from pre-trial or continuing trial hearing   £900-£1,250
   (ca) appeal from the Sheriff Appeal Court to the High Court under section 194ZB
        of the 1995 Act   £900–£1,250
   (cb) referral from the Sheriff Appeal Court to the High Court under section 175A
        of the 1995 Act   £900–£1,250
   (d) opinion   £350–£700

6A. *Advising hearing*
    Any hearing relative to proceedings of a type described in the preceding paragraphs
    held subsequent to the court making avizandum, if paragraph 11E of the notes on
    the operation of Schedule 2—
    (a) applies   £410
    (b) does not apply   £150

7. *Appeals written work other*
   (a) drafting devolution or compatibility minute   £150
   (b) drafting Petition to the Nobile Officium   £225
   (c) opinion in connection with an application under section 94(2A) of the Criminal
        Procedure (Scotland) Act 1995 (transcripts of record and documentary
        productions)   £50

8. *Consultations*   £250

9. *Travel*
   Supplementary fee chargeable in addition to any of the above fees where necessary
   travel is undertaken within Scotland, including travel to a Procurator Fiscal's office
   or elsewhere to view productions   £100

Supplementary fee chargeable in addition to any of the above fees where necessary
travel is undertaken furth of Scotland   £200

10. *Accommodation and associated subsistence*
    Payment of necessary accommodation and associated subsistence per day   £100.00
11. Opinion where, in the circumstance mentioned in paragraph 11F of the notes on the
    operation of Schedule 2, counsel concludes that there is no stateable case   £350-£1,400

PART 3
FEES OF COUNSEL FOR PROCEEDINGS IN THE SHERIFF AND DISTRICT COURT

CHAPTER 1 –
JUNIOR COUNSEL

	Junior as leader	Junior alone	Junior with leader
1A. *Written work*			
(a) petition to Nobile Officium	1,£225.00	1,£225.00	£225.00
(b) drafting devolution or compatibility minute	1,£150.00	1,£150.00	£150.00
(c) drafting section 275 application under the 1995 Act	1,£150.00	1,£150.00	£150.00
(d) drafting specification of documents	1,£125.00	1,£125.00	£125.00
(e) drafting interrogatories	1,£125.00	1,£125.00	£125.00
(f) drafting defence statement under section 70A of the 1995 Act or section 125 of the 2010 Act	£125.00	£125.00	£125.00
1B. *Early plea*			
Hearing under section 76 of the 1995 Act	£1,250.00	£1,250.00	£625.00
2. *Trial (per day)*			
Category Charges Prosecuted in the Sheriff Court			
(a) Culpable Homicide, Assault and Robbery (involving commercial premises), Importation of controlled drugs, Fraud and related offence, Section 1 of the 1988 Act (causing death by dangerous driving), Section 3A of the 1988 Act (causing death by careless driving when under the influence of drink or drugs) Sedition, Treason, Offences under the 2000 Act, Torture, War crimes, Rape, Multiple attempted murder, Offences under the Explosive Substances Act 1883, sections 372 to 333 and 339(1A) of the Proceeds of Crime Act 2002 (Money laundering, Firearms offences, Incest, Sodomy, Embezzlement, Lewd and libidinous behaviour against children under the age of 12, Section 2B of the 1988 Act, Section 3ZB of the 1988 Act, Sections 1, 2, 3(2)(a) and 18 to 27 of the 2009 Act	£647.50	£575.00	£360.00
(b) Attempted Murder, Assault to severe injury (with aggravations), Indecent assault, Assault and robbery (involving retail premises), Possession with intent to supply or being concerned in the supply of a class A drug, Attempted rape, Lewd and libidinous behaviour (other than under category (a) above), Offences under the Sexual Offences Act, Offences against children under the 1995 Consolidation Act, Offences under section 16A of the 1995 Consolidation Act, Abduction and/or unlawful imprisonment, Extortion, Counterfeiting, Bribery and corruption, Mobbing and rioting, Environmental protection prosecutions, Health and safety offences, Intellectual property offences, Indecent or obscene publications, Possession with intent to supply or being concerned in the supply of a class B or class C drug, Assault to severe injury, Assault and robbery, Wilful fire raising, Housebreaking, Opening lockfast places, Bigamy, Contempt of Court Perjury, Theft, Forgery, Uttering, Reset, Concealing a pregnancy, Deforcement of Sheriff's	£495.00	£430.00	£350.00

Officers, Malicious mischief, Brothel keeping, Public order offences (stirring up racial hatred, wearing of uniforms, disrupting lawful meetings) Harassment, Road traffic offences (other than section 1 or 3A of the 1988 Act), Possession of offensive weapons, Violation of sepulchres, Offences under the Immigration Act 1971, Offences under section 52 or 52A of the Civic Government (Scotland) Act 1982, Offences under section 12(1) of the Children and Young Persons (Scotland) Act 1937, All offences under the 2009 Act not otherwise prescribed in this Table of Fees

3. *Miscellaneous Hearings*

(a)	fee for a day in court for miscellaneous hearings other than those for which a fee is prescribed	£288.00	£252.00	£180.00
(aa)	judicial examination	£288.00	£252.00	£180.00
(b)	preliminary diet	£288.00	£252.00	£180.00
(c)	hearing under section 275 of the 1995 Act	£288.00	£252.00	£180.00
(d)	hearing on specification of documents	£288.00	£252.00	£180.00
(e)	hearing on a devolution or compatibility minute	£288.00	£252.00	£180.00
(f)	hearing on an application by the Crown for an extension of time	£288.00	£252.00	£180.00
(g)	hearing under section 72 of the 1995 Act	£144.00	£126.00	£90.00
(h)	hearing on a Motion to adjourn	£144.00	£126.00	£90.00
(i)	hearing on an application for special measures	£144.00	£126.00	£90.00
(j)	confiscation diet in which substantial evidence is led or where full settlement is agreed where the confiscation proceedings follow acceptance of a guilty plea to the charge or charges categorised as below or follow a trial as specified in this Chapter in–			
	(i) paragraph 2(a)	£647.50	£575.00	£360.00
	(ii) paragraph 2(b)	£495.00	£430.00	£305.00
(k)	confiscation diet where no substantial evidence is led	£288.00	£252.00	£180.00
(l)	deferred sentence where mitigation is led	£288.00	£252.00	£180.00
(m)	deferred sentence where no mitigation is led	£144.00	£126.00	£90.00
(ma)	drug treatment and testing order review	£144.00	£126.00	£90.00
(mb)	drug treatment and testing order review where mitigation led and order revoked	£288.00	£252.00	£180.00
(n)	adjourned trial diet	£144.00	£126.00	£90.00
(o)	adjourned trial diet (trial having commenced)	£288.00	£252.00	£180.00
(oa)	trial diet where there is more than one accused and counsel represents an accused who pled guilty at an earlier diet	£288.00	£252.00	£180.00
(p)	trial within a trial	Payable at the full rate for a trial (paragraph 2 above) depending on category of case and status of counsel.		
(pa)	commission on evidence and any other hearing, other than one for which a fee is prescribed, at which evidence is adduced	Payable at the full rate for a trial (paragraph 2 above) depending on the category of case and status of counsel.		
(q)	examination of the facts in a case of insanity or diminished responsibility	Payable at the full rate for a trial (paragraph 2 above) depending on category of case and status of counsel.		
(r)	proof in mitigation	Payable at the full rate for a trial (paragraph 2 above) depending on category of case and status of counsel.		
(s)	deferred sentence in which evidence is taken from an expert witness	Payable at the full rate for a trial (paragraph 2 above) depending on category of case and status of counsel.		
(t)	first diet	Payable at the full rate for a trial (paragraph 2 above) depending on category of case and status of counsel.		

4. *Fee for consultations, accused and counsel meetings and locus visits*

£178.00   £154.00   £108.00

4A. *Fee for abortive consultation*

	£89.00	£77.00	£54.00

5. *Fee for a necessary Note*

	£50.00	£50.00	£50.00

6. *Travel*
Supplementary fee chargeable in addition to any of the above £100.00 £100.00 £100.00
fees where necessary travel is undertaken

7. *Accommodation and associated subsistence*
Payment of necessary accommodation and associated subsistence £100.00 £100.00 £100.00
per day

CHAPTER 2 –
SENIOR COUNSEL

1A. *Written work*

(a)	petition to Nobile Officium	1,£225.00	1,£225.00	£225.00
(b)	drafting devolution or compatibility minute	1,£150.00	1,£150.00	£150.00
(c)	drafting section 275 application under the 1995 Act	1,£150.00	1,£150.00	£150.00
(d)	drafting specification of documents	1,£125.00	1,£125.00	£125.00
(e)	drafting interrogatories	1,£125.00	1,£125.00	£125.00
(f)	drafting defence statement under section 70A of the 1995 Act or section 125 of the 2010 Act	£125.00	£125.00	£125.00

1B. *Early plea*
Hearing under section 76 of the 1995 Act   £1,250.00 £1,250.00 £625.000

2. *Trial (per day)*
Category Charges Prosecuted in the Sheriff Court
   (a) Culpable Homicide, Assault and Robbery (involving commercial premises i.e.   £720.00
   banks, post offices, warehouses etc.), Importation of Controlled Drugs, Fraud
   and related offence. Section 1 of the 1988 Act (causing death by dangerous
   driving), Section 3A of the 1988 Act (causing death by careless driving when
   under the influence of drink or drugs), Sedition, Treason, Offences under
   the 2000 Act, Torture, War crimes, Multiple attempted murder, Offences
   under the Explosive Substances Act 1883, sections 327 to 333 and 339(1A) of
   the Proceeds of Crime Act 2002 (Money Laundering), Firearms offences,
   Incest, Sodomy, Embezzlement, Lewd and libidinous behaviour against children
   under the age of 12, Section 2B of the 1988 Act, Section 3ZB of the 1988 Act,
   Sections 1, 2, 3(2)(a) and 18 to 27 of the 2009 Act
   (b) Attempted Murder, Assault to severe injury (with aggravations), Indecent   £560.00
   assault, Assault and robbery (involving retail premises), Possession with
   intent to supply or being concerned in the supply of a class A drug,
   Attempted rape, Lewd and libidinous behaviour (other than under category
   (a) above), Offences under the Sexual Offences Act, Offences against
   children under the 1995 Consolidation Act Offences under section 16A of
   the 1995 Consolidated Act, Abduction and/or unlawful imprisonment,
   Extortion, Counterfeiting, Bribery and corruption, Mobbing and rioting,
   Mobbing, Environmental protection prosecutions, Health and safety
   offences, Intellectual property offences, Indecent or obscene publications,
   Possession with intent to supply or being concerned in the supply of a
   class B or class C drug, Assault to severe injury, Assault and robbery,
   Wilful fire raising, Housebreaking, Opening lockfast places, Bigamy,
   Contempt of Court, Perjury, Theft, Forgery, Uttering, Reset, Concealing
   a pregnancy, Deforcement of Sheriff's Officers, Malicious mischief,
   Brothel keeping, Public order offences (stirring up racial hatred, wearing
   of uniforms, disrupting lawful meetings), Harassment, Road traffic
   offences (other than section 1 or 3A of the 1988 Act), Possession of
   offensive weapons, Violation of sepulchres, Offences under the Immigration
   Act 1971, Offences under section 52 or 52A of the Civic Government
   (Scotland) Act 1982 , Offences under section 12(1) of the Children and
   Young Persons (Scotland) Act 1937, All offences under the 2009 Act
   not otherwise prescribed in this Table of Fees

3. *Miscellaneous Hearings*
   (a) fee for a day in court for miscellaneous hearings other than for which a fee is   £328.00
   prescribed
   (aa) judicial examination   £328.00
   (b) preliminary diet   £328.00

(c)	hearing under section 275 of the 1995 Act	£328.00
(d)	hearing on specification of documents	£328.00
(e)	hearing on a devolution or compatibility minute	£328.00
(f)	hearing on an application by the Crown for an extension of time	£328.00
(g)	hearing under section 72 of the 1995 Act	£164.00
(h)	hearing on a motion to adjourn	£164.00
(i)	hearing on an application for special measures	£164.00
(j)	confiscation diet in which substantial evidence is led or where full settlement is agreed where the confiscation proceedings follow acceptance of a guilty plea to the charge or charges categorised as below or follow a trial as specified in this Chapter in–	
	(i) paragraph 2(a)	£720.00
	(ii) paragraph 2(b)	£560.00
	(iii) paragraph 2(c)	£328.00
(k)	confiscation diet where no substantial evidence is led	£328.00
(l)	deferred sentence where mitigation is led	£328.00
(m)	deferred sentence where no mitigation is led	£164.00
(ma)	drug treatment and testing order review	£164.00
(mb)	drug treatment and testing order review where mitigation led and order revoked	£328.00
(n)	adjourned trial diet	£164.00
(o)	adjourned trial diet (trial having commenced)	£328.00
(oa)	trial diet where there is more than one accused and counsel represents an accused who pled guilty at an earlier diet	£328.00
(p)	trial within a trial	Payable at the full rate for a trial (paragraph 2 above) depending on category of case.
(pa)	commission on evidence and any other hearing, other than one for which a fee is prescribed, at which evidence is adduced	Payable at the full rate for a trial (paragraph 2 above) depending on the category of case and status of counsel.
(q)	examination of the facts in a case of insanity or diminished responsibility depending on category of case.	Payable at the full rate for a trial (paragraph 2 above)
(r)	proof in mitigation	Payable at the full rate for a trial (paragraph 2 above) depending on category of case.
(s)	deferred sentence in which evidence is taken from an expert witness	Payable at the full rate for a trial (paragraph 2 above) depending on category of case.
(t)	first diet	Payable at the full rate for a trial (paragraph 2 above) depending on category of case.

4. *Fee for consultations, accused and counsel meetings and locus visits* £200.00

4A. *Fee for abortive consultation* £100.00

5. *Fee for a necessary Note* £50.00

6. *Travel*

Supplementary fee chargeable in addition to any of the above fees where necessary travel is undertaken within Scotland, including travel to a Procurator Fiscal's office or elsewhere to view productions £100.00

Supplementary fee chargeable in addition to any of the above fees where necessary travel is undertaken furth of Scotland £200.00

7. *Accommodation and associated subsistence*

Payment of necessary accommodation and associated subsistence per day £75.00

SCHEDULE 3
Regulation 4

FEES OF COUNSEL FOR PROCEEDINGS IN THE SUPREME COURT

Notes on the operation of Schedule 3

1. Subject to the following provisions of this Schedule, fees shall be calculated by the Board, and in the event of a question or dispute by the auditor, in accordance with the Table of Fees in this Schedule.

2. In the assessment and taxation of counsel's fees–

(a) where higher fees than those set out in the Table of Fees are sought, they must be explained in a note from counsel;

(b) for proceedings under paragraph 1 of the Table of Fees–
  (i) subject to any higher fees allowable under sub-paragraph (a), no other payments are permitted;
  (ii) there is a working assumption that a single fee is allowed for one junior counsel even where sanction is authorised for two counsel and that it would only be in the most exceptional cases that fees are allowable for two counsel; and
  (iii) a fee for senior counsel may be allowed instead of junior counsel if it is held to be necessary because of the difficulty or complexity of the case or for other good reason; and

(c) for proceedings under paragraph 2 of the Table of Fees–
  (i) counsel's fees are allowed only where the Board has sanctioned the employment of counsel or where counsel is automatically available;
  (ii) except on cause shown, the auditor shall not have regard to any information produced by counsel at taxation which was not made available to the Board at the time the Board made the offer to counsel which is subject to taxation;
  (iii) in cases where junior counsel has undertaken most of the work on a particular item the auditor shall allow such fee to senior and junior counsel as appears appropriate to provide reasonable remuneration for the work;
  (iv) there is a working assumption that counsel for an appellant commands a higher fee than counsel for a respondent;
  (v) only one counsel's fee is permitted on a petition of appeal and on attending judgment; and
  (vi) the brief fee shall include all work on the brief, the case and the first day of attendance at the Supreme Court.

TABLE OF FEES

		Junior Counsel	Senior Counsel
1.	*Petition for leave to appeal*		
	(a) Drafting application for permission to appeal	£800.00	£1000.00
	(b) Preparing respondents' objections	£550.00	£750.00
	(c) Attending Supreme Court	£1100.00	£1600.00
2.	*Appeals and References*		
	(a) Drafting Petition of appeal	£75.00	£75.00
	(b) Statement of Facts and Issues	£1750.00	£3500.00
	(c) Authorities	£600.00	£1200.00
	(d) Consultations (each, up to a maximum of three)	£350.00	£700.00
	(e) Brief (based on a 1 day hearing)	£6250.00	£12500.00
	(f) Brief (based on a 2 day hearing)	£8000.00	£16000.00
	(g) Refresher (from day two of the hearing)	£1250.00	£2500.00
	(h) Judgment	£150.00	£150.00

NOTE: WHERE THE UNDERNOTED REGULATIONS APPLY, THE FIXED PAYMENTS REPLACE THE FEES AND OUTLAYS PAYABLE IN TERMS OF THE CRIMINAL LEGAL AID (SCOTLAND) (FEES) REGULATIONS 1989 (SI 1989 NO 1491) — SEE PP 104–131.

The Criminal Legal Aid (Fixed Payments) (Scotland) Regulations 1999 (SI 1999 No 491)

[These Regulations are printed as amended by:
The Scotland Act 1998 (Consequential Modifications) (No 2) Order 1999 (SI 1999 No 1820) which came into force on 1st July 1999;
Criminal Legal Aid (Fixed Payments) (Scotland) Amendment Regulations 1999 (SSI 1999 No 48) which came into force on 1st October 1999;
Criminal Legal Aid (Fixed Payments) (Scotland) Amendment Regulations 2001 (SSI 2001 No 307) which came into force on 15th October 2001;
Criminal Legal Aid (Fixed Payments) (Scotland) Amendment Regulations 2002 (SSI 2002 No 247) which came into force on 17th June 2002;
Criminal Legal Aid (Fixed Payments) (Scotland) Amendment (No 2) Regulations 2002 (SSI 2002 No 442) which came into force on 1st November 2002.]
Criminal Legal Aid (Youth Courts) (Scotland) Regulations 2003 (SSI 2003 No 249) which came into force on 2nd June 2003;
Criminal Legal Aid (Fixed Payments) (Scotland) Amendment Regulations 2004 (SSI 2004 No 51) which came into force on 11th March 2004;

Criminal Legal Aid (Fixed Payments) (Scotland) Amendment (No 2) Regulations 2004 (SSI 2004 No 126) which came into force on 2nd April 2004;

Criminal Legal Aid (Fixed Payments) (Scotland) Amendment (No 3) Regulations 2004 (SSI 2004 No 263) which came into force on 28th June 2004;

Criminal Legal Aid (Fixed Payments) (Scotland) Amendment Regulations 2005 (SSI 2005 No 93) which came into force on 23rd March 2004;

Criminal Legal Aid (Summary Justice Pilot Courts and Bail Conditions) (Scotland) Regulations 2006 (SSI 2006 No 234) which came into force on 12th June 2006;

Criminal Legal Assistance (Fees and Informaiton etc.) (Scotland) Regulations 2008 (SSI 2008 No 240) which came into force on 30th June 2008;

Criminal Legal Aid (Fixed Payments) (Scotland) Amendment Regulations 2010 (SSI 2010 No 237) which came into force on 5th July 2010;

Criminal Legal Aid (Fixed Payments) (Scotland) Amendment (No 2) Regulations 2010 (SSI 2010 No 267) which came into force on 4th July 2010;

Criminal Legal Assistance (Fees) (Scotland) Regulations 2010 (SSI 2010 No 270) which came into force on 8th July 2010

Criminal Legal Assistance (Fees) (No 2) (Scotland Regulations 2010 (SSI 2010 No 312) which came into force on 30th September 2010;

The Advice and Assistance and Legal Aid (Online Applications etc.) (Scotland) Regulations 2011 (SSI 2011 No 161) which came in to force on 1st April 2011;

The Criminal Legal Aid (Fixed Payments) (Scotland) Amendment Regulations 2011 (SSI 2011 No 162) which came into force on 22nd March 2011;

The Criminal Legal Assistance (Fees) (Scotland) Regulations 2011 (SSI 2011 No 333) which came into force on 31st October 2011;

Scotland Act 2012 (Transitional and Consequential Provisions) Order 2013 (SSI 2013 No 7) which came into force on 22nd April 2013;

Criminal Legal Aid (Fixed Payments) (Scotland) Amendment Regulations 2013 (SSI 2013 No 92 which came into force on 26th April 2013;

Criminal Legal Aid (fixed Payments and Assistance by Way of Representation) (Scotland) (Miscellaneous Amendments) Regulations 2014 (SSI 2014 No 366) which came into force on 17th December 2014;

Legal Aid (Miscellaneous Provisions (Scotland) Regulations 2015 (SSI 2015 No 337) which came into force on 22nd September 2015]

Citation and commencement

1. These Regulations may be cited as the Criminal Legal Aid (Fixed Payments) (Scotland) Regulations 1999 and shall come into force on 1st April 1999.

Interpretation

2.—(1) In these Regulations, unless the context otherwise requires—

"the Act" means the Legal Aid (Scotland) Act 1986;

"the 1995 Act" means the Criminal Procedure (Scotland) Act 1995;

"diet of deferred sentence" includes those diets where the case has been adjourned for inquiries or reports under sections 201 (power of court to adjourn case before sentence), section 202 (deferred sentence) or section 203 (reports) of the 1995 Act;

"adjourned trial diet" means a diet that follows a rial that has commenced by the leading of evidence;

"assisted person" means a person to whom criminal legal aid or (as the case may be) assistance by way of representation has been made available in relation to the proceedings in question;

"continued diet" means a diet which takes place on a separate date from the diet at which a victim statement is laid before the court;

"excluded proceedings" means—

    (a) summary proceedings arising following a reduction from solemn proceedings;

    (b) proceedings in relation to which legal aid is only available by virtue of section 22(1)(a) of the Act (identification parades held by or on behalf of the prosecutor in contemplation of criminal proceedings);

    (c) proceedings in relation to which legal aid is only available by virtue of section 22(1)(c) of the Act (assisted person in custody or liberated by police on undertaking to appear), except where those proceedings are before a court which has been designated as a drug court by the sheriff principal;

    (d)   proceedings in relation to which legal aid is only available by virtue of section 22(1)(da) of the Act (plea of insanity in bar of trial);

    (e)   proceedings in relation to which legal aid is only available by virtue of section 22(1)(db) of the Act (examination of facts);

    (f)   proceedings in relation to which legal aid is made available by virtue of regulation 15 of the Criminal Legal Aid (Scotland) Regulations 1996 (matters of special urgency);

    (g)   any reference in connection with proceedings under article 234 of the EEC Treaty;

    (h)   any reference on a devolution issue under paragraph 9 of Schedule 6 to the Scotland Act 1998;

    (i)   proceedings under section 9 of the Extradition Act 1989;

    (j)   proceedings under section 5 of the International Criminal Court Act 2001;

    (k)   proceedings in relation to which legal aid is only available by virtue of section 22(1) (dd) of the Act (solicitor appointed by court for person accused of sexual offence);

    (l)   proceedings in an appeal under section 174(1) (appeals relating to preliminary pleas) of the 1995 Act;

    (m) any reference on a compatibility issue under section 2882B(1) or (2) of the 1995 Act.

"proof in mitigation" includes those diets where a proof in mitigation take place at the same time as a proof of a victim statement;

"relevant ABWOR" means assistance by way of representation provided by a solicitor in relation to summary criminal proceedings other than excluded proceedings;

"relevant criminal legal aid" means criminal legal aid provided by a solicitor in relation to summary proceedings other than excluded proceedings;

"victim statement" means a statement made for the purposes of section 14 of the Criminal Justice (Scotland) Act 2003.

(2) In these Regulations, unless the context otherwise requires, any reference to a numbered regulation is to one of these Regulations.

(3) For the purposes of these Regulations, a trial, proof in mitigation or proof of a victim statement shall be taken to commence when the first witness is sworn.

Application

3.—(1) For the purposes of these regulations, the references in section 33(3A) and (3B) of the Act to criminal legal assistance relate to relevant criminal legal aid and relevant ABWOR.

    (2) These Regulations shall apply—

    (a)   in respect of relevant criminal legal aid first made available in terms of sections 22 or 24(7) of the Act, only in relation to any case where criminal legal aid is first so available on or after 1st April 1999; and

    (b)   in respect of relevant criminal legal aid first made available otherwise, only in relation to any case where an application for criminal legal aid is granted on or after that date.

    (3) These Regulations apply also in respect of relevant ABWOR.

Fixed payments allowable to solicitors

4.—(1) There shall be made to a solicitor who provides relevant criminal legal aid in summary proceedings, in respect of the professional services provided by him and the outlays specified in paragraph (2) below, and in accordance with the provisions of this regulation, the fixed payments specified in Schedule 1 or 1A.

(1A) In the application of paragraph (1) above in relation to the assisted person's case, fixed payments are payable under one of those Schedules only (as alternatives to each other) where–

    (a)   Schedule 1 is for the purpose of–

       (i)   cases in the JP court (other than before a stipendiary magistrate);

      (ii)   cases in the JP court (before a stipendiary magistrate) or the sheriff court which proceed beyond the first 30 minutes of a trial;

    (b)   Schedule 1A is for the purpose of cases in the JP court (before a stipendiary magistrate) or the sheriff court which do not proceed.

(1B) Those Schedules are to be read and applied accordingly.

(1C) There is to be made (in accordance with the other provisions of this regulation) to a solicitor who provides relevant ABWOR in summary proceedings, in respect of the professional services provided by the solicitor and the outlays mentioned in paragraph (2) below, the fixed payments specified in Schedule 1B.

(1D) Schedule 1B is for the purpose of cases in the JP court (before a stipendiary magistrate or otherwise) or the sheriff court.

    (2) The outlays specified in this paragraph are all outlays in connection with—

    (a)   the taking, drawing, framing and perusal of precognitions;

(b) the undertaking by another solicitor of any part of the work; and

(c) photocopying.

(3) Except where proceedings have been brought under section 185 of the 1995 Act, for the purposes of the references to summary proceedings in paragraph (1) and 1(C) above the following are to be treated as a single matter

(a) a single summary complaint or complaints which arise out of the same incident; and

(b) proceedings under section 22, 22ZA(1)(a), 27(1)(a), 28 or 150(8) of the 1995 Act arising out of the complaint or complaints referred to in sub-paragraph (a).

(4) Where in such proceedings a solicitor acts for more than one assisted person a separate fixed payment shall be made to him in respect of each such assisted person, in accordance with paragraph (5) below.

(5) Where a solicitor represents 2 or more assisted persons he shall be paid in respect of the first assisted person 100% of such of the fixed payments as are appropriate to that assisted person, in respect of a second assisted person 40% of the appropriate fixed payments, and in respect of a third and each subsequent assisted person 20% of those payments.

(5A) Where—

(a) a solicitor provides relevant ABWOR to an assisted person when, in the same court on the same day, that person is first brought before a court to answer to two or more summary complaints which are not to be treated as a single matter by virtue of paragraph (3); and

(b) a guilty plea is tendered to a charge libelled in any of the complaints at the first diet at which the assisted person was called upon to plead, resulting in the disposal of the case,

the amount payable under paragraph 1 of Part 1 of Schedule 1B is 100% of the prescribed amount in respect of the first complaint, 40% of that amount in respect of the second complaint and 20% in respect of any other complaints.

(5B) The amount payable under paragraph 1 of Part 1 of Schedule 1 or, as the case may be, paragraph 1 of Schedule 1A is half the amount that would otherwise be payable if the assisted person—

(a) was represented by a solicitor arranged by the Board to provide criminal legal aid in accordance with regulation 7(1) of the Criminal Legal Assistance (Duty Solicitors) (Scotland) Regulations 2011;

(b) tendered a plea of not guilty to any charge libelled in a complaint at the first diet at which the assisted person was called upon to plead; and

(c) before the commencement of the trial tendered a plea of guilty to that charge or any other charge in that complaint resulting in the disposal of the case.

(6) Where a solicitor represents an assisted person who has been remanded in custody at or subsequent to the first calling of the case and that assisted person is at any time during that remand under 21 years of age the fixed payment specified in paragraph 1 of Part 1 of Schedule 1 shall be increased by £100.

(6ZA) Where paragraphs (5B) and (6) both apply, the amount payable under paragraph 1 of Part 1 of Schedule 1 is to be halved in accordance with paragraph (5B) and £100 added to the quotient in accordance with paragraph (6).

(6A) [Revoked by SSI 2011 No 333]

(6B) [Revoked by SSI 2011 No 333]

(6BA) [Revoked by SSI 2011 No 333]

(6C) [Revoked by SSI 2011 No 333]

(7) Where the Board grants an application for a change of solicitor under regulation 17(3) of the Criminal Legal Aid (Scotland) Regulations 1996 there shall be paid to each of the solicitors who act for the assisted person in the relevant proceedings

(a) an equal part of the total amount payable under paragraph 1 of Part 1 of Schedule 1 or (as the case may be) under paragraph 1 of Schedule 1A; and

(b) where Schedule 1 applies the amounts payable under paragraphs 2 to 13 of Part 1 of Schedule 1 shall be payable to the solicitor who carries out the work described in those paragraphs;

(c) where Schedule 1A applies, the amounts payable under paragraph 1 of Schedule 1A so far as applying by reference to paragraphs 10, 10AA and 13 of Part 1 of Schedule 1, or under paragraph 2 of Schedule 1A, are payable to the solicitor who carries out the work concerned (despite, in the case of paragraph 1 of Schedule 1A, the reference in sub paragraph (a) above to that paragraph).

(7A) Paragraph (7) above is subject to paragraph (1A) above (and, accordingly, does not affect the restriction imposed by it).

(7B) Where, in relation to relevant ABWOR, there is a change of solicitor by virtue of regulation 14A(2) and (3) of the Advice and Assistance (Scotland) Regulations 1996, there is to be paid–

(a)   to each of the solicitors who act for the assisted person in the relevant proceedings, an equal part of the total amount payable under paragraph 1 or 2 of Part 1 of Schedule 1B; and

(b)   to the solicitor who carries out work described in the other paragraphs of that Part of that Schedule, the amount payable under those paragraphs in respect of the work.

(8)   Where the work done by a solicitor constitutes a supply of services in respect of which value added tax is chargeable, there may be added to the amount of payments allowed to the solicitor an amount equal to the amount of value added tax chargeable.

(9)   Where a solicitor represents an assisted person (having relevant criminal legal aid) in a court which has been designated as a drug court by the sheriff principal —

(a)   Part 1 of Schedule 1 shall not apply to those proceedings; and

(b)   where that assisted person has been remanded in custody at or subsequent to the first calling of the case and is at any time during that remand under 21 years of age, there shall be payable in addition to the fixed payments specified in Part 2 of Schedule 1 a payment of £100.

(10)   Where a solicitor represents an assisted person (having relevant ABWOR) in a court which has been so designated–

(a)   Part 1 of Schedule 1B does not apply; and

(b)   the fixed payment specified in Part 2 of that Schedule is payable instead.

Exceptional cases

4A.—(1) A solicitor who provides relevant criminal legal aid or relevant ABWOR shall —

(a)   where the circumstances prescribed at paragraph (3) exist; and

(b)   subject to the conditions prescribed at paragraph (5),

instead of receiving the fixed payments specified (as the case may be) in Schedule 1, Schedule 1A or Schedule 1B, be paid out of the Fund in accordance with regulations made under section 33(2) and (3) of the Act.

(2)   It shall be for the Board to determine whether the circumstances prescribed at paragraph (3) exist, and whether the conditions prescribed at paragraphs (5) and (9) are met.

(3)   The circumstances referred to in paragraph (1)(a) are where an assisted person would be deprived of the right to a fair trial in any case because of the amount of the fixed payments payable for the criminal legal assistance provided.

(4)   The factors to be taken into account by the Board in considering whether the circumstances prescribed at paragraph (3) exist shall include —

(a)   the number, nature and location of witnesses;

(b)   the number and nature of productions;

(c)   the complexity of the law (including procedural complexity);

(d)   whether the assisted person, or any witnesses, may be unable to understand the proceedings because of age, inadequate knowledge of English, mental illness, other mental or physical disability or otherwise.

(5)   The conditions referred to in paragraph (1)(b) are as follows —

(a)   the solicitor providing relevant criminal legal aid or relevant ABWOR shall make an application to the Board —

(i)   in such manner and form, which may include an online form; and

(ii)   containing such information,

as it may specify, at as early a stage in the provision of the relevant criminal legal aid or relevant ABWOR as is reasonably practicable and that solicitor shall, if required by the Board to do so, supply such further information or such documents as the Board may require to enable it to determine the application; and

(b)   that solicitor shall keep proper records of all professional services provided by way of an outlays incurred in the provision of that relevant criminal legal aid or relevant ABWOR, whether before or after the Board exercises its power to determine whether the conditions prescribed at paragraph (5)(a) are met.

(6)   An application for a review under section 33(3K) of the Act shall —

(a)   omitted by SSI 2011 No 161;

(b)   subject to paragraph (7), be lodged with the Board within 15 days of the time when notice of refusal of the application was given to the applicant;

(c)   include a statement of any matters which the applicant wishes the Board to take into account in reviewing the application; and

(d)   be accompanied by such additional precognitions and other documents as the applicant considers to be relevant to the review.

(7) Paragraph (6)(b) shall not apply where the Board considers that there is a special reason for it to consider a late application for review.

(8) Where the Board has granted an application for a change of solicitor under regulation 17(3) of the Criminal Legal Aid (Scotland) Regulations 1996[3], any solicitor who provided relevant criminal legal aid prior to that grant shall, where the Board has determined that the circumstances prescribed in Schedule 1, be paid out of the Fund in accordance with regulations made under section 33(2) and (3) of the Act.

(9) A solicitor to whom paragraph (8) applies shall only be paid where that solicitor has kept proper records of all professional services provided by way of and outlays incurred in the provision of that relevant criminal legal aid.

(10) Where the Board has granted an application for change of solicitor under regulation 14A(2) of the Advice and Assistance (Scotland) Regulations 1996, any solicitor who has provided relevant ABWOR prior to that grant is, where the Board has determined that the circumstances prescribed at paragraph (3) exist, instead of receiving the fixed payments specified in Schedule 1B, to be paid out of the Fund in accordance with regulations made under section 33(2) and (3) of the Act.

(11) A solicitor to whom paragraph (10) applies is only to be paid where that solicitor has kept proper records of all professional services provided by way of, and outlays incurred in the provision of, that relevant ABWOR.

Submission of accounts

5.—(1) A claim for a fixed payment in accordance with these Regulations shall be made by submitting to the Board not later than 4 months after the date of conclusion of the proceedings in respect of which the relevant legal aid or assistance was granted, an account specifying the fixed payments which are claimed in relation to the proceedings, together with any fees and outlays which are claimed in relation to those proceedings by virtue of the Criminal Legal Aid (Scotland) (Fees) Regulations 1989 or Advice and Assistance (Scotland) Regulations 1996).

(2) The Board may accept accounts submitted later than the 4 months referred to in paragraph (1) if it considers that there is special reason for late submission.

SCHEDULE 1 PART 1   Regulation 4

	Where professional services are provided in relation to proceedings in the JP Court (other than where proceedings are marked for prosecution before a Stipendiary Magistrate)	*Where professional services are provided in relation to proceedings in the Sheriff Court (other than proceedings in a Court specified in Schedule 2) or the JP Court (where proceedings are marked for prosecution before a Stipendiary Magistrate)*	*Where professional services are provided in relation to proceedings in the Sheriff Court and those proceedings are brought in a Court specified in Schedule 2*
1. All work up to and including: (i) any diet at which a plea of guilty is made and accepted or plea in mitigation is made: (ii) the first 30 minutes of conducting a proof in mitigation, or a proof of a victim statement, other than in the circumstances where paragraph 3 below applies; (iii) the first 30 minutes of conducting any trial; and (iiia) a first or second diet of deferred sentence; and	£295; or £270 where criminal legal aid has been made available in the circumstances referred to in paragraphs 11 or 12 below	£485 in relation to proceedings in the sheriff court; £460 where criminal legal aid has been made available in the circumstances referred to in paragraphs 11 or 12 in relation to proceedings in the sheriff court; £390 in relation to proceedings in the JP court; or £365 where criminal legal aid has been made available in the circumstances referred to in paragraphs 11 or 12 in relation to proceedings in the JP court	£535; or £510 where criminal legal aid has been made available in the circumstances referred to in paragraphs 11 or 12 below

	Where professional services are provided in relation to proceedings in the JP Court (other than where proceedings are marked for prosecution before a Stipendiary Magistrate)	Where professional services are provided in relation to proceedings in the Sheriff Court (other than proceedings in a Court specified in Schedule 2) or the JP Court (where proceedings are marked for prosecution before a Stipendiary Magistrate)	Where professional services are provided in relation to proceedings in the Sheriff Court and those proceedings are brought in a Court specified in Schedule 2
(iv) advising, giving an opinion and taking final instructions on the prospects of an appeal against conviction, sentence, other disposal or acquittal, together with any subsequent or additional work other than that specified in paragraphs 2–13 below.			
2. All work mentioned in paragraph 1 above that is done in connection with a complaint under section 22ZA(1)(b), 22ZB or 27(1)(b) of the 1995 Act.	£147.50	£195.00	£242.50
3. All work done in connection with a grant of legal aid under section 23(1)(b) of the Act ncluding ithe first 30 minutes of conducting a proof in mitigation, or a proofof a victim statement.	£25	£50	£50
4. Conducting a trial or proof in mitigation for the first day (after the first 30 minutes).	£50	£100	£100
4A. Conducting an adjourned trial diet, during which no evidence is led, where there was no intention nor anticipation that evidence would be led, the only matter in consideration being the determination of the further procedure of the trial proceedings.	£25	£50	£50

SCHEDULE 1 PART 1   Regulation 4

	Where professional services are provided in relation to proceedings in the JP Court (other than where proceedings are marked for prosecution before a Stipendiary Magistrate)	*Where professional services are provided in relation to proceedings in the Sheriff Court (other than proceedings in a Court specified in Schedule 2) or the JP Court (where proceedings are marked for prosecution before a Stipendiary Magistrate)*	*Where professional services are provided in relation to proceedings in the Sheriff Court and those proceedings are brought in a Court specified in Schedule 2*
4B. Conducting an adjourned trial diet, during which no evidence is led, where there was an intention and an anticipation that the trial would proceed through the continued leading of evidence.	£50	£100	£100
5. Conducting a trial or proof in mitigation for the second day	£50	£200	£200
6. Conducting a trial or proof in mitigation for the third and subsequent days (per day)	£100	£400	£400
7. Representation in court at a continued diet following a victim statement having been laid before the court where the court determines sentence or fixes a proof of a victim statement, or adjourns such a proof without hearing evidence.		£50	
8. Conducting a proof of a victim statement where there has been no trial or proof in mitigation for the first day (after the first 30 minutes), and thereafter for subsequent days (per day).		£200	

SCHEDULE 1 PART 1   Regulation 4

	Where professional services are provided in relation to proceedings in the JP Court (other than where proceedings are marked for prosecution before a Stipendiary Magistrate)	*Where professional services are provided in relation to proceedings in the Sheriff Court (other than proceedings in a Court specified in Schedule 2) or the JP Court (where proceedings are marked for prosecution before a Stipendiary Magistrate)*	*Where professional services are provided in relation to proceedings in the Sheriff Court and those proceedings are brought in a Court specified in Schedule 2*
9. Conducting a proof of a victim statement at a continued diet following a concluded trial or proof in mitigation (per day).		£200	
10. Representation, per appearance— (a) in a court which has been designated as a youth court by the sheriff principal; (b) in a court which has been designated as a domestic abuse court by the sheriff principal; (c) at a hearing in respect of a community supervision order.	£25	£50	£50
10ZA. Representation in court, per appearance, at a deferred sentence hearing other than where a fee is payable by virtue of paragraph 1(iiia) in respect of a first or second diet of deferred sentence.	£25 where the hearing relates to one complaint; or £37.50 where the hearing relates to more than one complaint	£50 where the hearing relates to one complaint; or £75 where the hearing relates to more than one complaint	£50 where the hearing relates to one complaint; or £75 where the hearing relates to more than one complaint.
10A. Omitted by SSI 2008 No 240	—		—
10AA. Representation at a first or second diet of deferred sentence (one only) at which the court considers a report required under section 203 of the 1995 Act and where the case is disposed of (as an additional payment).	£25	£25	£25

SCHEDULE 1 PART 1   Regulation 4

	Where professional services are provided in relation to proceedings in the JP Court (other than where proceedings are marked for prosecution before a Stipendiary Magistrate)	*Where professional services are provided in relation to proceedings in the Sheriff Court (other than proceedings in a Court specified in Schedule 2) or the JP Court (where proceedings are marked for prosecution before a Stipendiary Magistrate)*	*Where professional services are provided in relation to proceedings in the Sheriff Court and those proceedings are brought in a Court specified in Schedule 2*
11. All work done where the accused is in custody and has tendered a plea of not guilty until determination of the application for legal aid.	£25	£25	£25
12. All work done by virtue of section 24(7) of the Act until determination of the application for legal aid.	£25	£25	£25
13. (a) All work done in connection with a bail appeal under section 32 of the 1995 Act, or an appeal under section 201(4) of the 1995 Act, other than under paragraph (b) or (c)	£50	£50	£50
(b) Representation in such an appeal where counsel not employed.	£30	£30	£30
(c) Representation at a continued diet in such an appeal where counsel not employed.	£30	£30	£30

SCHEDULE 1A

	Where professional services are provided in relation to proceedings in the Sheriff Court or the JP court (where proceedings are marked for prosecution before a Stipendiary Magistrate)	*Where professional services are provided in relation to proceedings in the Sheriff Court and those proceedings are brought in a Court specified in Schedule 2*
1. All work up to and including– (a) any diet at which a plea of guilty is made and accepted or plea in mitigation is made;	£485 in relation to proceedings in the sheriff court; £460 where criminal legal aid has been made available in the circumstances referred to in paragraphs 11 or 12 of Part 1 of Schedule 1 in relation to proceedings in the sheriff court; £390 in relation to proceedings in	£485; or £460 where criminal legal aid has been made available in the circumstances referred to in paragraphs 11 or 12 of Part 1 of Schedule 1

SCHEDULE 1A

	Where professional services are provided in relation to proceedings in the Sheriff Court or the JP court (where proceedings are marked for prosecution before a Stipendiary Magistrate)	Where professional services are provided in relation to proceedings in the Sheriff Court and those proceedings are brought in a Court specified in Schedule 2
(b) the first 30 minutes of conducting any trial; (c) a first or second diet of deferred sentence; and (d) advising, giving an opinion and taking final instructions on the prospects of an appeal against conviction, sentence, other disposal or cquittal, together with any subsequent or additional work other than that of the kind specified in paragraphs 10 to 13 of Part 1 of Schedule 1 above.	the JP court; or £365 where criminal legal aid has been made available in the circumstances referred to in paragraphs 11 or 12 of Part 1 of Schedule 1 in relation to proceedings in the JP court	
2. All work mentioned in paragraph 1 above that is done in connection with a complaint under section 27(1)(b) of the 1995 Act.	£195.00 in relation to proceedings before a Stipendiary Magistrate; £242.50 in relation to proceedings in the sheriff court	£257.50

SCHEDULE 1B PART 1

	Where professional services are provided in relation to proceedings in the JP court (other than where proceedings are marked for prosecution before a Stipendiary Magistrate)	Where professional services are provided in relation to proceedings in the Sheriff Court or the JP court (where proceedings are marked for prosecution before a Stipendiary Magistrate)
1. All work up to and including– (a) any diet at which a plea of guilty is made and accepted or plea in mitigation is made; (b) the first 30 minutes of conducting a proof in mitigation, or a proof of a victim statement, other than in the circumstances where paragraph 3 below applies;		£485; or £390 in relation to proceedings in the JP court

SCHEDULE 1B PART 1

	Where professional services are provided in relation to proceedings in the JP court (other than where proceedings are marked for prosecution before a Stipendiary Magistrate)	*Where professional services are provided in relation to proceedings in the Sheriff Court or the JP court (where proceedings are marked for prosecution before a Stipendiary Magistrate)*
(c) a first or second diet of deferred sentence; and		
(d) advising, giving an opinion and taking final instructions on the prospects of an appeal against conviction, sentence, other disposal or acquittal, together with any subsequent or additional work other than that specified in paragraphs 8, 8A, 9 and 10 below.		
2. All work prior to, and attendance at–	£150	
(a) any diet at which a plea to the competency or relevancy of the complaint or proceedings, or a plea in bar of trial, is tendered;		
(b) any diet at which a question within the meaning of Rule 31.1 of the Act of Adjournal (Criminal Procedure Rules) 1996 is raised;		
(c) any diet from or to which the case has been adjourned under section 145 of the 1995 Act (including preparation for such a diet where the diet has not subsequently taken place);		
(d) any diet at which there is tendered a plea of guilty or a plea in mitigation is made;		
(e) any diet at which the court is considering the accused's plea of guilty to the charges		

SCHEDULE 1B PART 1

Where professional services are provided in relation to proceedings in the JP court (other than where proceedings are marked for prosecution before a Stipendiary Magistrate)	*Where professional services are provided in relation to proceedings in the Sheriff Court or the JP court (where proceedings are marked for prosecution before a Stipendiary Magistrate)*
and where there has been no change of plea; and	
(f) any diet at which the court is considering the accused's change to plea of guilty to the charges, and where no application for criminal legal aid has been made, together with–	
(i) the first 30 minutes of conducting a proof in mitigation;	
(ii) a first or second diet of deferred sentence;	
(iii) any subsequent or additional work other than that specified in paragraphs 4 and 8 to 13 below.	
3. All work mentioned in paragraph 1 or 2 above that is done in connection with a complaint under section 27(1)(b) of the 1995 Act. £150	£195.00 in relation to proceedings before a Stipendiary Magistrate; £242.50 in relation to proceedings in the sheriff court
4. Conducting a proof in mitigation for the first day (after the first 30 minutes). £50	
5. Representation in court at a continued diet following a victim statement having been laid before the court where the court determines sentence or fixes a proof of a victim statement, adjourns such a proof without hearing evidence.	
6. Conducting a proof of a victim statement where there has been no proof in mitigation for the first day (after the	

SCHEDULE 1B PART 1

	Where professional services are provided in relation to proceedings in the JP court (other than where proceedings are marked for prosecution before a Stipendiary Magistrate)	*Where professional services are provided in relation to proceedings in the Sheriff Court or the JP court (where proceedings are marked for prosecution before a Stipendiary Magistrate)*
first 30 minutes), and thereafter for subsequent days (per day).		
7. Conducting a proof of a victim statement at a continued diet following a concluded trial or proof in mitigation (per day).		
8. Representation, per appearance— (a) in a court which has been designated as a youth court by the sheriff principal; (b) in a court which has been designated as a domestic abuse court by the sheriff principal; (c) at a hearing in respect of a community supervision order	£25	£50
8A. Representation in court, per appearance, at a deferred sentence hearing other than where a fee is payable by virtue of paragraph 1(c) in respect of a first or second diet of deferred sentence.	£25 where the hearing relates to one complaint; or £37.50 where the hearing relates to more than one complaint	£50 where the hearing relates to one complaint; or £75 where the hearing relates to more than one complaint.
9. Representation at a first or second diet of deferred sentence (one only) at which the court considers a report required under section 203 of the 1995 Act and where the case is disposed of (as an additional payment).	£25	£25
10. All work done in connection with a bail appeal under section 32 of the 1995 Act, or on appeal under section 201(4) of the 1995 Act.	£50	£50

SCHEDULE 1B PART 1

		Where professional services are provided in relation to proceedings in the JP court (other than where proceedings are marked for prosecution before a Stipendiary Magistrate)	Where professional services are provided in relation to proceedings in the Sheriff Court or the JP court (where proceedings are marked for prosecution before a Stipendiary Magistrate)
12.	Conducting a special reasons proof or hearing on exceptional hardship (where both, they to be regarded as one only even if conducted separately).	£150	£150
13.	Conducting a back-duty proof (but only if in the case no fee is payable under paragraph 12 above).	£50	

PART 2

		Where professional services are provided in relation to proceedings in a sheriff court which has been designated as a drug court by the Sheriff Principal
1.	All work done in connection with any appearance of an assistance person (per appearance).	£50

SCHEDULE 1 PART 2

		Where professional services are provided in relation to proceedings in a Sheriff Court which has been designated as a drug court by a Sheriff Principal
1.	All work done under section 22(1)(c) of the Act up to and including the first appearance of an assisted person.	£100
2.	All work done (other than work done in terms of paragraph 1) in 101 (per appearance)	£50

SCHEDULE 2 PART 2

Campeltown	Oban
Dunoon	Portree
Fort William	Rothesay
Kirkwall	Stornoway
Lerwick	Wick
Lochmaddy	

3. Civil Legal Aid

Civil Legal Aid (Scotland) (Fees) Regulations 1989 (SI 1989 No 1490)

[This Statutory Instrument is printed as amended by:
Civil Legal Aid (Scotland) (Fees) Amendment Regulations 1990 (SI 1990 No 473) (counsel's fees);
Civil Legal Aid (Scotland) (Fees) Amendment (No 2) Regulations 1990 (SI 1990 No 1036) (solicitors' fees);
Civil Legal Aid (Scotland) (Fees) Amendment Regulations 1991 (SI 1991 No 565) (solicitors' and counsel's fees) which came into force on 1st April 1991;
Civil Legal Aid (Scotland) (Fees) Amendment Regulations 1992 (SI 1992 No 372) (solicitors' and counsel's fees) which came into force on 1st April 1992;
Civil Legal Aid (Scotland) (Fees) Amendment Regulations 1994 (SI 1994 No 1015) (solicitors' fees) which came into force on 5th May 1994;
Civil Legal Aid (Scotland) (Fees) Amendment (No 2) Regulations 1994 (SI 1994 No 1233) (solicitors' fees) which came into force on 27th May 1994;
Civil Legal Aid (Scotland) (Fees) Amendment Regulations 1995 (SI 1995 No 1044) which came into force on 5th May 1995;
Civil Legal Aid (Scotland) (Fees) Amendment Regulations 1997 (SI 1997 No 689) which came into force on 1st April 1997;
The Scotland Act 1998 (Consequential Modifications) (No 1) Order 1999 (SI 1999 No 1042) which came into force on 6th May 1999;
Civil Legal Aid (Scotland) (Fees) Amendment Regulations 2002 (SSI 2002 No 496) which came into force on 1st December 2002;
Civil Legal Aid (Scotland) (Fees) Amendment Regulations 2003 (SSI 2003 No 178) which came into force on 1st October 2003;
The Civil Legal Aid (Scotland) (Fees) Amendment Regulations 2007 (SSI 2007 No 14) which came into force on 10th February 2007;
The Civil Legal Aid (Scotland) (Fees) Amendment (No 2) Regulations 2007 (SSI 2007 No 181) which came into force on 29th March 2007;
The Civil Legal Aid (Scotland) (Fees) Amendment (No 3) Regulations 2007 (SSI 2007 No 438) which came into force on 1st November 2007;
The Civil Legal Aid (Scotland) (Fees) Amendment Regulations 2009 (SSI 2009 No 203) which came into force on 22nd June 2009;
Legal Aid (Supreme Court) (Scotland) Regulations 2010 (SSI 2009 No 312) which came into force on 1st October 2009;
The Advice and Assistance and Civil Legal Aid (Transfer of Tribunal Functions) (No. 1) (Scotland) Regulations 2010 (SSI 2010 No 166) which came into force on 9th June 2010;
The Legal Aid and Advice and Assistance (Solicitors' Travel Fees) (Scotland) Regulations 2011 (SSI 2011 No 41) which came into force on 28th February 2011;
The Civil Legal Aid (Scotland) (Fees) Amendment Regulations 2011 (SSI 2011 No 160) which came into force on 1st April 2011;
Scotland Act 2012 (transitional and Consequential Provisions) Order 2013 (SSI 213 No 7) which came into force on 22nd April 2013;
The Children's Legal Assistance (Fees) (Miscellaneous Amendments) (Scotland) Regulations 2013 (SSI 2013 No 144) which came into force on 24 June 2013;
Legal Aid and Advice and Assistance (Photocopying Fees and Welfare Reform) (Miscellaneous Amendments) (Scotland) Regulations 2013 (SSI 2013 No 250) which came into force on 31st October 2013;
Legal Aid (Miscellaneous Amendments) (Scotland) Regulations 2015 (SSI 2015 No 337) which came into force on 22nd September 2015;
The Civil Legal Aid (Scotland) (Miscellaneous Amendments) Regulations 2015 (SSI 2015 No 380) which came into force on 1st January 2016]

Fees and outlays allowable to solicitors

4. Subject to the provisions of regulations 5 and 7 regarding the calculation of fees, regulations 6 and 7 regarding the calculation of outlays, and the provisions of regulations 7A and 8 regarding the submission of accounts, a solicitor shall be allowed such amount of fees and outlays as shall be determined by the Board to be reasonable remuneration for work actually, necessarily and reasonably done and outlays actually, necessarily and reasonably incurred, for conducting the proceedings in a proper manner, as between solicitor and client, third party paying.

5.—(1) A solicitor's fees in relation to proceedings in the Court of Session shall be calculated in accordance with Schedule 5.

(1A) A solicitor's fees in relation to proceedings in the Sheriff Appeal Court shall be calculated in accordance with either Schedule 5 or Schedule 6 but it shall not be competent to charge fees partly on the basis of Schedule 5 and partly on the basis of Schedule 6.

(2) A solicitor's fees in relation to proceedings in the sheriff court–

    (a) shall, subject to sub-paragraphs (b) and (c), be calculated in accordance with chapters I and II of Schedule 6;

    (b) which are listed in Schedule 7 shall be calculated in accordance with Schedule 5; and

    (c) which consist of a summary cause or executry business shall be calculated in accordance with chapter III or IV respectively of Schedule 2.

(2A) For the purpose of calculating the fees set out in Schedule 6, a unit has the value of £21.00.

(2B) Where a solicitor does work which comes within chapter I of Schedule 6 (undefended cases) and, in the same case, does work which comes within chapter II of that Schedule (defended cases) the fee for all work in that case shall be calculated on the basis of the fees set out in chapeter II of that Schedule.

(2C) Subject to paragraph (2D), the Board may at its discretion allow a fee additional to the fees prescribed in chapter II of Schedule 6 where it is satisfied that any of the circumstances prescribed in chapter III of that Schedule exists, and have a significant effect on the conduct of the case.

(2D) The additional fee allowable in accordance with paragraph (2C) shall be 15% of the fee authorised by Chapter II of Schedule 6 in respect of each of the circumstances specified in paragraphs 1 to 5A of Chapter III of that Schedule and 20% of the said fee authorised in respect of each of the circumstances specified in paragraphs 6 and 7 of said Chapter III, up to a maximum in any case of 50% of that fee.

(2E) Fees for sequestration in bankruptcy (other than summary sequestrations) shall be chargeable only on the basis of Schedule 3 and fees for summary sequestrations shall be chargeable only on the basis of 80 per cent of the fees in that Schedule.

(3) A solicitor's fees in relation to proceedings in the Supreme Court on appeal from the Court of Session or, under paragraph 10 or 33 of Schedule to the Scotland Act 1998, Employment Appeal Tribunal, Lands Valuation Appeal Court, Scottish Land Court or Lands Tribunal for Scotland or before the Upper Tribunal or the Social Security Commissioners, shall be calculated in accordance with Schedule 5.

(4) In all Court of Session proceedings or proceedings in the Sheriff Appeal Court a fee, additional to those set out in Schedule 5 and not exceeding 50 per cent of those fees, may be allowed at the discretion of the court to cover the responsibility undertaken by a solicitor in the conduct of the proceedings. In the sheriff court, in proceedings of importance or requiring special preparation, the sheriff may allow a percentage increase in a cause on the Summary Cause Roll, not exceeding 100 per cent, of the fees authorised by Schedules 2 or 3 to cover the responsibility undertaken by the solicitor in the conduct of the proceedings. The Court of Session, or as the case may be the Sheriff Appeal Court, in deciding whether to allow an additional fee and the auditor in determining that fee or the sheriff in fixing the amount of a percentage fee increase shall take into account the following factors —

    (a) the complexity of the proceedings and the number, difficulty or novelty of the questions involved;

    (b) the skill, specialised knowledge and responsibility required of and the time and labour expended by the solicitor;

    (c) the number and importance of the documents prepared or perused;

    (d) the place and circumstances of the proceedings or in which the solicitor's work of preparation for and conduct of it has been carried out;

    (e) the importance of the proceedings or the subject matter thereof to the client;

    (f) the amount or value of money or property involved;

    (g) the steps taken with a view to settling the proceedings, limiting the matters in dispute or limiting the scope of any hearing; and

    (h) any other fees and allowances payable to the solicitor in respect of other items in the same proceedings and otherwise charged for in the account.

(5) The auditor of the Court of Session shall have power to increase or decrease any inclusive fee set out in Schedule 1 in any appropriate circumstances.

(6) The auditor shall have the power to apportion any fees set out in Schedules 1, 2 or 6 between solicitors in appropriate circumstances or to modify any such fees in the case of a solicitor acting for more than one party in the same proceedings or in the case of the same solicitor acting in more than one proceeding arising out of the same circumstances or in the event of the proceedings being settled or disposed of at a stage when the work covered by any inclusive fee has not been completed.

(7) Where work done by a solicitor constitutes a supply of services in respect of which value-added tax is chargeable, there may be added to the amount of fees calculated in accordance with the foregoing paragraphs of this regulation an amount equal to the amount of value-added tax chargeable.

6. A solicitor's outlays shall include a charge in respect of posts and incidents of 12 per cent of the amount of the fees allowable to the solicitor in Schedules 1 and 2 (excluding any amount added in accordance with regulations 5 (4) and (7)). In Schedule 5 or 6, without prejudice to any other claims for outlays, a solicitor shall not be allowed outlays representing posts and incidents.

7. Where any work is carried out in the preparation for or conduct of the proceedings and that work could more economically have been done by instructing a local solicitor, only such fees and outlays shall be allowed as would have been allowable if a local solicitor had been instructed, including reasonable fees for instructing and corresponding with him, unless it was reasonable in the interests of the client that the solicitor in charge of the proceedings, or a solicitor or clerk authorised by him, should attend personally.

Single account where other solicitor employed

7A.—(1) Paragraphs (2) and (3) apply where a solicitor ("the nominated solicitor") instructs another solicitor to carry out work in relation to proceedings (other than proceedings in the Sheriff Appeal Court, the Court of Session or the Supreme Court).

(2) Accounts in respect of fees and outlays allowable to solicitors shall be submitted to the Board only by the nominated solicitor, payment of the other solicitor being a matter for adjustment between the nominated solicitor and the other solicitor out of the fees and outlays allowed to the nominated solicitor.

(3) In determining the sum to be allowed to the nominated solicitor, the Board shall take into account also the work carried out by the other solicitor.

Accounts in respect of solicitors' fees and outlays

8.—(1) Subject to paragraph (2) below, accounts prepared in respect of fees and outlays allowable to solicitors and fees allowable to counsel shall be submitted to the Board not later than 4 months after the date of completion of the proceedings in respect of which that legal aid was granted.

(2) The Board may accept accounts submitted in respect of fees and outlays allowable to solicitors and fees allowable to counsel later than the 4 months referred to in paragraph (1) if it considers that there is a special reason for late submission.

Fees allowable to counsel

9. Subject to the provisions of regulation 8 regarding the submission of accounts, and the provisions of regulation 10 regarding the calculation of fees, the fees allowable to counsel shall be fees for such work as shall be determined by the Board to have been actually and reasonably done, due regard being had to economy.

10.—(1) Counsel's fees in relation to proceedings in the Court of Session, Sheriff Appeal Court and sheriff court shall be calculated in accordance with Schedule 4.

(2) Counsel's fees for any work in relation to proceedings in the Supreme Court, Employment Appeal Tribunal, Lands Valuation Appeal Court, Scottish Land Court or Lands Tribunal for Scotland, or before the Upper Tribunal or the Social Security Commissioners shall be 90 per cent of the amount of fees which would be allowed for that work on a taxation of expenses between solicitor and client, third party paying, if the work done were not legal aid.

(2A) The fees of a solicitor — advocate for any work in relation to proceedings in the Supreme Court, shall be 90 per cent of the amount of fees which would be allowed for that work on a taxation of expenses between solicitor and client, third party paying, if the work done were not legal aid.

(3) Where work done by counsel constitutes a supply of services in respect of which value-added tax is chargeable, there may be added to the amount of fees calculated in accordance with the foregoing paragraphs of this regulation an amount equal to the amount of value-added tax chargeable thereon.

Payments to account

11.—(1) A solicitor acting for, or counsel instructed on behalf of, a person receiving civil legal aid may prior to the completion of the proceedings for which the legal aid was granted submit a claim to the Board, in such form and complying with such terms and containing such information as the Board may require for assessment purposes, for payment of sums to account of his fees necessarily and reasonably incurred in connection with these proceedings.

(2) A claim by counsel under this regulation may be made only in relation to any case where—

    (a)   a period of no less than 6 months has elapsed since the date on which the Board gave notice in writing of the grant of civil legal aid;

    (b)   an interval of no less than 6 months has elapsed since the immediately preceding claim was made; or

    (c)   counsel reasonably anticipates not receiving further instructions in the proceedings.

(3) The amount of any payment in respect of a claim by counsel under this regulation in relation to proceedings referred to in regulation 10(2) and (2A) shall be limited to 75% of the fees that will become eligible for payment and earned during the period covered by the claim.

(4) When assessing the fee payable to a solicitor in respect of legal aid the Board may have regard to any payment, or payments, made to account under advice and assistance in relation to the same matter and,

where the work in respect of which such payment, or payments, is made might reasonably have been carried out under legal aid, it may reduce the amount of the fee payable accordingly.

(5) The making of a claim under this regulation shall not be regarded as an account of expenses nor shall the claim affect in any way the provisions of regulation 8 above with regard to the submission and acceptance of accounts prepared in respect of fees and outlays allowable to solicitors.

(6) Where payment has been made in accordance with the provisions of this regulation but the payment made exceeds in the case of any solicitor acting for the assisted person the total fees and outlays allowable to that solicitor in respect of the legal aid or in the case of any counsel instructed on behalf of the assisted person the total fees allowable to that counsel in respect of the legal aid, the excess shall be repaid to the Fund by such solicitor or counsel as the case may be:

Provided that where by reason of a failure to comply with the requirements of regulation 8 above with regard to submission of an account of his fees and outlays the amount of the fees and outlays allowable to a solicitor to whom payment has been made under this regulation cannot be ascertained, the Board may require such solicitor to repay to the Fund the whole amount paid under this regulation or such part thereof which it is satisfied may have been overpaid to the solicitor.

Taxation of fees and outlays

12.—(1) If any question or dispute arises between the Board and a solicitor or counsel as to the amount of fees or outlays allowable to the solicitor, or as to the amount of fees allowable to counsel, from the Fund under these Regulations, other than regulation 11 above, the matter shall be referred for taxation by the auditor.

(2) A reference to the auditor under paragraph (1) above may be at the instance of the solicitor concerned or, where the question or dispute affects the fees allowable to counsel, of the counsel concerned, or of the Board, and the auditor shall give reasonable notice of the diet of taxation to the solicitor or counsel as appropriate and to the Board.

(3) Subject to regulaton 12A the Board and any other party to a reference to the auditor under paragraph (1) above shall have the right to state written objections to the court in relation to the auditor's report within 14 days of the issue of that report, and may be heard thereon; and where the court is the Court of Session rule 349 of the Act of Sederunt (Rules of Court, consolidation and amendment) 1965 shall apply to the determination of any such objections.

(4) For the purposes of this regulation the expression "the court" means —

    (a)   in relation to any report of the Auditor of the Court of Session, the Court of Session;

    (aa) in relation to any report of the auditor of a sheriff court in relation to proceedings in the Sheriff Appeal Court, the Sheriff Appeal Court;

    (b)   in relation to any report of the auditor of a sheriff court (other than a report in relation to proceedings in the Sheriff Appeal Court), the sheriff; and

    (c)   in relation to any report of the Auditor of the Scottish Land Court, the Chairman of the Scottish Land Court.

12A.—(1) In relation to proceedings in the Supreme Court, the Board and any other party to a reference to the auditor who is dissatisfied with all or part of a taxation shall have the right to lodge a petition to the Supreme Court within 14 days of the taxation setting out the items objected to and the nature and grounds of the objections.

(2) The petition shall be served on the Board, any such other party who attended the taxation and any other party to whom the auditor directs that a copy should be delivered.

(3) Any party upon whom such a petition is delivered may within 14 days after such delivery lodge a response to the petition which shall be served on the Board, any such other party who attended the taxation and any other party to whom the auditor directs that a copy should be delivered.

(4) The petition and responses, if any, shall be considered by a panel of Justices, as defined by rule 3(2) of the Supreme Court Rules 2009, which may allow or dismiss the petition without a hearing, invite any or all of the parties to lodge submissions or further submissions in writing or direct that an oral hearing be held.

SCHEDULE 1

Regulation 5

FEES OF SOLICITORS FOR PROCEEDINGS IN THE COURT OF SESSION

1.   In this Schedule, unless the context otherwise requires —

    "the court" means the Court of Session; and

    "session fee" means the fee set out in paragraph 21 of Part V of the Table of Fees in this Schedule.

TABLE OF FEES

Part I — Undefended Actions (other than Consistorial Actions)

£

1. Inclusive fee to pursuer's solicitor in all undefended cases where no proof is led, to cover all work from taking instructions up to and including obtaining extract decree 95.80

Part II — Undefended Consistorial Actions (other than Actions to which Part III Applies)

1. Fee for all work (other than precognitions) up to and including the calling of summons in court 136.20

Note: Precognitions to be charged as in Part V, paragraph 5 of this Schedule

2. *Incidental procedures*

   Fixing diet, enrolling action, preparation for proof, citing witnesses, etc 77.10

3. *Amendment*

   (a) Where summons amended, where re-service is not ordered, and motion is not starred..   19.40

   (b) Where summons amended, where re-service is not ordered and motion is starred 28.40

   (c) Where summons amended and re-service is ordered 36.00

4. *Commissions to take evidence on interrogatories*

   (a) Basic fee to cover all work up to and including lodging completed interrogatories 28.40

   (b) Additional fee for completed interrogatories, including all copies — per sheet 6.05

5. *Commissions to take evidence on open commission*   £

   (a) Basic fee to solicitor applying for commission but excluding attendance at execution thereof 32.10

   (b) Attendance at execution of commission — per half hour 16.50

6. Where applicable the fees set out in paragraphs 6, 7, 10, 14, 16 and 21 of Part V of this Schedule may be charged

7. Proof and completion fee — excluding accounts of expenses but including instructing counsel for proof, attendance at proof, settling with witnesses, borrowing and returning productions, procuring interlocutor, and obtaining extract decree of divorce 95.80

8. Accounts

   Framing and lodging account and attending taxation 30.60

Part III — Undefended Consistorial Actions: Affidavit Procedure

1. In any undefended action of divorce or separation where —

   (a) the facts set out in section 1(2)(b) (unreasonable behaviour) of the Divorce (Scotland) Act 1976 are relied upon; and

   (b) the pursuer seeks to prove those facts by means of affidavits,

the pursuer's solicitor may in respect of the work specfied in column 1 of Table A in this paragraph charge, in a case where he is an Edinburgh solicitor acting alone, the inclusive fee specfied in respect of that work in column 2 of that Table, and, in any other case, the inclusive fee specfied in respect of that work in column 3 of that Table.

TABLE A

Column 1 *Work done*	Column 2 *Inclusive fee Edinburgh solciitor acting alone*	Column 3 *Inclusive fee any other case*
1. All work to and including calling of the summons	£198.60	£227.10
2. All work from calling to and including swearing affidavits	£141.90	£170.40

3. All work from swearing affidavits to and including sending extract decree	£42.60	£63.80
4. All work to and including sending extract decree	£383.20	£461.20
Add session fee to item 4	of 7.5 %	of 10%

2. In any undefended action of divorce or separation where —

    (a) the facts set out in section 1(2)(a) (adultery), 1(2)(c) (desertion), 1(2)(d) (two years' non-cohabitation and consent) or 1(2)(e) (five years' non-cohabitation) of the Divorce (Scotland) Act 1976 are relied on; and

    (b) the pursuer seeks to prove these facts by means of affidavits,

the pursuer's solicitor may in respect of the work specified in column 1 of Table B in this paragraph charge, in a case where he is an Edinburgh solicitor acting alone, the inclusive fee specified in respect of that work in column 2 of that Table, and, in any other case, the inclusive fee specified in respect of that work in column 3 of that Table.

TABLE B

Column 1 Work done	Column 2 Inclusive fee Edinburgh solciitor acting alone	Column 3 Inclusive fee any other case
1. All work to and including calling of the summons	£163.20	£191.60
2. All work from calling to and including swearing affidavits	£78.10	£99.30
3. All work from swearing affidavits to and including sending extract decree	£42.60	£63.80
4. All work to and including sending extract decree	£282.80	£354.70
Add session fee to item 4	of 7.5 %	of 10%

3. If —

    (a) the pursuer's solicitor charges an inclusive fee under either paragraph 1 or paragraph 2 of this Part; and

    (b) the action to which the charge relates includes a conclusion relating to an ancillary matter,

in addition to that fee, he may charge in respect of the work specified in column 1 of Table C in this paragraph the inclusive fee specified in respect of that work in column 2 of that Table.

TABLE C

Column 1 Work done	Column 2 Inclusive fee
1. All work to and including calling of the summons	£39.80
2. All work from calling to and including swearing affidavits	£45.40
4. All work under items 1 and 2	£85.10

Add session fee to item 3 of 7.5% in the case of an Edinburgh solicitor acting alone and 10% in any other case.

PART IV — OUTER HOUSE PETITIONS

A. *Unopposed petitions*   £

1. Fee for all work, including precognitions and all copyings, up to and obtaining extract decree —

    (a) in the case of an Edinburgh solicitor acting alone 200.70

    (b) in any other case 280.10

Note: Outlays including duplicating charges to be allowed in addition.

B. *Opposed petitions*

2. Fee for all work (other than precognitions) up to and including lodging petition, obtaining and
    executing warrant for service 136.20

Note: Outlays including duplicating charges to be allowed in addition.

3. Where applicable, the fees set out in paragraphs 5, 6, 7, 10, 12, 14, 18, 19, 20 and 21 of Part
    V of this Schedule may be charged.

4. Reports —

    (a) For each report by Accountant of Court 24.00

    (b) For any other report as under Part V, paragraph 6 of this Schedule.

5. Obtaining Bond of Caution 24.00

PART V — DEFENDED ACTIONS

1. *Instruction fee*   £

    (a) To cover all work (apart from precognitions) until lodgement of open record 188.60

    (b) Instructing re-service where necessary 20.20

    (c) If counter-claim lodged, additional fee for solicitor for each party 39.80

2. *Record fee*

    (a) To cover all work in connection with adjustment and closing of record including
         subsequent work in connection with By Order Adjustment Roll 200.70

    (b) To cover all work as above, so far as applicable, where action settled or disposed of
         before record closed 125.00

    (c) If consultation held before record closed, additional fees may be allowed as follows:

         (i)   Arranging consultation 20.20
         (ii) Attendance at consultation — per half hour 16.50

    (d) Additional fee (to include necessary amendments) to the solicitors for the existing
         pursuer and each existing defender, to be allowed for each pursuer, defender or third
         party brought in before the record is closed, each of 59.10

    (e) Additional fee to the solicitors for existing pursuer and each existing defender, to be
         allowed for each pursuer, defender, or third party brought in after the record is closed,
         each of 88.30

3. *Procedure Roll or Debate Roll*

    (a) Preparing for discussion and all work incidental thereto including instruction of
         counsel 39.80

    (b) Attendance at court — per half hour 16.50

    (c) Advising and work incidental thereto 30.00

4. *Adjustment of issues and counter-issues*

    (a) Fee to solicitor for pursuer to include all work in connection with and incidental to the
         lodging of an issue, and adjustment and approval thereof 38.20

    (b) If one counter-issue, additional fee to solicitor for pursuer 10.60

    (c) If more than one counter-issue, additional fee to solicitor for pursuer for each additional
         counter-issue 4.55

    (d) Fee to solicitor for defender or third party for all work in connection with lodging of
         counter-issue and adjustment and approval thereof 38.20

    (e) Fee to solicitor for defender or third party for considering issue where no counter-issue
         lodged 10.60

    (f) Fee to solicitor for defender or third party for considering each additional counter-
         issue 4.55

5. *Precognitions*

    Taking and drawing precognitions — per sheet 19.40

Note: (i) In addition each solicitor shall be entitled to charge for copies of the precognitions for the use of counsel and himself.

    (ii) Where a skilled witness prepares his own precognition or report the solicitor shall be allowed, for revising and adjusting it, half of the taking and drawing fee per sheet.

6. *Reports obtained under order of court excluding auditor's report*   £

    (a) Fee for all work incidental thereto 42.00

    (b) Additional fee per sheet of report to include all copies required (maximum £42.35) 6.05

7. *Specification of documents*

    (a) Basic fee to cover instructing counsel, revising and lodging and all incidental procedures to obtain a diligence up to and including obtaining interlocutor 39.80

    (b) Fee to opponent's solicitor 19.40

    (c) If commission executed, additional fee — per half hour 16.50

    (d) If alternative procedure adopted, fee per person upon whom order served 15.80

8. *Commission to take evidence on interrogatories*

    (a) Basic fee to solicitor applying for commission to cover all work up to and including lodging report of commission with completed interrogatories and cross interrogatories 80.10

    (b) Basic fee to opposing solicitor if cross-interrogatories lodged 64.40

    (c) Fee to opposing solicitor if no cross-interrogatories lodged 24.00

    (d) Additional fee to solicitor for each party for completed interrogatories or cross-interrogatories, including all copies — per sheet 6.05

9. *Commission to take evidence on open commission*

    (a) Basic fee to solicitor applying for commission up to and including lodging report of commission, but excluding attendance at execution thereof 88.30

    (b) Basic fee to opposing solicitor 39.80

    (c) Attendance at execution of commission — per half hour 16.50

10. *Miscellaneous motions where not otherwise covered by this Schedule*

    (a) Where attendance of counsel and/or solicitor not required 10.60

    (b) Where attendance of counsel and/or solicitor required, inclusive of instruction of counsel — not exceeding half hour 30.00

    (c) Thereafter attendance fee — per additional half hou 16.50

11. *Incidental procedure (not chargeable prior to approval of issue or allowance of proof)*

Fixing diet, obtaining note on the line of evidence, etc, borrowing and returning process, lodging productions, considering opponent's productions, and all other work prior to the consultation on the sufficiency of evidence 112.40

12. *Amendment of record*

    (a) Amendment of conclusions only — fee to solicitor for pursuer 30.00

    (b) Amendment of conclusions only — fee to solicitor for opponent 10.60

    (c) Amendment of pleadings after record closed, where no answers to the amendment are lodged — fee to solicitor for proposer 43.50

          £

    (d) In same circumstances — fee to solicitor for opponent 20.20

    (e) Amendment of pleadings after record closed where answers are lodged — fee for solicitor for each party lodging answers 102.50

    (f) Fee for adjustment of minute and answers, where applicable, to be allowed in addition to solicitor for each party 56.20

13. *Preparation for trial or proof to include fixing consultation on the sufficiency of evidence and attendance thereat, fee-funding precept, adjusting minute of admissions, citing witnesses, all work checking and writing up process, and preparing for trial or proof*

(a) If action settled before trial or proof, or the trial or proof lasts only one day, to include, where applicable, instruction of counsel 272.50

(b) For each day or part of a day after the first, including instruction of counsel 24.00

(c) To cover preparing for adjourned diet and all work incidental as in (a), if diet postponed more than 5 days 49.50

14. *Copying fees —*

Where a document is copied and it is necessary to take a copy of more than 20 sheets (whether 20 of 1 sheet, 5 of 4 sheets or whatever), for each sheet copied a fee of 0.08

Note: a "sheet" shall consist of 250 words or numbers.

15. *Settlement by tender — fees for solicitor for either party*

(a) Basic fee for lodging, or for considering, first tender 59.10

(b) Fee for lodging, or for considering, each further tender 39.80

(c) Additional fee if tender accepted 39.80

16. *Extra-judicial settlement*

Fee inclusive of joint minute (not based on a judicial tender) 102.50

17. *Proof or trial*

Attendance fee — per half hour 16.50

18. *Accounts* — to include framing and lodging account, intimating diet, and attending taxation, uplifting account and noting and intimating taxations 71.80

19. *Ordering and obtaining extract* 15.00

20. *Final procedure*

(a) If case goes to trial or proof, to include all work to close of litigation, so far as not otherwise provided for, including in particular settling with witnesses and procuring and booking verdict, or attendance at judgment 80.10

(b) If case disposed of before trial or proof 24.00

21. *Session fee — to cover communications with client and counsel*

(a) Where no correspondent — 7.5% of total fees (including copying fees) allowed on taxation.

(b) Where correspondent involved — 10% of total fees (including copying fees) allowed on taxation.

PART VI — INNER HOUSE BUSINESS

	£
1. *Reclaiming motions*	
(a) Fee for solicitor for appellant for all work up to interlocutor sending case to roll	59.10
(b) Fee for solicitor for respondent	30.00
(c) Additional fee for solicitor for each party for every 50 pages of appendix	24.70
2. *Appeals from inferior courts*	£
(a) Fee for solicitor for appellant	71.80
(b) Fee for solicitor for respondent	35.20
(c) Additional fee for solicitor for each party for every 50 pages of appendix	24.70

3. *Summar or Short Roll*

(a) Preparing for discussion, instructing counsel, and preparing appendix 59.10

(b) Attendance fee — per half hour 16.50

4. Where applicable the fees set out in Part V of this Schedule may be charged.

5. *Special cases and Inner House petitions*
According to circumstances of the case.

6. Obtaining Bond of Caution 24.00

PART VII — ADMIRALTY AND COMMERCIAL CASES, SEQUESTRATION IN BANKRUPTCY, APPLICATIONS FOR SUMMARY TRIAL UNDER SECTION 26 OF THE COURT OF SESSION ACT 1988 AND CASES REMITTED FROM THE SHERIFF COURT

The fees shall be based on this Schedule or Schedule 3 according to the circumstances.

SCHEDULE 2

Regulation 5

FEES OF SOLICITORS FOR PROCEEDINGS IN THE SHERIFF COURT

1. Subject to the following provisions of this Schedule fees shall be calculated in accordance with the Table of Fees in this Schedule.

2. Chapter III of the Table of Fees in this Schedule shall have effect subject to the following provisions:—

   (a) in paragraph 2 of Part I and paragraph 7 of Part II, no fee is allowable for attendance at a continuation of the first calling, unless specifically authorised by the court;

   (b) in Part I, in relation to actions for reparation there are allowable such additional fees for precognitions and reports as are necessary to permit the framing of the summons;

   (c) in Part II, in respect of paragraph 22 (final procedure),no fee shall be allowed in respect of accounts of expenses when the hearing on the claim for expenses takes place immediately on the sheriff or sheriff principal announcing his decision;

   (d) unless the sheriff, on an incidental application in that behalf, otherwise directs, all fees chargeable under Chapter III shall be reduced by 50% in respect of—

   i(i) undefended actions for recovery of heritable property;

   (ii) actions under the Tenancy of Shops (Scotland) Act 1949(3) or section 3 of the Sheriff Courts (Civil Jurisdiction and Procedure) (Scotland) Act 1963(4).

2A. In Chapter III of the Table of Fees in this Schedule—

"attendance at court" means waiting for and conducting any hearing unless specifically provided for elsewhere in the Chapter;

"half hour" shall be read as if immediately followed by the words "(or part thereof)";

"a page" consists of 125 words or numbers; and

"a sheet" consists of 250 words or numbers.

TABLE

Actions	Percentage Reduction
1. For recovery of possession of heritable property in undefended actions	50%
2. Under the following enactments:-	50%
(i) Tenancy of Shops (Scotland) Act 1949, and	
(ii) Section 3 of the Sheriff Courts (Civil Jurisdiction and Procedure) (Scotland) Act 1963	

Provided that for the purposes of this sub-paragraph "value", in relation to any action in which a counter-claim has been lodged, is the total of the sums craved in the writ and in the counter-claim.

3. In this Schedule "process fee" means the fee set out in paragraph 23 of Chapter II of the Table of Fees in this Schedule.

TABLE OF FEES

NOTE

THE UNDERNOTED FEES APPLY ONLY TO CAUSES COMMENCED ON OR AFTER 1ST JANUARY 1994. THE FEES APPLICABLE TO CAUSES COMMENCED BEFORE 1ST JANUARY 1994 CAN BE FOUND IN THE FEES SUPPLEMENT 1998 AT PAGES 109–116.

CHAPTER I — UNDEFENDED ACTIONS (OTHER THAN ACTIONS TO WHICH CHAPTER III OR IV APPLIES)

Part I — All actions except those actions of divorce or separation and aliment to which Part II applies

£

1. Actions (other than those specified in paragraph 2 of this Part) in which decree is granted without proof —

Inclusive fee to cover all work from taking instructions up to and including obtaining extract decree ... 79.30

In cases where settlement is effected after service of a writ but before the expiry of the period of notice ... 65.90

Note: If the pursuer's solicitor elects to charge this inclusive fee he shall endorse a minute to that effect on the initial writ before ordering extract decree. Outlays such as court dues for deliverance and posts shall be chargeable in addition and taxation shall be unnecessary.

2. Actions of separation and aliment (not being actions to which Part II of this Chapter applies), adherence and aliment or custody and aliment where proof takes place —

Inclusive fee to cover all work from taking instructions up to and including obtaining extract decree ... 280.10

Part II — Actions of divorce or separation and aliment where proof is by means of affidavits

1. In any undefended action of divorce or of separation and aliment where —

    (a) the facts set out in section 1(2)(b) (unreasonable behaviour) of the Divorce (Scotland) Act 1976 are relied upon; and

    (b) the pursuer seeks to prove those facts by means of affidavits,

the pursuer's solicitor may in respect of the work specified in column 1 of Table A in this paragraph charge the inclusive fee specified in respect of that work in column 2 of that Table.

TABLE A

	Column 1 *Work done*	Column 2 *Inclusive fee*
1.	All work to and including the period of notice	£198.60
2.	All work from the period of notice to and including swearing affidavits	£141.90
3.	All work from swearing affidavits to and including sending extract decree	£42.60
4.	All work to and including sending extract decree	£383.20
	Add process fee to item 4	of 10%

2. In any undefended action of divorce or separation and aliment where —

    (a) the facts set out in section 1(2)(a) (adultery), 1(2)(c) (desertion), 1(2)(d) (two years' non-cohabitation and consent) or 1(2)(e) (five years' non-cohabitation) of the Divorce (Scotland) Act 1976 are relied on; and

    (b) the pursuer seeks to prove those facts by means of affidavits,

the pursuer's solicitor may in respect of the work specified in column 1 of Table B in this paragraph charge the inclusive fee specified in respect of that work in column 2 of that Table.

TABLE B

Column 1 Work done	Column 2 Inclusive fee
1. All work to and including the period of notice	£163.20
2. All work from the period of notice to and including swearing affidavits	£78.10
3. All work from swearing affidavits to and including sending extract decree	£42.60
4. All work to and including sending extract decree	£283.80
Add process fee to item 4	of 10%

3. If —

   (a) the pursuer's solicitor charges an inclusive fee under either paragraph 1 or paragraph 2 of this Part; and

   (b) the action to which the charge relates includes a crave relating to an ancillary matter,

in addition to that fee, he may charge in respect of the work specified in column 1 of Table C in this paragraph the inclusive fee specified in respect of that work in column 2 of that Table.

TABLE C

Column 1 Work done	Column 2 Inclusive fee
1. All work to and including the period of notice	£77.30
2. All work from the period of notice to and including swearing affidavits	£45.40
3. All work under items 1 and 2	£122.60
Add process fee to item 3	of 10%

CHAPTER II — DEFENDED ACTIONS (OTHER THAN ACTIONS TO WHICH CHAPTER III OR IV APPLIES)

£

1. *Instruction fee* —

   (a) To cover all work (except as hereinafter otherwise specially provided for in this Chapter) to the lodging of defences including copying 217.30

   (b) Additional fee where separate statement of facts and counterclaim and answers lodged 40.20

2. *Precognitions* — taking and drawing — per sheet 19.00

Note: Where a skilled witness prepares his own precognition or report, the solicitor shall be allowed half of above drawing fee for revising and adjusting it.

3. *Productions* —

   (a) For lodging productions — each inventory 20.60

   (b) For considering opponent's productions — each inventory 10.30

4. *Adjustment fee* — To cover all work (except as otherwise specially provided for in this Chapter) in connection with the adjustment of the Record including making up and lodging certified copy Record —

   (a) Fee to solicitor for any party 99.90

   (b) Fee to each original party's solicitor if action settled before Options Hearing 58.70

   (c) Additional fee to each original party's solicitor if additional defender brought in before Options Hearing 24.70

   (d) Additional fee to each original party's solicitor if additional defender brought in after Options Hearing 31.90

£

5. *Fee for framing affidavits* — per sheet 8.25

6. *Options Hearing* — Fee to include preparation for and conduct of Options Hearing (or First Hearing in defended family actions) and noting interlocutor —

   (a) Where hearing does not exceed one half hour 82.40

   (b) Where hearing exceeds one half hour — for every extra quarter hour 12.40

   (c) For lodging and intimating or for considering note of basis of preliminary plea — for each note lodged 20.60

7. *Additional Procedure* — For all work subsequent to Options Hearing including preparation for and attendance at procedural hearing —

   Where hearing does not exceed one half hour 82.40

   For every extra quarter hour 12.40

8. *Debate (other than on evidence)* —

   (a) Where counsel not employed —

      (i) To include preparation for and all work in connection with any hearing or debate other than on evidence 62.80

      (ii) For conduct of debate — per quarter hour 11.30

   (b) Where counsel employed, fee to solicitor appearing with counsel — per quarter hour . 8.25

9. *Interim Interdict Hearings* —

   (a) Preparation for each hearing — each party 39.10

   (b) Fee to conduct hearing — per quarter hour 11.30

   (c) If counsel employed, fee to attend hearing per quarter hour 8.25

10. *Reports obtained under order of court, excluding auditor's report* —

   (a) Fee for all work incidental thereto 43.30

   (b) Additional fee per sheet of report to include all copies required (maximum £28.25) 5.65

11. *Commissions to take evidence* —

   (a) On interrogatories —

      (i) Fee to solicitor applying for commission to include drawing, intimating and lodging motion, drawing and lodging interrogatories, instructing commissioner and all incidental work (except as otherwise specially provided for in this Chapter) but excluding attendance at execution of commission 119.50

      (ii) Fee to opposing solicitor if cross-interrogatories prepared and lodged 79.30

      (iii) If no cross-interrogatories lodged 23.70

   (b) Open Commissions —

      (i) Fee to solicitor applying for commission to include all work (except as otherwise specially provided in this Chapter) up to lodging report of commission but excluding attendance thereat 79.30

      (ii) Fee to solicitor for opposing party 40.20

      (iii) Fee for attendance at execution of commission — per quarter hour 11.30

      (iv) If counsel employed, fee for attendance of solicitor — per quarter hour 8.25

      (v) Travelling time — per quarter hour 8.25

12. *Specification of documents* —

   (a) Fee to cover drawing, intimating and lodging specification and relative motion —

      (i) Where motion unopposed 41.30

      (ii) Where motion opposed — additional fee per quarter hour 11.30

£

(b) Fee for considering opponent's specification and relative motion —

    (i) Where motion not opposed 23.70

    (ii) Where motion opposed — additional fee per quarter hour 11.30

(c) Fee for citation of havers, preparation for and attendance before commissioner at execution of commission —

    (i) Where attendance before commissioner does not exceed 1 hour 43.30

    (ii) For each additional quarter hour after the first hour 14.00

(d) If optional procedure adopted — fee per person upon whom order is served 10.30

(e) Fee for perusal of documents recovered — per quarter hour 11.30

13. *Amendment of Record* —

(a) (i) Fee to cover drawing, intimating and lodging minute of amendment and relative motion 39.10

    (ii) Fee for perusal of answers 15.50

    (iii) Fee for any court appearance necessary — per quarter hour 11.30

(b) (i) Fee to opposing solicitor — for perusing minute of amendment 31.90

    (ii) Fee for preparation of answers 15.50

    (iii) Fee for any court appearance necessary — per quarter hour 11.30

(c) Fee for adjustment of minute and answers where applicable to be allowed in addition to each party 39.10

14. *Motions and minutes* —

(a) Fee to cover drawing, intimating and lodging any written motion or minute, including a reponing note, and relative attendances at court (except as otherwise provided in for in this Chapter) —

    (i) Where opposed 55.60

    (ii) Where unopposed (including for each party a joint minute other than under paragraph 20(b)) 23.70

(b) Fee to cover considering opponent's written motion, minute or reponing note and relative attendances at court —

    (i) Where motion, minute or reponing note opposed 55.60

    (ii) Where motion, minute or reponing note unopposed 20.60

15. *Hearing Limitation* —

Fee to include work (except as otherwise specially provided for in this Chapter) undertaken with a view to limiting the scope of any hearing, and including the exchange of documents, precognitions and expert reports, agreeing any fact, statement or document not in dispute, preparing and intimating any Notice to Admit or Notice of Non- Admission and preparing and lodging any Joint Minute, not exceeding 195.70

16. *Procedure preliminary to proof* —

(a) Fee to cover all work, preparing for proof (except as otherwise specially provided in this Chapter) —

    (i) If action settled or abandoned not later than 14 days before the diet of proof 127.70

    (ii) In any other case 233.80

(b) Fee to cover preparing for adjourned diet and all incidental work as in (a) if diet postponed for more than 6 days, for each additional diet 51.50

(c) Fee for attendance inspecting opponent's documents — per quarter hour 12.40

17. *Conduct of proof*

(a) Fee to cover conduct of proof and debate on evidence if taken at close of proof — per quarter hour 11.30

(b) If counsel employed, fee to solicitor appearing with counsel — per quarter hour 8.25

18. *Debate on evidence*   £

    (a) Where debate on evidence not taken at conclusion of proof, fee for preparing for debate 39.10

    (b) Fee for conduct of debate — per quarter hour 11.30

    (c) If counsel employed, fee to solicitor appearing with counsel — per quarter hour 8.25

19. *Appeals*

    (a) Omitted by SSI 2015 No 380

    (b) To Court of Session —

        Fee to cover instructions, marking appeal or noting that appeal marked and instructing Edinburgh correspondents 39.10

20. *Settlements*

    (a) Judicial tender —

        (i)   Fee for preparation and lodging or for consideration of minute of tender 43.30

        (ii) Fee on acceptance of tender, to include preparation and lodging or consideration of minute of acceptance and attendance at court when decree granted in terms thereof 35.00

    (b) Extra-judicial settlement —

        Fee to cover negotiations resulting in settlement, framing or revising joint minute and attendance at court when authority interponed thereto 80.30

    (c) Whether or not fees are payable under (a) or (b) above where additional work has been undertaken with a view to effecting settlement, including offering settlement, although settlement is not agreed — not exceeding 80.30

21. *Final procedure*

    (a) Fee to cover settling with witnesses, enquiries for cause at avizandum, noting final interlocutor 59.70

    (b) Fee to cover drawing account of expenses, arranging, intimating and attending diet of taxation and obtaining approval of auditor's report and adjusting account with opponent where necessary, ordering, procuring and examining extract decree or adjusting account with opponent 47.90

    (c) Fee to cover considering opponent's account of expenses and attending diet of taxation or adjusting account with opponent 15.00

22. *Copying fees*

Where a document is copied and it is necessary to take a copy of more than 20 sheets (whether 20 of 1 sheet, 5 of 4 sheets or whatever), for each sheet copied a fee of 0.08

Note: A "sheet" shall consist of 250 words or numbers.

23. *Process fee*

Fee to cover all consultations between solicitor and client during the progress of the cause and all communications, written or oral, passing between them:

10% on total fees (including copying fees) allowed on taxation.

24. *Instruction of counsel*

    (a) Fee for instructing counsel to revise pleadings 24.70

    (b) Fee for instructing counsel to attend court 51.50

    (c) Fee for attending consultation with counsel —

        (i)   Where total time engaged does not exceed one hour 51.50

        (ii) For each additional quarter hour 11.30

Note: In each case to cover all consultations, revisal of papers and all incidental work.

CHAPTER III

Part I —Undefended Actions

1. The fee for citation, service or re-service after the first citation—

    (a) to any destination by post £6.74

    (b) by advertisement £19.01

2. The fee for attendance at court £19.01

3. The fee for all other work £53.50

Part II —Defended Actions

1. The instruction fee—

(a) for the pursuer's solicitor, including taking instructions, framing summons and statement of claim, obtaining warrant for service, enquiring for the form of response and noting defence £81.16

(b) for the defender's solicitor, for all work from taking instructions (including instructions for a counter-claim) up to and including lodging the form of response £81.16

2. Where an additional defender or third party enters the cause, an additional fee for each of the original parties' solicitors for all consequent work... £40.61

3. The fee for citation, service or re-service, except as provided for in paragraph 19(e), by—

(a) post, to a destination—

    (i) within the United Kingdom, Isle of Man, Channel Islands or the Republic of Ireland £6.74

    (ii) other than one specified in paragraph (i) £14.42

(b) sheriff officer, to include instructing sheriff officer, perusing execution of citation and settling sheriff officer's fee £6.74

(c) advertisement, to include framing and instructing the advertisement £21.11

4. In connection with the first hearing of the cause—

(a) the fee for attendance at court, including noting the outcome of the hearing £70.17

(b) if waiting for and conducting the hearing exceeds an hour and a half, the fee for attendance at court for each subsequent half hour £21.11

5. The fee for attendance at court, except as specifically provided for elsewhere in this Chapter, per half hour... £21.11

6. The fee for drawing precognitions, including instructions, attendances with witnesses and all relative meetings and correspondence, per sheet... £31.27

7. The fee for perusing, revising and adjusting a report or precognition prepared by a skilled witness, per sheet £15.64

8. In connection with reports commissioned by order of Court, the fee for—

(a) all incidental work, including instructing the report £21.11

(b) each half hour perusing the report £21.11

9. The fee, per inventory, for—

(a) lodging productions £31.27

(b) perusing the opposition's productions £14.42

10. The fee for framing affidavits, per sheet.. £15.64

11. Except as provided for by paragraphs 17, 18 and 19 the fee for—

(a) drawing, intimating and lodging any written minute or incidental application including any relative attendance at court, where that minute or application is—

    (i) opposed £44.53

    (ii) unopposed £26.74

(b) considering a written minute or incidental application intimated by the opposition including any relative attendance at court, where that minute or application is—

(i)	opposed	£36.63
(ii)	unopposed	£21.11

12. In connection with a hearing to which paragraph 11 applies, if waiting for and conducting that hearing exceeds half an hour, the fee for attendance at court for each subsequent half hour ... £21.11

13. In connection with a proof the fee for all work, except as specifically provided for elsewhere in this Chapter, preparatory to—

(a) the first scheduled proof, if—

    (i) the cause is settled or abandoned 7 or more days before the scheduled proof £73.26

    (ii) paragraph (i) does not apply £87.96

(b) any adjourned proof, if the postponement from the hearing previously scheduled exceeds 6 days and—

    (i) the cause is settled or abandoned 7 or more days before the scheduled proof £36.63

    (ii) paragraph (i) does not apply £43.98

14. The fee for each half hour inspecting the opposition's documents either at court or at a place fixed by the opposition.................. £21.11

15. In connection with a proof or a trial and debate on evidence taken at the close of proof, the fee for each half hour—

(a) conducting that hearing £21.11

(b) waiting in court for that hearing £11.22

16. In connection with a debate on evidence not taken at the close of proof, the fee for—

(a) all preparatory work £49.06

(b) attendance at court, per half hour £21.11

17. In connection with a minute of judicial tender—

(a) the fee for consideration of, preparing and lodging the minute £44.53

(b) on acceptance of the tender, the fee for consideration of, preparing and lodging the minute of acceptance and attendance at court when decree is granted in terms of that minute £31.27

(c) on rejection of the tender, the fee for considering it £31.27

18. The fee for each party where the case is settled extra-judicially, including all relative negotiations, framing or revising the joint minute and attendance at court when authority is interponed thereto.................. £73.26

19. In connection with an incidental application for commission and diligence to recover documents or an order under section 1 of the Administration of Justice (Scotland) Act 1972(6), the fee for—

(a) drawing, intimating and lodging the application and, where relevant, specification and any relative attendance at court, where the application is—

    (i) opposed £48.95

    (ii) unopposed £26.74

(b) considering the application and, where relevant, specification intimated by the opposition and any relative attendance at court, where the application is—

    (i) opposed £36.63

    (ii) unopposed £21.11

(c) each subsequent half hour, where attendance at court exceeds half an hour £21.11

(d) citing havers and preparing for and appearing before the commissioner or sheriff at the execution of the commission, per half hour £21.11

(e) serving an order on each person, if optional procedure is adopted £14.42

(f) each half hour perusing the documents recovered £21.11

20. In connection with an open commission to take evidence, the fee for—

(a) all work, excluding attendance at the commission, by the—

    (i) solicitor applying for the commission £49.06

    (ii) the opposing solicitor £21.11

(b) each half hour attending the execution of the commission £21.11

21. Omitted by SSI 2015 No 380.

22. At the conclusion of the cause, the fee for—

(a) settling with witnesses and noting the final decree £44.53

(b) the successful party to cover drawing the account of expenses, arranging, intimating and attending a diet of taxation and obtaining approval of the auditor's report and, where necessary, ordering, procuring and examining extract decree or adjusting account with opponent £44.53

(c) the unsuccessful party to cover considering the opponent's account of expenses and, where necessary, adjusting the account with opponent or attending a diet of taxation £21.11

CHAPTER IV — EXECUTRY BUSINESS

£

1. *Petition for decree dative*

Inclusive fee for taking instructions to present petition, drawing petition and making necessary copies, lodging and directing publication, attendance at court, moving for decreedative, extracting decree where necessary and all matters incidental to petition 33.70

2. *Restriction of Caution*

Inclusive fee for taking instructions to prepare petition, drawing petition and making necessary copies, lodging, instructing advertisement and all matters incidental to petition ... 33.70

3. Fees for other work shall be chargeable according to Schedule 3.

SCHEDULE 3

Regulation 4

TABLE OF DETAILED FEES CHARGEABLE BY SOLICITORS FOR PROCEEDINGS IN THE COURT OF SESSION AND SHERIFF COURT

£

1. The fee for —

   (a) Any time up to the first half hour spent by a solicitor conducting a proof or hearing ... 28.20

   (b) Each quarter hour (or part thereof) subsequent to the first half hour 14.10

2. The fee for —

   (a) Each quarter hour (or part thereof) spent by a solicitor in carrying out work other than that prescribed in paragraphs 1 and 3 to 6 hereof, provided that any time is additional to the total time charged for under paragraph 1 above 10.90

   (b) Each quarter hour (or part thereof) spent by a solicitor's clerk in carrying out work other than that prescribed in paragraphs 3 to 6 hereof 5.40

3. The fee for —

   Framing affidavits — per sheet (or part thereof) 9.25

4. The fee for —

   (a) Framing and drawing all necessary papers, other than affidavits or papers of a formal character

   (b) Each citation of a party, witness or haver including execution thereof

   (c) Instructing messengers-at-arms and sheriff officers, including examining execution and settling fee

   (d) Agency accepting service of any writ

   (e) Lodging first step of process

   (f) Lengthy telephone calls (of over 4 minutes and up to 10 minutes duration)

(g) Letters including instructions to counsel — per page (or part thereof), subject to paragraph 5(f) below

(h) Perusing any document (other than a letter) consisting of not more than 12 sheets — for the first 2 sheets and each 2 sheets thereafter —

Note: Where the document perused consists of more than 12 sheets the fee for perusing the whole document shall be charged in accordance with paragraph 2 above.

in each of sub-paragraphs (a)-(h) 6.20

5. The fee for —

(a) Attendance at court offices for carrying out formal work including making up process and each necessary lodging in (other than first step), uplifting from or borrowing of process (to include return of same) or enquiry for documents due to be lodged;

(b) Revising papers drawn by counsel, open and closed records etc or where revisal ordered — per 5 sheets (or part thereof);

(c) Framing formal papers such as inventories, title pages and accounts of expenses per sheet (or part thereof);

(d) Certifying or signing a document;

(e) Short telephone calls (of up to 4 minutes duration);

(f) Short letters of a formal nature, intimations, and letters confirming telephone calls — in each of sub-paragraphs (a) to (f) 2.45

5A. The fee for each quarter hour (or part thereof) spent travelling—

(a) by a solicitor 5.45

(b) by a solicitor's clerk 2.70

6. Where a document is copied and it is necessary to take a copy of more than 20 sheets (whether 20 of 1 sheet, 5 of 4 sheets or whatever), for each sheet copied a fee of 0.08

Interpretation

In this Table —

"court" means court or tribunal as the case may be;

a "sheet" shall consist of 250 words or numbers; and

a "page" shall consist of 125 words or numbers.

SCHEDULE 4

Regulation 10

FEES OF COUNSEL FOR PROCEEDINGS IN THE COURT OF SESSION AND SHERIFF COURT

1. Subject to the following provisions of this Schedule, the fees of counsel shall be calculated by the Board, or in the event of dispute by the auditor, in accordance with the fees prescribed in the Tables of Fees set out after paragraph 17 to this Schedule, and the fee of a solicitor-advocate for undertaking an item of work in the Court of Session shall be—

(a) where that person is acting as a junior solicitor-advocate, the same as that allowable to a junior counsel for undertaking an item of work equivalent to that undertaken by the solicitor-advocate; or

(b) where that person is acting as a senior solicitor-advocate, the same as that allowable to a senior counsel for undertaking an item of work equivalent to that undertaken by the solicitor-advocate.

2. Where the Tables of Fees in this Schedule prescribe a range of fees for any item of work the Board, or as the case may be the auditor, shall allow such fee as appears to provide reasonable remuneration for the work, subject to the following—

(a) it shall be for counsel to identify any factors justifying a higher fee than the minimum prescribed;

(b) where a fee relates to the drafting of any document the length of the document shall be a subordinate consideration to the content of the document;

(c) in determining the appropriate fee for drafting a summons, petition, defences, or answers regard shall be had to the volume of documentation that required to be considered, and the novelty or difficulty of the work involved;

(d) in determining the appropriate level of fee for a consultation, regard shall be had to the length of the consultation and any reasonable and proportionate preparation required which has not otherwise been reflected in an additional fee for preparation, or in a fee for a proof or other hearing; and

(e) in determining the appropriate fee for drafting a note, regard shall be had to the issues involved, the importance, novelty or complexity of the applicable law and, as appropriate, the absence of previous authority or the existence of adverse authority.

3. Where the Tables of Fees in this Schedule do not prescribe a fee for any class of proceedings or any item of work, the Board, or as the case may be the auditor, shall allow such fee as appears to be appropriate to provide reasonable remuneration for the work with regard to all the circumstances, including the general levels of fees in the Tables of Fees.

4. Subject to paragraphs 5 to 7, the fees prescribed in the Tables of Fees in this Schedule include all associated preparation work.

5. Subject to paragraph 6, an additional fee for preparation shall only be allowed if it relates to a proof, debate or like hearing and the hearing—

(a) does not proceed (a date or dates having been assigned for the hearing);

(b) does not exceed a day in duration;

(c) does not exceed four days in duration, and the Board is satisfied that the case is abnormal in magnitude, difficulty or any other respect; or

(d) exceeds four days in duration, and the Board is satisfied that the case is abnormal in magnitude, difficulty of any other respect, and also that counsel required to consider an abnormally large quantity of documentation.

6. An additional fee for preparation as provided for in paragraph 5 above shall be allowed only on the following conditions—

(a) the fee is only chargeable in respect of work undertaken following the instruction of counsel for the hearing;

(b) in respect of any hearing, except on cause shown, such a fee is allowable only once to junior or senior counsel, or as the case may be junior and senior counsel, notwithstanding that the applicant or assisted person is represented by more than one junior or senior counsel during the course of the proceedings;

(c) the Board, or as the case may be the auditor, must be satisfied that the time engaged in preparation was reasonable and proportionate in all the circumstances of the case; and

(d) counsel shall provide the Board with a detailed summary of the work undertaken and the documentation perused at each stage of the process and shall, if required by the Board, provide details of authorities referred to, the time engaged, dates and locations as to when and where the work was undertaken, and any contemporaneous records or notes made in the course of preparation.

7. The additional fee for preparation shall be calculated by dividing the time allowed, as determined in accordance with paragraphs 5 and 6, into units of 8 hours, each unit being payable at the rate of two thirds of the daily rate applicable to that hearing as prescribed in the Tables of Fees.

8. The fees prescribed in the Tables of Fees for drafting any summons, petition, other initiating document, defences or answers include any work involved in revising such a document.

9. Paragraphs 10 and 11 apply where, in respect of any hearing, counsel claims a fee for keeping free from other commitments ("a commitment fee"), and regulation 9 shall apply subject to those paragraphs.

10. A commitment fee is allowable only where—

(a) counsel has accepted instructions to appear at a proof, debate or similar hearing assigned for 8 days or more over consecutive weeks;

(b) the proceedings settle on or before the first day of the hearing;

(c) counsel is notified that the hearing is not proceeding no more than two working days before the start of the hearing; and

(d) in the case of a hearing assigned for fewer than 12 days, counsel is not otherwise entitled to a fee for attendance at the first day of the hearing.

11. Where a commitment fee is allowable the fee is payable at a unit rate equal to the daily rate applicable to the hearing to which it relates, as prescribed in the Tables of Fees, and—

(a) 2 units shall be payable in the case of a hearing assigned for 12 days or more where counsel is not otherwise entitled to a fee for attendance at the first day of the hearing; and

(b) 1 unit shall be payable in any other case.

12. In the calculation of counsel's fees—

(a) counsel's fees are allowable only where the Board has approved the employment of counsel or where the approval of the Board is not required;

(b) junior counsel shall only be allowed the fees prescribed in Part 1 of the applicable Table of Fees even where sanction has been granted for the employment of senior counsel;

(c) except on cause shown, fees to counsel shall be allowed for no more than two consultations in the course of proceedings;

(d) notwithstanding that sanction may have been granted for the employment of senior counsel, or for the employment of a second junior counsel, fees shall not be payable for the attendance of two counsel at a hearing which by its nature does not require the attendance of a second counsel, or for the attendance of senior counsel at a hearing that by its nature does not require the attendance of senior counsel; and

(e) correspondence, telephone calls and meetings between counsel acting for the same assisted person are not allowable as separate items and shall be subsumed within the fees prescribed for the associated item of work in the Tables of Fees.

13. In the calculation of counsel's fees for proceedings in the sheriff court or the Sheriff Appeal Court—

(a) no fee shall be allowed to counsel for drafting defences in skeleton form;

(b) except on cause shown, no fee shall be allowed to counsel for drafting or revising a motion or for attendance at the calling of a motion; and

(c) except on cause shown, no fee shall be allowed to counsel for attendance at hearings which are routine, or procedural in nature, or unopposed.

14. The fee for time engaged in necessary travel specified in paragraph 13 of Chapter 6 of Part 1 and paragraph 7 of Part 2 of Table of Fees A and in paragraph 10 of Part 1 and paragraph 7 of Part 2 of Table of Fees B is chargeable only as follows—

(a) the travel undertaken must involve a round trip exceeding 60 miles in each direction;

(b) counsel shall, if required, produce vouching of the travel undertaken; and

(c) the fee is chargeable only once in respect of each round trip, irrespective of the number of cases for which the travel is undertaken.

15.—(1) Travel costs are chargeable as an outlay only in circumstances where a fee for time engaged in necessary travel is chargeable under paragraph 14.

(2) Counsel shall if required provide vouching of the costs incurred.

16.—(1) The cost of necessary accommodation and subsistence is chargeable as an outlay up to the level specified in paragraph 14 of Chapter 6 of Part 1 and paragraph 8 of Part 2 of Table of Fees A and in paragraph 11 of Part 1 and paragraph 8 of Part 2 of Table of Fees B only in circumstances where a fee for time engaged in necessary travel is chargeable under paragraph 14, and on cause shown.

(2) Counsel shall if required provide vouching of the costs incurred.

17. In any taxation of counsel's fees in terms of regulation 12, the auditor shall have regard to information not previously made available to the Board only if the information was not available to be provided to the Board at the time it made the offer to counsel which is the subject of taxation, or on cause shown.

TABLE OF FEES A
FEES OF COUNSEL FOR PROCEEDINGS IN THE COURT OF SESSION SHERIFF APPEAL COURT AND SHERIFF COURT

PART I — JUNIOR COUNSEL

CHAPTER I — FAMILY ACTIONS

	£
1. *Summons or other initiating writ*	300.00
2. *Minute*	£
(a) minute relating to orders for parental responsibilities or parental rights and/or aliment or financial provision	200.00

    (b)   any other minute containing a conclusion or crave 150.00

3. *Defences or answers*   £

    (a)   Defences or answers in purely skeleton form to preserve the rights of parties 50.00

    (b)   Defences or answers to which sub-paragraph (a) does not apply 275.00

4. *Joint minute or minute of agreement regulating aliment, financial provision, orders relating to parental responsibilities or parental rights or any other matter in respect of which orders may be sought*

    (a)   straightforward cases 50.00

    (b)   other cases 125.00

    (c)   minute of agreement 200.00

5. *Minute for decree* 50.00

6. *All other work*

    The fees prescribed in Chapter 6 shall apply

CHAPTER 2 — PETITIONS (OTHER THAN PETITIONS TO WHICH CHAPTERS 3 TO 5 APPLY)

1. *Petition*

    (a)   petition for interdict

        (i)   straightforward cases 200.00

        (ii)   other cases... 300.00

    (b)   other Outer House petitions 300.00

    (c)   the fee for Inner House petitions shall be as appears to the Board, or as the case may be the auditor, to provide reasonable remuneration for the work having regard to the level of fees in this Table of Fees

2. *Answers*

    (a)   petition for interdict 150.00

    (b)   other Outer House petitions 150.00

    (c)   the fee for Inner House petitions shall be as appears to the Board, or as the case may be the auditor, to provide reasonable remuneration for the work having regard to the level of fees in this Table of Fees

3. *All other work*

    The fees prescribed in Chapter 6 shall apply

CHAPTER 3 — PETITIONS FOR JUDICIAL REVIEW

1. *Petition for judicial review* 350.00

2. *Oral hearing at permission stage or procedural hearing*

    (a)   where the hearing does not exceed 30 minutes 60.00

    (b)   where the hearing exceeds 30 minutes, for each subsequent half hour or part thereof 50.00

3. *Substantive hearing (per day)*

    (a)   junior alone 900.00

    (b)   junior with senior.. 650.00

4. *Written statement of arguments* 200.00

5. *All other work*

    The fees prescribed in Chapter 6 shall apply

CHAPTER 4 – PETITIONS ON CHILD ABDUCTION AND ON THE RECOGNITION AND ENFORCEMENT OF DECISIONS RELATING TO CHILDREN

		£
1.	*Petition*	325.00
2.	*Answers*	325.00

3. *Motion for interim orders*

(a)	where the hearing does not exceed 30 minutes	60.00
(b)	where the hearing exceeds 30 minutes, for each subsequent half hour or part thereof....	50.00

4. *First or second hearing (per day)*

(a)	junior alone	900.00
(b)	junior with senior	650.00

5.	*Revising any affidavit which requires to be lodged*	50.00

6. *All other work*

The fees prescribed in Chapter 1, which failing Chapter 6 shall apply

CHAPTER 5 — APPLICATIONS FOR ADOPTION ORDERS, CONVENTION ADOPTION ORDERS AND PERMANENCE ORDERS AND OTHER PROCEEDINGS UNDER THE ADOPTION AND CHILDREN (SCOTLAND) ACT 2007(1)

1.	*Petition*	300.00
2.	*Revising any affidavit which requires to be lodged*	50.00
3.	*Note for revocation of permanence order or other note in the adoption process*	200.00
4.	*Hearing to set timetable or determine procedure (per half hour)*	50.00

5. *All other work*

The fees prescribed in Chapter 1, which failing Chapter 6 shall apply

CHAPTER 6 – ORDINARY ACTIONS

1.	*Summons*	300.00

2. *Defences*

(a)	where in purely skeleton form to preserve rights of parties	50.00
(b)	otherwise	275.00

3. *Adjustment of pleadings*

(a)	adjustment of skeleton defences	225.00
(b)	otherwise (each occasion)	75.00

4. *Specification of documents*

(a)	specification with standard calls only	50.00
(b)	other specification of documents	125.00

5. *Minutes etc*

(a)	formal amendments or answers	75.00
(b)	amendments or answers other than formal	150.00
(c)	drafting, revising and signing tender or acceptance	50.00
(d)	note of exceptions	50.00
(e)	abandonment, sist, restriction, etc.	50.00
(f)	issue or counter issue	75.00

6. *Notes* £

    (a) note on liability and/or quantum 150.00–
        350.00

    (b) note advising on tender or extra-judicial offer, where not merely confirming advice at
        consultation 125.00

    (c) note on line of evidence 200.00–
        400.00

    (d) other types of note 150.00

7. *Consultations*

    (a) before proof or trial, or otherwise involving a significant degree of preparation or
        lengthy discussion—

        (i) junior alone 250.00–
            400.00

        (ii) junior with senior 200.00–
            300.00

    (b) other consultations—

        (i) junior alone 125.00–
            250.00

        (ii) junior with senior 100.00
            200.00

8. *Pre-trial meetings*

Pre-trial meeting with opponent with a view to settlement of the case (to include preparation
of minute of pre-trial meeting and any associated joint minute)

        (i) junior alone 450.00

        (ii) junior with senior 350.00

9. *Motions (including By Order hearings)*

    (a) where the hearing does not exceed 30 minutes 60.00

    (b) where the hearing exceeds 30 minutes, for each subsequent half hour or part thereof.... 50.00

9A. *Any other hearing where no other fee is specified*

    (a) where the hearing does not exceed 30 minutes £60.00

    (b) where the hearing exceeds 30 minutes, for each subsequent half hour or part thereof.... £50.00

10. *Procedure roll, proof or jury trial (per day)*

    (a) junior alone 900.00

    (b) junior with senior 650.00

11. *Inner House*

    (a) Single Bills

        (i) where the hearing does not exceed 30 minutes 75.00

        (ii) where the hearing exceeds 30 minutes, for each subsequent half hour or part
            thereof 50.00

    (b) reclaiming motion (per day)

        (i) junior opening or appearing alone 1,000.00

        (ii) junior otherwise 700.00

    (c) motion for new trial (per day)

        (i) junior opening or appearing alone 750.00

        (ii) junior otherwise 500.00

12. *Attendance at judgment*

    (a) Outer House 50.00

    (b) Inner House 50.00

13. *Time engaged in necessary travel*   £

Supplementary fee chargeable in addition to any of the above fees where necessary travel is
undertaken 100.00

14. *Accommodation and associated subsistence*

Payment of necessary accommodation and associated subsistence per day 100.00

PART 2 – SENIOR COUNSEL FAMILY ACTIONS, PETITIONS (INCLUDING JUDICIAL REVIEW, ABDUCTION
AND ADOPTION) AND ORDINARY ACTIONS

1. *Drafting or revisal of pleadings*   £

   (a)   drafting of summons, defences, petition or answers 425.00–
500.00

   (b)   revisal of summons, defences, petition or answers 150.00

   (c)   adjustment fee (open record) (each occasion) 125.00

2. *Minutes, etc – revisal fees*

   (a)   amendments (other than formal) or answers 200.00

   (b)   admissions, tender or acceptance (in appropriate cases) 75.00

   (c)   note of exceptions 100.00

3. *Notes*

   (a)   note on liability and/or quantum 225.00–
550.00

   (b)   advice on tender or extra-judicial offer when not merely confirming advice at
consultation 200.00

   (c)   note on line of evidence 300.00–
600.00

   (d)   other notes 225.00

4. *Consultations*

before proof or trial, or otherwise involving a significant degree of preparation or lengthy
discussion with senior alone or with senior and junior 300.00–
550.00

5. *Pre-trial meetings*

Pre-trial meetings with opponent with a view to settlement of case (to include preparation of
minute of pre-trial meeting and any associated joint minute) 650.00

6. *Day in court*

   (a)   Inner House 1,500.00

   (b)   Outer House 1,350.00

7. *Time engaged in necessary travel*

Supplementary fee chargeable in addition to any of the above fees where necessary travel is
undertaken 100.00

8. *Accommodation and associated subsistence*

Payment of necessary accommodation and associated subsistence per day 100.00

TABLE OF FEES B
FEES OF COUNSEL FOR PROCEEDINGS IN THE SHERIFF COURT AND THE SHERIFF
APPEAL COURT

PART I — JUNIOR COUNSEL

                                                         £

1. *Initial writ (or minute in family action)* 275.00

2. *Defences (or answers to minute in family action)* 225.00

3. *Adjustment of pleadings*   £

    Adjustment fee (each occasion) 67.50

4. *Specification of documents*

    (a) straightforward cases 45.00

    (b) other cases 110.00

5. *Minutes, etc.*

    (a) formal amendments or answers 45.00

    (b) amendments or answers other than formal 115.00

    (c) drafting, revising and signing tender or acceptance 45.00

    (d) note of exceptions 40.00

    (e) abandonment, sist, restriction, etc. 40.00

6. *Notes*

    (a) note on liability and/or quantum 135.00–
                                                                      315.00

    (b) note advising on tender or extra-judicial offer, where not merely confirming advice at
        consultation 110.00

    (c) note on line of evidence 180.00–
                                                                      360.00

    (d) other notes 135.00

7. *Applications for adoption orders and permanence orders and other proceedings under the Adoption and Children (Scotland) Act 2007*

    (a) petition 275.00

    (b) minute for revocation of permanence order or other minute in the adoption process 225.00

    (c) revising each affidavit 45.00

    (d) hearing to set timetable or determine procedure 45.00

8. *Applications under section 85(1) of the Children (Scotland) Act 1995(2)*

    Written application under section 85(1) for a review of establishment of grounds of referral   225.00

9. *Motions*

    Attendance at opposed motion for up to half hour, and for each subsequent half hour or part
    thereof 45.00

10. *Time engaged in necessary travel*

    Supplementary fee chargeable where necessary travel undertaken 100.00

11. *Accommodation and associated subsistence*

    Payment of necessary accommodation and associated subsistence per day 100.00

	Junior with senior	Junior alone
12. *Consultations (including joint consultations with opponent with a view to negotiating settlement)*	£	£
Before proof, or otherwise involving a significant degree of preparation or lengthy discussion	180.00–270.00	225.00–360.00
13. *Child welfare hearing*		
Attendance up to half hour, and for each subsequent half hour or part thereof	£40.00	£55.00
14. *Hearings under Part II of Chapter 3 of the Children (Scotland) Act 1995*		
(a) under section 55 to defend an application for a child assessment order	£40.00	£55.00
(b) under section 60(7) for an application to set aside or vary a child protection order	£40.00	£55.00
(c) under section 67 to defend a warrant for further detention of a child	£40.00	£55.00

15. *Proof, debate (or like hearing) or appeal under section 51(1) of the Children (Scotland) Act 1995 (per day)*

		£	£
(a)	up to 20 days	£625.00	£810.00
(b)	subsequent days	£562.50	£729.00

16. *Appeal to the Sheriff Appeal Court(per day)* £650.00 £850.00

17. *Any other hearing where no other fee is specified*

Attendance for up to half hour, and for each subsequent half hour or part thereof £55.00

PART 2 — SENIOR COUNSEL

£

1. *Revisal of pleadings*
   - (a) revisal of initial writ, defences, petition or answers 135.00
   - (b) adjustment fee (open record) (each occasion) 112.50

2. *Other revisal fees*
   - (a) amendments (other than formal) or answers 180.00
   - (b) admissions, tender or acceptance (in appropriate cases) 67.50

3. *Notes*
   - (a) note on liability and/or quantum 202.50–500.00
   - (b) advice on tender or extra-judicial offer where not merely confirming advice at consultation 270.00
   - (c) note on line of evidence 270.00–540.00
   - (d) other notes 202.50

4. *Consultations (including joint consultations with opponent with a view to negotiating settlement)*

   Before proof, or otherwise involving a significant degree of preparation or lengthy discussion 270.00–500.00

5. *Proof, debate (or like hearing) or appeal under section 51(1) of the Children (Scotland) Act 1995 (per day)* ....
   - (a) up to 20 days 1,215.00
   - (b) subsequent days 1,093.50

6. *Appeal to Sheriff Appeal Court (per day)* 1,300.00

7. *Time engaged in necessary travel*

   Supplementary fee chargeable in addition to any of the above fees where necessary travel is undertaken 100.00

8. *Accommodation and associated subsistence* ....

   Payment of necessary accommodation and associated subsistence per day 100.00

SCHEDULE 5

Regulations 5 and 6

TABLE OF DETAILED FEES CHARGEABLE BY SOLICITORS FOR PROCEEDINGS IN THE COURT OF SESSION AND THE SHERIFF APPEAL COURT, PROCEEDINGS LISTED AT REGULATION 5(3) AND PROCEEDINGS IN THE SHERIFF COURT LISTED IN SCHEDULE 7

1. The fee for –   £
   - (a) Any time to the first half hour spent by a solicitor conducting a proof or hearing 37.58
   - (b) Each quarter hour (or part thereof) subsequent to the first half hour 18.79

2. The fee for –
   - (a) Each quarter hour (or part thereof) spent by a solicitor in carrying out work other than that prescribed in paragraphs 1 and 3 to 6 hereof, provided that any time is additional to the total time charged for under paragraph 1 above 14.53

£

(b)   Each quarter hour (or part thereof) spent by a solicitor's clerk in carrying out work other than that prescribed in paragraphs 3 to 6 hereof 7.18

3.   The fee for –

Framing affidavits – per sheet (or part thereof) 12.32

4.   The fee for –

(a)   Framing and drawing all necessary papers, other than affidavits or papers of a formal character

(b)   Each citation of a party, witness or haver including execution thereof

(c)   Instructing messengers-at-arms and sheriff officers, including examining execution and settling fee

(d)   Agency accepting service of any writ

(e)   Lodging first step of process

(f)   Lengthy telephone calls (of over 4 minutes and up to 10 minutes duration)

(g)   Letters, including instructions to counsel – per page (or part thereof), subject to paragraph 5(f) below

(h)   Perusing any document (other than a letter) consisting of not more than 12 sheets – for the first 2 sheets and each 2 sheets thereafter-

Note: Where the document perused consists of more than 12 sheets the fee for perusing the whole document shall be charged in accordance with paragraph 2 above

in each of sub paragraphs (a)–(h) 8.29

5.   The fee for –

(a)   Attendance at court offices for carrying out formal work including making up process and each necessary lodging in (other than first step) uplifting from or borrowing of process (to include return of same) or enquiry for documents due to be lodged

(b)   Revising papers drawn by counsel, open and closed records etc. or where revisal ordered – per 5 sheets (or part thereof)

(c)   Framing formal papers such as inventories, title pages and accounts of expenses per sheet (or part thereof)

(d)   Certifying or signing a document

(e)   Short telephone calls (of up to 4 minutes duration)

(f)   Short letters of a formal nature, intimations, and letters confirming telephone calls

in each of sub paragraphs (a) to (f) 3.26

5A. The fee for each quarter hour (or part thereof) spent travelling—

(a)   by a solicitor...   7.27

(b)   by a solicitor's clerk...   3.59

6.   (a)   There is no fee for photocopying—

       (i)   where fewer than 20 sheets are copied at any one time;

       (ii)   in relation to the first 20 sheets copied at any one time.

(b)   Subject to sub-paragraph (a), the fee for all photocopying in relation to proceedings is—

       (i)   for each sheet copied for up to 10,000 sheets 0.05

       (ii)   for each sheet copied in addition to the first 10,000 sheets 0.01

Interpretation

In this Table –

     'court' means court or tribunal as the case may be;

     a 'sheet' shall consist of 250 words or numbers; and

     a 'page' shall consist of 125 words or numbers

SCHEDULE 6

Regulations 5 and 6

TABLE OF FEES CHARGEABLE BY SOLICITORS FOR PROCEEDINGS IN THE SHERIFF COURT (EXCEPT SUMMARY CAUSE AND EXECUTRY PROCEEDINGS AND THE PROCEEDINGS LISTED IN SCHEDULE 7) AND IN THE SHERIFF APPEAL COURT

CHAPTER I

SHERIFF COURT CIVIL FEES (UNDEFENDED)

Notes on the operation of Chapter I

Payment of the fees set out in the table in this chapter is subject to the following provisions.

1. A fee is payable under paragraph 2 of Part I where it can be demonstrated that following the grant of legal aid significant work was undertaken by the solicitor by way of negotiation with the opponent and/or the opponent's solicitor. Where this fee is claimed the work done must be clearly documented on the file, for perusal, if required, by the Board.

2. The factors that the Board or, as the case may be, the Auditor shall take into account in assessing a claim based on any of the paragraphs within Part I are a lengthy meeting or series of meetings or correspondence or other communication between the parties which, together, justify the conclusion that, but for this significant work, the case would have proceeded further at potential cost to the Fund or the parties.

3. The fee provided in paragraph 2 of Tables A to C includes all the costs incurred in the swearing of affidavits, including defender's affidavits where appropriate.

4. A fee is payable under either Table A or Table B. The fee under Table C relating to matters ancillary to those in Tables A and B is payable only once.

5. The fees payable under this chapter include all travel to court, except as otherwise provided for by paragraph 6.

6. In addition to the fees payable under Part II of this chapter, travel time is payable at £7.27 per 15 minutes and is allowable only in relation to an attendance at court, subject to the following conditions:–

(a)   the solicitor claiming travel time is a solicitor with whom the client has had significant contact in relation to the conduct of the case;

(b)   the solicitor's attendance is necessary for the advancement of the case;

(c)   the distance travelled is at least 10 miles in each direction from the solicitor's normal place of work;

(d)   when payment for travel time is claimed for more than one case, the time shall be apportioned equally among the various cases for which the solicitor attended court (including non legally aided cases).

7. Travel expenses may be incurred only where travel time is chargeable.

8. Where it would be more cost effective to travel by public transport the solicitor shall do so.

Work Done	Inclusive Fee in Units
PART I – NEGOTIATION	
1. Cases where settlement is effected without an action being raised where through negotiation, discussion, voluntary disclosure, meetings, correspondence and, as the case may be, other forms of participation by the solicitor a negotiated settlement is reached and minute of agreement or separation agreement, as the case may be, is entered into (subject to a maximum charge of 19); or	10–19
2. Cases where settlement is not effected but where without an action being raised the outcome or disposal is effected through negotiation, discussion, voluntary disclosure, meetings, correspondence and, as the case may be, other forms of participation by the solicitor (subject to a maximum charge of 10).	5–10

PART II – ALL ACTIONS EXCEPT THOSE ACTIONS OF DIVORCE OR SEPARATION AND
ALIMENT TO WHICH PART III APPLIES

	Inclusive fee in Units
1. Actions (other than those specified in paragraph 2 of this Part) in which decree is granted without proof–	10–19
Inclusive fee to cover all work from taking instructions up to and including obtaining extract decree.	10
Note: In cases where settlement is effected after service of a writ but before the expiry of the period of notice.	5

Additional fee to cover–

(a) drawing, intimating and lodging any written motion for or minute (including any Motion for an interim Order) or diligence, including the first quarter hour of argument, even if involving appearances on different dates (to include instructing service and implementation);	6
(b) thereafter, waiting for or attending by solicitor at the conduct of any hearing not otherwise prescribed (including any continued hearing and ancillary hearing on expenses or other miscellaneous subsequent hearing) per quarter hour.	1
To framing all necessary affidavits per sheet (to include notarial fee unless on cause shown the affidavit cannot be notarised within the principal agent's firm, in which case a fee to the external notary is 1 unit).	1

Note: Charges levied by notaries outwith the United Kingdom shall be payable according to the circumstances of the case; and

affidavits in this Part do not include those required to prove a divorce.

Report Fee – to instructing (if required) perusing and taking instructions on any report extending to at least four sheets obtained from a professional or expert person, either–

(i) where the report is commissioned by the solicitor for the assisted person; or

(ii) where the report is commissioned by order of Court.

Attendance at Hearing – Paragraph 19 of the Notes on the operation of Chapter II in relation to the calculation of time shall apply in relation to attendance of a hearing under Part II of Chapter I.

2. Actions of separation and aliment (not being actions to which Part III of this chapter applies) or residence and aliment where proof takes place– inclusive fee to cover all work from taking instructions up to and including obtaining extract decree.	20

PART III – ACTIONS OF DIVORCE OR SEPARATION AND ALIMENT WHERE PROOF
IS BY MEANS OF AFFIDAVITS

1. In any undefended action of divorce or separation and aliment where–

(a) the facts set out in section 1(2)(b) (unreasonable behaviour) of the Divorce (Scotland) Act 1976(a) are relied upon; and

(b) the pursuer seeks to prove those facts by means of affidavits,

the pursuer's solicitor may in respect of the work specified in column 1 of Table A in this paragraph charge the inclusive fee specified in respect of that work in column 2 of that Table.

TABLE A

Column 1	Column 2 Inclusive fee in Units
1. All work to and including the period of notice.	16
2. All work from the period of notice to and including swearing affidavits.	13
3. All work from swearing affidavits to and including sending extract decree.	3
4. All work to and including sending extract decree.	32

(a) 1976 *c.*39.

2. In any undefended action of divorce or separation and aliment where–
   (a) the facts set out in section 1(2) (adultery), 1(2)(d) (one year's non-cohabitation and consent) or 1(2)(e) (two years' non-cohabitation) of the Divorce (Scotland) Act 1976(b) are relied on; and
   (b) the pursuer seeks to prove those facts by means of affidavits,

the pursuer's solicitor may, in respect of the work specified in column 1 of Table B in this paragraph, charge the inclusive fee specified in respect of that work in column

TABLE B

Column 1	Column 2
	Inclusive fee in Units
1. All work to and including the period of notice.	13
2. All work from the period of notice to and including swearing affidavits.	8
3. All work from swearing affidavits to and including sending extract decree.	3
4. All work to and including sending extract decree.	24

3. If–
   (a) the pursuer's solicitor charges an inclusive fee under paragraph 1 or 2 of this Part; and
   (b) the action to which the fee relates includes a crave relating to an ancillary matter,

in addition to that fee, he may charge in respect of the work specified in column 1 of Table C in this paragraph the inclusive fee specified in respect of that work in column 2 of that Table.

TABLE C

Column 1	Column 2
	Inclusive fee in Units
1. All work to and including the period of notice.	6
2. All work from the period of notice to and including swearing affidavits.	3.5
3. All work under items 1 and 2.	9.5

CHAPTER II
SHERIFF COURT CIVIL FEES (DEFENDED)

Notes on the operation of chapter II

Payment of the fees set out in the table in this chapter is subject to the following provisions.

1. In assessing any account lodged with the Board on a solicitor and client, third party paying basis, regard shall be had to-
   (a) what would be considered reasonable in a judicial taxation, on a party and party basis, for conducting the proceedings in a proper manner; and
   (b) any work or expense specifically sanctioned, certified or authorised by the Board.

2. It shall be competent for the Auditor to disallow any fee which he shall judge irregular or unnecessary.

3. In the taxation of accounts where counsel is employed-
   (a) counsel's fees are allowed only where the Board has sanctioned the employment of counsel;
   (b) except on cause shown, fees to counsel for only two consultations in the course of the cause are allowed; and
   (c) except on cause shown, fees to counsel shall not be payable for attendance at hearings which are routine or procedural or which do not advance the cause.

(**b**) Section 1(2)(d) and (e) was amended by the Family Law (Scotland) Act 2006 (asp 2), section 11.

4. A fee in respect of a Minute of Amendment is only payable to the solicitor bringing the amendment where—

    (a) the Minute was necessary due to a new development in the case;

    (b) relevant information which was previously unknown to the solicitor came to the solicitor's attention; or

    (c) the work could not have been done at an earlier stage in the proceedings.

5. The fees set out in this chapter include-

    (a) all correspondence, telephone calls or communication of whatever nature with the Board;

    (b) all fees incurred by any other solicitor in relation to work done in any part of the case, which shall not be a chargeable outlay; and

    (c) copyings,

and include not only the work expressly set out within the terms of each paragraph but also (unless specifically provided for) all meetings, correspondence, precognitions, negotiation ancillary thereto, and all posts and incidental expenses.

6. The fee under paragraph 1(d) is payable on each transfer of agency but is not payable where an advice and assistance account in respect of the same matter is charged to the Board or the client. Where there is a transfer of agency, the solicitor from whom agency is transferred shall be paid the whole fee for work done by that solicitor in respect of any paragraph or sub-paragraph; and where work done under any paragraph or sub-paragraph is only partially completed by that solicitor, the fee payable in respect of that work shall be apportioned equally between the solicitor from whom agency is transferred and the solicitor to whom agency is transferred.

7. A fee is payable under paragraph 2(a)(i), (ii) or (iii); more than one fee cannot be claimed. The fee under paragraph 2(a)(ii) is only payable where it is unlikely that the action would have settled without the input of the solicitor and the solicitor certifies that settlement took place in consequence of one or both of the following circumstances:—

    (a) settlement was expressed within an extraneous Minute of Agreement or a Joint Minute (other than a Joint Minute for dismissal or decree simpliciter) encompassing an outcome materially different from the terms of any interim order of court in force immediately prior to the execution of that Joint Minute or Minute of Agreement;

    (b) settlement followed upon an exercise of sustained negotiation involving a significant level of discussion between solicitor, the client or the opponent (or their agent) taking place after the conclusion of the work payable under paragraph 1 and clearly documented on the file for perusal, if required, by the Board.

7A. The fee under paragraph 2(a)(iii) is payable only where–

    (a) no settlement is achieved but an outcome or disposal is reached and the solicitor can demonstrate that an exercise of sustained negotiation involving a significant level of discussion between the solicitor, the client and, as the case may be, the opponent (or the opponent's agent) took place;

    (b) the Board is satisfied that all the additional work carried out by the solicitor was reasonable and necessary in all the circumstances of the case; and

    (c) the work is clearly documented on the file and may be persued by the Board as required.

8. The factors that the Board or, as the case may be, the Auditor shall take into account in assessing a claim based on paragraph 2(a)(ii) or (iii) will be a lengthy meeting or series of meetings or correspondence or other communication between the parties which, together, justify the conclusion that, but for this significant work, the case would have proceeded further at potential cost to the Fund or the parties.

9. The fee under paragraph 3(a) is payable only in relation to time engaged in the conduct of the hearing and any continued hearing including a hearing under Rule 18.3 of the Ordinary Cause Rules in Schedule 1 to the Sheriff Courts (Scotland) Act 1907. The conduct of the hearing is the actual time involved in the substantive argument and does not include any formal attendance at a hearing for the purpose of seeking an adjournment or other formal attendance not devoted to the stating of the argument

10. The fee payable under paragraph 3(a)(i) includes the first quarter hour of argument, even if involving appearances on different dates. The fee is not chargeable on a quarter hour block but rather on the total number of minutes taken up in argument at a hearing or continued hearings.

11. The fee payable under paragraph 4(a) includes the notarial fee unless, on cause shown, the affidavit cannot be notarised within the principal agent's firm, in which case a fee of one unit is payable to the external notary. Charges levied by notaries outwith the United Kingdom shall be paid according to the circumstances of the case.

12. The fees under paragraph 4(b), (c), (d) and (e) are payable only once in any case.

13. The fee under paragraph 4(e) is payable only where the settlement conference or negotiation takes place in one location or by telephone. This fee is payable in relation to one meeting (including a continued meeting) in relation to any case and is payable only where

    (a) negotiation commences at least 14 days prior to the proof; and

    (b) the fee under paragraph 4(f) is not charged in the case, and where this fee is claimed the work done should be clearly documented on the file, for perusal, if required, by the Board.

14. The fee under paragraph 4(f) is payable only where no other attendance fee is charged in relation to any appearance at which authority is interponed to the Joint Minute and is not payable in addition to any fee under paragraph 5(a)(ii) to (iii).

14A. The fee under paragraph 4(k) in contentious contact dispute cases is payable only where the additional work is necessary as a result of a material issue and not due to ones party's refusal to resolve any contact issue.

14B. The fee under paragraph 4(k) is payable in respect of each of the circumstances specified in that sub-paragraph.

15. The fee under paragraph 5(a) is only payable once in any case and the fee under paragraph 5(a)(iii) includes preparation for a debate on evidence.

16. The fee under paragraph 5(b) is payable only in respect of a debate in law.

17. Omitted by SSI 2007/14.

18. Notwithstanding paragraph 5(e), the taking of an appeal to the Sheriff Appeal Court is a distinct proceeding and shall require a separate application for civil legal aid and nothing in this table shall imply otherwise.

19. The fee under paragraph 6 is payable on the total time engaged per day and is payable cumulatively between waiting and conduct time, rounded up too the nearest 15 minutes. The fee is payable-

    (a) from the time appointed by the court for the hearing; or

    (b) from the conclusion of any other business (including non legal aid cases) ending prior to the hearing,

whichever is the shorter.

20. The fees payable under this chapter include all travel to court, except as otherwise provided for by paragraph 21.

21. In addition to the fees payable under this chapter, travel time, is payable at £7.27 per 15 minutes and is allowable only in relation to an attendance at court, subject to the following conditions:-

    (a) the solicitor claiming travel time is a solicitor with whom the client has had significant contact in relation to the conduct of the case;

    (b) the solicitor's attendance is necessary for the advancement of the case;

    (c) the distance travelled is at least 10 miles in each direction from the solicitor's normal place of work;

    (d) when payment for travel time is claimed for more than one case, the time shall be apportioned equally among the various cases for which the solicitor attended court (including non legally aided cases).

22. Travel expenses may only be incurred where travel time is chargeable.

23. Where it would be more cost effective to travel by public transport the solicitor shall do so.

24. Unless otherwise prescribed no fee is allowable unless the work for which the fee is payable has been completed in its entirety.

Fee Payable	Units
1. Instruction Fee	
(a) To cover all work from the taking of instructions to the conclusion of proceedings where no fee is payable under paragraph (b).	10
(b) To cover all work from the taking of instructions to–	20
(i) commence proceedings until the lodging of a Notice of Intention to Defend or the first appearance of the defender; or	
(ii) to defend proceedings until the date appointed for the lodging of defences, the making of an order dispensing with written defences, the first appearance of the defender or the issue of the usual procedural timetable (except as specifically provided below).	
(c) Counterclaim – Additional fee where a counterclaim is lodged.	4

(d) Transfer of Agency – receiving instructions after a transfer of agency, where defences have, or should already have been, lodged, to include familiarising the incoming agent with the file.   8

2. Progress Fees

(a) (i) To cover all additional work (including adjustment and attendance at Options Hearing) from the conclusion of the work in Paragraph 1 until the allowance of a Proof or Debate or other court hearing fixed for the purpose of settlement (except as specifically provided below);   19

    (ii) To cover all additional work (e.g. negotiation, discussion, voluntary disclosure and all meetings and correspondence) involving the active participation of agents and resulting, prior to the allowance of a Proof, Debate, or other court hearing fixed for the purpose of settlement, in the negotiated settlement of the action (except as specifically provided below); or   19

    (iii) To cover all additional work (e.g. negotiation, discussion, voluntary disclosure and all meetings and correspondence) involving the active participation of agents where, prior to the allowance of a Proof or Debate, or other court hearing fixed for the purpose of settlement, an outcome or disposal is effected (subject to a maximum charge of 10 units) (except as specifically provided below);   10

(b) Fee to cover all work for the preparation and attendance at any Continued Options Hearing including the preparation of an amended Record.   2

3. Motions and Minutes etc.

(a) Fee to cover drawing, intimating, lodging, receiving and opposing (if so advised) any reponing note or written motion or minute (including Motions for interim orders) for any party-

    (i) where opposed or unopposed and involving a hearing before the Sheriff, to include the first quarter hour of argument, even if involving appearances on different dates   6

    (ii) where unopposed and not involving a hearing   2

    (iii) thereafter attendance fee per quarter hour, including any continuation of the diet ordered by the Sheriff to allow a minute of amendment to be received and answered   1

(b) Fee to cover drawing, or receiving Minute of Amendment, in addition to motion fee, if appropriate-

    (i) where assisted person is party bringing amendment and no answers lodged;   4

    (ii) where amendment is sought by another party and no answers lodged by assisted person;   2

    (iii) where answered, to include adjustment as required, for any party.   6

(c) Specification of Documents, in addition to motion fee, if appropriate-

    (i) fee to cover drawing, intimating and lodging Specification   4

    (ii) fee to opposing solicitor.   2

4. Miscellaneous Fees

(a) Affidavits – to framing all necessary affidavits, per sheet.   1

(b) Contact Arrangements – fee arranging or attempting to arrange interim contact arrangements where appropriate.   6

(c) Notice to Admit – preparing and serving/receiving a Notice to admit and serving a counter notice if required.   4

(d) Joint Minute of Admissions – preparing and/or considering and executing a joint minute of admissions with a view to avoiding unnecessary evidence or disposing of some (but not all) craves.   4

(e) Settlement conference/negotiation – participating in a settlement conference or negotiation after the allowance of a proof or debate where the solicitor making the claim is authorised in advance by the client to participate, per quarter hour (subject to a maximum charge of 8 units).   1

(f) Extra Judicial Settlement – fee to cover work to formalise settlement.   8

(g) Minute of Agreement – to drawing/revising Minute of Agreement necessary to accomplish or record overall settlement per sheet (subject to a maximum charge of 8 units).   1

(h) Report Fee – to instructing (if required) perusing and taking instructions on any report extending to at least four sheets obtained from a professional or expert person, either

    (i) where the report is commissioned by the solicitor for the assisted person; or   4

    (ii) the report is commissioned by order of Court.

(i) Additional Procedure – additional fee where Additional Procedure invoked in terms of Chapter 10 of the Ordinary Cause Rules in Schedule 1 to the Sheriff Courts (Scotland) Act 1907 (to include attendance at any procedural hearing(s).   4

(j) Additional fee where the action involves a third party minuter at any stage.   4

(k) Additional fee where the action involves–   4

    (i) a complex financial dispute leading to protracted negotiations;

    (ii) a complex pension sharing arrangement; or

    (iii) a contentious contact dispute.

(l) Peremptory diet – fee to cover all work in connection with a peremptory diet (excluding attendance at court).   3

5. Preparation

(a) *Preparation for proof or evidential child welfare hearing*

    (i) If action settled or abandoned not later than 14 days before the diet of proof or evidential child welfare hearing.   18

    (ii) Where the action settles within 14 days of, or on the day of, or after the diet of proof or evidential child welfare hearing but without evidence being lead.   24

    (iii) In any other case where evidence is led (to include settling with witnesses and enquiring for cause at avizandum (if required).   36

(aa) *Preparation for Child Welfare Hearing*

    (i) Fee to cover all work preparing for first hearing   6

    (ii) Fee to cover all work preparing for each subsequent hearing   3

(b) Preparation for Debate- Fee to cover all work in connection with preparing for any debate, where such debate takes place prior to proof or Proof Before Answer.   8

(c) Omitted by SSI 2007/14.

(d) Commission to Take Evidence – Fee to cover all work preparing for the taking of evidence or executing specification on open commission or proceeding as provided in (iii) below-

    (i) For solicitor arranging commission.   8

    (ii) For opposing solicitor.   4

    (iii) If optional procedure adopted-fee for each person on whom specification is served.   1

    (iv) Fee for perusing documents recovered-per quarter hour.   1

(e) Preparing for Appeal – Fee to cover all work preparing for an appeal to the Sheriff Appeal Court (to include marking appeal or noting marking of appeal).   12

6. Conduct & Waiting

To waiting for or attending by solicitor at the conduct of any hearing not otherwise prescribed (including any continued hearing and ancillary hearing on expenses or other miscellaneous subsequent hearing) per quarter hour.   1

CHAPTER III

CIRCUMSTANCES IN WHICH THE BOARD MAY ALLOW A FEE ADDITIONAL TO THE FEES PRESCRIBED IN CHAPTER II

1. That the assisted person's inadequate knowledge of English—

    (a) required instructions through an interpreter; or

    (b) significantly increased the duration of meetings necessary to take instructions.

2. That although able to attend at the solicitor's office the assisted person suffered throughout or for a significant period of the case from—

    (a) a severe substance abuse problem; or

    (b) a mental disorder within the meaning of section 328 of the Mental Health (Care and Treatment) (Scotland) Act 2003.

3. That the assisted person suffered from a physical disability which necessitated a significantly lengthier process than would normally have been encountered in the taking and obtaining of instructions.

4. That the assisted person was, for a significant period in relation to the overall duration of the case, unable to attend at the solicitor's office by reason of disability, illness or imprisonment.

5. That the nature or circumstances of the case necessitated significant attendance to its progress outwith normal office hours.

5A. That the assisted person or any other witness in the case is a vulnerable witness in terms of section 11 of the Vulnerable Witnesses (Scotland) Act 2004 and this has necessitated significant additional work in seeking, or opposing, or implementing a special measure for the taking of evidence from a vulnerable witness by virtue of sections 11, 12, 13 and 18(1)(a) and/or (b) of that Act.

6. That the law in relation to the matter at issue was particularly complex and involved an area of law with which a solicitor engaged in general court practice would be unlikely to be familiar.

7. That the case raised unusually complex issues of fact, including detailed consideration of extensive documentary evidence.

Note on the application of Chapter III

    (a) Except where an uplift is granted under paragraph 5, 6 or 7 above, the element of the solicitor's fee subject to an uplift will exclude any amount charged in relation to time spent waiting or appearing at, court.

    (b) Only 1 of paragraphs 2, 3 and 4 may be claimed in any case.

    (c) An uplift may not be granted under paragraph 7 above where a fee under paragraph 4(k) of the table of fees in Chapter II of Schedule 6 is claimed.

    (d) the solicitor of an assisted person, who is a vulnerable witness, may not claim in respect of the assisted person the additional fee under paragraphs 2, 3 or 4, if there is a claim under paragraph 5A in respect of the assisted person as a vulnerable witness.

SCHEDULE 7

Regulation 5

SHERIFF COURT PROCEEDINGS FOR WHICH FEES FOR WORK DONE SHALL ONLY BE PAYABLE UNDER SCHEDULE 5

Adoptions;

conveyancing work required to implement an Order of the Court;

division and sale of heritable property

exceptional cases;

fatal accident inquiries;

minute procedure in a closed process;

proceedings arising under the Mortgage Rights (Scotland) Act 2001 proceedings in an all-Scotland sheriff court within the meaning of section 42(7) of the Courts Reform (Scotland) Act 2014;

proceedings where the assisted person is a curator *ad litem*;

proceedings where the assisted person is a third party minuter;

work carried out under Regulation 18 of the Civil Legal Aid (Scotland) Regulations 2002 in a case which does not proceed to a grant of civil legal aid;

work in connection with a motion for modification of expenses of the assisted person, drafting and submitting an account of expenses, or disputing (on receipt) an opponent's account of expenses, including attendance at taxation and taking/opposing Notes of Objections, including taxations instructed by the Board; and

work in connection with letters of inhibition;

work in connection with the registration and enforcement of a decree;

summary applications.

Interpretation

1.—(1) For the purposes of this Schedule an "exceptional case" means any case certified as such by the Board on the application of the solicitor involved.

(2) The solicitor involved may apply to the Board not later than 4 months after the conclusion of a case to have it certified as an exceptional case.

(3) The Board will certify a case as exceptional only if satisfied that—

    (a)   the other party, or as the case may be at least one of the other parties, was a party litigant;

    (b)   there were concurrent proceedings before a children's hearing;

    (c)   the solicitor involved had to apply for a transfer of agency after the fixing of a diet of proof, debate or any other hearing fixed for the purposes of settlement; or

    (d)   payment in accordance with Schedule 6 would not provide reasonable remuneration for the word actually, necessarily and reasonably done because the case involved—

        i(i)   unusual court procedure for which a fee is not otherwise prescribed; or

        (ii)   a significantly greater volume of work than is usual for a case of that type.

SOLICITORS' OUTLAYS

Table of Fees payable in the Court of Session and Offices connected therewith

The Court of Session etc. Fees Order 2015 (SSI 2015 No 261),

which came into force on 22nd September 2015, revoking all earlier Orders.

Exemption of certain persons from fees

4.—(1) A fee provided for by this Order is not payable by a person if paragraph (2) or (3) applies.

(2) This paragraph applies where the person is a debtor in connection with any proceedings under the Debtors (Scotland) Act 1987.

(3) This paragraph applies where—

(a) the person or the person's partner is in receipt of income support under the Social Security Contributions and Benefits Act 1992;

(b) the person is in receipt of an income-based jobseeker's allowance under the Jobseekers Act 1995;

(c) the person is in receipt of universal credit under Part 1 of the Welfare Reform Act 2012;

(d) the person is in receipt of civil legal aid within the meaning of section 13(2) of the Legal Aid (Scotland) Act 1986 in respect of the matter in the Table of Fees in connection with which the fee is payable;

(e) the fee is payable in connection with a simplified divorce or dissolution of a civil partnership application and the person is in receipt of advice and assistance from a solicitor under the Legal Aid (Scotland) Act 1986 in respect of that application;

(f) the person's solicitor is undertaking work in relation to the matter in the Table of Fees in connection with which the fee is payable on the basis of any regulations made under section 36 of the Legal Aid (Scotland) Act 1986 providing for legal aid in a matter of special urgency;

(g) the person or the person's partner is in receipt of guarantee credit under the State Pension Credit Act 2002;

(h) the person or the person's partner is in receipt of working tax credit, provided that—

(i) child tax credit is being paid to the party, or otherwise following a claim for child tax credit made jointly by the members of a couple (as defined in section 3(5A) of the Tax Credits Act 2002) which includes the party; or

(ii) there is a disability element or severe disability element (or both) to the tax credit received by the party;

and that the gross annual income taken into account for the calculation of the working tax credit is £16,642 or less; or

(i) the person or the person's partner is in receipt of income-related employment and support allowance under the Welfare Reform Act 2007.

Exemption of certain motions from fees

5.—(1) This article applies to motions which are enrolled in the process of the cause or made orally at the bar in accordance with rule 23.2 of the Rules of Court (enrolment of motions).

(2) The fees specified in items B21 and C17 of the Table of Fees are not payable in respect of motions which operate solely so as to activate further steps of procedure and any opposition to such motions.

(3) Without prejudice to the generality of paragraph (2) above, a motion which is exempt from the payment of fees includes a motion under any of the following rules of the Rules of Court—

(a) rule 19.1 (decrees in absence);

(b) rule 22.3(5)(a) (closing record);

(c) rule 36.13 (death, disability, retiral, etc. of Lord Ordinary);

(d) r ules 37.1(2)(b), 37.1(6) and 37.1(7) (applications for jury trial);

(e)   rule 37.10 (application of verdicts); and

(f)   rule 38.17(1) (amendment of pleadings in reclaiming motion).

Calculation of certain fees payable

6.—(1) Subject to article 5, the fees specified in items B21 and C17 of the Table of Fees are payable in addition to those fees which are specified in items B2, B6 and C5 of the Table of Fees.

(2) The fees specified in items B21 and C17 of the Table of Fees are not payable in addition to those fees which are specified in items B9, B10 and B13 and C9 of the Table of Fees.

SCHEDULE

TABLE OF FEES

(Fees payable from 1st April 2016)

Column 1 *(Matters)*	Column 2 *(Fee payable)* £	Column 3 *(Fee formerly Payable)* £
PART I – FEES IN THE CENTRAL OFFICE OF THE COURT		
A. Signeting		
Signeting of any writ or summons if attendance is necessary outwith normal office hours.	125	123
B. General Department		
1. Appeal, application for leave to appeal, summons, or other writ or step by which any cause or proceeding, other than a family action, is originated in either the Inner or Outer House (to include signeting in normal office hours).	214	210
2. Defences, answers or other writ (including a joint minute) or step in process or enrolment or opposition to a motion in a pending process by which a party other than an originating party first makes an appearance in a cause or proceeding, other than a family action.	214	210
3. Writ by which a family action is originated (other than a simplified divorce or dissolution of a civil partnership application) – inclusive fee (to include signeting within normal office hours and, if applicable, issue to the pursuer of an extract in terms of item G5(a) of this Table, and to the defender, if appropriate, a duplicate thereof).	166	163
4. Simplified divorce or dissolution of a civil partnership application (inclusive of all procedure other than that specified in item B5 of this Table).	125	123
5. In relation to a simplified divorce or dissolution of a civil partnership application, citation of any persons under rule 16.1(1)(a)(i), (ii) or (iii), as applied by rule 49.76, of the Rules of Court, or intimation to any person or persons under rule 16.1(1)(a)(i), (ii) or (iii), as applied by rule 49.76, of those Rules, where such intimation is required.	£12 plus messenger at arms fee to serve document	£11 plus messenger at arms fee to serve document
6. Defences, answers or other writ (including a joint minute) or step in process or enrolment of or opposition to a motion in a pending process by which a party other than an originating party first makes appearance in a family action.	166	163
7. Initial lodging of affidavits in a family action where proof by affidavit evidence has been allowed.	71	70
8. Special case—		
for each party	107	105
maximum fee payable per case	435	426

Column 1 *(Matters)*	Column 2 *(Fee payable)* £	Column 3 *(Fee formerly* *Payable)* £
9. Application by minute or motion for variation of an order in a family action.	36	35
10. Answers or opposition to an application under item B9 of this Table.	36	35
11. Letter of request to a foreign court.	54	53
12. Citation of each jury, to include outlays incurred in citing and countermanding - payable on receipt of instruments for issue of precept.	298	292
13. Reclaiming motion - payable by party enrolling motion.	214	210
14. Closed record – payable by each party on the lodging of the closed record or, where no closed record is lodged, when mode of enquiry is determined.	107	105
15. Allowing proof, etc. - payable by each party on diet of proof, jury trial, procedure roll or summar roll hearing being allowed.	59	58
16. Court hearing (in normal hours) before a single judge – payable by each party for every 30 minutes or part thereof. *Note:* This fee does not apply to the first 30 minutes of the hearing of a motion.	96	94
17. Court hearing (in normal hours) before 3 or more judges – payable by each party for every 30 minutes or part thereof. *Note:* This fee does not apply to the first 30 minutes of the hearing on the single bills.	239	234
18. Court hearing (out of hours) before a single judge – payable by each party for every 30 minutes or part thereof.	115	113
19. Court hearing (out of hours) before 3 or more judges – payable by each party for every 30 minutes or part thereof.	287	281
20. Cancellation of court hearing before 3 or more judges, by a party or parties, within 28 days of court hearing date – fee payable is shared equally between the parties.	50% of fee that would have been payable under this Table had the court hearing taken place as planned	50% of fee that would have been payable under this Table had the court hearing taken place as planned
21. Fee payable by any party enrolling a motion or making a motion orally at the bar and any party opposing any such motion.	54	53
C. Petition Department		
1. Petition of whatever nature presented to the Inner or Outer House other than a petition under item C3 or C4 of this Table, whether in respect of the first or any subsequent step of process, and any application for registration or recognition of a judgment under the Civil Jurisdiction and Judgments Act 1982.	214	210
2. Additional fee payable when a petition in terms of item C1 of this Table is presented outwith normal office hours.	125	123
3. Petition to be admitted as a notary public—for each applicant	161	158
4. Petition to be admitted as a solicitor—for each applicant	161	158
5. Answers, objection or other writ (including a joint minute) or step in process or enrolment or opposition to a motion in a pending process by which a party other than an originating party first makes appearance in a proceeding to which item C1 of this Table applies.	214	210
6. Caveat	48	47
7. No fee.	—	—
8. Registering official copies of orders of courts in England and Wales or Northern Ireland.	18	18

Column 1 *(Matters)*	Column 2 *(Fee payable)* £	Column 3 *(Fee formerly Payable)* £
9. Reclaiming motion – payable by party enrolling motion.	214	210
10. Closed record – payable by each party on the lodging of the closed record or, when no closed record is lodged, when mode of enquiry is determined.	107	105
11. Allowing proof, etc. – payable by each party on diet of proof, procedure roll, summar roll or judicial review hearing being allowed.	59	58
12. Court hearing (in normal hours) before a single judge – payable by each party for every 30 minutes or part thereof. *Note:* This fee does not apply to the first 30 minutes of the hearing of a motion.	96	94
13. Court hearing (in normal hours) before 3 or more judges – payable by each party for every 30 minutes or part thereof. *Note:* This fee does not apply to the first 30 minutes of the hearing on the single bills.	239	234
14. Court hearing (out of hours) before a single judge – payable by each party for every 30 minutes or part thereof.	115	113
15. Court hearing (out of hours) before 3 or more judges – payable by each party for every 30 minutes or part thereof.	287	281
16. Cancellation of court hearing before 3 or more judges, by a party or parties, within 28 days of court hearing date – fee payable is shared equally between parties.	50% of fee that would have been payable under this Table had the court hearing taken place as planned	50% of fee that would have been payable under this Table had the court hearing taken place as planned
17. Fee payable by any party enrolling a motion or making a motion orally at the bar and any party opposing any such motion.	54	53
18. Lodging of notice of appointment or intention to appoint an administrator out of court under the Insolvency Act 1986(**2**).	214	210
D. Court for hearing appeals relating to the registration of electors Appeal – inclusive fee.	214	210
E. Election court 1. Parliamentary election petition.	214	210
2. Statement of matters.	18	18
3. Any other petition, application, answers or objections submitted to the court.	54	53
4. Certificate of judgment.	54	53
F. Lands valuation appeal court 1. Appeal - inclusive fee.	214	210
2. Answers - inclusive fee.	214	210
G. Extracts department 1. Extract decree following upon a summons, petition or appeal, or after protestation of a note, whether in absence or otherwise.	59	58
2. Extract of admission as a solicitor.	54	53
3. Extract of protestation.	54	53
4. Certificate under the Civil Jurisdiction and Judgments Act 1982.	54	53
5. Documentation evidencing divorce, nullity or dissolution of marriage or civil partnership including—	30	29

Column 1 *(Matters)*	Column 2 *(Fee payable)* £	Column 3 *(Fee formerly Payable)* £
(a) extract from Consistorial Register of Decrees of decree pronounced on or after 23rd September 1975 if not issued in terms of item B3 or B4 of this Table;		
(b) certificate of divorce in decree pronounced prior to 23rd September 1975;		
(c) certified copy interlocutor in decree pronounced prior to 23rd September 1975.		
6. Extract from the Register of Acts and Decrees – per sheet or part thereof.	30	29
7. Sealing and certifying any document for exhibition in a foreign jurisdiction or otherwise.	30	29
8. Acknowledgement of receipt of a notice under section 19(6) or 21(2) of the Conveyancing and Feudal Reform (Scotland) Act 1970.	54	53

PART II – FEES IN THE OFFICE OF THE ACCOUNTANT OF COURT

H. Office of the accountant of court

I. In Factories

1. Registering case and receiving and delivering up bond of caution.	22	22
2. Examining factor's inventory – 0.333% of the value of the estate as disclosed		
(a) minimum fee payable;	30	29
(b) maximum fee payable.	721	707
3. Auditing each account, based on estate value		
(a) £0 – £30,000;	112	110
(b) £30,001 – £50,000;	225	221
(c) £50,001 – £250,000;	562	551
(d) £250,001 – £500,000;	845	828
(e) £500,001 and above.	1,126	1,104
4. Reporting with regard to discharge, special powers, other special matters, surplus estate or scheme of division.	56	55
5. For certificate under seal.	17	17

II. In Consignations

6. Lodging consignation.	32	31
7. Producing or delivering up consignation, based on consignation value—		
(a) consignation value £0 – £50 and less than 7 years since lodged;	No charge	No charge
(b) consignation value over £51 and less than 7 years since lodged;	32	31
(c) consignation value £0 –£70 and over 7 years since lodged;	No charge	No charge
(d) consignation value over £71 and over 7 years since lodged.	53	52

PART III – FEES IN THE OFFICE OF THE AUDITOR OF THE COURT OF SESSION

I. Office of the auditor of the court of session

1. Taxing accounts of expenses incurred in judicial proceedings (including proceedings in the High Court of Justiciary) remitted to the Auditor of the Court of Session for taxation—		
(a) on lodging account for taxation;	43	42
(b) taxing accounts for expenses etc.—		
(i) up to £400;	20	20
(ii) for every additional £100 or part thereof	5	5

Column 1 *(Matters)*	Column 2 *(Fee payable)* £	Column 3 *(Fee formerly* *Payable)* £
Note: fee to be determined by the Auditor of the Court of Session on amount of account as submitted.		
2. Fee for assessing account remitted to the Auditor to determine whether an additional fee should be paid.	287	281
3. Fee for cancellation of diet of taxation—		
(a) where written notice of cancellation received from receiving party after 4.00 pm on the fourth working day before the day of the diet of taxation;	50% of fee that would be payable under item I1(b) of this Table	50% of fee that would be payable under item I1(b) of this Table
(b) where written notice of cancellation received from receiving party after 4.00 pm on the second working day before the day of the diet of taxation.	75% of fee that would be payable under item I1(b) of this Table	75% of fee that would be payable under item I1(b) of this Table

PART IV – FEES COMMON TO ALL OFFICES

J. Miscellaneous

1. Certified copy of proceedings for appeal to the Supreme Court.	214	210
2. Certifying of any other document (plus copying charges if necessary).	18	18
3. Recording, extracting, engrossing or copying- all documents (exclusive of search fee)—		
(a) copying of each document, up to 10 pages;	6	6
(b) copying of each further page or part thereof;	0.50	0.50
(c) copying of each document in electronic form.	6	6
4. Any search of records or archives, per 30 minutes or part thereof.	12	11
In addition, correspondence fee where applicable.	12	11
5. Captions—		
(a) marking caption when ordered;	12	11
(b) warrant for caption when issued.	12	11
6. Change of party name where more than 10 cases are registered – per case.	2	2

Bankruptcy Fees etc. (Scotland) Regulations 2012
(SI 2012 No 118)

[This Table of Fees came into force on 1st June 2012; revoking SI 1993 No 486; SI 1999 No 752; SSI 2007 No 220; SSI 2008 No 5; SSI 2008 No 79; SSI 2008 No 97; SSI 2010 No 76; SSI 2011 No 142]

SCHEDULE

TABLE OF FEES

PART I
FEES FOR ACCOUNTANT IN BANKRUPTCY AS INTERIM TRUSTEE OR TRUSTEE IN SEQUESTRATION

Column 1 (Functions)	Column 2 (Rates)	Column 3 (Former rates)
1. In respect of each hour of work in the exercise by the Accountant in Bankruptcy of that office's functions as interim trustee in a sequestration where the Accountant in Bankruptcy is not appointed as trustee in that sequestration........................	£100 per hour	£39 per hour for first 5 hours; £69 per hour for each subsequent hour
2. In respect of each hour of work in the exercise by the Accountant in Bankruptcy of that office's functions as interim trustee or trustee in a sequestration, other than in respect of the realisation of assets in the sequestrated estate............................	£100 per hour	£39 per hour for first 21 hours; £69 per hour for each subsequent hour
3. In respect of the exercise by the Accountant in Bankruptcy of that office's functions as trustee in a sequestration in relation to the realisation of assets in the sequestrated estate—		
(a) in respect of the total price paid in a transaction by the purchaser of heritable property, including any interest paid thereon, but after the deduction of any sums paid to secured creditors in respect of their securities over that property—		
(i) on the first £10,000 or fraction thereof;	15% of that amount	5% of that amount
(ii) on the next £10,000 or fraction thereof;	5% of that amount	1% of that amount
(iii) on all further sums;	2% of that amount	0.5% of that amount
(b) in respect of the proceeds of the sale of moveable property, after the deduction of the expenses of sale and any sums paid to secured creditors in respect of their securities over that property—		5% of the proceeds of sale (across all sums)
(i) on the first £10,000 or fraction thereof;	15% of that amount	

Column 1	Column 2	Column 3
(Functions)	*(Rates)*	*(Former rates)*
(ii) on the next £10,000 or fraction thereof;	5% of that amount	
(iii) on all further sums;	2% of that amount	0.5% of that amount
4. In respect of the exercise by the Accountant in Bankruptcy of that office's functions as trustee in relation to the payment of dividends to creditors..	25% of funds ingathered	None
5. In respect of the exercise by the Accountant in Bankruptcy of that office's functions as trustee in relation to the payment of dividends to creditors—..		£78 plus £39 in respect of each creditor who is paid a dividend
(i) on the first £10,000 or fraction thereof;	10% of that amount	
(ii) on the next £10,000 or fraction thereof;	5% of that amount	
(iii) on all further sums.	2% of that amount	

PART II

FEES FOR OTHER FUNCTIONS OF THE ACCOUNTANT IN BANKRUPTCY

Column 1	Column 2	Column 3
(Functions)	*(Fee payable)*	*(Fee formerly payable)*
	£	£
1. For registering award of sequestration..	20.00	*(No change)*
2. For admistration of a creditor's petition		
(a) any petition by a creditor, trustee under a protected trust deed or the executor of a deceased debtor;	100.00	200.00
(b) any such petition where following award of sequestration the Accountant in Bankruptcy is the trustee (in addition to item 2(a)).	200.00	None
3. For supervising proceedings in sequestration—		
(a) where commissioners have been elected;..	139.00	*(No change)*
(b) where no commissioners have been elected;	210.00	*(No change)*
(c) where the Accountant in Bankruptcy is the trustee	139.00	*(No change)*
4. For supervising payment of dividend to creditors where no commissioners have been elected	69.00	*(No change)*
5. For any special report to the court..	69.00	*(No change)*

	Column 1	Column 2	Column 3
	(Functions)	*(Fee payable)*	*(Fee formerly payable)*
		£	£

6. For considering and issuing a determination in an appeal against a determination of commissioners as to the outlays and remuneration payable to a trustee — 5% of the sum remaining on deduction from the sum of outlays and remuneration determined by the Accountant in Bankruptcy of any outlays incurred by way of statutory fees, trading expenses or expenses of realisation — *(No change)*

7. For issuing a determination fixing the outlays and remuneration payable to—
   (a) an interim trustee; or
   (b) a trustee

   17.5% of the sum remaining on deduction from the sum of outlays and remuneration determined of any outlays incurred by way of statutory fees, trading expenses or expenses of realisation — *(No change)*

8.	For examination of the sederunt book and related work, in connection with the discharge of a permanent trustee	36.00	*(No change)*
9.	For granting a certificate of discharge to an interim trustee	36.00	*(No change)*
10.	For granting a certificate of discharge to a debtor	11.00	*(No change)*
11.	For providing a certified copy of an entry in the register of insolvencies	24.00	*(No change)*
12.	For the certifying of any other document (excluding copying charges)	17.00	*(No change)*

13. For providing a copy of any document—
    (a) by photocopying—

	(i) 10 pages or less	11.00	*(No change)*
	(ii) each page after first 10	0.32	*(No change)*
	(b) in an electronic medium or by printout from records held on computer — per document	£0.13	*(No change)*
14.	For attendance at any meeting of creditors – fee per hour or part thereof, including travelling time.	£69.00	*(No change)*
15.	For calling any meeting of creditors.	69.00	*(No change)*
16.	For attendance at any examination of the debtor — fee per hour or part thereof, including travelling time	69.00	*(No change)*

17. In respect of protected trust deeds—

	(a) for registering a protected trust deed	36.00	*(No change)*

(b) for supervision of the trustee of a protected trust deed — £100.00 per 12 month period of supervision beginning on the date of registration of the protected trust deed and ending on the discharge of the trustee (or part of such period). — 250.00

	Column 1	Column 2	Column 3
	(Functions)	*(Fee payable)*	*(Fee formerly payable)*
		£	£
18.	For auditing the accounts of a trustee under a protected trust deed and fixing the trustee's remuneration.	5% of the sum remaining on deduction from the sum of outlays and remuneration determined of any outlays incurred by way of statutory fees, trading expenses or expenses of realisation.	*(No change)*
19.	For lodging any unclaimed dividend in an appropriate bank or institution set aside for payment to a creditor or creditors, in respect of each creditor on consignation	26.00	*(No change)*
20.	For uplifting any unclaimed dividend consigned in an appropriate bank or institution, in respect of each creditor	26.00	*(No change)*
21.	For determination of a debtor application	200.00	100.00
22.	For an application for a bankruptcy restrictions order	250.00	*(No change)*
23.	For accepting and issuing a bankruptcy restrictions undertaking	150.00	*(No change)*
24.	For registering a court order appointing a replacement trustee	19.00	*(No change)*
25.	For petitioning for the replacement of a trustee acting in more than one sequestration	200.00	*(No change)*

Table of Fees payable in the High Court of Justiciary

High Court of Justiciary Fees Order 2015
(SSI 2015 No 262),

which came into force on 22nd September 2015, revoking all earlier Orders.

SCHEDULE

TABLE OF FEES

(Payable from 1st April 2016)

	Column 1	Column 2	Column 3
	(Matters)	*(Fee payable)*	*(Fee formerly payable)*
		£	£
1.	Petitions to the nobile officium and applications for criminal letters (inclusive fee covering all steps in procedure).	107	105
2.	Certified copy of any document other than an extract conviction	18	18
3.	Copying of–		
	(a) each document, up to 10 pages;	6	6
	(b) each further page or part thereof	0.50	0.50
	(c) each document in electronic form	6	6
4.	Any search of records or archives, per 30 minutes or part thereof.	12	11
.	In addition, correspondence fee where applicable..	12	11
5.	Petition for removal of disqualification from driving.	89	87

Table of Fees payable in the Sheriff Appeal Court

The Sheriff Appeal Court Fees Order 2015
(SSI 2015 No 379)

Exemption of certain persons from fees

3.—(1) A fee provided for by this Order is not payable by a person if—

(a)   the person or the person's partner is in receipt of income support under the Social Security Contributions and Benefits Act 1992;

(b)   the person is in receipt of an income-based jobseeker's allowance under the Jobseekers Act 1995;

(c)   the person is in receipt of universal credit under Part 1 of the Welfare Reform Act 2012;

(d)   the person is in receipt of civil legal aid within the meaning of section 13(2) of the Legal Aid (Scotland) Act 198 in respect of the matter in the Table of Fees in Schedule 1, 2 or 3 in connection with which the fee is payable;

(e)   the fee is payable in connection with a simplified divorce or dissolution of a civil partnership application and the person is in receipt of advice and assistance from a solicitor under the Legal Aid (Scotland) Act 1986 in respect of that application;

(f)   the person's solicitor is undertaking work in relation to the matter in the Table of Fees in Schedule 1, 2 or 3 in connection with which the fee is payable on the basis of any regulations made under section 36 of the Legal Aid (Scotland) Act 1986 providing for legal aid in a matter of special urgency;

(g)   the person or the person's partner is in receipt of guarantee credit under the State Pension Credit Act 2002

(h)   the person or the person's partner is in receipt of working tax credit, provided that—

    (i)   child tax credit is being paid to the party, or otherwise following a claim for child tax credit made jointly by the members of a couple (as defined in section 3(5A) of the Tax Credits Act 2002 which includes the party; or

    (ii)   there is a disability element or severe disability element (or both) to the tax credit received by the party;

    and that the gross annual income taken into account for the calculation of the working tax credit is £16,642 or less; or

(i)   the person or the person's partner is in receipt of income-related employment and support allowance under the Welfare Reform Act 2007.

(2) In this article "partner" means a person to whom a person is married or with whom the person is in a civil partnership.

Exemptions relating to particular proceedings

4.—(1) The fees provided for by this Order do not apply to any appeal to the Sheriff Appeal Court under or by virtue of the Children's Hearings (Scotland) Act 2011.

(2) The fees provided for by this Order do not apply to a debtor or creditor in any appeal to the Sheriff Appeal Court under the Debtors (Scotland) Act 1987 or the Debt Arrangement and Attachment (Scotland) Act 2002.

SCHEDULE

TABLE OF FEES

(Payable from 1st April 2016)

Column 1 (Matters)	Column 2 (Fee payable) £	Column 3 (Fee formerly payable) £
1. Lodging or opposing a motion.	48	47
2. Fixing a hearing date.	54	53
3. Lodging an appeal in a cause other than a summary cause; lodging an application under section 69 or 71 of the Courts Reform (Scotland) Act 2014.	113	111
4. Hearing fee per day or part thereof (bench of 1).	227	223
(*Note*: This fee does not apply to the first 30 minutes of the hearing.)		
5. Hearing fee per day or part thereof (bench of 3 or more).	568	557
(NOTE: This fee does not apply to the first 30 minutes of the hearing.)		
6. Copying of—		
(a) each document, up to 10 pages;	6	6
(b) each further page or part thereof;	0.5	0.5
(c) each document in electronic form.	6	6
7. Any search of records or archives, per 30 minutes or part thereof.	12	11
In addition, correspondence fee where applicable.	12	11
8. Taxing accounts of expenses incurred in judicial proceedings remitted to the auditor of court for taxation—		
(a) lodging account for taxation;	43	42
(b) taxing accounts of expenses etc.—		
(i) up to £400;	20	20
(ii) for every additional £100 or part thereof.	5	5
(*Note:* Fee to be determined by auditor of court on amount of account as submitted.)		
(c) cancellation of diet of taxation—		
(i) where written notice of cancellation received from receiving party after 4.00 pm on the fourth working day before the day of diet of taxation;	50% of fee that would have been payable under sub-paragraph (b) of this paragraph	50% of fee that would have been payable under sub-paragraph (b) of this paragraph
(ii) where written notice of cancellation received from receiving party after 4.00 pm on the second working day before the day of the diet of taxation.	75% of fee that would have been payable under sub-paragraph (b) of this paragraph	75% of fee that would have been payable under sub-paragraph (b) of this paragraph

Table of Fees payable in the United Kingdom Supreme Court

The Supreme Court Fees Order 2009
(SI 2009 No 2131)

[This Schedule is printed as amended by Supreme Court Fees (Amendment) Order 2011 (SI 2011 No 1737) which came into force on 5 August 2011.]

SCHEDULE 1

Fees payable in the Supreme Court

(1) Number and description of fee	(2) Amount of fee	(3) Amount of fee
1 Application for permission to appeal		
1.1 On filing an application for permission to appeal.	£1,000	£400
1.2 On filing notice of objection to an application for permission to appeal.	£160	£160
2 Appeals etc		
2.1 On filing notice under rule 18(1)(c) of the 2009 Rules of an intention to proceed with an appeal.	£800	£400
2.2 On filing a notice of appeal.	£1600	£400
2.3 On filing a reference under the Supreme Court's devolution jurisdiction. No fee is payable where the reference is made by a court.	n/a	£200
2.4 On filing notice under rule 21(1) of the 2009 Rules (acknowledgement by respondent).	£320	£160
2.5 On filing a statement of relevant facts and issues and an appendix of essential documents.	£4820	£800
3 Procedural applications		
3.1 On filing an application for a decision of the Registrar to be reviewed.	£1500	£200
3.2 On filing an application for permission to intervene in an appeal.	£800	£200
3.3 On filing any other procedural application.	£350	£200
3.4 On filing notice of objection to a procedural application.	£150	£150
4 Costs		
4.1 On submitting a claim for costs.	2.5% of the sum claimed	2.5% of the sum claimed
4.2 On certification by the Registrar under rule 52 of the 2009 Rules of the amount of assessed costs, or on receipt of an order showing the amount.	2.5% of the sum allowed	2.5% of the sum allowed
5 Copying		
5.1 On a request for a copy of a document (other than where fee 5.2 or 5.3 applies)—		
(a) for ten pages or less;	£5	£5
(b) for each subsequent page.	50p	50p
5.2 On a request for a copy of a document to be provided on a computer disk or in other electronic form, for each such copy.	£5	£5
5.3 On a request for a certified copy of a document.	£20	£20

Table of Fees payable in the Sheriff Court

The Sheriff Court Fees Order 2015
(SSI 2015 N0 264),

which came into force on 22nd September 2015, revoking all earlier Orders.

SCHEDULE

TABLE OF FEES

(Payable from 1st April 2016)

Column 1 (Matters)	Column 2 (Fee Payable) £	Column 3 (Fee Formerly Payable) £
PART I — COMMISSARY PROCEEDINGS		
1. Petition for—		
(a) appointment of executor;	18	18
(b) restriction of caution;	18	18
(c) special warrant;	18	18
(d) sealing up of repositories or the like;	18	18
(e) appointment of Commissary factor.	18	18
(NOTE: the fee for all petitions in paragraph 1 includes issue of extract decree).		
2. Sealing up repositories or the like, per hour.	30	29
3.		
(a) Receiving and examining inventory of estate, except where sub paragraph (b) or (c) of this paragraph applies—		
(i) where the amount of the estate vested in or belonging beneficially to the deceased, of which confirmation is required, or for which resealing under the Colonial Probates Act 1892 is required does not exceed—		
£10,000;	No fee	No fee
£50,000;	225	221
(ii) where the amount of the estate exceeds £50,000;	225	221
(b) Receiving and examining additional or corrective inventory of estate or inventory of estate *ad non executa;*	225	221
(c) Receiving and examining inventory of estate where it is declared that confirmation is not required.	The fees payable are 50% of those specified in sub paragraph (a) or (b) of this paragraph. If confirmation is subsequently required the remaining 50% of the fees specified in sub paragraph (a) or (b) are payable	The fees payable are 50% of those specified in sub paragraph (a) or (b) of this paragraph. If confirmation is subsequently required the remaining 50% of the fees specified in sub paragraph (a) or (b) are payable

Column 1 *(Matters)*	Column 2 *(Fee Payable)* £	Column 3 *(Fee Formerly Payable)* £
4. Commissary copying and extracting.		
(1) Issuing certificate of confirmation—		
(a) if ordered when lodging inventory, each certificate;	7	6
(b) if ordered subsequent to lodging inventory—		
(i) first certificate, including search fee;	18	17
(ii) each subsequent certificate.	7	6
(2) Copy or duplicate confirmation—		
(a) if ordered when lodging inventory;	12	11
(b) if ordered subsequent to lodging inventory—		
(i) duplicate confirmation, including search fee;	24	23
(ii) each subsequent duplicate confirmation if ordered at the same time as the duplicate confirmation in head (i).	12	11
(3) Certified extract confirmation and will (if any)—		
(a) if ordered when lodging inventory;	24	23
(b) if ordered subsequent to lodging inventory—		
(i) certified extract, including search fee;	36	35
(ii) each subsequent certified extract if ordered at the same time as the certified extract in head (i).	24	23
(4) Copy will—		
(a) if ordered when lodging inventory;	7	6
(b) if ordered subsequent to lodging inventory—		
(i) copy will, including search fee;	18	17
(ii) each subsequent copy will if ordered at the same time as the copy will in head (i).	7	6

PART II — SHERIFF COURT PROCEEDINGS

Initial Writ

5. Initial writ in any proceedings not being proceedings for which any other paragraph of this Table prescribes a fee (NOTE: fee covers issue of extract decree).	96	94
6. European Order for payment in terms of EU Regulation 1896/2006 – application for European Order for payment.	96	94

Divorce and dissolution of civil partners

7. Initial writ in an action of divorce or dissolution of a civil partnership (other than a simplified divorce or dissolution of a civil partnership application) (NOTE: fee covers issue of extract decree).	150	147

Application for simplified divorce and simplified dissolution of civil partnership

8. Any application (inclusive of all procedures other than those specified at paragraphs 9 and 38) (NOTE: fee covers issue of extract decree).	113	111
9. Subsequent application upon change of circumstances by party.	30	29

Summary warrant

10. Application for summary warrant.	71	70

Bankruptcy

11. Petition for sequestration of estates or petition for recall of award of sequestration.	113	111
12. Miscellaneous applications, including appeals under the Bankruptcy (Scotland) Act 1985.	59	58
13. Application for the approval of composition.	36	35

Column 1 *(Matters)*	Column 2 *(Fee Payable)* £	Column 3 *(Fee Formerly* *Payable)* £
Declarator and petitions for completion of title for the Sheriff of Chancery		
14. Application for declarator and petitions for completion of title to the Sheriff of Chancery.	227	223
15. Issue of chancery extract.	107	105
Summary cause		
16. Summons - summary cause (including small claim and European small claim procedure) (NOTE: fee covers issue of extract decree)—		
(a) actions for payment of money of £200 or less (or 250 euros for European small claims);	18	18
(b) other actions;	78	76
(c) on the marking of an appeal.	59	58
Criminal procedure		
17. Complaint.	36	35
Road Traffic Offenders Act 1988(2)		
18. Petition for removal of disqualification.	89	87
Miscellaneous		
19. Application under section 4 of the Requirements of Writing (Scotland) Act 1995.	18	18
20. Caveat.	36	35
21. Any proceedings under section 12 or 18 of the Civil Jurisdiction and Judgments Act 1982.	24	23
22. Note in a liquidation or judicial factory.	36	35
Defender's responses		
23. First writ, reponing note, application for recall of decree or attendance to state a defence or oppose an interim order (fee payable by each defender or compearer) (NOTE: fee covers issue of extract decree)—		
(a) in proceedings to which paragraph 5 of this Table applies;	96	94
(b) in an action of divorce or dissolution of a civil partnership (other than a simplified divorce or dissolution of civil partnership).	150	147
Civil court procedure		
PAYABLE BY PURSUER		
24. Lodging of a certified copy record under the Ordinary Cause Rules (NOTE: fee payable only once in respect of a cause).	113	111
25. Lodging of a certified closed record under the additional procedure of the Ordinary Cause Rules.	113	111
26. Fixing, allocating or assigning of a proof, a debate or a hearing in a summary or miscellaneous application on the merits of the cause.	54	53
27. For each day or part thereof of proof, debate or hearing in a summary or miscellaneous application on the merits of the cause (NOTE: not payable if the proof, debate or hearing does not proceed on that day).	227	223
28. Initial lodging of affidavits in a family action where proof by affidavit evidence has been allowed.	66	65
Payable by any party (including pursuer)		
29. Lodging of a written motion or minute and the lodging of any written opposition to any such motion or minute.	48	47

Column 1 *(Matters)*	Column 2 *(Fee Payable)* £	Column 3 *(Fee Formerly Payable)* £
30. Marking an appeal to the Sheriff Principal in any proceedings (other than as provided for in paragraph 16(c) of this Table).	113	111
Sheriff court books		
31. Recording protest of a bill or promissory note (NOTE: Extracts to be charged as in paragraph 36 of this Table).	24	23
32. Preservation of deeds, each deed (NOTE: This includes recording and engrossing. If extracts are required, a separate fee is to be charged as in paragraph 36 of this Table).	12	11
Miscellaneous office procedures		
33. Lodging each set of plans or other Parliamentary deposit.	71	70
34. Inspection of report of auction and the auditor of court's report.	18	18
35. Search and report service as instructed by a trade protection society, licensed credit reference agency or trade publication of protests of relevant court records as allowed as appropriately included in the Ordinary Cause Rules with the fees below payable in advance—		
weekly for 12 months;	346	339
36. Recording, engrossing, extracting, printing or copying of all documents, except as provided for at paragraph 4 of this Table (if a search is required an additional fee will be charged as per paragraph 37 of this Table)—		
(a) by photocopying or otherwise producing a printed or typed copy—		
(i) up to 10 pages;	6	6
(ii) each page or part thereof in excess of 10 pages;	0.50	0.50
(b) for a copy of a document in electronic form.	6	6
(NOTE: Recording in Sheriff Court Register of Deeds to be charged as in paragraph 31.)		
37. Any search of records or archives, except as provided for at paragraph 4 of this Table, per 30 minutes or part thereof.—	12	11
In addition, correspondence fee where applicable.	12	11
38. Citation of, or intimation to, any person or persons by sheriff officer as instructed by the sheriff clerk.	12 plus sheriff officer's fee	11 plus sheriff officer's fee

PART III — AUDITOR OF COURT

39. Taxing accounts of expenses incurred in judicial proceedings remitted to the auditor of court for taxation—		
(a) lodging account for taxation.	43	42
(b) taxing accounts of expenses etc.—		
(i) up to £400;	20	20
(ii) for every additional £100 or part thereof;	5	5
(NOTE: Fee to be determined by auditor of court on amount of account as submitted.)		
(c) cancellation of diet of taxation—		
(i) where written notice of cancellation received from receiving party after 4.00 pm on the fourth working day before the day of diet of taxation;	50% of fee that would have been payable under sub-paragraph (b) of this paragraph	550% of fee that would have been payable under sub-paragraph (b) of this paragraph

Column 1 (Matters)	Column 2 (Fee Payable) £	Column 3 (Fee Formerly Payable) £
(ii) where written notice of cancellation received from receiving party after 4.00 pm on the second working day before the day of the diet of taxation.	75% of fee that would have been payable under sub-paragraph (b) of this paragraph	75% of fee that would have been payable under sub-paragraph (b) of this paragraph

PART 2

Sheriff Personal Injury Court

(Payable from 1st April 2016)

Column 1 (Matters)	Column 2 (Fee Payable) £	Column 3 (Fee Formerly Payable) £
1. Lodging of a written motion or minute and the lodging of any written opposition to any such motion or minute.	54	53
2. Fixing, allocating or assigning of a proof or trial, a debate or a hearing on the merits of the cause	59	58
3. Hearing fee: per 30 minutes or part thereof.	77	75
4. Lodging a certified copy closed record. (NOTE: fee payable only once in respect of a cause).	107	105
5. Initial writ. (NOTE: fee covers issue of extract decree).	214	210
6. Lodging defences (fee payable by each defender or compearer). (NOTE: fee covers issue of extract decree).	214	210
7. Citation of a civil jury. (NOTE: includes outlays incurred in citing and countermanding, and is payable on the lodging of a proposed issue for jury trial.)	298	292
8. Certified copy of a document	18	18

Table of Fees payable in the Justice of Peace Courts

Justice of the Peace Court Fees (Scotland) Order 2012
(SSI 2012 No 292)

[This Table of Fees is printed as amended by:
The Justice of the Peace Court Fees (Scotland) Order 2015 (SSI 2015 No 263) which came into force on
22nd September 2015.]

SCHEDULE

TABLE OF FEES

(Payable from 1st April 2016)

Column 1	Column 2	Column 3
(Matters)	*(Fee payable)*	*(Fee formerly payable)*
	£	£
1. Application for utility warrants	11	11
2. Copying of—		
(a) each document, up to 10 pages;	6	6
(b) each further page or part thereof;	0.5	0.5
(c) each document in electronic form	6	6
3. Any search of records or archives, per 30 minutes or part thereof.	12	11
In addition, correspondence fee where applicable.	12	11
4. Petition for removal of disqualification from driving.	89	87

Table of Fees payable to Messengers-at-Arms

Act of Sederunt (Fees of Messengers-at-Arms) (No 2) 2002
(SSI 2002 No 566))

[This Schedule is printed as amended by:

Act of Sederunt (Fees of Messengers-at-Arms) 2004 (SSI 2004 No 515) which came into force on 1st January 2005;

Act of Sederunt (Fees of Messengers-at-Arms) 2005 (SSI 2005 No 582) which came into force on 1st January 2006;

Act of Sederunt (Fees of Messengers-at-Arms) 2006 (SSI 2006 No 540) which came into force on 1st January 2007;

Act of Sederunt (Fees of Messengers-at-Arms) 2007 (SSI 2007 No 532) which came into force on 1st January 2008;

Act of Sederunt (Fees of Messengers-at-Arms) 2008 (SSI 2008 No 481) which came into force on 12th January 2009;

Act of Sederunt (Fees of Messengers-at-Arms) (Diligence) 2009 (SSI 2009 No 383) which came into force on 23rd November 2009;

Act of Sederunt (Fees of Messengers-at-Arms) 2011 (SSI 2011 No 48) which came into force on 1st March 2011;

Act of Sederunt (Fees of Messengers-at-Arms) (No 2) 2011 (SSI 2011 No 431) which came into force on 23rd January 2012;

Act of Sederunt (Fees of Messengers-at-Arms) (Amendment) 2012 (SSI 2012 No 8) which came into force on 22nd January 2012;

Act of Sederunt (Fees of Messengers-at-Arms) (Amendment) (No. 2) 2012 (SSI 2012 No 340) which came into force on 8th January 2013;

Act of Sederunt (Fees of Messengers-at-Arms) 2013 (SSI 2013 No 346) which came into force on 27th January 2014;

Act of Sederunt (Fees of Messengers-at-Arms) 2016 (SSI 2016 No 101) which came into force on 1st April 2016.]

SCHEDULE 1
GENERAL REGULATIONS

1. Subject to the following paragraphs, the fees payable to a messenger-at-arms shall be calculated in accordance with the Table of Fees in this Schedule and shall be payable in respect of all forms of service or intimation of a document, citation of a person or execution of diligence and all other work authorised by the court and executed by a messenger-at-arms during the normal business hours of 9.00 am to 5.00 pm.

2. Fees in relation to service or intimation of a document, citation of a person or diligence which, of necessity, is executed outwith normal business hours shall be surcharged by the levying of an additional fee of —

   (a) 33¹/³ per cent of the fee specified in the Table of Fees, where it is executed on a week day between the hours of 5.00 pm and 10.00 pm; and

   (b) 75 per cent of the fee specified in the Table of Fees, where it is executed on a week day after 10.00 pm or before 9.00 am or on a Saturday, Sunday or a public holiday.

3. Where the service or intimation of a document or inhibition is executed in a remote rural area the fees specified in the Table of Fees at Item 1(a)(i), 2(a)(i) and 2(b)(i) shall be surcharged by the levying of an additional fee of 30 per cent of the fee specified in the Table of Fees.

3A. Where the value of an action is over £100,000 the fees specified in the Table of Fees at Item 1(a), 2, 3(b), 3(c) and 12 shall be surcharged by the levying of an additional fee of 0.01 percent of the value of the action.

4. An additional fee may be negotiated between the messenger-at-arms and the instructing agent by prior agreement in the following circumstances:

   (a) where the messenger-at-arms is standing by awaiting the delivery or uplifting of a document for immediate service;

   (b) where the messenger-at-arms has to instruct an huissier or other officer of court outwith Scotland to serve a document; or

   (c) where there is no prescribed fee and the importance, urgency and value of the work involved necessitates an additional fee.

5. All reasonable outlays, including postage and any recorded delivery costs in respect of items 1(b) and

1(c) in the Table of Fees, necessarily incurred by a messenger-at-arms in carrying out lawful instructions shall be charged in addition to a fee specified in the Table of Fees.

6. Every fee note rendered by a messenger-at-arms shall be so detailed that the fees charged by him may be easily checked against the Table of Fees; and any fees agreed under paragraph 4 above and any allowable outlays shall be clearly narrated as such. The fee note shall be reviewed by the messenger-at-arms to ensure that it is fair and reasonable in the circumstances and shall be adjusted by him if necessary.

7. Discounting of fees is permitted only between messengers-at-arms.

8. Any restriction or modification made by a messenger-at-arms of fees recoverable from a person shall be passed on to that person only.

9. Time shall be charged in units of 30 minutes or part thereof; and, except in relation to time under paragraph 10, 11 or 12 below —

    (a) time shall apply from the end of the first hour at the place of execution until completion; or

    (b) time shall apply after the messenger-at-arms has travelled a distance of 30 miles from his place of business until he returns to a distance of 30 miles from that place.

10. Where a messenger-at-arms has to use a ferry, he and any witness shall be allowed the necessary cost of the ferry, all reasonable subsistence and the time for boarding, crossing and returning, which shall be charged on a time basis.

11. Where a messenger-at-arms is required to attend before a notary public, commissioner or other person or as a witness, a fee for such attendance by the messenger-at-arms and any witness shall be chargeable on a time basis.

12. Where enquiries are necessary in order to execute service, intimation, citation, diligence or any other work authorised by the court, a fee for such enquiries shall be chargeable on a time basis.

12A. Where, in relation to a money attachment, a messenger-at-arms is required to realise the value of the money attached and dispose of same under section 184 of the Act of 2007 and deposit cash and proceeds of foreign currency (including conversion of foreign currency) the fee for such work shall be chargeable on a time basis.

13.—(1) Where, in an attachment, the appraised value of an article exceeds the sum recoverable, the fee specified in the Table of Fees shall be calculated in accordance with the sum recoverable and not the appraised value.

(2) Where, in an attachment, a debtor or other occupier of the premises claims that goods are subject to a hire purchase agreement or are otherwise the property of someone other than the debtor, but refuses, or is unable, to produce evidence to that effect, the messenger-at-arms may poind the goods and shall add a note on the schedule of the poinding stating that the debtor has claimed that the goods are subject to a hire purchase agreement or are otherwise the property of someone other than the debtor, as the case may be.

13A.—(1) Where, in a money attachment, the value of the money exceeds the sum recoverable, the fee specified in the Table of Fees shall be calculated in accordance with the sum recoverable and not the value.

(2) Where, in a money attachment, a debtor or other occupier of the premises claims that money is the property of someone other than the debtor but refuses, or is unable to produce evidence to that effect, the messenger-at-arms may attach the money and shall add a note on the schedule of the attachment stating that the debtor claims that the money is the property of someone other than the debtor.

14. A messenger-at-arms supplying services to any person in respect of which fees are payable to him under this Schedule shall —

    (a) if he is a taxable person within the meaning of the Value Added Tax Act 1983; and

    (b) if the supply is a taxable supply within the meaning of that Act,

make charges to that person in addition to the charges in respect of that fee, being such additional charge as amounts to the value-added tax payable under that Act in respect of the supply of those services.

15. In this Schedule, unless the context otherwise requires —

    "the Act of 2002" means the Debt Arrangement and Attachment (Scotland) Act 2002 (asp 7)

    "the Act of 2007" means the Bankruptcy and Diligence etc. (Scotland) Act 2007 (asp 3);

    "the Act of 1987" means the Debtors (Scotland) Act 1987;

    "apprehension" means apprehending, detaining and taking to and from court or prison;

    "arranging" means accepting instructions, checking for competency, reserving time, advising instructing agent, making all necessary arrangements, intimation and service (where necessary) prior to execution;

    "possession" means searching, taking possession and delivery;

"postal diligence" means service of any diligence, which may be served by post, by registered post or the first class recorded delivery service;

"postal service" means service or intimation by registered post or the first class recorded delivery service;

"remote rural area" means an area classified as such in the Scottish Government's Urban/Rural Classification 2009-2010.

"service" means service or intimation of any document under a rule of court or an order of the court and includes accepting instructions, preparation, postage and service or intimation of any ancillary form or other ancillary document.

SCHEDULE

TABLE OF FEES

(Payable from 1st April 2016)

Item	£
1. *Service or intimation of a document*	
(a) Service	
(i) each person at a different address	101.15
(ii) each additional person at the same address or additional copy required to be served or intimated under the Act of 1987 and the Act of 2002	19.95
(b) Postal service	28.75
(c) Postal diligence	43.80
2. *Inhibitions*	
(a) Inhibitions only	
(i) each person at a different address	101.15
(ii) each additional person at the same address	32.55
(b) Inhibition and service	
(i) each person at a different address	120.75
(ii) each additional person at the same address	52.45
(c) Inhibition, service and interdict	
(i) each person at a different address	200.55
(ii) each additional person at the same address	85.25
3. *Interdicts (including non-harassment orders under the Protection from Harassment Act 1997)*	
(a) Interdict only	
(i) each person at a different address	147.80
(ii) each additional person at the same address	32.55
(b) Interdict and service	
(i) each person at a different address	167.95
(ii) each additional person at the same address	52.45
(c) Interdict, service and inhibition	
(i) each person at a different address	200.55
(ii) each additional person at the same address	85.25
4. *Attachments*	
(a) Service notice of entry	11.20
(b) Arranging attachment and endeavouring but being unable to execute the same for whatever reason	83.80

£

    (c)   Arranging and executing attachment where appraised value is—
- (i)   £690 or under   98.05
- (ii) over £690 and up to £2,773   152.00
- (iii) over £2,773 and up to £27,922 – 10% of the appraised value
- (iv) over £27,922 and up to £139,601 – 10% of the first £27,922, 5% thereafter
- (v) over £139,601 – 10% of the first £27,922, 5% thereafter up to £139,601 and 1% thereafter

    (d)   Reporting attachment   9.30

5. *Attachment of motor vehicles, heavy plant or machinery*

    (a)   Arranging and executing attachment where appraised value is—
- (i)   £690 or under   98.05
- (ii) over £690 and up to £3,067   152.00
- (iii) over £3,067 and up to £139,601 – 5% of the appraised value
- (iv) over £139,601 – 5% of the first £139,601 and 1% thereafter

    (b)   Reporting attachment   9.30

6. *Money attachments under the Act of 2007*

    (a)   Arranging attachment and endeavouring but being unable to execute the same for whatever reason   83.80

    (b)   Arranging and executing attachment, including removal of attached money, where value of money is—
- (i)   £690 or under   98.05
- (ii) over £690 and up to £2,773   152.00
- (iii) over £2,773 and up to £27,922 – 10% of the value
- (iv) over £27,922 and up to £139,601 – 10% of the first £27,922, 5% thereafter
- (v) over £139,601 – 10% of the first £27,922, 5% thereafter up to £139,601 and 1% thereafter

    (c)   Reporting attachment   9.30

7. *Auctions*

    (a)   Arranging auction, preparing advertisement and giving public notice   24.25

    (b)   Serving copy of warrant of auction and intimating the place and date of auction and if necessary the date of removal of attached effects – as in item 1(a) or (b) above, as the case may be   80.05

    (c)   Officer and witness attending auction but auction not executed for whatever reason   80.05

    (d)   Officer and witness attending auction sale   147.80

8. *Ejections*

    (a)   Arranging ejection   80.05

    (b)   Arranging and executing ejection   124.25

9. *Taking possession of effects*

    (a)   Arranging possession   80.05

    (b)   Arranging and effecting possession   147.80

10. *Apprehensions*

    (a)   Arranging apprehension   80.05

    (b)   Arranging and apprehending   147.80

11. *Taking possession of children*

    (a)   Arranging to take possession   80.05

    (b)   Taking possession of each child   147.80

£

12. *Arresting vessels, aircraft and cargo*

    (a) Arranging to arrest   80.05

    (b) Arranging and effecting arrestment   244.60

13. *Miscellaneous*

    (a) Making any report or application under the Act of 1987, the Act of 2002 or the Act of 2007 with the exception of reporting an attachment or a money attachment   18.60

    (b) Granting any receipt required to be issued under the Act of 1987 or the Act of 2002   9.30

    (c) Arranging locksmith or tradesman to be in attendance   5.95

    (d) Granting certificate of displenishment or providing any other certificate or report, registering any document or making any application to a court or the creditor   18.60

    (e) Executing warrant to open lockfast places   18.60

    (f) Time

        (i) with witness – £29.80 per unit

        (ii) without witness – £22.20 per unit

    (g) Photocopies

        (i) first page document – £2.10

        (ii) subsequent pages – per page £1.15

    (h) Service of a document in Scotland under Regulation (EC) No 1393/2007 of the European Parliament and of the Council of 13th November 2007 on the service in the Member States of judicial and extrajudicial documents in civil or commercial matters (service of documents), and repealing Council Regulation (EC) No 1348/2000—

        (i) where service is effected by a method mentioned in rule 16.1(1)(a)(i), (ii), (iii) or (b)(i) of the Rules of the Court of Session 1994 (methods and manner of service on a person)   138.90

        (ii) where service is effected by a method mentioned in rule 16.1(1)(a)(iv) or (b)(ii) of the Rules of the Court of Session 1994 (postal service)   44.25

Table of Fees payable to Sheriff Officers

Act of Sederunt (Fees of Sheriff Officers) (No 2) 2002 (SSI 2002 No. 567)

[This Schedule is printed as amended by:

Act of Sederunt (Fees of Sheriff Officers) 2003 (SSI 2003 No 538) which came into force on 1st January 2004;

Act of Sederunt (Fees of Sheriff Officers) 2004 (SSI 2004 No 513) which came into force on 1st January 2005;

Act of Sederunt (Fees of Sheriff Officers) 2005 (SSI 2005 No 538) which came into force on 1st January 2006;

Act of Sederunt (Fees of Sheriff Officers) 2006 (SSI 2006 No 539) which came into force on 1st January 2007;

Act of Sederunt (Fees of Sheriff Officers) 2007 (SSI 2006 No 550) which came into force on 14th January 2008;

Act of Sederunt (Fees of Sheriff Officers) 2008 (SSI 2008 No 430) which came into effect on 26th January 2009;

Act of Sederunt (Fees of Sheriff Officers) (Diligence) 2009 (SSI 2009 No 379) which came into force on 23rd November 2009;

Act of Sederunt (Fees of Sheriff Officers) 2011 (SSI 2009 No 47) which came into force on 1st March 2011;

Act of Sederunt (Fees of Sheriff Officers) (No 2) 2011 (SSI 2011 No 432) which came into force on 23rd January 2012;

Act of Sederunt (Fees of Sheriff Officers) (Amendment) 2012 (SSI 2012 No 7) which came into force on 22nd January 2012;

Act of Sederunt (Fees of Sheriff Officers) (Amendment) (No. 2) 2012 (SSI 2012 No 341) which came into force on 8th January 2013;

Act of Sederunt (Fees of Sheriff Officers) 2013 (SSI 2013 No 345) which came into force on 27th January 2014;

Act of Sederunt (Fees of Sheriff Officers) 2016 (SSI 2016 No 100) which came into force on 1st April 2016.]

SCHEDULE 1

GENERAL REGULATIONS

1. Subject to the following paragraphs, the fees payable to a sheriff officer in relation to an ordinary cause or a summary cause, as the case may be, shall be calculated in accordance with the Table of Fees in this Schedule and shall be payable in respect of (a) all forms of service or intimation of a document, citation of a person or execution of diligence and all other work authorised by the court and (b) recovery of rates, charges or taxes by summary warrant, any of which is executed by a sheriff officer during the normal business hours of 9.00 am to 5.00 pm.

1A. Column A of the Table of Fees specifies the fees payable in relation to —

    (a)   a summary cause commenced before 14th January 2008; and

    (b)   a summary cause commenced on or after that date where the value of the claim when the cause is commenced is £1,500 or less (exclusive of interest and expenses).

1B. A summary cause falling within paragraph (c) of section 35(1) of the Sheriff Courts (Scotland) Act 1971 (actions *ad factum praestandum* and actions for the recovery of possession of heritable or moveable property)(4) falls within paragraph (b) of general regulation 1A where it contains no additional or alternative crave for decree for payment of money or where the value of such crave is £1,500 or less (exclusive of interest and expenses).

1C. Column B of the Table of Fees specifies the fees payable in relation to —

    (a)   a summary cause not falling within general regulation 1A; and

    (b)   an ordinary cause.

2. Fees in relation to service or intimation of a document, citation of a person or diligence which, of necessity, is executed outwith normal business hours shall be surcharged by the levying of an additional fee of —

    (*a*)   33^{1}/$_{3}$ per cent of the fee specified in the Table of Fees, where it is executed on a week day between the hours of 5.00 pm and 10.00 pm; and

    (*b*)   75 per cent of the fee specified in the Table of Fees, where it is executed on a week day after 10.00 pm or before 9.00 am or on a Saturday, Sunday or a public holiday.

3. Where the service or intimation of a document or inhibition is executed in a remote rural area the fees specified in the Table of Fees at Item 1(a)(i), 2(a)(i) and 2(b)(i) shall be surcharged by the levying of an additional fee of 30 per cent of the fee specified in the Table of Fees.

3A. In General Regulation 9 for "2, 4A(b), 5(c), 6(b)(i) and (ii), 7(b), 8(b), 9(b), 10(b), 11(b)" substitute "3, 6(b), 7(c) and (d), 8(b), 9(b), 10(b), 11(b), 12(b).

4. An additional fee may be negotiated between a sheriff officer and the instructing agent by prior agreement in the following circumstances —

    (*a*) where the sheriff officer is standing by awaiting the delivery or uplifting of a document for immediate service;

    (*b*) where the sheriff officer has to instruct an huissier or other officer of court outwith Scotland to serve a document; or

    (*c*) where there is no prescribed fee and the importance, urgency and value of the work involved necessitates an additional fee

5. All reasonable outlays, including postage and any recorded delivery costs in respect of items 1(b) and 1(c) in the Table of Fees, necessarily incurred by a sheriff officer in carrying out lawful instructions shall be charged in addition to a fee specified in the Table of Fees in this Schedule.

6. Every fee note rendered by a sheriff officer shall be so detailed that the fees charged by him may be easily checked against the Table of Fees; and any fees agreed under paragraph 4 above and any allowable outlays shall be clearly narrated as such. The fee note shall be reviewed by the sheriff officer to ensure that it is fair and reasonable in the circumstances and shall be adjusted by him if necessary.

7. Discounting of fees is permitted only between sheriff officers.

8. Any restriction or modification made by a sheriff officer of fees recoverable from a person shall be passed on to that person only.

9. Time will be charged in units of 30 minutes or part thereof; and, in respect of the following items in the Table of Fees, shall apply from the end of the first hour at the place of execution until completion: 2, 4A(b), 5(c), 6(b)(i) and (ii), 7(b), 8(b), 9(b), 10(b) and 11(b).

10. Where a sheriff officer has to use a ferry, he and any witness shall be allowed the necessary cost of the ferry, all reasonable subsistence and the time for boarding, crossing and returning, which shall be charged on a time basis.

11. Where a sheriff officer is required to attend before a notary public, commissioner or other person or as a witness, a fee for such attendance by the sheriff officer and any witness shall be chargeable on a time basis.

12. Where enquiries are necessary in order to execute service, intimation, citation, diligence or any other work authorised by the court, a fee for such enquiries shall be chargeable on a time basis.

12A. Where, in relation to a money attachment, a sheriff officer is required to realise the value of the money attached and dispose of same under section 184 of the Act of 2007 and deposit cash and proceeds of foreign currency (including conversion of foreign currency) the fee for such work shall be chargeable on a time basis.

13. Where personal service is to be carried out under item 1(a)(i) in the Table of Fees and more than one visit is required, each additional visit shall be charged at 50 per cent of the fee specified in that item.

14.—(1) Where, in an attachment, the appraised value of an article exceeds the sum recoverable, the fee specified in the Table of Fees in this schedule shall be calculated in accordance with the sum recoverable and not the appraised value.

14A.—(1) Where, in a money attachment, the value of the money exceeds the sum recoverable, the fee specified in the Table of Fees shall be calculated in accordance with the sum recoverable and not the value.

(2) Where, in a money attachment, a debtor or other occupier of the premises claims that money is the property of someone other than the debtor but refuses, or is unable to produce evidence to that effect, the sheriff officer may attach the money and shall add a note on the schedule of the attachment stating that the debtor claims that the money is the property of someone other than the debtor.

(2) Where, in an attachment, a debtor or other occupier of the premises claims that goods are subject to a hire purchase agreement or are otherwise the property of someone other than the debtor, but refuses or is unable to produce evidence to that effect, the sheriff officer may attach the goods and shall add a note on the schedule of the attachment stating that the debtor has claimed that the goods are subject to a hire purchase agreement or are otherwise the property of someone other than the debtor, as the case may be.

15. The fees payable to a sheriff officer in respect of recovery of rates, charges or taxes by summary warrant shall be calculated in accordance with the fees specified in Column B of the Table of Fees.

16. A sheriff officer supplying services to any person in respect of which fees are payable to him under this Schedule shall —

    (*a*) if he is a taxable person within the meaning of the Value Added Tax Act 1983; and

    (*b*) if the supply is a taxable supply within the meaning of that Act,

make charges to that person in addition to the charges in respect of that fee, being such additional charge as amounts to the value-added tax payable under the Act in respect of the supply of those services.

17. In this Schedule, unless the context otherwise requires —

"the Act of 2002" means the Debt Arrangement and Attachment Act 2002 (asp 17);

"the Act of 2007 means the Bankruptcy and Diligence etc. (Scotland) Act 2007 (asp 3);

"the Act of 1987" means the Debtors (Scotland) Act 1987;

"apprehension" means apprehending, detaining and taking to and from court or prison;

"arranging" means accepting instructions, checking for competency, reserving time, advising instructing agent, making all necessary arrangements, intimation and service (where necessary) prior to execution;

"possession" means searching, taking possession and delivery;

"postal diligence" means service of any diligence, which may be served by post, by registered post or the first class recorded delivery service;

"postal service" means service or intimation by registered post or the first class recorded delivery service;

"remote rural area" means an area classified as such in the Scottish Government's Urban/Rural Classification 2009-2010.

"service" means service or intimation of any document under a rule of court or an order of the court and includes accepting instructions, preparation, postage and service or intimation of any ancillary form or other ancillary document.

SCHEDULE

TABLE OF FEES

(Payable from 1st April 2016)

Item	Column A £	Column B £
1. *Service or intimation of a document*		
(a) Service		
(i) each person at a different address	50.70	79.10
(ii) each additional person at the same address or additional copy required to be served or intimated under the Act of 1987 and the Act of 2002	11.05	17.85
(b) Postal service	15.50	26.25
(c) Postal diligence	24.05	39.45
2. *Inhibitions*		
(a) Inhibitions only		
(i) each person at a different address	65.35	101.15
(ii) each additional person at the same address	21.05	32.55
(b) Inhibition and service		
(i) each person at a different address	76.30	117.85
(ii) each additional person at the same address	33.15	51.20
(c) Inhibition, service and interdict		
(i) each person at a different address		195.75
(ii) each additional person at the same address		83.30
3. *Interdicts (including non-harassment orders under the Protection from Harassment Act 1997 and antisocial behaviour orders under the Antisocial Behaviour etc. (Scotland) Act 2004)*		
(a) Interdict only		
(i) each person at a different address		147.80
(ii) each additional person at the same address		32.55
(b) Interdict and service		
(i) each person at a different address		166.15
(ii) each additional person at the same address		50.60

Item	Column A £	Column B £
4. *Attachments*		
(a) Service notice of entry	7.25	11.20
(b) Arranging attachment and endeavouring but being unable to execute the same for whatever reason	57.25	83.80
(c) Arranging and executing attachment where appraised value is—		
(i) £690 or under	98.05	98.05
(ii) over £690 and up to £2,773	152.00	152.00
(iii) over £2,773 and up to £27,922 – 10% of the appraised value		
(iv) over £27,922 and up to £139,601 – 10% of the first £27,922, 5% thereafter		
(v) over £139,601 – 10% of the first £27,922 5% thereafter up to £139,601 and 1% thereafter		
(d) Reporting attachment	9.30	9.30
5. *Attachment of motor vehicles, heavy plant or machinery*		
(a) Arranging and executing attachment where appraised value is—		
(i) £690 or under	98.05	98.05
(ii) over £690 and up to £3,067	152.00	152.00
(iii) over £3,067 and up to £139,601 – 5% of the appraised value		
(iv) over £139,601 – 5% of the first £139,601 and 1% thereafter		
(b) Reporting attachment	9.30	9.30
6. *Money attachments under the Act of 2007*		
(a) Arranging attachment and endeavouring but being unable to execute the same for whatever reason	57.25	83.80
(b) Arranging and executing attachment, including removal of attached money, where value of money is—		
(i) £690 or under	98.05	98.05
(ii) over £690 and up to £2,773	152.00	152.00
(iii) over £2,773 and up to £27,922 – 10% of the value		
(iv) over £27,922 and up to £139,601 – 10% of the first £27,564 5% thereafter		
(v) over £139,601 – 10% of the first £27,922, 5% thereafter up to £139,601 and 1% thereafter		
(c) Reporting attachment	9.30	9.30
7. *Auctions*		
(a) Arranging auction, preparing advertisement and giving public notice	24.25	24.25
(b) Intimating the place and date of auction and if necessary the date of removal of attached effects – as in items 1(a) or (b) above, as the case may be		
(c) Officer and witness attending auction but auction not executed for whatever reason	53.35	80.05
(d) Officer and witness attending auction	147.80	147.80
8. *Ejections*		
(a) Arranging ejection	53.35	80.05
(b) Arranging and executing ejection	109.55	124.25
9. *Taking possession of effects*		
(a) Arranging possession	53.35	80.05
(b) Arranging and effecting possession	109.55	147.80

Item	Column A £	Column B £
10. *Apprehensions*		
(a) Arranging apprehension		80.05
(b) Arranging and apprehending		147.80
11. *Uplifting children*		
(a) Arranging uplift		80.05
(b) Uplifting of each child		147.80
12. *Arresting vessels, aircraft and cargo*		
(a) Arranging to arrest	53.35	80.05
(b) Arranging and effecting arrestment	134.55	244.60
13. *Miscellaneous*		
(a) Making any report or application under the Act of 1987, the Act of 2002 or the Act of 2007 with the exception of reporting an attachment or a money attachment	18.60	18.60
(b) Granting any receipt required to be issued under the Act of 1987 or the Act of 2002	9.30	9.30
(c) Arranging locksmith or tradesman to be in attendance	5.95	5.95
(d) Granting certificate of displenishment or providing any other certificate or report, registering any document or making any application to a court or the creditor	18.60	18.60
(e) Executing warrant to open lockfast places	18.60	18.60
(f) Time		
(i) with witness – £29.80 per unit		
(ii) without witness – £22.20 per unit		
(g) Photocopies		
(i) first page of document – £2.10		
(ii) subsequent pages – per page £1.15		

Table of Fees payable in the Scottish Land Court

Scottish Land Court (Fees) Order 1996 (SI 1996 No 680)

[Came into force on 1st April 1996.]

SCHEDULE

TABLE OF FEES

		£
(1) Small Landholders (Scotland) Acts 1886 to 1931 and Crofters (Scotland) Act 1993		
(a)	Application for a record of a holding or a croft	
	Principal application (each applicant)	60.00
	For each respondent	10.00
(b)	Recording agreements for loan by —	
	(i) The Scottish Office Agriculture, Environment And Fisheries Department And	
	(ii) Highlands And Islands Enterprise	
	Each agreement	70.00
(c)	Other applications	
	Principal application	28.00
	When more than one applicant (each additional applicant)	18.00
	For each respondent	4.00
(d)	Appeals and motions for rehearing	
	Each appellant or motioner	50.00
	Each respondent	6.00
(e)	Hearing and inspection fee payable by applicant in all applications. For each day or part thereof the court sits or inspects	60.00
(f)	Additional fee	
	(i) Where the application is granted, dismissed or withdrawn after the hearing order has been received by each party but before the commencement of the hearing — payable by the applicant	70.00
	(iii) Where the principal clerk of court executes a conveyance following upon an order of the court under section 16(2) of the crofters (scotland) act 1993 — payable by the applicant	65.00
(2) Agricultural Holdings (Scotland) Act 1991		
(a)	Valuation of sheep stocks	
	Awards not exceeding £100	6.00
	Awards exceeding £100:	
	For the first £100 thereof	6.00
	For every additional £100 or part thereof	3.00
	Where application dismissed or withdrawn before valuation	75.00
(b)	Arbitration as to rents	
	Rental as fixed by court, not exceeding £500	50.00
	Rental as fixed by court exceeding £500:	
	For The First £500	50.00
	For every additional £100 or part thereof	7.50
	Where application dismissed or withdrawn before rent fixed	80.00

(c) Appeals against award by an arbiter   £

Fee payable on lodging appeal 65.00

Rental as fixed by court not exceeding £500 .... 30.00

Rental as fixed by court exceeding £500:

For the first £500 .... 30.00

For every additional £100 or part thereof.. 3.00

Where application dismissed or withdrawn before rent fixed 85.00

(d) Claims for compensation

Awards not exceeding £100 .... 12.00

Awards exceeding £100:

For the first £100 thereof 12.00

For every additional £100 or part thereof 5.00

Where application dismissed or withdrawn before compensation fixed 80.00

(e) Other applications

Principal application 100.00

When more than one applicant (each additional applicant) 50.00

For each respondent 45.00

(f) Appeals and motions for rehearing

Each Appellant Or Motioner... 60.00

(g) Hearings And Inspections

For every day or part thereof the court sits or inspects — payable by the applicant 120.00

(h) Additional fee

Where the application is granted, dismissed or withdrawn after the hearing order has been received by each party but before the commencement of the hearing — payable by the applicant 120.00

(3) Miscellaneous

(a) for making a copy or copies of the principal application or any part of it, or any order in it, or any original deed, writ, or document in process

For each sheet 1.20

For certifying such copy 7.00

(b) Applications not otherwise specified

Principal application 100.00

When more than one applicant (each additional applicant) 50.00

For each respondent 45.00

(c) Hearings And Inspections

For every day or part thereof the court sits or inspects — payable by the applicant 120.00

(d) Additional Fee

Where the application is granted, dismissed or withdrawn after the hearing order has been received by each party but before the commencement of the hearing — payable by the applicant 120.00

(e) Search Fee

For searches in records arising from postal or other enquiries — for each search.......... 9.00

Table of Fees payable in the Lands Tribunal for Scotland

Lands Tribunal for Scotland Rules 1971 (SI 1971 No 218)

[This Schedule is printed as amended by:

Lands Tribunal for Scotland (Amendment) (Fees) Rules 1993 (SI 1993 No 296) which came into force on 1st April 1993;

Lands Tribunal for Scotland (Amendment) (Fees) Rules 1994 (SI 1994 No 218) which came into force on 1st April 1994;

Lands Tribunal for Scotland (Amendment) (Fees) Rules 1995 (SI 1995 No 308) which came into force on 1st April 1995;

Lands Tribunal for Scotland (Amendment) (Fees) Rules 1996 (SI 1996 No 519) which came into force on 1st April 1996.

Lands Tribunal for Scotland (Amendment) (Fees) Rules 2003 (SI 2003 No 521) which came into force on 1st November 2003;

Lands Tribunal for Scotland Amendment (Fees) Rules 2004 (SSI 2004 No 480) which came into force on 28th November 2004;

Lands Tribunal Scotland Amendment (Fees) Rules 2009 (SSI 2009 No 260) which came into force on 1st July 2009;

Lands Tribunal for Scotland Amendment (Fees) Rules 2014 (SSI 2014 No 24) which came into force on 6th March 2014;

Lands Tribunal for Scotland Amendment (Fees) Rules 2015 (SSI 2015 No 199) which came into force on 30 June 2015.]

SCHEDULE 2

FEES

Applications etc. £

1. On an application under the Conveyancing and Feudal Reform (Scotland) Act 1970 —

    (i)   section 1 (land obligations) — initial application 130.00

    (ii) section 1 — subsequent application 65.00

    (iii) section 4 (feu duties) 75.00

2. On an application relating to disputed compensation under Part III of these Rules or where the Tribunal is acting under a reference by consent under section 1(5) of the Lands Tribunal Act 1949 —

    (i)   where the disputed amount does not exceed £20,000.00 being either a lump sum or a rent or other annual payment 78.00

    (ii) where the disputed amount exceeds £20,000.00 being either a lump sum or a rent or other annual payment 130.00

    (iii) where the application or reference does not involve a disputed amount 78.00

3. On an appeal under section 1(3A) of the Lands Tribunal Act 1949 (valuation for rating) —

    (i)   where the net annual value does not exceed £10,000.00 .... 100.00

    (ii) where the net annual value exceeds £10,000.00 but not £50,000.00 .... 150.00

    (iii) where the net annual value exceeds £50,000.00 but not £100,000.00 .... 300.00

    (iv) where the net annual value exceeds £100,000.00 .... 500.00

4. On an appeal under section 1(3BA) of the Lands Tribunal Act 1949 (non-referral of valuation appeal or complaint)... 78.00

5. On an appeal under section 25 of the Land Registration (Scotland) Act 1979 (appeal from action or omission of the Keeper of the Registers of Scotland)... 78.00

6. On any other application (not being an appeal under Part IV or Part VA or a reference under Part V of these Rules) 52.00

Hearing fees, etc.

7. (a) On the hearing of an application under section 1 of the   £155.00 for each day on which the
        Conveyancing and Feudal Reform (Scotland) Act 1970   Tribunal sits
    (b) On the making of an order under—
        (i) section 1 of the Conveyancing and Feudal Reform
            (Scotland) Act 1970   £88.00
        (ii) section 4 of that Act   £88.00

8. On the hearing of an application under Part III or an appeal under Part VC of these Rules or where the
    Tribunal is acting under a reference by consent —
    (a) Where the amount is determined in terms of a lump   £50.00 in respect of every
        sum—   £5,000.00 or part of £5,000.00 of
           such lump sum but not less than
           £155.00 for each day on which the
           Tribunal sits and not exceeding in
           any case £5,000.00
    (b) Where the amount is determined in terms of rent or   £50.00 in respect of every
        other annual payment —   £500.00 or part of £500.00 of
           such rent or other annual payment
           but not less than £155.00 for each
           day on which the Tribunal sits and
           not exceeding in any case
           £5,000.00
    (c) Where there is a settlement as to amount, for each day   £155.00
        on which the Tribunal sits

9. On the hearing of any other application or appeal or
    reference including the hearing of preliminary pleas-in-law
    or legal debates in which no fee is payable by reference to an   £155.00 for each day on which
    amount determined   the Tribunal sits

Miscellaneous fees

10. On certifying a copy of an order or determination of the
    Tribunal   £7.50

11. For each sheet of a copy of all or part of any document   £1.20

12. On a case for the decision of the Court of Session or the Lands
    Valuation Appeal Court (in respect of references under Part VC
    of these Rules) — an application for appeal by way of stated
    case (to include drafting of case and any necessary copies)   £55.00

13. On the placing of an advertisement under section 1 of the   100 per cent of the cost of the
    Conveyancing and Feudal Reform (Scotland) Act 1970   advertisement in an appropriate
    (*Note:* advertisements are invariably required in applications   newspaper (charge is restricted
    involving (a) missing superiors, (b) alcohol and (c) major   to the cost of one advertisement
    developments which may have widespread implications)   irrespective of the number of
       advertisements placed)

14. On an application for the cancellation of a hearing   £75.00

15. On an application during the course of proceedings which is
    not specifically referred to in the above table of fees (*eg* an
    application for (i) an extension to the period in which answers
    or adjustments are required to be lodged, or (ii) the
    continuation or sisting of an application)   £35.00

16. On an application under section 90 or 91 of the Title   £150.00
    Conditions (Scotland) Act 2003

17. On an application under the Land Reform (Scotland) Act 2003   £150.00

17A. On an application under article 22 or 23 of the Title
    Conditions (Scotland) Act 2003 (Development Management
    Scheme) Order 2009   £150

18. On a referral under section 86(5) of the Title Conditions (Scotland) Act 2003 or section 44 of the Abolition of Feudal Tenure etc. (Scotland) Act 2000 — £150.00

19. On the hearing of an application or referral under items 16,17, 17A or 18 above — £155 for each day on which the Tribunal sits

20. On the making of an order under the Abolition of Feudal Tenure etc. (Scotland) Act 2000, the Land Reform (Scotland) Act 2003 or the Title Conditions (Scotland) Act 2003 — £88 plus 100% of the cost of registering the order where the Tribunal is obliged to do so

21. For placing an advertisement in connection with applications under section 20 of the Abolition of Feudal Tenure etc. (Scotland) Act 2000 and sections 90 and 91 of the Title Conditions (Scotland) Act 2003 or the Title Conditions (Scotland) Act 2003 (Development Management Scheme) Order 2009 — 100% of the cost of the advertisement in an appropriate newspaper (charge is restricted to the cost of one advertisement irrespective of the number of advertisements placed)

22. On making representatives as respects an application under section 90(1) or 91 of the Title Conditions (Scotland) Act 2003 and article 22 or 23 of the Title Conditions (Scotland) Act 2003 (Development Management Scheme) Order 2009 — £25

23. On a referral under section 102 of the Title Conditions (Scotland) Act 2003 and article 22 or 23 of the Title Conditions (Scotland) Act 2003 (Development Management Scheme) Order 2009 — £150

24. On a referral under section 102 of the Title Conditions (Scotland) Act 2003 — £150

25. On an application under section 21, 44 or 69 of the Long Leases (Scotland) Act 2012(1) — £150

26. On an application under section 78 of the Long Leases (Scotland) Act 2012 where a determination is not sought under any other provision — £150

27. On a referral under section 55 or 77 of the Long Leases (Scotland) Act 2012 — £150

28. On hearing an application or referral under items 25 and 26 above — £155 for each day on which the Tribunal sits

29. On the making of an order under section 21, 44, 55, 69 or 77 of the Long Leases (Scotland) Act 2012 — £88

30. On the making of a determination under section 78 of the Long Leases (Scotland) Act 2012 not made with an order under any other provision — £88

31. For placing an advertisement in connection with applications under section 22 or 69 of the Long Leases (Scotland) Act 2012 — 100 per cent of the cost of the advertisement in an appropriate newspaper (charge is restricted to the cost of one advertisement irrespective of the number of advertisements placed)

31A. On an application under section 67(2), 69(1), 70(1) or 71(1) of the Land Registration etc. (Scotland) Act 2012 — £45

32. On a referral under section 82 of the Land Registration etc. (Scotland) Act 2012(2) — £150

33. On an appeal under section 103 of the Land Registration etc. (Scotland) Act 2012 — £150

34. On hearing a referral or appeal under items 32 and 33 above — £155 for each day on which the Tribunal sits

35. On the issue of a notice of determination under section 82 of the Land Registration etc. (Scotland) Act 2012 — £88

36. On the making of an order under section 103 of the Land Registration etc. (Scotland) Act 2012 — £88

Table of Fees payable to the Edinburgh Gazette

Authorised Scale of Charges for Notices and Advertisements

2016 Price List

All charges are exclusive of VAT at the prevailing rate, currently 20% No VAT is payable on printed copies	Public sector placing mandatory notices or State notices		All other advertisers.	
	XML, Webform, Gazette template Ex VAT	Other Ex VAT	XML, Webform, Gazette template Ex VAT	Other Ex VAT
1. Corporate and personal insolvency notices	£0.00	£20.60	£58.25	£79.40
(2–5 Related companies/individuals charged double the single company rate)	£0.00	£41.20	£116.50	£158.80
(6–10 Related companies/individuals charged treble the single company rate)	£0.00	£61.80	£174.75	£238.20
[Pursuant to the Insolvency Act 1986, the Insolvency Rules 1986, Companies (Forms) (Amendment) Regulations 1987 and any subsequent amending legislation]				
2. Deceased estate notices	£0.00	£20.60	£58.25	£79.40
3. All other notices – charged by event	£0.00	£20.60	£58.25	£79.40
(2–5 Related events will be charged at double the single event rate)	£0.00	£41.20	£116.50	£158.80
(6–10 Related events will be charged at treble the single company rate)	£0.00	£61.80	£174.75	£238.20
4. Offline Proofing		£36.00		£36.00
5. Late Advertisements		£36.00		£36.00

(6–10 Related events will be charged at treble the single company rate)
Examples,
- One event
- Appointments to a single role
- Specification for a single coin
- Single traffic order
- Application for a permit for one premises
- Petition to transfer one business
- A case transfer between insolvency practitioners
- Multiple events
- If you have two to five traffic orders then you pay double rate
- If you have six to ten traffic orders then you pay treble rate

- **London** – accepted after 11.30am, 2 days prior to publication

- **Edinburgh** – accepted after 9.30am, 1 day prior to publication

- **Belfast** – accepted after 3.00pm, 1 day prior to publication

All charges are exclusive of VAT at the prevailing rate, currently 20%	Public sector placing mandatory notices or State notices		All other advertisers.	
	XML, Webform, Gazette template	Other	XML, Webform, Gazette template	Other
No VAT is payable on printed copies	Ex VAT	Ex VAT	Ex VAT	Ex VAT
6. Withdrawal of Notices		£20.60	£58.25	£79.40
• **London** – after 11.30am, 2 days prior to publication				
• **Edinburgh** – after 9.30am, 1 day prior to publication				
• **Belfast** – after 3.00pm, 1 day prior to publication				
7. Other Services				
• A brand, logo, map, signature image	£51.50	£51.50	£53.00	£53.00
• Forwarding service for deceased estates	£51.50	£51.50	£53.00	£53.00

For those interested in purchasing voucher copies or subscriptions the following pricing applies:

	London	Edinburgh	Belfast
Print voucher copy (zero VAT)	£2.25	£1.50	£1.25
PDF voucher copy (+VAT)	£2.25	£1.50	£1.25
Annual subscription to the printed copy	£450.10	£105.70	£79.40
Annual subscription to the pdf copy	£529.50	211.90	£105.70

For more information and pricing for our datafeeds services, please call 01603 696701, or email data@thegazette.co.uk.

For more information or to buy a subscription, call +44 (0)333 202 5070, or email customer.services@thegazette.co.uk.

Table of Fees payable in the Registers of Scotland

The Registers of Scotland (Fees) Order 2014 (SSI 2014 No 188)

[The Schedule and Table of Fees are printed as amended by:

The Registers of Scotland (Voluntary Registration, Amendment of Fees, etc) Order 2015 (SSI 2015 No 265) which came into force on 30th June 2015.]

SCHEDULE 1

Article 3(a)

PART 1— LAND REGISTER OF SCOTLAND

Applications for deeds (other than heritable securities) and voluntary registration

1.—(1) Where an application mentioned in sub-paragraph (2) is made, subject to sub-paragraphs (4) to (7), the fee is calculated on the—

    (a)   amount of the consideration paid; or

    (b)   value of the plot of land,

whichever is the greater.

(2) This sub-paragraph applies to an application for registration of—

    (a)   disposition, a notice of title, a lease or an assignation of lease; or

    (b)   an unregistered plot of land by virtue of section 27(1) of the Act.

(3) Where an application mentioned in sub-paragraph (2) is made, subject to sub-paragraphs (8) to (11), the fee is at the rates shown in the Table of Fees in Part 3 of this Schedule—

    (a)   for an application mentioned in sub-paragraph (2)(a)—

        (i)   in column 2 of that Table; or

        (ii) where the application may be, and is, made using the ARTL system, in column 3 of that Table; or

    (b)   for an application mentioned in sub-paragraph (2)(b), in column 4 of that   Table.

(4) Where the application is to register a plot of land excambed, the fee is calculated on the value of the land transferred.

(5) Where the consideration consists of a yearly or periodical payment, the consideration is calculated at 10 years' purchase.

(6) Where the application is to register the grant of a lease, the fee is calculated on the consideration (if any) provided for that grant plus 10 times the relevant rent.

(7) Where the application is made to register the assignation of a lease, the fee is calculated on the consideration (if any) provided for the assignation plus 10 times the relevant rent payable at the date of the application.

(8) Where an application affects a number of title sheets, the fee is at the rates shown in the Table of Fees in Part 3 of this Schedule plus an additional fee of £60 for every title sheet affected other than the first.

(9) The additional fee of £60 mentioned in sub-paragraph (8) does not apply to a—

    (a)   shared plot title sheet designated under section 17(2) of the Act where the first title sheet affected is a sharing plot; or

    (b)   shared lease title sheet designated under schedule 1, paragraph 2(a) of the Act where the first title sheet affected is a sharing lease.

(10) Where the application is to register a disposition relating to a registered plot of land—

    (a)   for the sole purpose of evacuating a survivorship destination; and

    (b)   the name and designation of the proprietor in the proprietorship section remains the same, the fee is £60 for each title sheet affected.

(11) Where an application mentioned in sub-paragraph (2)(b) is made which is—

(a) entered in the application record on the same date as an application to register a standard security; and

(b) the standard security relates to the whole extent of that plot of land, no fee is payable in respect of the application mentioned in sub-paragraph (2)(b).

Heritable securities

2. Where an application is made for registration in respect of a heritable security, including the constitution, transfer, variation, postponement, corroboration or extinction of a security, the fee is—

(a) £60 for each title sheet affected; or

(b) where an application may be, and is, made using the ARTL system, £50 for each title sheet affected.

Related fees and services

3.—(1) Subject to sub-paragraph (1A), where an application is—

(a) rejected under section 21(3) of the Act; or

(b) withdrawn under section 34(1)(a) of the Act, the fee is £30.

(1A) Sub-paragraph (1) does not apply to an application which is rejected or withdrawn for the sole reason that another application in respect of the same land or title number, to which paragraph (1) does apply, has been rejected or withdrawn.

(2) In respect of an application for—

(a) an advance notice under section 57(1) of the Act; or

(b) a discharge of an advance notice under section 63(1) of the Act, the fee is £10.

(3) In respect of an application to make an entry in, or remove an entry from, a title sheet—

(a) where an order is granted by the court under—

    (i) section 67(3) of the Act, for warrant to place a caveat on a title sheet;

    (ii) section 69(2) of the Act, for warrant to renew a caveat;

    (iii) section 70(2) of the Act to restrict a caveat; or

    (iv) section 71(2) of the Act, to recall a caveat; or

(b) where, under section 72 of the Act, a person discharges a caveat, the fee is £60.

(4) Where an application is received in respect of a registered plot of land, to request the Keeper to vary warranty under section 76(2) of the Act, the fee is £60.

Article 3(b)

PART 2—REGISTER OF SASINES

Completion of title

4. Where the recording of completion of title by decree or a notice of title is made, the fee is—

(a) calculated on the value of the heritable subjects to which the recording relate; and

(b) at the rates shown in column 2 of the Table of Fees in Part 3 of this Schedule.

Heritable securities

5. In respect of the recording of a heritable security, including the constitution, transfer, variation, postponement, corroboration or extinction of a security, the fee is £60.

Recording by memorandum

6. Where any writ is presented in the Register of Sasines for recording by memorandum, the fee is £60 for each memorandum.

Additional extract or plain copy

7. Where a deed is being recorded, in respect of an additional extract or plain copy requested at the date of the application for recording, the fee is £10 plus VAT.

Article 3(a) and (b)

PART 3—FEES FOR REGISTRATIONS AND RECORDINGS IN THE LAND REGISTER OF SCOTLAND AND THE REGISTER OF SASINES

Industrial and Provident Society receipts

8. No fee is payable in respect of an application for registration or recording of receipts under the Industrial and Provident Societies Act 1965(1).

Other deeds

9. Where an application for registration is made under section 21 of the Act, or for recording in the Register of Sasines, of other deeds not referred to in Parts 1 and 2 of this Schedule, the fee is—

    (a) £60 for each title sheet affected or each deed recorded; or

    (b) where the application may be, and is, made using the ARTL system, £50 for each title sheet affected or each deed recorded.

Dual registration

10. Where an application for registration under section 21 of the Act or for recording a deed in the Register of Sasines comprises an application for dual registration or an application for variation of a title condition and no fee is provided in respect of such application in Parts 1 and 2 of this Schedule, the fee is £60 in respect of that application plus £60 for every title sheet other than the first affected by that application and for each deed recorded.

Table of Fees

"Column 1 Consideration paid or value £		Column 2 Fee £	Column 3 ARTL Fee £	Column 4 Voluntary registration Fee £
Not exceeding	50,000	60	50	45
	100,000	120	90	90
	150,000	240	180	180
	200,000	360	270	270
	300,000	480	360	360
	500,000	600	450	450
	700,000	720	540	540
	1,000,000	840	660	630
	2,000,000	1,000	800	750
	3,000,000	3,000	2,500	2,250
	5,000,000	5,000	4,500	3,750
Exceeding	5,000,000	7,500	7,000	5,625"

Article 3(c)

PART 4 — THE CHANCERY AND JUDICIAL REGISTERS

Registration Fees

Register	*Product/Service*	*Fee*
Register of Inhibitions	For each document	£15
Register of Deeds and Probative Writs in the Books of Council and Session	For each document (including first extract)	£10
Register of Protests	For each document (including first extract)	£10
Register of Judgments	For each document (including first extract)	£10
Register of the Great Seal	For a charter of incorporation	£250
	For a Commission	£630
Register of the Cachet Seal	For each impression	£30
Register of the Quarter Seal	For each gift of *ultimus haeres* or *bona vacantia*	£130
All	When a document is being registered, an additional extract or plain copy requested at the date of the application for registration	£10 plus VAT
None	For each certificate issued under the Civil Jurisdiction and Judgments Act 1982	£30

Article 3(d)

PART 5 — THE CROFTING REGISTER

Applications for registration and updating a registration schedule

Product/Service	*Fee*
Registration of a croft under section 4(1) or (2) of the Crofting Reform (Scotland) Act 2010 ("2010 Act")	£90
Updating the registration schedule of a registered croft following an event under section 5(1) of the 2010 Act	£90
Registration of a common grazing under section 24(1)(a) or (b) of the 2010 Act	£90
Updating the registration schedule of a registered common grazing under section 25(1) of the 2010 Act	£90
Registration of land held runrig under section 32(1) of the 2010 Act	£90
Updating the registration schedule of registered land held runrig following an event under section 32(5) of the 2010 Act	£90

Article 3(e)

PART 6 — THE REGISTER OF COMMUNITY INTERESTS IN LAND

Product/service	*Fee*
Initial registration of a tenant's interest	£40
Subsequent registration of an existing or previously registered interest	£25

Article 3(f)

PART 7 — FEES FOR ACCESS TO A REGISTER UNDER THE MANAGEMENT AND CONTROL OF THE KEEPER AND INFORMATION MADE AVAILABLE BY THE KEEPER

Register	*Product/service*	*Fee*
All registers under the management and control of the Keeper(2)	Request in writing by letter or email or electronically by submitting the form on Registers of Scotland website for inspection of a register in respect of one title (including one plain copy or copy of search sheet or minute)	£20 plus VAT
All registers under the management and control of the Keeper	Request made in person at a Registers of Scotland Customer Service Centre(3) for inspection of a register in respect of one title (including one plain copy or copy of search sheet or minute)	£30 plus VAT
Land Register	Extract(4) of— • Title sheet and part of the cadastral map • Title sheet • Part of a title sheet • Part of cadastral map • Document from the archive record • Part of document from the archive record • Application • Advance notice • Document in the application record • Part of document in application record Certified copy(5) of— • Application • Advance notice • Document in the application record • Part of document in application record	£30 plus VAT
Land Register	Plain copy of— • Title sheet and part of the cadastral map • Title sheet • Part of a title sheet • Part of cadastral map • Document from the archive record • Part of document from the archive record • Application • Advance notice • Document in the application record • Part of document in application record	£16 plus VAT
Register of Sasines	Extract of recorded deed	£30 plus VAT
Register of Sasines	Plain copy of recorded deed	£16 plus VAT
Register of Sasines	Copy of search sheet where request in writing provides search sheet number	£16 plus VAT
Register of Inhibitions	Plain copy of document where request in writing provides minute number	£16 plus VAT
Register of Deeds and Probative Writs in the Books of Council and Session	Extract of document where request in writing provides minute number	£30 plus VAT

Register of Deeds and Probative Writs in the Books of Council and Session	Plain copy of document where request in writing provides minute number	£16 plus VAT
Crofting Register	• Office copy of a registration schedule of a croft, common grazing or land held runrig	£30 plus VAT
	• Information provided by the Keeper regarding the suitability of an applicant's map for registration purposes in the Crofting Register	
Crofting Register	• Plain copy of a registration schedule of a croft, common grazing or land held runrig	£16 plus VAT
	• Copy of an Ordnance Survey map supplied for the purpose of registration in the Crofting Register	
Register of Community Interests in Land	• Extract of registration	£30 plus VAT
	• Plan (colour)	
Register of Community Interests in Land	• Plain copy of registration	£16 plus VAT
	• Plan (black and white)	

* Paragraph 3(1) of Part 1 to Schedule 1 came into force on 9th February 2015

(1) 1965(c.12), There are no relevant amendments.

(2) The Crofting Register, the Register of Community Interests in Land and the Register of Sites of Special Scientific Interest may be searched online for no fee at http://www.ros.gov.uk/customerservices/index.html.

(3) Meadowbank House, 153 London Road, Edinburgh EH8 7AU or Hanover House, 23 Douglas Street, Glasgow G2 7NQ.

(4) Section 104(1) of the Land Registration etc. (Scotland) Act 2012.

(5) Section 104(2) of the Land Registration etc. (Scotland) Act 2012.

Table of Fees payable in The National Archives of Scotland

Act of Sederunt (Fees in the National Archives of Scotland) 2003
(SSI 2003 No 234)

This Table of Fees is printed as amended by: Act of Sederunt (Fees in the National Archives of Scotland) 2005 (SSI 2005 No 77) which came into force on 1st March 2005.)

SCHEDULE
TABLE OF FEES

PART I — INSPECTION FEES

Column 1	Column 2
For the inspection of each volume, document or process, and the production of associated copies for each document or process therein	£6.00
Note: Fees are remitted for the inspection of records for historical or literary purposes in terms of section 10 of the Public Records (Scotland) Act 1937.	

PART II — SEARCH FEES

Column 1	Column 2
For personal searches in the records, for each search	£40.00
Notes:	
(1) The Keeper of the Records of Scotland may carry out a search in the records of the National Archives of Scotland for any person, and for any search the Keeper shall —	
(i) impose an additional charge based on the cost of carrying out that search, which cost shall include the cost of any copying requested or required as part of that search;	
(ii) provide an estimate to that person of the amount of that additional charge; and	
(iii) require that person to pay a deposit of a sum not exceeding £40 before carrying out that search.	
(2) The Keeper of the Records of Scotland may reduce or waive the charge or	

deposit payable for any search.

PART III — COPYING FEES	
Column 1	Column 2
1. Reprographic services, including digital images and output to microfilm and microfiche, are provided on a cost recovery basis, and National Archives of Scotland will provide an estimate of the cost on request.	As estimated
Notes:	
(1) A minimum charge of £6.00 will be payable for any of the above services.	
(2) An additional charge may be payable for work of unusual difficulty, or requiring special attention.	
2. Authentication: for each extract or certified copy, in addition to the reprographic charge and handling charge.	£4.00

PARTY LITIGANTS

Act of Sederunt (Expenses of Party Litigants) 1976 (SI 1976 No 1606)

[Amended by Act of Sederunt (Expenses of Party Litigants) (Amendment) 1983 (SI 1983 No 1438).]

2.—(1) Where in any proceedings in the Court of Session or the sheriff court, any expenses of a party litigant are ordered to be paid by any other party to the proceedings or in any other way, the auditor may, subject to the following provisions of this Rule, allow as expenses such sums as appear to the auditor to be reasonable having regard to all the circumstances in respect of —

    (a) work done which was reasonably required in connection with the cause, up to the maximum of two- thirds of the sum allowable to a solicitor for that work under the table of fees for solicitors in judicial proceedings; and

    (b) outlays reasonably incurred for the proper conduct of the cause.

(2) Without prejudice to the generality of paragraph (1) above, the circumstances to which the auditor shall have regard in determining what sum, if any, to allow in respect of any work done, shall include —

    (a) the nature of the work;

    (b) the time taken and the time reasonably required to do the work;

    (c) the amount of time spent in respect of which there is no loss of earnings;

    (d) the amount of any earnings lost during the time required to do the work;

    (e) the importance of the cause to the party litigant;

    (f) the complexity of the issues involved in the cause.

(3) In this Rule —

    (a) the word "auditor" includes any person taxing or otherwise determining a claim for expenses incurred in any proceedings in the Court of Session or in the sheriff court;

    (b) the expression "remunerative time" in relation to a litigant, means time when he is earning or would have been earning but for work done in or in connection with proceedings in court;

    (c) the expression "leisure time" in relation to a litigant, means time other than remunerative time.

    (d) the expression "table of fees for solicitors in judicial proceedings" means —

        (i) in relation to a cause in the Court of Session, the table of fees in Rule 347 of the Rules of Court in force at the time the work is done; and

        (ii) in relation to an ordinary action in the sheriff court, the table of fees in Schedule 2 to the Act of Sederunt (Alteration of Sheriff Court Fees) 1971 in force at the time the work is done.

The Land and Buildings Transaction Tax (Scotland)

The Land and Buildings Transaction Tax (LBTT) replaced the old system of Stamp Duty Land Tax (SDLT) on 1 April 2015.

Administration of LBTT

Revenue Scotland will administer LBTT, supported by Registers of Scotland.

Exemptions from LBTT

Schedule 1 to the LBTT Act 2013 sets out the exemptions that will be available under LBTT. These include:

- Transactions for which there is no chargeable consideration. What constitutes the chargeable consideration for the purposes of a land transaction is set out in Schedule 2 to the Act. Paragraph 1 of Schedule 2 provides that the chargeable consideration is, unless otherwise provided, any consideration in money or money's worth for the transaction.

- Acquisitions by the Crown

- Transfers of property on divorce, separation or the end of a civil partnership

- Grants of residential leases (other than 'qualifying leases' which are due to convert to ownership under the Long Leases (Scotland) Act 2012)

- Property transferred to a person in relation to the will of a deceased person or the intestacy of a deceased person.

Tax reliefs from LBTT

Certain reliefs from LBTT are provided for in Schedules 3–16 to the LBTT Act:

- Sale and Leaseback arrangements – the leaseback element is not charged to avoid double counting (Schedule 3)

- Where a developer or property trader buys a residential property in part exchange for a new residential property (Schedule 4)

- Transfers involving multiple dwellings (Schedule 5)

- Certain acquisitions by Registered Social Landlords (Schedule 6)

- Where Alternative Finance Products (Schedule 7) and Alternative Finance Investment Bonds (AFIB) (Schedule 8) are used (which includes Islamic finance transactions) to ensure that they are not taxed more than conventional loans.

- Crofting community right to buy (Schedule 9)

- Group relief which enables groups to move property between companies for commercial reasons without having to consider stamp duty land tax implications (Schedule 10)

- Certain transactions in connection with the reconstruction and acquisition of companies (Schedule 11)

- On the incorporation of limited liability partnerships (Schedule 12)

- Charities and charitable trusts, subject to certain conditions (Schedule 13)

- Where compulsory purchase orders are used by a local authority (Schedule 14)

- Land transactions resulting from compliance with planning obligations such as requiring a developer to provide affordable housing (Schedule 15)

- Transfers involving public bodies (Schedule 16)

All of these reliefs are currently available under SDLT.

Application of LBTT to Leases

LBTT will be applied to non-residential leases. Residential leases are only subject to LBTT where an ultra-long lease, exceeding 175 years, exists, albeit such leases will convert to ownership under the Long Leases (Scotland) Act 2012. Licences to occupy property are exempt interests, except licences that are of a description prescribed by Scottish Ministers under section 53(1) of the LBTT Act. Please see the consultation on subordinate legislation for further information regarding licences.

The chargeable consideration includes rent and other monies, such as a premium, payable over the term of the lease (Schedule 19, Part 1). The amount of tax chargeable is determined by calculating the net present value (NPV) and applying the relevant tax rates (Schedule 19, Part 2).

The taxpayer must review the amount of tax paid on every third anniversary of the lease and submit a return to the tax authority to ensure the correct tax is paid (Schedule 19, Part 4).

The revised tax rates and bands for residential property transactions are as follows:

Band	Rate
Up to £145,000	-
£145,001 to £250,000	2.0%
£250,001 to £325,000	5.0%
£325,001 to £750,000	10.0%
£750,001 and over	12.0%

Tax calculators are available on the Revenue Scotland website.

Additional Dwelling Supplement - LBTT rates and bands

The Land and Buildings Transaction Tax (Amendment) (Scotland) Act 2016 provides for an Additional Dwelling Supplement (ADS) of LBTT to be applied on purchases of additional residential properties in Scotland (such as buy-to-let properties and second homes) of £40,000 or more. The current rate of ADS is 3% of the 'relevant consideration' (usually the purchase price). Paragraph 4 of Schedule 2A sets out how ADS is calculated and the parameters for defining the relevant consideration. The supplement may apply to parts of some non-residential transactions, which will be determined by the concept of "just and reasonable apportionment".

STAMP TAXES

Stamp Duty Land Tax, Stamp Duty and Stamp Duty Reserve Tax

General notes:

This section covers the following three taxes: (A) Stamp Duty Land Tax, (B) Stamp Duty and (C) Stamp Duty Reserve Tax.

Notes follow below on each of these taxes.

A. STAMP DUTY LAND TAX

The stamp duty land tax regime came into effect (subject to transitional provisions) on 1 December 2003. The main provisions relating thereto are contained in the Finance Act 2003, as amended.

Finance Act 2003

Amount of tax chargeable

55 Amount of tax chargeable: general

(1) The amount of tax chargeable in respect of a chargeable transaction is a percentage of the chargeable consideration for the transaction.

(2) That percentage is determined by reference to whether the relevant land—

    (a) consists entirely of residential property (in which case Table A below applies), or

    (b) consists of or includes land that is not residential property (in which case Table B below applies),

and, in either case, by reference to the amount of the relevant consideration.

Table A: Residential

Relevant consideration	Percentage
Up to £125,000*	0
Over £125,000 but not more than £250,000	1
Over £250,000 but not more than £500,000	3
Over £500,000 but not more than £1 million	4
Over £1 million to £2 million	5
Over £2 million from 22 March 2012	7
Over £2 million (purchased by certain persons, including corporate bodies) from 21 March 2012	15

*£250,000 for first-time buyers where completion is from 25.03.2010 to 24.03.2012.

Table B: Non-residential or mixed

Relevant consideration	Percentage
Not more than £150,000 — annual rent is under £1,000	0
Not more than £150,000 — annual rent is £1,000 or more	1
More than £150,000 but not more than £250,000	1
More than £250,000 but not more than £500,000	3
More than £500,000	4

(Special rules apply to land situated in a designated disadvantaged area)

(3) For the purposes of subsection (2)—

    (a) the relevant land is the land an interest in which is the main subject-matter of the transaction, and

    (b) the relevant consideration is the chargeable consideration for the transaction,

subject as follows.

(4) If the transaction in question is one of a number of linked transactions—

    (a) the relevant land is any land an interest in which is the main subject-matter of any of those transactions, and

    (b) the relevant consideration is the total of the chargeable consideration for all those transactions.

(5) This section has effect subject to—

section 74 (exercise of collective rights by tenants of flats), and

section 75 (crofting community right to buy),

(which provide for the rate of tax to be determined by reference to a fraction of the relevant consideration).

(6) In the case of a transaction for which the whole or part of the chargeable consideration is rent this section has effect subject to section 56 and Schedule 5 (amount of tax chargeable: rent).

(7) References in this Part to the "rate of tax" are to the percentage determined under this section.

56 Amount of tax chargeable: rent

Schedule 5 provides for the calculation of the tax chargeable where the chargeable consideration for a transaction consists of or includes rent.

Schedule 5

Stamp duty land tax: amount of tax chargeable: rent

Introduction

1. This Schedule provides for calculating the tax chargeable—

    (a) in respect of a chargeable transaction for which the chargeable consideration consists of or includes rent, or

    (b) where such a transaction is to be taken into account as a linked transaction.

Amounts payable in respect of periods before grant of lease

1A For the purposes of this Part "rent" does not include any chargeable consideration for the grant of a lease that is payable in respect of a period before the grant of the lease.

Calculation of tax chargeable in respect of rent

2.—(1) Tax is chargeable under this Schedule in respect of so much of the chargeable consideration as consists of rent.

(2) The tax chargeable is the total of the amounts produced by taking the relevant percentage of so much of the relevant rental value as falls within each rate band.

(3) The relevant percentages and rate bands are determined by reference to whether the relevant land—

    (a) consists entirely of residential property (in which case Table A below applies), or

    (b) consists of or includes land that is not residential property (in which case Table B below applies).

Table A: Residential

Rate bands from 1 December 2003 to 16 March 2005	Percentage
£0 to £60,000	0
Over £60,000	1
Rate bands from 17 March 2005 to 22 March 2006	*Percentage*
£0 to £120,000	0
Over £120,000	1
Rate bands from 23 March 2006	*Percentage*
£0 to £125,000	0
Over £125,000	1

Table B: Non-residential or mixed	
Rate bands	*Percentage*
£0 to £150,000	0
Over £150,000	1

(Special rules apply to land situated in a designated disadvantaged area)

(4) For the purposes of sub-paragraphs (2) and (3)—

    (a)   the relevant rental value is the net present value of the rent payable over the term of the lease, and

    (b)   the relevant land is the land that is the subject of the lease.

(5) If the lease in question is one of a number of linked transactions for which the chargeable consideration consists of or includes rent, the above provisions are modified.

(6) In that case the tax chargeable is determined as follows.

First, calculate the amount of the tax that would be chargeable if the linked transactions were a single transaction, so that—

    (a)   the relevant rental value is the total of the net present values of the rent payable over the terms of all the leases, and

    (b)   the relevant land is all land that is the subject of any of those leases.

Then, multiply that amount by the fraction:

$$\frac{\text{NPV}}{\text{TNPV}}$$

where—

NPV is the net present value of the rent payable over the term of the lease in question, and

TNPV is the total of the net present values of the rent payable over the terms of all the leases.

Net present value of rent payable over the term of a lease

3. The net present value (v) of the rent payable over the term of a lease is calculated by applying the formula:

$$v = \sum_{i=1}^{n} \frac{r_i}{(1+T)^i}$$

where—

ri is the rent payable in respect of year i,

i is the first, second, third, etc year of the term,

n is the term of the lease , and

T is the temporal discount rate (see paragraph 8).

Temporal discount rate

8—(1) For the purposes of this Schedule the "temporal discount rate" is 3.5% or such other rate as may be specified by regulations made by the Treasury.

(2) Regulations under this paragraph may make any such provision as is mentioned in subsection (3)(b) to (f) of section 178 of the Finance Act 1989 (c 26) (power of Treasury to set rates of interest).

(3) Subsection (5) of that section (power of Inland Revenue to specify rate by order in certain circumstances) applies in relation to regulations under this paragraph as it applies in relation to regulations under that section.

Tax chargeable in respect of consideration other than rent: general

9—(1) Where in the case of a transaction to which this Schedule applies there is chargeable consideration other than rent, the provisions of this Part apply in relation to that consideration as in relation to other chargeable consideration (but see paragraph 9A).

(2) If the relevant rental figure exceeds £600 a year, the 0% band in the Tables in subsection (2) of section 55 does not apply and any case that would have fallen within that band is treated as falling within the 1% band. [sub-paragraphs (2), (2A) and (3) repealed by FA 2008, sec 92]

(2A) For the purposes of sub-paragraph (2) the relevant rental figure is—

    (a)   the annual rent in relation to the transaction in question, or

    (b)   if that transaction is one of a number of linked transactions for which the chargeable consideration consists of or includes rent, the total of the annual rents in relation to all those transactions.

(3) In sub-paragraph (2A) the "annual rent" means the average annual rent over the term of the lease or, if—

    (a)   different amounts of rent are payable for different parts of the term, and

    (b)   those amounts (or any of them) are ascertainable at the effective date of the transaction, the average annual rent over the period for which the highest ascertainable rent is payable.

(4) Tax chargeable under this Schedule is in addition to any tax chargeable under section 55 or Schedule 6B in respect of consideration other than rent.

(5) Where a transaction to which this Schedule applies falls to be taken into account for the purposes of that section or Schedule as a linked transaction, no account shall be taken of rent in determining the relevant consideration.

Tax chargeable in respect of consideration other than rent: 0% band

9A (1) This paragraph applies in the case of a transaction to which this Schedule applies where there is chargeable consideration other than rent.

(2) If—

    (a)   the relevant land consists entirely of land that is non-residential property, and

    (b)   the relevant rent is at least £1,000,

the 0% band in Table B in section 55(2) does not apply in relation to the consideration other than rent and any case that would have fallen within that band is treated as falling within the 1% band.

(3) Sub-paragraphs (4) and (5) apply if—

    (a)   the relevant land is partly residential property and partly non-residential property, and

    (b)   the relevant rent attributable, on a just and reasonable apportionment, to the land that is non-residential property is at least £1,000.

(4) For the purpose of determining the amount of tax chargeable under section 55 in relation to the consideration other than rent, the transaction (or, where it is one of a number of linked transactions, that set of transactions) is treated as if it were two separate transactions (or sets of linked transactions), namely—

    (a)   one whose subject-matter consists of all of the interests in land that is residential property, and

    (b)   one whose subject-matter consists of all of the interests in land that is non-residential property.

(5) For that purpose, the chargeable consideration attributable to each of those separate transactions (or sets of linked transactions) is the chargeable consideration so attributable on a just and reasonable apportionment.

(6) In this paragraph "the relevant rent" means—

    (a)   the annual rent in relation to the transaction in question, or

    (b)   if that transaction is one of a number of linked transactions for which the chargeable consideration consists of or includes rent, the total of the annual rents in relation to all of those transactions.

(7) In sub-paragraph (6) the "annual rent" means the average annual rent over the term of the lease or, if—

    (a)   different amounts of rent are payable for different parts of the term, and

    (b)   those amounts (or any of them) are ascertainable at the effective date of the transaction, the average annual rent over the period for which the highest ascertainable rent is payable.

(8) In this paragraph "relevant land" has the meaning given in section 55(3) and (4). [inserted by FA 2008, sec 95]

B. STAMP DUTY

The following provisions apply to instruments executed on or after 28th March 2000 except, with certain exceptions, one giving effect to a contract made before 21st March 2000.

Following the introduction of Stamp Duty Land Tax with effect from 1 December 2003, Stamp Duty generally only applies to the following:

1. Instruments relating to stock or marketable securities.

2. Land where the conveyance or transfer is pursuant to a contract entered into on or before 10 July 2003 even if the conveyance or transfer is executed after 1 December 2003.

3. Transfers of certain interests in partnerships.

In some cases it is Stamp Duty Reserve Tax ("SDRT") that applies to transactions involving shares and securities: see section C below. SDRT generally applies where the transaction is an electronic "paperless" share transaction.

The provisions noted below are contained in the Finance Act 1999, as amended by the Finance Act 2000.

However, with effect from 1 December 2003, the stamp duty land tax regime (see Part A) came into force, subject to transitional provisions.

Instruments chargeable and rates of duty are contained in Schedule 13 of Finance Act 1999, as amended by the Finance Act 2000 and subsequent Acts.

FA 1999 Schedule 13

STAMP DUTY: INSTRUMENTS CHARGEABLE AND RATES OF DUTY

PART I

CONVEYANCE OR TRANSFER ON SALE

Charge

1.—(1) Stamp duty is chargeable on a transfer on sale.

(2) For this purpose "transfer on sale" includes every instrument, and every decree or order of a court or commissioners, by which any property, or any estate or interest in property, is, on being sold, transferred to or vested in the purchaser or another person on behalf of or at the direction of the purchaser.

(3) Sub-paragraph (1) is subject to sub-paragraphs (3A) to (6).

(3A) Stamp duty is not chargeable under sub-paragraph (1) on a transfer of stock or marketable securities where—

(a) the amount or value of the consideration for the sale is £1,000 or under, and

(b) the instrument is certified at £1,000.

(4) Where a company acquires any shares in itself by virtue of section 690 of the Companies Act 2006 (power of company to purchase own shares) or otherwise, sub-paragraph (1) does not apply to any instrument by which the shares are transferred to the company.

(5) Where a company holds any shares in itself by virtue of section 724 of that Act (treasury shares) or otherwise, sub-paragraph (1) does not apply to any instrument to which sub-paragraph (6) applies [as amended by FA 2008, Sch 32, para 10].

(6) This sub-paragraph applies to any instrument for the sale or transfer of any of the shares by the company, other than an instrument which, in the absence of sub-paragraph (5), would be an instrument in relation to which—

(a) section 67(2) of the Finance Act 1986 (transfer to person whose business is issuing depositary receipts etc), or

(b) section 70(2) of that Act (transfer to person who provides clearance services etc), applied.

Rates of duty

2. Duty under this Part is chargeable by reference to the amount or value of the consideration for the sale.

3. In the case of a transfer of stock or marketable securities the rate is 0.5%.

4. In the case of any other transfer on sale the rates of duty are as follows—

    1. Where the amount or value of the consideration is £175,000 or under and the instrument is certified at £175,000 .... Nil

    2. Where the amount or value of the consideration is £250,000 or under and the instrument is certified at £250,000 .... 1%

    3. Where the amount or value of the consideration is £500,000 or under and the instrument is certified at £500,000 .... 3%

    4. Any other case 4%

5. The above provisions are subject to any enactment setting a different rate or setting an upper limit on the amount of duty chargeable.

Meaning of instrument being certified at an amount

6.—(1) The references in paragraphs 1(3A) and 4 above to an instrument being certified at a particular amount mean that it contains a statement that the transaction effected by the instrument does not form part of a larger transaction or series of transactions in respect of which the amount or value, or aggregate amount or value, of the consideration exceeds that amount.

(2) For this purpose a sale or contract or agreement for the sale of goods, wares or merchandise shall be disregarded—

    (a) in the case of an instrument which is not an actual transfer of the goods, wares or merchandise (with or without other property);

    (b) in the case of an instrument treated as such a transfer only by virtue of paragraph 7 contracts or agreements chargeable as conveyances on sale);

and any statement as mentioned in sub-paragraph (1) shall be construed as leaving out of account any matter which is to be so disregarded.

Contracts or agreements chargeable as conveyances on sale

7.—(1) A contract or agreement for the sale of—

    (a) any equitable estate or interest in property, or

    (b) any estate or interest in property except—

        (i)ii lands, tenements, hereditaments or heritages, or property locally situate out of the United Kingdom,

        (ii)i goods, wares or merchandise,

        (iii) stock or marketable securities,

        (iv) any ship or vessel, or a part interest, share or property of or in any ship or vessel, or

        (v)i property of any description situated outside the United Kingdom.

Is chargeable with the same *ad valorem* duty, to be paid by the purchaser, as if it were an actual conveyance on sale of the estate, interest or property contracted or agreed to be sold.

(2) Where the purchaser has paid *ad valorem* duty and before having obtained a transfer of the property enters into a contract or agreement for the sale of the same, the contract or agreement is chargeable, if the consideration for that sale is in excess of the consideration for the original sale, with the ad valorem duty payable in respect of the excess consideration but is not otherwise chargeable.

(3) Where duty has been paid in conformity with sub-paragraphs (1) and (2), the transfer to the purchaser or sub-purchaser, or any other person on his behalf or by his direction, is not chargeable with any duty.

(4) In that case, upon application and upon production of the contract or agreement (or contracts or agreements) duly stamped, the Commissioners shall either—

    (a) denote the payment of the *ad valorem* duty upon the transfer, or

    (b) transfer the *ad valorem* duty to the transfer.

8.—(1) Where a contract or agreement would apart from paragraph 7 not be chargeable with any duty and a transfer made in conformity with the contract or agreement is presented to the Commissioners for stamping with the *ad valorem* duty chargeable on it—

(a) within the period of six months after the execution of the contract or agreement, or

(b) within such longer period as the Commissioners may think reasonable in the circumstances of the case,

the transfer shall be stamped accordingly, and both it and the contract or agreement shall be deemed to be duly stamped.

(2) Nothing in this paragraph affects the provisions as to the stamping of a transfer after execution.

9.—The *ad valorem* duty paid upon a contract or agreement by virtue of paragraph 7 shall be repaid by the Commissioners if the contract or agreement is afterwards rescinded or annulled or is for any other reason not substantially performed or carried into effect so as to operate as or be followed by a transfer.

[NOTE — By virtue of the Finance Act 2001, sec 92, no stamp duty shall be chargeable on a transfer of an estate or interest in land, or a lease of land, if the land is situated in a disadvantaged area, and the instrument is executed on or after a date to be specified by the Treasury. The specified date is 30 November 2001 (by virtue of SI 2001/3748). Finance Act 2002, sec 116, Sch 37 abolishes the duty on instruments executed after 23rd April 2002 relating to goodwill.]

PART II

LEASE

Charge

10. Stamp duty is chargeable on a lease.

Rates of duty

11. In the case of a lease for a definite term less than a year the duty is as follows—

1. Lease of furnished dwelling-house or apartments where the rent for the term exceeds £5000	£5
2. Any other lease of land	The same duty as for a lease for a year at the rent reserved for the definite term

12.—(1) In the case of a lease for any other definite term, or for an indefinite term, the duty is determined as follows.

(2 If the consideration or part of the consideration moving to the lessor or to any other person consists of any money, stock, security or other property, the duty in respect of that consideration is the same as that on a conveyance on a sale for the same consideration.

But if—

(a) part of the consideration is rent, and

(b) that rent exceeds £600 a year,

the duty is calculated as if paragraph 1 of the Table in paragraph 4 of Part I of Schedule 13 to the Finance Act 1999 were omitted.

(3) If the consideration or part of the consideration is rent, the duty in respect of that consideration is determined by reference to the rate or average rate of the rent (whether reserved as a yearly rent or not), as follows:—

1. Term not more than 7 years or indefinite—	Nil
(a) if the rent is £5000 or less	1%
(b) if the rent is more than £5000	
2. Term more than 7 years but not more than 35 years	2%
3. Term more than 35 years but not more than 100 years	12%
4. Term more than 100 years	24%

[The amending provisions in relation to leases of not more than seven years apply to instruments executed on or after 1st October 1999. Transitional provisions are contained in Schedule 32 of the Act for instruments executed on or after 1st October 1999 but before 28th March 2000.]

13. Stamp duty of £5 is chargeable on a lease not within paragraph 11 or 12 above.

Agreement for a lease charged as a lease

14.—(1) An agreement for a lease is chargeable with the same duty as if it were an actual lease made for the term and consideration mentioned in the agreement.

(2) Where duty has been duly paid on an agreement for a lease and subsequent to that agreement a lease is granted which either—

(a)   is in conformity with the agreement, or

(b)   relates to substantially the same property and term as the agreement,

the duty which would otherwise be charged on the lease is reduced by the amount of the duty paid on the agreement.

(3) Sub-paragraph (1) does not apply to missives of let in Scotland that constitute an actual lease.

Subject to that, references in this paragraph to an agreement for a lease include missives of let in Scotland.

Lease for fixed term and then until determined

15.—(1) For the purposes of this Part a lease granted for a fixed term and thereafter until determined is treated as a lease for a definite term equal to the fixed term together with such further period as must elapse before the earliest date at which the lease can be determined.

(2) Paragraph 5 (agreement for a lease charged as a lease) shall be construed accordingly.

[NOTE — By virtue of the Finance Act 2001, sec 92, no stamp duty shall be chargeable on a conveyance or transfer of an estate or interest in land, or a lease of land, if the land is situated in a disadvantaged area, and the instrument is executed on or after a date to be specified by the Treasury. The specified date is 30 November 2001 (by virtue of SI 2001/3748)]

Part III

Other Instruments

Conveyance or transfer otherwise than on sale

[repealed by FA 2008, Sch 32 para 10 with effect for instruments executed on or after 13 March 2008 and not stamped before 19 March 2008]

16.—(1) Stamp duty of £5 is chargeable on a transfer of property otherwise than on sale.

(2) In sub-paragraph (1) "transfer" includes every instrument, and every decree or order of a court or commissioners, by which any property is transferred to or vested in any person.

Declaration of use or trust

[repealed by FA 2008, Sch 32 para 10 with effect for instruments executed on or after 13 March 2008 and not stamped before 19 March 2008]

17.—(1) Stamp duty of £5 is chargeable on a declaration of any use or trust of or concerning property unless the instrument constitutes a transfer on sale.

(2) This does not apply to a will.

Dispositions in Scotland

18.—(1) The following are chargeable with duty as a conveyance on sale—

(a)   a disposition of heritable property in Scotland to singular successors or purchasers;

(b)   a disposition of heritable property in Scotland to a purchaser containing a clause declaring all or any part of the purchase money a real burden upon, or affecting, the heritable property thereby disported, or any part of it;

(c)   a disposition in Scotland containing constitution of feu or ground annual right.

(2) A disposition in Scotland of any property, or any right or interest in property, that is not so chargeable is chargeable with stamp duty of £5.[repealed by FA 2008, Sch 32 para 10 with effect for instruments executed on or after 13 March 2008 and not stamped before 19 March 2008]

Duplicate or counterpart

19.—(1) A duplicate or counterpart of an instrument chargeable with duty is chargeable with duty of £5. [repealed by FA2008, Sch 32 para 10 with effect for instruments executed on or after 13 March 2008 and not stamped before 19 March 2008]

(2) The duplicate or counterpart of an instrument chargeable with duty is not duly stamped unless—

    (a) it is stamped as an original instrument, or

    (b) it appears by some stamp impressed on it that the full and proper duty has been paid on the original instrument of which it is the duplicate or counterpart.

(3) Sub-paragraph (2) does not apply to the counterpart of an instrument chargeable as a lease, if that counterpart is not executed by or on behalf of any lessor or grantor.

Instrument increasing rent

20.—(1) An instrument (not itself a lease)—

    (a) by which it is agreed that the rent reserved should be increased, or

    (b) which confirms or records any such agreement made otherwise than in writing,

is chargeable with the same duty as if it were a lease in consideration of the additional rent made payable by it.

(2) Sub-paragraph (1) does not apply to an instrument giving effect to provision in the lease for periodic review of the rent reserved by it.

Partition or division

21.—(1) Where on the partition or division of an estate or interest in land consideration exceeding £100 in amount or value is paid or given, or agreed to be paid or given, for equality, the principal or only instrument by which the partition or division is effected is chargeable with the same *ad valorem* duty as a conveyance on sale for the consideration, and with that duty only.

(2) Where there are several instruments for completing the title of either party, the principal instrument is to be ascertained, and the other instruments shall be charged with duty, as provided by sections 58(3) and 61 of the Stamp Act 1891 in the case of several instruments of conveyance.

(3) Stamp duty of £5 is chargeable on an instrument effecting a partition or division to which the above provisions do not apply. [repealed by FA2008, Sch 32 para 10 with effect for instruments executed on or after 13 March 2008 and not stamped before 19 March 2008]

Release or renunciation

22.—Stamp duty of £5 is chargeable on a release or renunciation of property unless the instrument constitutes a transfer on sale. [repealed by FA 2008, Sch 32 para 10 with effect for instruments executed on or after 13 March 2008 and not stamped before 19 March 2008]

Surrender

23.—Stamp duty of £5 is chargeable on a surrender of property unless the instrument constitutes a transfer on sale.[repealed by FA2008, Sch 32 para 10 with effect for instruments executed on or after 13 March 2008 and not stamped before 19 March 2008]

PART IV

GENERAL EXEMPTIONS

24. The following are exempt from stamp duty under Schedule 13 to the Finance Act 1999—

    (a) transfers of shares in the government or parliamentary stocks or funds or strips (within the meaning of section 47 of the Finance Act 1942) of such stocks or funds;

    (b) instruments for the sale, transfer, or other disposition (absolutely or otherwise) of any ship or vessel, or any part, interest, share or property of or in a ship or vessel; [repealed by FA 2011 Sch 26, para 7(1)]

    (c) testaments, testamentary instruments and dispositions mortis causa in Scotland;

(d) renounceable letters of allotment, letters of rights or other similar instruments where the rights under the letter or other instrument are renounceable not later than six months after its issue.

25. Stamp duty is not chargeable under Schedule 13 to the Finance Act 1999 on any description of instrument in respect of which duty was abolished by—

(a) section 64 of the Finance Act 1971 or section 5 of the Finance Act (Northern Ireland) 1971 (abolition of duty on mortgages, bonds, debentures etc.), or

(b) section 173 of the Finance Act 1989 (life insurance policies and superannuation annuities).

26. Nothing in Schedule 13 to the Finance Act 1999 affects any other enactment conferring exemption or relief from stamp duty.

FA 1999, Schedule 15

STAMP DUTY: BEARER INSTRUMENTS

PART I
CHARGING PROVISIONS

Charge on issue of instrument

1.—(1) Stamp duty is chargeable—

(a) on the issue of a bearer instrument in the United Kingdom, and

(b) on the issue of a bearer instrument outside the United Kingdom by or on behalf of a UK company.

(2) This is subject to the exemptions in Part II of Schedule 15 to the Finance Act 1999.

Charge on transfer of stock by means of instrument

2.—Stamp duty is chargeable on the transfer in the United Kingdom of the stock constituted by or transferable by means of a bearer instrument if duty was not chargeable under paragraph 1 on the issue of the instrument and—

(a) duty would be chargeable under Part 1 of Schedule 13 (transfer on sale) if the transfer were effected by an instrument other than a bearer instrument, or

(b) the stock constituted by or transferable by means of a bearer instrument consists of units under a unit trust scheme.

Meaning of "bearer instrument"

3.—In Schedule 15 to the Finance Act 1999 "bearer instrument" means—

(a) a marketable security transferable by delivery;

(b) a share warrant or stock certificate to bearer or instrument to bearer (by whatever name called) having the like effect as such a warrant or certificate;

(c) a deposit certificate to bearer;

(d) any other instrument to bearer by means of which stock can be transferred; or

(e) an instrument issued by a non-UK company that is a bearer instrument by usage.

Rates of duty

4.—The duty chargeable under this Schedule is 1. 5% of the market value of the stock constituted by or transferable by means of the instrument, unless paragraph 5 or 6 applies.

5.—In the case of—

(a) a deposit certificate in respect of stock of a single non-UK company, or

(b) an instrument issued by a non-UK company that is a bearer instrument by usage (and is not otherwise within the definition of "bearer instrument" in paragraph 3),

the duty is 0.2% of the market value of the stock constituted by or transferable by means of the instrument.

6.—In the case of an instrument given in substitution for a like instrument stamped *ad valorem* (whether under Schedule 15 to the Finance Act 1999 or not) the duty is £5.[repealed by FA 2008, Sch 32 para 10 with effect for instruments executed on or after 13 March 2008 and not stamped before 19 March 2008]

Ascertainment of market value

7.—(1) For the purposes of duty under paragraph 1 (charge on issue of instrument) the market value of the stock constituted by or transferable by means of the instrument is ascertained as follows.

(2) If the stock was offered for public subscription (whether in registered or in bearer form) within twelve months before the issue of the instrument, the market value shall be taken to be the amount subscribed for the stock.

(3) In any other case the market value shall be taken to be—

    (a) the value of the stock on the first day within one month after the issue of the instrument on which stock of that description is dealt in on a stock exchange in the United Kingdom, or

    (b) if stock of that description is not so dealt in, the value of the stock immediately after the issue of the instrument.

8.—(1) For the purposes of duty under paragraph 2 (charge on transfer of stock by means of instrument) the market value of the stock constituted by or transferable by means of the instrument is ascertained as follows.

(2) In the case of a transfer pursuant to a contract of sale, the market value shall be taken to be the value of the stock on the date when the contract is made.

(3) In any other case, the market value shall be taken to be the value of the stock on the day preceding that on which the instrument is presented to the Commissioners for stamping, or, if it is not so presented, on the date of the transfer.

Meaning of "deposit certificate"

9.—In this Schedule a "deposit certificate" means an instrument acknowledging the deposit of stock and entitling the bearer to rights (whether expressed as units or otherwise) in or in relation to the stock deposited or equivalent stock.

Bearer instruments by usage

10.—(1) In Schedule 15 to the Finance Act 1999 a "bearer instrument by usage" means an instrument—

    (a) which is used for the purpose of transferring the right to stock, and

    (b) delivery of which is treated by usage as sufficient for the purposes of a sale on the market, whether that delivery constitutes a legal transfer or not.

(2) A bearer instrument by usage is treated—

    (a) as transferring the stock on delivery of the instrument, and

    (b) as issued by the person by whom or on whose behalf it was first issued, whether or not it was then capable of being used for transferring the right to the stock without execution by the holder.

Meaning of "company", "UK company" and "non-UK company"

11.—In Schedule 15 to the Finance Act 1999—

"company" includes any body of persons, corporate or unincorporate;

"UK company" means

    (a) a company that is formed or established in the United Kingdom other than an SE which has its registered office outside the United Kingdom following a transfer in accordance with Article 8 of Council Regulation (EC) 2157/2001 on the Statute for a European Company (Societas Europaea)), or

    (b) an SE which has its registered office in the United Kingdom following a transfer in accordance with Article 8 of that Regulation; and

"non-UK company" means a company that is not a UK company.

Meaning of "stock" and "transfer"

12.—(1) In Schedule 15 to the Finance Act 1999 "stock" includes securities.

(2) References in that Schedule to stock include any interest in, or in any fraction of, stock or in any dividends or other rights arising out of stock and any right to an allotment of or to subscribe for stock.

(3) In that Schedule "transfer" includes negotiation, and "transferable", "transferred" and "transferring" shall be construed accordingly.

PART II

EXEMPTIONS

Substitute instruments

12A (1) Stamp duty is not chargeable on a substitute instrument.

(2) A substitute instrument is a bearer instrument given in substitution for a like instrument stamped *ad valorem* (whether under this Schedule or otherwise) ("the original instrument").

(3) The substitute instrument shall not be treated as duly stamped unless it appears by some stamp impressed on it that the full and proper duty has been paid on the original instrument." [inserted by FA 2008, sch 32, with effect for instruments executed on or after 13 March 2008 and not stamped before 19 March 2008]

Foreign loan securities

13.—Stamp duty is not chargeable on a bearer instrument issued outside the United Kingdom in respect of a loan which is expressed in a currency other than sterling and which is not—

    (a) offered for subscription in the United Kingdom, or

    (b) offered for subscription with a view to an offer for sale in the United Kingdom of securities in respect of the loan.

Stock exempt from duty on transfer

14.—Stamp duty is not chargeable under Schedule 15 to the Finance Act 1999 on an instrument constituting, or used for transferring, stock (other than units in a unit trust) that is exempt from all stamp duties on transfer.

Instruments in respect of which duty previously abolished

15.—Stamp duty is not chargeable under Schedule 15 to the Finance Act 1999 on any description of instrument in respect of which duty was abolished by—

    (a) section 64 of the Finance Act 1971 or section 5 of the Finance Act (Northern Ireland) 1971 (abolition of duty on mortgages, bonds, debentures etc.), or

    (b) section 173 of the Finance Act 1989 (life insurance policies and superannuation annuities).

Renounceable letters of allotment

16.—Stamp duty is not chargeable under Schedule 15 to the Finance Act 1999 on renounceable letters of allotment, letters of rights or other similar instruments where the rights under the letter or other instrument are renounceable not later than six months after its issue.

Instruments relating to non-sterling stock

17.—(1) Stamp duty is not chargeable under Schedule 15 to the Finance Act 1999 on the issue of an instrument which relates to stock expressed—

    (a) in a currency other than sterling, or

    (b) in units of account defined by reference to more than one currency (whether or not including sterling),

or on the transfer of the stock constituted by or transferable by means of any such instrument.

(2) Where the stock to which the instrument relates consists of a loan for the repayment of which there is an option between sterling and one or more other currencies, sub-paragraph (1) applies if the option is exercisable only by the holder of the stock and does not apply in any other case.

18.—Where the capital stock of a company is not expressed in terms of any currency, it shall be treated for the purposes of paragraph 17 as expressed in the currency of the territory under the law of which the company is formed or established.

19.—(1) A unit under a unit trust scheme or a share in a foreign mutual fund shall be treated for the purposes of paragraph 17 as capital stock of a company formed or established in the territory by the law of which the scheme or fund is governed.

(2) A "foreign mutual fund" means a fund administered under arrangements governed by the law of a territory outside the United Kingdom under which subscribers to the fund are entitled to participate in, or receive payments by reference to, profits or income arising to the fund from the acquisition, holding, management or disposal of investments.

(3) In relation to a foreign mutual fund "share" means the right of a subscriber, or of another in his right, to participate in or receive payments by reference to profits or income so arising.

Variation of original terms or conditions

20.—Where a bearer instrument issued by or on behalf of a non-UK company in respect of a loan expressed in sterling—

(a) has been stamped *ad valorem*, or

(b) has been stamped in accordance with paragraph 12A, or, or

(c) has been stamped with the denoting stamp referred to in paragraph 21(2)(b) below,

duty is not chargeable under Schedule 15 to the Finance Act 1999 by reason only that the instrument is amended on its face pursuant to an agreement for the variation of any of its original terms or conditions.

PART III

SUPPLEMENTARY PROVISIONS

Duty chargeable on issue of instrument

21.—(1) This paragraph applies where duty is chargeable under paragraph 1 of Schedule 15.

(2) The instrument—

(a) shall before being issued be produced to the Commissioners together with such particulars in writing of the instrument as the Commissioners may require, and

(b) shall be deemed to be duly stamped if and only if it is stamped with a particular stamp denoting that it has been produced to the Commissioners.

(3) Within six weeks of the date on which the instrument is issued, or such longer time as the Commissioners may allow, a statement in writing containing the date of the issue and such further particulars as the Commissioners may require in respect of the instrument shall be delivered to the Commissioners.

(4) The duty chargeable in respect of the instrument shall be paid to the Commissioners on delivery of that statement or within such longer time as the Commissioners may allow.

22.—(1) If default is made in complying with paragraph 21—

(a) the person by whom or on whose behalf the instrument is issued, and

(b) any person who acts as the agent of that person for the purposes of the issue,

are each liable to a penalty not exceeding the aggregate of £300 and the duty chargeable.

(2) Those persons are also jointly and severally liable to pay to Her Majesty—

(a) the duty chargeable, and

(b) interest on the unpaid duty from the date of the default until the duty is paid.

Duty chargeable on transfer of stock by means of instrument

23.—(1) This paragraph applies where duty is chargeable under paragraph 2 of Schedule 15.

(2) Where the instrument is presented to the Commissioners for stamping—

(a) the person presenting it, and

(b) the owner of the instrument,

shall furnish to the Commissioners such particulars in writing as the Commissioners may require for determining the amount of duty chargeable.

(3) If the instrument is not duly stamped each person who in the United Kingdom—

(a) transfers any stock by or by means of the instrument, or

(b) is concerned as broker or agent in any such transfer,

is liable to a penalty not exceeding the aggregate of £300 and the amount of duty chargeable.

(4) Those persons are also jointly and severally liable to pay to Her Majesty—

(a) the duty chargeable, and

(b) interest on the unpaid duty from the date of the transfer in question until the duty is paid.

Supplementary provisions as to interest

24.—(1) The following provisions apply to interest under paragraph 22(2) or 23(4).

(2) If an amount is lodged with the Commissioners in respect of the duty, the amount on which interest is payable is reduced by that amount.

(3) Interest is payable at the rate prescribed under section 178 of the Finance Act 1989 for the purposes of section 15A of the Stamp Act 1891 (interest on late stamping).

(4) The amount of interest shall be rounded down (if necessary) to the nearest multiple of £5.

No interest is payable if the amount is less than £25.

(5) The interest shall be paid without any deduction of income tax and shall not be taken into account in computing income or profits for any tax purposes.

Penalty for false statement

25.—A person who in furnishing particulars under this Part wilfully or negligently furnishes particulars that are false in any material respect is liable to a penalty not exceeding the aggregate of £300 and twice the amount by which the stamp duty chargeable exceeds that paid.

26.—An instrument in respect of which duty is chargeable under paragraph 2 of above which—

(a) has been stamped *ad valorem*, or

(b) has been stamped with a stamp indicating that it is chargeable with a fixed duty under paragraph 6 (instrument in substitution for one stamped *ad valorem*) and has been stamped under that paragraph,[repealed by FA 2008, Sch 32 para 10 with effect for instruments executed on or after 13 March 2008 and not stamped before 19 March 2008]

shall be treated as duly stamped for all purposes other than paragraph 25.

Regulations applicable to Instruments Generally

Stamp Act 1891 (as amended by Finance Act 1999)

Charge of duty upon instruments

All duties to be paid according to regulations of Act

Sec. 2.—All stamp duties for the time being chargeable by law upon any instruments are to be paid and denoted according to the regulations in this Act contained, and except where express provision is made to the contrary all stamp duties are to be denoted by impressed stamps only.

How instruments are to be written and stamped

Sec. 3.—(1) Every instrument written upon stamped material is to be written in such manner, and every instrument partly or wholly written before being stamped is to be so stamped, that the stamp may appear on the face of the instrument, and cannot be used for or applied to any other instrument written upon the same piece of material.

(2) If more than one instrument be written upon the same piece of material, every one of the instruments is to be separately and distinctly stamped with the duty with which it is chargeable.

Instruments to be separately charged with duty in certain cases

Sec. 4.—Except where express provision to the contrary is made by this or any other Act:

(a) an instrument containing or relating to several distinct matters is to be separately and distinctly charged, as if it were a separate instrument with duty in respect of each of the matters;

(b) an instrument made for any consideration in respect whereof it is chargeable with *ad valorem* duty, and also for any further or other valuable consideration, is to be separately and distinctly charged, as if it were a separate instrument with duty in respect of each of the considerations.

Facts and circumstances affecting duty to be set forth in instruments

Sec. 5.—All the facts and circumstances affecting the liability of any instrument to duty, or the amount of the duty with which any instrument is chargeable, are to be fully and truly set forth in the instrument; and every person who, with intent to defraud Her Majesty:

(a) executes any instrument in which all the said facts and circumstances are not fully and truly set forth; or

(b) being employed or concerned in or about the preparation of any instrument, neglects or omits fully and truly to set forth therein all the said facts and circumstances;

shall incur a penalty not exceeding £3,000.

Mode of calculating *ad valorem* duty in certain cases

Sec. 6.—(1) Where an instrument is chargeable with *ad valorem* duty in respect of

(a) any money in any foreign or colonial currency, or

(b) any stock or, marketable security

the duty shall be calculated on the value, on the day of the date of the instrument, of the money in British currency according to the current rate of exchange, or of the stock or security according to the average price thereof.

(2) Where an instrument contains a statement of current rate of exchange, or average price, as the case may require, and is stamped in accordance with that statement, it is, so far as regards the subject matter of the statement, to be deemed duly stamped, unless or until it is shown that the statement is untrue, and that the instrument is in fact insufficiently stamped.

Denoting stamps

Sec. 11.—Where the duty with which an instrument is chargeable depends in any manner upon the duty paid upon another instrument, the payment of such last mentioned duty shall, upon application to the commissioners, and production of both the instruments, be denoted on the first-mentioned instrument in such manner as the commissioners think fit. (See Finance Act 1984, sec.111).

Adjudication stamps

Adjudication by Commissioners

Sec. 12.—(1) Subject to such regulations as the Commissioners may think fit to make, the Commissioners may be required by any person to adjudicate with reference to any executed instrument upon the questions:

    (a)   whether it is chargeable with any duty;

    (b)   with what amount of duty it is chargeable.

    (c)   whether any penalty is payable for late stamping, and

    (d)   what penalty is in their opinion correct and adequate.

(2) The Commissioners may require to be furnished with an abstract of the instrument and with such evidence as they may require as to the facts and circumstances relevant to those questions.

(3) The Commissioners shall give notice of their decision upon those questions to the person by whom the adjudication was required.

(4) If the Commissioners decide that the instrument is not chargeable with any duty, it may be stamped with a particular stamp denoting that it has been the subject of adjudication and is not chargeable with any duty.

(5) If the Commissioners decide that the instrument is chargeable with duty and assess the amount of duty chargeable, the instrument when stamped in accordance with their decision may be stamped with a particular stamp denoting that it has been the subject of adjudication and is duly stamped.

(6) Every instrument stamped in accordance with subsection (4) or (5) shall be admissible in evidence and available for all purposes notwithstanding any objection relating to duty.

Adjudication: supplementary provisions

Sec 12A.—(1) An instrument which has been the subject of adjudication by the Commissioners under section 12 shall not, if it is unstamped or insufficiently stamped, be stamped otherwise than in accordance with the Commissioners' decision on the adjudication.

(2) If without reasonable excuse any such instrument is not duly stamped within 30 days after the date on which the Commissioners gave notice of their decision, or such longer period as the Commissioners may allow, the person by whom the adjudication was required is liable to a penalty not exceeding £300.

(3) A statutory declaration made for the purposes of section 12 shall not be used against the person making it in any proceedings whatever, except in an inquiry as to the duty with which the instrument to which it relates is chargeable or as to the penalty payable on stamping that instrument.

(4) Every person by whom any such declaration is made shall, on payment of the duty chargeable upon the instrument to which it relates, and any interest or penalty payable on stamping, be relieved from any penalty to which he may be liable by reason of the omission to state truly in the instrument any fact or circumstance required by this Act to be so stated.

Appeal against Commissioners' decision on adjudication

Sec 13.—(1) A person who is dissatisfied with a decision of the Commissioners on an adjudication under section 12 may appeal against it.

(2) The appeal must be brought within 30 days of notice of the decision on the adjudication being given under section 12(3).

(3) An appeal may only be brought on payment of—

    (a)   duty and any penalty in conformity with the Commissioners' decision, and

    (b)   any interest that in conformity with that decision would be payable on stamping the instrument on the day on which the appeal is brought.

(4) An appeal which relates only to the penalty payable on late stamping may be brought to the Special Commissioners in accordance with section 13A.

(5) Any other appeal may be brought in accordance with section 13B to the High Court of the part of the United Kingdom in which the case has arisen.

The following provisions apply in relation to instruments executed on or after 1st October 1999.

Stamping after execution

Sec 15.—(1) An unstamped or insufficiently stamped instrument may be stamped after being executed on payment of the unpaid duty and any interest or penalty payable.

(2) Any interest or penalty payable on stamping shall be denoted on the instrument by a particular stamp.

Late stamping: interest

Sec 15A.—(1) Interest is payable on the stamping of an instrument which—

    (a) is chargeable with *ad valorem* duty, and

    (b) is not duly stamped within 30 days after the day on which the instrument was executed (whether in the United Kingdom or elsewhere).

(2) Interest is payable on the amount of the unpaid duty from the end of the period of 30 days mentioned in subsection (1)(b) until the duty is paid.

If an amount is lodged with the Commissioners in respect of the duty, the amount on which interest is payable is reduced by that amount.

(3) Interest shall be calculated at the rate applicable under section 178 of the Finance Act 1989 (power of Treasury to prescribe rates of interest).

(4) The amount of interest shall be rounded down (if necessary) to the nearest multiple of £5.

No interest is payable if that amount is less than £25.

(5) Interest under this section shall be paid without any deduction of income tax and shall not be taken into account in computing income or profits for any tax purposes.

Late stamping: penalties

Sec 15B.—(1) A penalty is payable on the stamping of an instrument which is not presented for stamping within 30 days after—

    (a) if the instrument is executed in the United Kingdom or relates to land in the United Kingdom, the day on which it is so executed;

    (b) if the instrument is executed outside the United Kingdom and does not relate to land in the United Kingdom, the day on which it is first received in the United Kingdom.

(1A) For the purposes of subsection (1) every instrument that (whether or not it also relates to any other transaction) relates to a transaction which to any extent involves land in the United Kingdom is an instrument relating to land in the United Kingdom.

(2) If the instrument is presented for stamping within one year after the end of the 30-day period mentioned in subsection (1), the maximum penalty is £300 or the amount of the unpaid duty, whichever is less.

(3) If the instrument is not presented for stamping until after the end of the one-year period mentioned in subsection (2), the maximum penalty is £300 or the amount of the unpaid duty, whichever is greater.

(4) The Commissioners may, if they think fit, mitigate or remit any penalty payable on stamping.

(5) No penalty is payable if there is a reasonable excuse for the delay in presenting the instrument for stamping.

Allowance for Spoiled Stamps

Stamp Duties Management Act 1891 (as amended by Finance Act 1999)

Note: The Commissioners may by concession allow repayment where a duplicate has been stamped, or free stamp a duplicate, where a stamped instrument has been lost.

Procedure for obtaining allowance

Sec. 9. Subject to such regulations as the Commissioners may think proper to make, and to the production of such evidence by statutory declaration or otherwise as the Commissioners may require, allowance is to be made by the Commissioners for stamps spoiled in the cases hereinafter mentioned:

(1) The stamp on any material inadvertently and undesignedly spoiled, obliterated, or by any means rendered unfit for the purpose intended, before the material bears the signature of any person or any instrument written thereon is executed by any party.

(4) The stamp on any bill of exchange signed by or on behalf of the drawer which has not been accepted or made use of in any manner whatever or delivered out of his hands for any purpose other than by way of tender for acceptance.

(5) The stamp on any promissory note signed by or on behalf of the maker which has not been made use of in any manner whatever or delivered out of his hands.

(6) The stamp on any bill or promissory note which from any omission or error has been spoiled or rendered useless, although the same, being a bill of exchange, may have been accepted or indorsed, or being a promissory note may have been delivered to the payee, provided that another completed and duly stamped bill or promissory note is produced identical in every particular, except in the correction of the error or omission, with the spoiled bill or note.

(7) The stamp used for any of the following instruments: that is to say —

    (a) an instrument executed by any party thereto, but afterwards found to be absolutely void from the beginning;

    (b) an instrument executed by any party thereto, but afterwards found unfit, by reason of any error or mistake therein, for the purpose originally intended;

    (c) an instrument executed by any party thereto which has not been made use of for any purpose whatever, and which, by reason of the inability or refusal of some necessary party to sign the same or to complete the transaction according to the instrument, is incomplete and insufficient for the purpose for which it was intended;

    (d) an instrument executed by any party thereto, which by reason of the refusal of any person to act under the same, or for want of registration within the time required by law, fails of the intended purpose or becomes void;

    (e) an instrument executed by any party thereto which becomes useless in consequence of the transaction intended to be thereby effected being effected by some other instrument duly stamped.

Provided as follows:

    (a) that the application for relief is made within two years after the stamp has been spoiled or become useless, or in the case of an executed instrument after the date of the instrument, or, if it is not dated, within two years after the execution thereof by the person by whom it was first or alone executed, or within such further time as the Commissioners may prescribe in the case of any instrument sent abroad for execution, or when from unavoidable circumstance any instrument for which another has been substituted cannot be produced within the said period;

    (b) That in the case of an executed instrument no legal proceeding has been commenced in which the instrument could or would have been given or offered in evidence, and that the instrument is given up to be cancelled.

Allowance for misused stamps

Sec. 10. When any person has inadvertently used for an instrument liable to duty a stamp of greater value than was necessary, or has inadvertently used a stamp for an instrument not liable to any duty, the commissioners may, on application made within two years after the date of the instrument, or, if it is not dated, within two years after the execution thereof by the person by whom it was first or alone executed, and upon the instrument, if liable to duty, being stamped with the proper duty, cancel and allow as spoiled the stamp so misused.

Allowance, how to be made

Sec. 11. In any case in which allowance is made for spoiled or misused stamps the commissioners may give in lieu thereof other stamps of the same denomination and value, or, if required, and they think proper, stamps of any other denomination to the same amount in value, or in their discretion, the same value in money.

Lost or spoiled instruments

Sec. 12A.—(1) This section applies where the Commissioners are satisfied that:

   (a) an instrument which was executed and duly stamped ("the original instrument") has been accidentally lost or spoiled; and

   (b) in place of the original instrument, another instrument made between the same persons and for the same purpose ("the replacement instrument") has been executed; and

   (c) an application for relief under this section is made to the Commissioners; and either

   (d) where the original instrument has been lost, the applicant undertakes to deliver it up to the Commissioners to be cancelled if it is subsequently found; or

   (e) where the original instrument has been spoiled;

      (i)ii the application is made within two years after the date of the original instrument, or if it is not dated, within two years after the time when it was executed, or within such further time as the Commissioners may allow; and

      (ii)i no legal proceeding has been commenced in which the original instrument has been or could or would have been given or offered in evidence; and

      (iii) the original instrument is delivered up to the Commissioners to be cancelled.

(2) Where this section applies:

   (a) the replacement instrument shall not be chargeable with any duty, but shall be stamped with the duty with which it would otherwise have been chargeable in accordance with the law in force at the time when it was executed, and shall be deemed for all purposes to be duly stamped; and

   (b) if any duty, interest or penalty was paid in respect of the replacement instrument before the application was made, the Commissioners shall pay to such person as they consider appropriate an amount equal to the duty, interest or penalty so paid.

(3) For the purposes of this section the Commissioners may require the applicant to produce such evidence by statutory declaration or otherwise as they think fit.

Notes: This section, which was inserted by Finance Act 1996, Sch 39, Part III, has effect from 29th April 1996.

The amendments made by this section shall not apply in relation to an instrument which has been accidentally spoiled if an application for allowance under sec 9 of the Management Act was made before 29th April 1996.

C. Stamp Duty Reserve Tax

Stamp Duty Reserve Tax ("SRT") is payable under Part IV of the Finance Act 1986 on certain transactions in securities which do not attract Stamp Duty. SDRT generally applies where the transaction is an electronic "paperless" share transaction.

SDRT is normally payable at 0.5% although the charge is 1.5% in relation to the transfer of securities into depository receipt schemes and clearance services. According to an announcement made by HMRC on 27 April 2012 following the decisions in two recent cases, the 1.5% SDRT is no longer applicable to issues of UK shares and securities to depositary receipt issuers and clearance services anywhere in the world. However, HMRC does not consider that the recent court decisions have any impact upon transfers (on sale or otherwise than on sale) of shares and securities to depositary receipt systems or clearance services that are not an integral part of an issue of share capital. In HMRC'S view the SDRT charge therefore continues to apply to such transactions.

Fees applicable to Companies under the Companies Acts

There is no stamp duty chargeable on the memorandum or articles of association.

Company Incorporation & Registration	WebFiled	Software	Paper
Incorporation (*excludes CICs, Welsh companies filing in Welsh, Unlimited companies & s1040 companies*)		£13.00	£40.00
Web Incorporation	£15.00		
Same-day incorporation		£30.00	£100.00
Change of name	£8.00	£8.00	£10.00
Same-day change of name	£30.00	£30.00	£50.00
Same-day simultaneous re-registration and change of name			£100.00
Re-registration			£20.00
Same-day re-registration			£50.00
Annual document processing fee payable with Annual Return	£13.00	£13.00	£40.00
Voluntary Strike Off			£10.00
Mortgage charge registration	£10.00	£10.00	£13.00
Reduction of capital by solvency statement			£10.00
Same day reduction of capital by solvency statement			£50.00
Reduction of capital by court order			£10.00
Same day reduction of capital by court order			£50.00
Administrative Restoration			£100.00
Application to make an address unavailable for public inspection by an individual			£55.00*
Application to make an address unavailable for public inspection by the company: for any list of members (other than a long list) in hard copy form			£55.00*
Application to make an address unavailable for public inspection by the company: for any list of members (other than a long list) filed electronically			£55.00*
Application to make an address unavailable for public inspection by the company: for a long list of members delivered on CD-ROM or DVD-ROM			£55.00*
Application to make an address unavailable for public inspection by the company: for a long list of members in hard copy form			£55.00*
Application to make an address unavailable for public inspection by a person who registers a charge			£55.00*
* Please note all fees are per document suppressed			
Section 243 application to make protected usual residential address information unavailable to a Credit Reference Agency			£100.00

Limited Liability Partnership (LLPs)	WebFiled	Software	Paper
Incorporation of a LLP (excludes Welsh LLPs filing in Welsh)		£13.00	£40.00
Same day incorporation of a LLP		£30.00	£100.00
LLP annual document processing fee payable with annual return	£13.00	£13.00	£40.00
LLP change of name		£8.00	£10.00
Same day LLP change of name		£30.00	£50.00
LLP Voluntary Strike Off			£10.00
Mortgage charge registration by a LLP	£10.00	£10.00	£13.00
Administrative Restoration of a LLP			£100.00
Application to make an address unavailable for public inspection by an individual member			£55.00*
Application to make an address unavailable for public inspection by a person who registers a charge			£55.00*
• Please note all fees are per document suppressed			

Overseas Companies	Paper
Registration of a UK establishment of an Overseas Company	£20.00
Same day registration of a UK establishment of an Overseas Company	£100.00
Change of corporate name or alternative name of an Overseas Company	£10.00
Same day change of corporate name or alternative name of an Overseas Company	£50.00
Annual document processing fee payable with the Overseas Company accounts	£20.00

European Economic Interest Groupings (EEIGs)		*Paper*
Registration of an EEIG in UK under Regulation 9		£20.00
Registration of an EEIG in UK under Regulation 12		£20.00
Change of name of an EEIG		£10.00
Registration of charge by an EEIG		£13.00

European Companies: Registration of a European Company (SE)		*Paper*
By merger in accordance with Article 2(1)		£20.00
By the formation of a holding SE in accordance with Article 2(2)		£20.00
By the formation of a subsidiary SE in accordance with Article 2(3)		£20.00
By the transformation of a PLC in accordance with Article 2(4)		£20.00
By the formation of a subsidiary SE in accordance with Article 3(2)		£20.00
Registration of a PLC by conversion of an SE in accordance with Article 66		£20.00
Registration of an SE on transfer to UK in accordance with Article 8		£20.00

Community Interest Company and 'other' incorporations	*Paper*	*CIC Regulator's fee*
Registration of a Community Interest Company in accordance with section 36 of the Companies (Audit, Investigations and Community Enterprise) Act 2004	£20.00	£15.00
Registration of a company or LLP with constitutional documents in Welsh	£20.00	
Registration of a company authorised to register in accordance with section 1040 of the Companies Act 2006	£20.00	
Registration of an Unlimited Company in accordance with section 14 of the Companies Act 2006	£20.00	

Limited Partnerships (LPs)		*Paper*
Registration of a Limited Partnership		£20.00
Same day registration of a Limited Partnership		£100.00

Income Tax

THIS SECTION HAS BEEN REVISED UP TO BUDGET 2016.

The main features of income tax are given in the table which reports the rates and allowances from 2010/11. Further details are given in the notes which follow, and which are referred to in the table by number.

RATES OF INCOME TAX

	2010/11	2011/12	2012/13	2013/14	2014/15	2015/16	2016/17
Lower Rate (Note 1)							
First £2,240	—	—	—	—	—	—	—
First £2,440	—	—	—	—	—	—	—
First £2,560	10%	—	—	—	—	—	—
First £2,710	—	10%	—	—	—	—	—
First £2,790	—	—	10%	10%	—	—	—
First £2,880	—	—	—	—	10%	—	—
First £5,000	—	—	—	—	—	0%	—
First £5,000	—	—	—	—	—	—	0%
Basic Rate (Note 1)							
Next £37,400	—	—	—	—	—	—	—
Next £37,400	—	—	—	—	—	—	—
Next £35,000	20%	—	—	—	—	—	—
Next £34,370	—	20%	—	—	—	—	—
Next £32,010	—	—	20%	20%	—	—	—
Next £31,865	—	—	—	—	20%	—	—
Next £31,785	—	—	—	—	—	20%	—
Next £32,000	—	—	—	—	—	—	20%
Higher Rates (Note 1)							
Over £37,400	—	—	—	—	—	—	—
£35,000–£150,000	—	—	—	—	—	—	—
£34,371–£150,000	—	40%	—	—	—	—	—
£32,011–£150,000	—	—	40%	—	—	—	—
£31,865–£150,000	—	—	—	—	40%	—	—
£31,785–£150,000	—	—	—	—	—	40%	—
£32,001 –£150,000	—	—	—	—	—	—	40%
Additional rate							
Over £150,000	—	—	—	—	45%		

2016/17	Tax band:	Rate of tax
Savings rate on savings income only	£0-£5,000	0%
Basic rate	£0-£32,000	20%
Higher rate	£32,001-£150,000	40%

Additional rate: 50% 45% from 6 April 2015	Over £150,000 N/A	Over £150,000 N/A	N/A Over £150,000

* The 10 per cent starting rate applies to savings income only. If, after deducting your Personal Allowance from your total income liable to Income Tax, your non-savings income is above this limit then the 10 per cent starting rate for savings will not apply. Non-savings income includes income from employment, profits from self-employment, pensions, income from property and taxable benefits.

The rates available for dividends are the 10 per cent ordinary rate, the 32.5 per cent dividend upper rate and the dividend additional rate of 42.5 per cent (the dividend additional rate is 37.5 per cent from 2013–14).

Allowances

	2010/11	2011/12	2012/13	2013/14	2014/15	2015/16	2016/17
Personal Allowance (Note 2)	£	£	£	£	£	£	£
(Born after 5 April 1948)	6,475	7,475	8,105	9,440	10,000	10,600	11,000
(Born 6 April 1938–5 April 1948)	9,490	9,940	10,500	10,500	10,500	N/A	11,000
(Born before 6 April 1938)	9,640	10,090	10,660	10,660	10,660	10,660	11,000
Income Limit (65 and over)	22,900	24,000	25,400	—	—	—	
Married Couple's Allowance (Note 3)							
minimum allowance	2,670	2,800	2,960	3,040	3,140	3,220	3,220
(Elder spouse born before 6/4/1935)	N/A	N/A	N/A	—	—	10% relief	
(Elder spouse 75 and over)	6,965	7,295	7,705	7,915	8,165	8,355	8,355
Income Limit (65 and over)	22,900	24,000	25,400	26,100	27,000	27,700	27,700
Blind Person's Allowance (Note 4)	1,890	1,980	2,100	2,160	2,230	2,290	2,290

Notes on tables

1. Lower, basic and higher rates (1973/74 onwards)

From 6th April 1993 dividends are taxed at 20%. From 6th April 1996, income from savings and distributions are also taxed at 20%. From 6th April 1999 dividends only carry a special 10% tax credit with other savings income continuing to be taxed at 20%. Where an individual is not subject to higher rate tax, the tax credit is deemed to satisfy any liability to the basic rate. From April 2010 a rate of Income Tax of 50% will apply to income over £150,000.

2. Personal allowance

For 1990/91 et seq. personal allowance replaced the single person's allowance.

A higher rate of allowance is available where a person is aged 65 or over. Where the individual's total income exceeds an income limit, that higher personal allowance is reduced by one-half of the excess until the allowance is the same as the ordinary personal allowance. From April 2010 the personal allowance will be reduced for incomes over £100,000 tapering down to zero. From 2016/17 onwards, all individuals will be entitled to the same personal allowance, regardless of the individuals' date of birth. This allowance is subject to the £100,000 income limit, which applies regardless of the individual's date of birth. The individual's personal allowance is reduced where their income is above this limit. The allowance is reduced by £1 for every £2 above the limit.

3. Married couple's allowance

This allowance is available from 2000/01 for a claimant who is, at any time in the year of assessment, a married man whose wife is living with him, and where at least one of them was born before 6th April 1935. From December 2005 this allowance may be claimed by registered civil partners if one partner was born before 6 April 1935, in which case it is claimed by the partner with the highest income for the tax year concerned.

Where the husband's (or the higher earner's) total income exceeds the income limit this allowance is reduced by one- half of the excess (less any reduction made in the claimant's personal allowance age increase) until the allowance is reduced to the minimum allowance. Income tax relief on this allowance is givne at 10%, but as a reduction in the claiment's tax liability, not as a reduction in total income.

For 1990/91 to 1999/00 this allowance was also available to claimants under the age of 65. Income tax relief on this allowance was restricted to 20% for 1994/95, 15% for 1995/96 to 1998/99 and 10% for 1999/00.

Where a claimant marries during a tax year, the allowance is reduced by one-twelfth of each fiscal month of the year ending before the date of marriage.

From 1993/94 and subsequent years, a wife may claim half the married couple's allowance or the husband and wife may jointly elect for the whole allowance to be given to the wife.

In the 2009/10 tax year all in the category of elder spouse 75 and over will become 75 and will therefore be entitled to the age 75 and over allowance.

4. Blind person's allowance

A claimant (a single person, or either of two spouses) must be registered as blind, but HMRC will by concession allow the relief in the previous tax year if evidnece of blindness had already been obtained by the edn of that year. If both spouses are blind, the allowance applies to each. The allowance is given in addition to the personal allowance and reduces the taxpayer's total income. .

Children's Tax Credit

Children's Tax Credit was an income tax relief for people with children. It was introduced by the Income and Corporation Taxes Act 1988, s 257AA and began on 6th April 2001. There was an additional tax credit for families with a baby born on or after 6th April 2002 in the tax year of their child's birth but this was stopped from 6 April 2011.

In April 2003 the Children's Tax Credit was replaced by the Child Tax Credit, introduced by the Tax Credits Act 2002, s 1(1). The income limit was reduced from £50,000 to £40,000 from 6 April 2011.

Retirement annuities and personal pension schemes

The provisions under secs. 226–229 of the Income and Corporation Taxes Act 1970 for retirement annuity contracts for the self-employed and those in non-pensionable employment are replaced with effect from 30th June 1988 by personal pension schemes (secs. 18–57 and Sched. 2, as amended by Finance Act 1988, secs. 54 and 55).

Retirement annuity schemes which are contracted before 30th June 1988 will continue to be dealt with under the existing provisions of secs. 620–629 ICTA 1988. The personal pension scheme provisions incorporate many of the features of those existing provisions.

Limits of relief

(a) Retirement annuity contracts

The following table summarises the maximum premium relief available from 1982/83 to 1986/1987.

Year of Birth	Percentage of individual's net relevant earnings
1934 or later	17½%
1916 to 1933	20
1914 or 1915	21
1912 or 1913	24
1910 or 1911	26½%
1908 or 1909	29½%
1907 or earlier	32½%

For 1987/88 and subsequent years the overall limit is 17½% of net relevant earnings increased for older individuals as follows:

Age range at beginning of year of assessment	Percentage
51 to 55	20
56 to 60	22½
61 or more	27½

(b) Personal pension plans

The maximum amount for which relief is available is 17½% of 'net relevant earnings', increased for older individuals as follows:

Age range at beginning of year of assessment	Percentage
36 to 45	20
46 to 50	25
51 to 55	30
56 to 60	35
61 or more	40

The permitted maximum net relevant earnings are as follows:

	£
1988/89	60,000
1989/90	60,000
1990/91	64,800
1991/92	71,400
1992/93	75,000
1993/94	75,000
1994/95	76,800
1995/96	78,600
1996/97	82,200
1997/98	84,000
1998/99	87,600
1999/00	90,600
2000/01	91,800
2001/02	95,400
2002/03	97,200
2003/04	99,000
2004/05	102,000
2005/06	105,600

From April 2006 the pension schemes earnings cap ceases. There will be two controls on an individual's savings:

	Annual Allowance.	Lifetime Allowance
2006/7	215,000	1,500,000
2007/8	225,000	1,600,000
2008/9	235,000	1,650,000
2009/10	255,000	1,750,000
2010/11	255,000	1,800,000
2011/12	50,000	1,800,000*
2012/13	50,000	1,500,000
2013/14	50,000	1,500,000
2014/15	40,000	

* Reduced to £1,500,000 from 6 April 2012.

Capital Gains Tax

Capital gains tax (CGT) was introduced by the Finance Act 1965 and commenced on 6th April of that year. It relates to gains in a year of assessment (*i.e.* a year ending on 5th April) accruing to individuals, personal representatives and trustees. The Capital Gains Tax Act 1979 (CGTA 1979) was re-enacted in the Taxation of Chargeable Gains Act 1992 (TCGA 1992) which contains the main current provisions in consolidated form. There are further provisions in subsequent Finance Acts.

Major changes in the scope of the tax were introduced by the Finance Act 1988. The original base date of 6th April 1965 was replaced by 31st March 1982 subject to the detailed provisions of assets held on 31st March 1982.

From 10th April 1962 to 5th April 1971 certain short-term capital gains were charged to income tax under Sched. D, Case VII. From 6th April 1971, both short- and long-term gains have been chargeable to capital gains tax. Accumulated short-term losses at 5th April 1971 are available thereafter for offset against capital gains generally (TCGA 1992, Sched. 11, para. 12).

Exemptions

The following is an abridged summary of the main exemptions or partial exemptions for capital gains tax purposes.

Private dwelling houses (where sole or main residence), private motor vehicles, savings certificates, charities, patent rights, foreign currency for personal expenditure, certain property transfers, Treasury listed government and public corporation securities (pre 2nd July 1986, exemption only if securities held for more than 12 months), tangible movable assets sold from 1989/90 onwards for £6,000 or less with marginal relief for sale proceeds exceeding £6,000. (From 1982/83 – 1988/89, limit was £3,000.)

Reference should be made to TCGA 1992 and subsequent Finance Acts for more details.

General reliefs

Reliefs are available for such matters as roll-over and hold-over relief for gifts and disposals of certain assets, roll-over relief on reinvestment in shares (entrepreneurial relief), investments in EIS companies/VCTs, etc.

Retirement relief ceased to apply in respect of disposals after 5th April 2003.

Indexation allowance

For disposals after 5th April 1982 (31st March 1982 for companies), the gain arrived at by deducting allowable expenditure from the amount realised or deemed to be realised on the disposal, is termed a "gross gain". From this "gross gain" there is to be deducted an "indexation allowance", which is the aggregate of the "indexed rise" in each item of "relevant allowable expenditure" provided the asset has been held for the "qualifying period". Qualifying period not applicable on disposals after 5th April 1985.

Special provisions apply to the calculation of the allowance in relation to disposals involving assets held on 31st March 1982 where made on or after the "1985 date" or, again, on or after 6th April 1988.

For disposals after 5th April 1985, indexation allowance can be claimed by reference to market value at 31st March 1982.

Reference should be made to Finance Act 1982 as amended by Finance Act 1985 (sec. 68 and Sched. 19) for full details relating to formula for calculating indexation allowance.

For disposals after 30th November 1994, indexation allowance cannot create or augment a capital loss. Transitional relief will be available for indexation losses arising in the period 30th November 1993 to 5th April 1995.

For disposals after 5th April 1998, indexation allowance will be available up to April 1998 but not beyond.

Re-basing to 31st March 1982

General re-basing rule is that on a disposal after 5th April 1988 of an asset held on 31st March 1982, it is to be assumed that the asset was sold on 31st March 1982 by the person making the disposal and immediately acquired by him at its market value on that date. However, if a smaller capital gain or loss would have been made by using the original cost then cost rather than 31st March 1982 value must be used in calculating the gain/loss. It was possible to make an election to have all assets rebased to their 31st March 1982 values. Reference should be made to Finance Act 1988, sec 96(1)(2).

Taper relief

Major changes in the scope of the indexation allowance were introduced by the Finance Act 1998. Companies, which pay corporation tax on chargeable gains, are not affected by these reforms.

For assets disposed of after 5th April 1998 and which were held at that date, the indexation allowance will be available up to April 1998 but not beyond. No indexation allowance will be available on disposals of assets acquired on or after 1st April 1998.

For disposals after 5th April 1998, a chargeable gain will be progressively reduced (tapered) according to the length of time the asset has been held. See the table below.

GAINS ON BUSINESS ASSETS

Number of complete years after 5/4/978 which asset held	Percentage of gain chargeable			Equivalent tax rates for higher rate taxpayer (2000/01 only)
	1989/99 to 1999/00	2000/01 to 2001/02	2002/03	
0	100	100	100	40
1	92.5	87.5	50	35
2	85	75	25	30
3	77.5	50	25	20
4	70	25	25	10
5	62.5	25	25	10
6	55	25	25	10
7	47.5	25	25	10
8	40	25	25	10
9	32.5	25	25	10
10 or more	25	25	25	10

For disposals in 1998/99 and 1999/00 an additional bonus holding year in respect of business assets held at 17th March 1998 was given. This no longer applies for disposals in 2000/01 and subsequent years.

GAINS ON NON-BUSINESS ASSETS

Number of complete years after 5/4/978 which asset held	Percentage of gain chargeable	Equivalent tax rates for higher rate taxpayer
0	100	40
1	100	40
2	100	40
3	95	38
4	90	36
5	85	34
6	80	32
7	75	30
8	70	28
9	65	26
10	60	24

For disposals of non-business assets held at 17th March 1998 an additional bonus year is given.

Reference should be made to the Finance Act 1998, secs. 119–120 for full details.

A consequence of the new taper relief rules is that the previous pooling arrangements will no longer apply to shares and securities. Disposals after 5th April 1998 will be identified with acquisitions in the following order:

—same day acquisitions;

—acquisitions within the following 30 days;

—other acquisitions after 5th April 1998 on a last in/first out basis;

—any shares in the pool at 5th April 1998;

—any shares held at 5th April 1982;

—any shares held at 6th April 1965;

—(if necessary) subsequent acquisitions.

'Bed and breakfasting'

For disposals of shares on or after 17th March 1998, 'bed and breakfasting', i.e. selling shares to realise a gain or loss and then buying them back shortly afterwards, will no longer have the desired effect for tax purposes. Any shares of the same class in the same company sold and repurchased within a 30-day period will instead be matched, so that the shares sold cannot be identified with those already held.

Rates

For 1996/97 and subsequent years capital gains will come within the new self-assessment rules. Tax will be payable by 31st January immediately after the year of assessment to which it relates.

Prior to 1996/97, tax was payable by 1st December, immediately after the year of assessment to which it related (6th July for tax relating to 1979/80 or earlier).

For 1977/78 and earlier years, the total charge was (generally) limited to additional income tax and investment income surcharge payable by an individual on one-half of net capital gains for the year, if under £5,000, or if greater, £2,500 plus the excess over £5,000. Losses could be set against gains. For 1967/71 an individual was exempt if the gains less allowable losses were not more than £50; Capital gains tax was charged on any excess.

For 1977/78 to 1979/80 the rates at which capital gains tax was charged are as follows:

Total net gains for year of assessment	Tax Chargeable
Not exceeding £1,000	Nil
£1,001–£5,000	15% on excess gains over £1,000
£5,001–£9,499	£600 + 50% on excess gains over £5,000
£9,500 or more	all gains at 30%

"Alternative charge" provisions still to apply for 1977/78 if less tax payable than under new provisions. The rates chargeable from 1980/81 to 1987/88 are as follows:

	Total net Gains	Tax chargeable
1980/81 and 1981/82	Not exceeding £3,000	Nil
	Over £3,000	30%
1982/83	Not exceeding £5,000	Nil
	Over £5,000	30%
1983/84	Not exceeding £5,300	Nil
	Over £5,300	30%
1984/85	Not exceeding £5,600	Nil
	Over £5,600	30%
1985/86	Not exceeding £5,900	Nil
	Over 5,900	30%
1986/87	Not exceeding £6,300	Nil
	Over £6,300	30%
1987/88	Not exceeding £6,600	Nil
	Over £6,600	30%

The exemption limits and rates chargeable from 1990/91 onwards are as follows:

Annual exemption limits

	Individuals	Trusts	Chattels
1990/91	£5,000	£2,500	£6,000
1991/92	£5,500	£2,750	£6,000
1992/93	£5,800	£2,900	£6,000
1993/94	£5,800	£2,900	£6,000
1994/95	£5,800	£2,900	£6,000
1995/96	£6,000	£3,000	£6,000
1996/97	£6,300	£3,150	£6,000
1997/98	£6,500	£3,250	£6,000
1998/99	£6,800	£3,400	£6,000
1999/00	£7,100	£3,550	£6,000
2000/01	£7,200	£3,600	£6,000
2001/02	£7,500	£3,750	£6,000
2002/03	£7,700	£3,850	£6,000
2003/04	£7,900	£3,950	£6,000
2004/05	£8,200	£4,100	£6,000
2005/06	£8,500	£4,250	£6,000
2006/07	£8,800	£4,400	£6,000
2007/08	£9,200	£4,600	£6,000
2008/09	£9,600	£4,800	£6,000
2009/10	£10,100	£5,050	£6,000
2010/11	£10,100	£5,050	£6,000
2011/12	£10,600	£5,300	£6,000
2012/13	£10,600	£5,300	£6,000
2013/14	£10,900	£5,450	£6,000
2014/15	£11,000	£5,500	£6,000
2015/16	£11,100	£5,550	£6,000
2016/17	£11,000	£5,500	£6,000

Rates of Tax

	Lower rate	Basic rate	Higher rate

(a)Individuals: Until 1991/92 the rate of capital gains tax was equivalent to the basic rate of income tax for the fiscal year. If income tax is chargeable at the higher rate in respect of any part of an individual's income for a year of assessment, the rate of capital gains tax is equivalent to the higher rate.

For 1992/93 to 1998/99, where no income tax is chargeable at the basic rate in respect of an individual's income but the amount on which he is chargeable to capital gains tax exceeds the unused part of his lower rate band, the rate of capital gains tax on that part of the amount chargeable to capital gains tax equal to the unused part of the lower rate band is equivalent to the lower rate. If, in the same circumstances, there is no such excess, the rate of capital gains tax equivalent to the lower rate applies to all the amount chargeable to capital gains tax.

From 1999/00 individuals chargeable at lower and basic rate tax for income tax purposes will be subject to capital gains tax at 20%. The rate for higher rate taxpayers will continue to be equivalent to the higher rate.

	Lower rate	Basic rate	Higher rate
1988/89 to 1991/92		25%	40%
1992/93	20%	25%	40%
1993/94	20%	25%	40%
1994/95	20%	25%	40%
1995/96	20%	25%	40%
1996/97	20%	24%	40%
1997/98	20%	23%	40%
1998/99	20%	23%	40%
1999/00	20%	20%	40%
2000/01	10%	20%	40%
2001/02	10%	20%	40%
2002/03	10%	20%	40%
2003/04	10%	20%	40%
2004/05	10%	20%	40%
2005/06	10%	20%	40%
2006/07	10%	20%	40%
2007/08	10%	20%	40%

(b) Trusts in general

1988/89 to 1995/96	25%		
1996/97	24%		
1997/98	23%		
1998/99 onwards	34%		

(c) Accumulation and discretionary trusts

1988/89 to 1995/96	35%		
1996/97 onwards	34%		

(d) Chattels: If the consideration exceeds the annual exemption figure, the chargeable gain is limited to five-thirds of the excess.

Corporation Tax

Corporation tax takes the place of income tax and profits tax for companies (and other corporate bodies and unincorporated associations) and operates generally as from 1966/67. Liability will normally first arise on profits and capital gains in the business year ending in the tax year 1965/66 and not by reference to the profits of the previous year.

Profits are generally to be calculated in accordance with income tax principles and include capital gains (less losses), interest and other charges on incomes as paid under deduction of income tax, which is then accounted for. Income tax was also deductible from dividends distributed up to 1972/73 and was paid over by the company.

Partnerships are still liable for income tax. The tax is not charged on the partnership, but on the individual partners, taking into account their respective profit shares.

Corporation tax is now generally payable within nine months from the end of the accounting period, although companies which make large profits are now required to pay in instalments.

The rate of tax was 40% for financial years 1964–67, $42^{1}/_{2}$% for 1967/68, 45% for 1968/70, 40% for 1970/73.

For the financial years 1973 to 1978 inclusive, the rate was increased to 52% with a small companies' rate of 42%. For the financial years 1979 to 1981, the full rate was retained at 52%, but the small companies' rate was reduced to 40%. For the financial year 1982 the full rate was 52%, and the small companies' rate 38%. The rates for the financial years 1983 to 1999 are as follows:

Financial year	Full rate	Small Companies' rate
1984	45%	30%
1985	40%	30%
1986	35%	29%
1987	35%	27%
1988	35%	25%
1989	35%	25%
1990	34%	25%
1991	33%	25%
1992	33%	25%
1993	33%	25%
1994	33%	25%
1995	33%	25%
1996	33%	24%
1997	31%	21%
1998	31%	21%
1999	30%	20%

From the financial year 2000 onwards a new starting rate of 10% was introduced as follows:

Financial year	Full rate	Small Companies' rate	Starting rate
2000	30%	20%	10%
2001	30%	20%	10%
2002	30%	20%	10%

However, from the financial year 2003 onwards, the starting rate was reduced to nil. For the financial year 2004, however, there have been changes. The nil rate still applies, but for distributions on or after 1 April 2004, a minimum rate of 19% applies where a company whose profits are below the threshold for the small companies' rate distributes profits to a non-company shareholder.

Marginal relief — starting rate

The upper and lower limits are as follows:

Financial year	Upper limit	Lower limit	Marginal fraction
2000	£50,000	£10,000	1/40
2001	50,000	10,000	1/40
2002	50,000	10,000	19/400
2003	50,000	10,000	19/400
2004	50,000	10,000	19/400
2005	50,000	10,000	19/400
2006	50,000	10,000	19/400

Marginal relief

The upper and lower limits are as follows:

Financial year	Upper limit	Lower limit	Standard fraction
1975	£50,000	£30,000	3/20
1976	65,000	40,000	4/25
1977	85,000	50,000	1/7
1978	100,000	60,000	3/20
1979	130,000	70,000	7/50
1980	200,000	80,000	2/25
1981	225,000	90,000	2/25
1982	500,000	100,000	7/200
1983	500,000	100,000	1/20
1984	500,000	100,000	3/80
1985	500,000	100,000	1/40
1986	500,000	100,000	3/200
1987	500,000	100,000	1/50
1988	500,000	100,000	1/40
1989	750,000	150,000	1/40
1990	1,000,000	200,000	9/400
1991	1,250,000	250,000	1/50
1992	1,250,000	250,000	1/50
1993	1,250,000	250,000	1/50
1994	1,500,000	300,000	1/50
1995	1,500,000	300,000	1/50
1996	1,500,000	300,000	9/400
1997	1,500,000	300,000	1/40
1998	1,500,000	300,000	1/40
1999	1,500,000	300,000	1/40
2000	1,500,000	300,000	1/40
2001	1,500,000	300,000	1/40
2002	1,500,000	300,000	11/400
2003	1,500,000	300,000	11/400
2004	1,500,000	300,000	11/400
2005	1,500,000	300,000	11/400
2006	1,500.000	300,000	11/400
2007	1,500.000	300,000	11/400
2008	1,500.000	300,000	1/400
2009	1,500,000	300,000	1/400
2010	1,500,000	300,000	1/400
2011	1,500,000	300,000	3/200
2012	1,500,000	300,000	1/100
2013	1,500,000	300,000	3/400
2014	1,500,000	300,000	1/400
2015	1,500,000	300,000	N/A
2016	1,500,000	300,000	N/A

Sec. 74 Finance Act 1987 enacts the reform of corporation tax on chargeable gains. Its effect is to remove the distinction hitherto made between income and capital profits.

Prior to 17th March 1987, companies' capital profits were taxed at 30%. From this date onwards companies' chargeable gains are included in full in taxable profits.

Advance corporation tax (ACT) was payable when dividends or distributions were made. The following is a summary of the ACT rates:

	Rates
1973/74	3/7ths
1974/75	33/67ths
1975/76	35/65ths
1967/77	35/65ths
1977/78	34/66ths
1978/79	33/67ths
1979/80	3/7ths
1980/81	3/7ths
1981/82	3/7ths
1982/83	3/7ths
1983/84	3/7ths
1984/85	3/7ths
1985/86	3/7ths
1986/87	29/71sts
1987/88	27/73rds
1988/89	1/3rd
1989/90	1/3rd
1990/91	1/3rd
1991/92	1/3rd
1992/93	1/3rd
1993/94	9/31sts
1994/95	1/4
1995/96	1/4
1996/97	1/4
1997/98	1/4
1998/99	1/4

Advance corporation tax is set against the company's total corporation tax liability. No income tax is deducted from dividends.

Advance corporation tax payments are abolished from 6th April 1999.

Inheritance Tax

Cumulative Chargeable Transfers (gross) £	Lifetime rate of tax %	Cumulative tax £	Death rate of tax %	Cumulative tax £
Commencing 17th March 1986				
Nil–£71,000	Nil	Nil	Nil	Nil
£71,001–£95,000	15	3,600	30	7,200
£95,001–£129,000	17½	9,550	35	19,100
£129,001–£164,000	20	16,550	40	33,100
£164,001–£206,000	22½	26,000	45	52,000
£206,001–£257,000	25	38,750	50	77,500
£257,001–£317,000	27½	55,250	55	110,500
Over £317,000	30		60	
After 17th March 1987				
Nil–£90,000	Nil	Nil	Nil	Nil
£90,001–£140,000	15	7,500	30	15,000
£140,001–£220,000	20	23,500	40	47,000
£220,001–£330,000	25	51,000	50	102,000
Over £330,000	30		60	

Lifetime rates do not apply to gifts between individuals

After 14th March 1988				
Nil £110,000	Nil		Nil	
Over £110,000	20		40	
After 5th April 1989				
Nil–£118,000	Nil		Nil	
Over £118,000	20		40	
After 5th April 1990				
Nil–£128,000	Nil		Nil	
Over £128,000	20		40	
After 5th April 1991				
Nil–£140,000	Nil		Nil	
Over £140,000	20		40	
After 9th March 1992				
Nil–£150,000	Nil		Nil	
Over £150,000	20		40	
After 5th April 1995				
Nil—£154,000	Nil		Nil	
Over £154,000	20		40	
After 5th April 1996				
Nil–£200,000	Nil		Nil	
Over £200,000	20		40	
After 5th April 1997				
Nil–£215,000	Nil		Nil	
Over £215,000	20		40	

Cumulative Chargeable Transfers (gross) £	Lifetime rate of tax %	Cumulative tax £	Death rate of tax %	Cumulative tax £
After 5th April 1998				
Nil–£223,000	Nil		Nil	
Over £223,000	20		40	
After 5th April 1999				
Nil–£231,000	Nil		Nil	
Over £231,000	20		40	
After 5th April 2000				
Nil–£234,000	Nil		Nil	
Over £234,000	20		40	
After 5th April 2001				
Nil–£242,000	Nil		Nil	
Over £242,000	20		40	
After 5th April 2002				
Nil–£250,000	Nil		Nil	
Over £250,000	20		40	
After 5th April 2003				
Nil–£250,000	Nil		Nil	
Over £250,000	20		40	
After 5th April 2004				
Nil–£263,000	Nil		Nil	
Over £263,000	20		40	
After 5th April 2005				
Nil–£275,000	Nil		Nil	
Over £275,000	20		40	
After 5th April 2006				
Nil–£285,000	Nil		Nil	
Over £285,000	20		40	
After 6th April 2007				
Nil–£300,000	Nil		Nil	
Over £300,000	20		40	
After 6th April 2008				
Nil–£312,000	Nil		Nil	
Over £312,000	20		40	
After 6th April 2009				
Nil–£325,000	Nil		Nil	
Over £325,000	20		40	
After 6th April 2010				
Nil–£325,000	Nil		Nil	
Over £325,000	20		40	
After 6th April 2011				
Nil–£325,000	Nil		Nil	
Over £325,000	20		40	
*After 6th April 2012				
Nil–£325,000	Nil		Nil	
Over £325,000	20		40	
After 6th April 2013				
Nil–£325,000	Nil		Nil	
Over £325,000	20		40	
After 6th April 2014				
Nil–£325,000	Nil		Nil	
Over £325,000	20		40	

After 6th April 2015		
Nil–£325,000	Nil	Nil
Over £325,000	20	40
After 6th April 2016		
Nil–325,000	Nil	Nil
Over 325,000	20	40

* From 6th April 2012 people who leave 10% or more of their net estate to charity can choose to pay a reduced rate of Inheritance Tax of 36%.

Tapering relief

The value of the estate on death is taxed as the top slice of cumulative transfers in the seven years before death. Transfers on or within seven years of death are taxed on their value at the date of the gift on the death rate scale, but using the scale in force at the date of death, subject to the following taper:

No of years between gift and death	Percentage of full charge at death rates
0–3	100
3–4	80
4–5	60
5–6	40
6–7	20

List of Principal Statutory Instruments Included

UPDATED CONTENT FOR THE SCOTTISH LAW DIRECTORY 2016

Geographical List of Law Firms

Aberdeen

Ledingham Chalmers LLP
Johnstone House, 52-54 Rose Street
Aberdeen AB10 1HA
Tel: 01224 408408
LP: 39 ABERDEEN 1
Email: mail@ledinghamchalmers.com
Web: www.ledinghamchalmers.com
Categories of Work
Adjudication
Adoption
Advice the Elderly & Powers of Attorney
Agriculture and estates
Agriculture and Estates (for the individual)
Agriculture, crofting and fishing
Competition
Construction
Debt (for the individual)
Disability
Discrimination
Employment
Employment Law
Environment (property)
EU / International
Family and Divorce
Health and Safety
Housing
Insolvency & Corporate Recovery
Insurance
Insurance (finance)
IT and Intellectual Property
Landlord & Tenant
Liquor Licensing
Media and entertainment
Medical Negligence – Claimant
Medical Negligence – Defender
Mergers and Acquisitions
Mining
Oil & Gas
Pensions (finance)
Personal Injury
Personal Injury – Defender
Planning
Planning (property)
Power and utilities
Property Litigation
Public Sector (corporate & commercial)
Residential Property
Road Traffic
Shipping
SME Business Advice
Social Housing

Software Licensing
Wills, executives and trusts
Alternative dispute resolution
Alternative investment market
Charities
Children
Contract & property disputes
Copyright, trademarks and design
Debt
Debt recovery, insolvency, bankruptcy
Environment
Environment (Business Premises)
Pensions (Company)
Planning (Business Premises)
Public sector
Unit Trusts, OEICs and investment trusts

Partners
Allan Collie
Graham William James Cooper
Michael Steven Cunningham
Tom Davidson
Graeme Mark Kynoch Edward
Malcolm Gregor Ferguson
Rodney Alphonsious Magil Hutchison
Alasdair Eoin MacLure
Marion Nancy McDonald
Alan Johnston Michie
Jody Bruce Mitchell
John Gillan Mitchell
Hazel Marion Moir
Stephen James Morrice
Peter Murray
Craig Andrew Pike
Nicola Wendy Reid
Hugh Stuart Robertson
David Stuart Scott
Daniel Stewart
Sarah Duncan Stuart
Timothy Robert Thomas
Douglas Morgan Watson
Jennifer Evelyn Young

Consultants
Lynne Burke
Carol Ann Cooper
Phyllis Garden
Shona Mhairi Hamilton
Malcolm Donald Laing
Eunice Margaret McConnach
Ronald Stuart Wadsworth

Associates
Erica Buchan
Catherine Anne Bury
Lucy Ann Cran
Lesley Ethel Currie
Nicola Jo Liddle
Sarah Louise Londragan
Stephen Charles McLaren
Veli-Matti Antinpoika Raikkonen
Hugh Kelvin Murray Richmond
Louise Simpson
Rebecca Clare Walker

Employees
Fraser Hugh Mackay
Katie Diane Spearman
Sally Ann Bowman
Jennifer Cham
Craig Stanley Falconer
Joanna Linda Lang
Raiya Law
Rachael Margaret Mackay
Keri Lyn Morrison
Kimberley Joan Smart
David Maughan Smith
Gillian Elizabeth Smith
Emma Margaret Suslak
Craig James Wilson

Edinburgh

M.J. Brown, Son & Co
Deanbank Lodge
10 Dean Bank Lane
Edinburgh EH3 5BS
Tel: 0131 3321200
Fax: 0131 3324600
DX: ED122 EDINBURGH
Email: jmat985725@aol.com
Partner
Joan Frances Matthew

Ledingham Chalmers LLP
3rd Floor, 68-70 George Street
Edinburgh EH2 2LR
Tel: 0131 2001000
LP: 98 EDINBURGH 2
Email: mail@ledinghamchalmers.com
Web: www.ledinghamchalmers.com
Categories of Work
Adjudication
Agriculture and estates
Agriculture and Estates (for the individual)
Competition
Construction
Debt (for the individual)
EU / International
Health and Safety
Insolvency & Corporate Recovery
Insurance (finance)
IT and Intellectual Property
Liquor Licensing
Media and entertainment
Medical Negligence – Claimant
Medical Negligence – Defender
Mergers and Acquisitions
Mining
Pensions (finance)
Personal Injury – Defender
Power and utilities
Property Litigation
Road Traffic
Shipping
SME Business Advice

Wills, executries and trusts
Agriculture, crofting and fishing
Alternative dispute resolution
Charities
Contract & property disputes
Copyright, trademarks and design
Debt
Debt recovery, insolvency, bankruptcy
Employment
Environment
Insurance
Medical negligence – defender
Pensions (Company)
Planning
Unit Trusts, OEICs and investment trusts
Partners
Neil Robert Anderson
John Alexander Gunn Chalmers
Sarah Elizabeth Morris
Consultants
John Edmund Gordon Hendry
David Kemlo Laing
Associates
Ian Brown Gilkison Scott
Anna Mhairi Watt
Employees
Megan Anne Georgeson
Anna Lindsay MacLeod
Marie Patricia Cartney
Amy Dawn McMillan

Urquharts
16 Heriot Row
Edinburgh EH3 6HR
Tel: 0131 5562896
Fax: 0131 5560046
LP: 29 EDINBURGH 2
DX: ED 206 EDINBURGH
E-mail: enquiries@urquharts.co.uk
Web: www.urquharts.co.uk
Categories of Work
Agriculture and estates
Advice for the elderly and powers of attorney
Contract and property disputes
Discrimination
Family and Divorce
Housing
Insolvency & Corporate Recovery
Insurance
Landlord & Tenant
Liquor Licensing
Mergers and Acquisitions
Personal Injury
Personal Injury – Defender
Personal Tax
Planning
Professional Negligence
Property Law and Litigation
Residential Property
SME Business Advice
Wills, executries and trusts

Alternative dispute resolution
Charities
Children
Contract & property disputes
Debt recovery, insolvency, bankruptcy
Partners
James Stevenson Baird
Gillian Stewart Black
Stephen Martin Blane
Roderick Macduff Urquhart
Associates
Gillian Fiona Andrew
David Alexander Sangster
Stephen William Webster
Employees
Sharon Gordon

Giffnock

Campbell Riddell Breeze Paterson LLP
229 Fenwick Road
Giffnock G46 6JQ
Tel: 0141 6387405
Fax: 0141 6382512
DX: 501607 GIFFNOCK
Email: rstewart@crbp.co.uk
Email: law@crbp.co.uk
Web: www.crbpsolicitorsglasgow.co.uk
Categories of Work
Commercial Property
Construction
Landlord & Tenant
Mergers & Acquisitions
Personal Tax
Residential Property
Advice the Elderly & Powers of Attorney

Glasgow

Campbell Riddell Breeze Paterson LLP
Floor 7, 80 St. Vincent Street
Glasgow G2 5UB
Tel: 0141 2042040
DX: GW18 GLASGOW
Email: law@crbp.co.uk
Web: www.crbpsolicitorsglasgow.co.uk
Categories of Work
Commercial Property
Construction
Landlord & Tenant
Mergers & Acquisitions
Personal Tax
Residential Property
Advice the Elderly & Powers of Attorney
Partners
John Harris Muir
Robert Crombie Stewart
Associate
Kenneth John Clunie Hay

Macnairs & Wilson Ltd
662 Alexandra Parade
Glasgow G31 3BU
Tel: 0141 5518185
Fax: 0141 5546235
LP: 1 ALEXANDRA PARADE
Email: glasgow@macnairswilson.co.uk
Directors
Lesley Catherine Mathieson
Employees
Louise Morgan Jones

Grangemouth

RGM Solicitors Ltd
9-11 La Porte Precinct
Grangemouth FK3 8AZ
Tel: 01324 482197
LP: 1 GRANGEMOUTH
Email: legal@rgmsolicitors.co.uk
Web: www.rgmsolicitors.co.uk
Categories of Work
Advice the Elderly & Powers of Attorney
Agriculture and Estates (for the individual)
Agriculture, crofting and fishing
Disability
Discrimination
Employment
Employment Law
Family and Divorce
Health and Safety
Housing
Human Rights
Insolvency & Corporate Recovery
Insurance
Insurance (finance)
Landlord & Tenant
Legal Aid – Civil
Liquor Licensing
Mental Health
Pensions (finance)
Personal Injury
Personal Injury – Defender
Planning
Property Litigation
Public Sector (corporate & commercial)
Residential Property
Road Traffic
SME Business Advice
Unit Trusts, OEICs and investment trusts
Wills, executries and trusts
Adoption
Agriculture and estates
Alternative dispute resolution
Alternative investment market
Children
Contract & property disputes
Debt recovery, insolvency, bankruptcy
Pensions (Company)
Public sector

Director
Samuel Harvey Waddell (Email: Harvey@rgmsolicitors.co.uk)
Employee
Leo Adair McGarvey

Inverness

Ledingham Chalmers LLP
Kintail House, Beechwood Business Park,
Inverness IV2 3BW
Tel: 01463 667400
LP: 1 INVERNESS 2
E-mail: mail@ledinghamchalmers.com
Web: www.ledinghamchalmers.com
Categories of Work
Adjudication
Agriculture and estates
Agriculture and Estates (for the individual)
Competition
Construction
Debt (for the individual)
Disability
Discrimination
Employment Law
Environment (property)
EU / International
Insolvency & Corporate Recovery
IT and Intellectual Property
Liquor Licensing
Mergers and Acquisitions
Mining
Oil & Gas
Planning (property)
Power and utilities
Property Litigation
Public Sector (corporate & commercial)
Road Traffic
Shipping
SME Business Advice
Software Licensing
Wills, executries and trusts
Agriculture, crofting and fishing
Alternative dispute resolution
Alternative investment market
Charities
Contract & property disputes
Copyright, trademarks and design
Debt
Employment
Environment
Environment (Business Premises)
Planning
Planning (Business Premises)
Public sector
Partners
Fiona Elizabeth Neilson
John Douglas Smart
William Kirkwood Mackenzie Tudhope
Associates
Karen Myra Shaw Cameron
Roderick Stewart Cormack

Victoria Jane Leslie
Sine MacConnell Mackay
Elisa Margaret Miller
Alison Jane Reid
Employees
Andrew Stott

Craig Wood Solicitors Ltd
16 Union Street
Inverness IV1 1PL
Tel: 01463 225544
LP: 22 INVERNESS 1
E-mail: nicola@craigwood.co.uk
Categories of Work
Criminal Legal Aid
Criminal Court Work
Directors
Ruaridh Howard Mackinnon Gowans
Shahid Latif
John Malcolm MacColl
Employee
Clare Frances Russell

Linlithgow

RGM Solicitors Ltd
19/21 High Street
Linlithgow EH49 7AB
Tel: 01506 847070
Fax: 01506 847090
LP: 3 LINLITHGOW
DX: 540886 LINLITHGOW
Email: linlithgow@rgmsolicitors.co.uk
Web: www.rgmsolicitors.co.uk
Categories of Work
Adoption
Alternative investment market
Children
Contract & property disputes
Employment
Insurance
Public sector
Unit Trusts, OEICs and investment trusts
Wills, executries and trusts
Director
Robert Gordon Marshall (Email: linlithgow@rgmsolicitors.co.uk)

Milngavie

Campbell Riddell Breeze Paterson LLP
21 Park Road
Milngavie G62 6PJ
Tel: 0141 9565454
LP: 1 MILNGAVIE
DX: 581600 MILNGAVIE
Email: law@crbp.co.uk
Web: www.crbpsolicitorsglasgow.co.uk
Categories of Work
Commercial Property
Construction
Landlord & Tenant

Mergers & Acquisitions
Personal Tax
Residential Property
Advice the Elderly & Powers of Attorney
Partners
Richard Leggett

Paisley

Macnairs & Wilson Ltd
9-11 New Street
Paisley PA1 1XU
Tel: 0141 8875181
Fax: 0141 8872775
LP: 1 PAISLEY
Email: paisley@macnairswilson.co.uk
Directors
Douglas Mitchell
Stuart Fraser Wilson
Associates
Christine Anne Hirst

Stirling

Ledingham Chalmers LLP
Suite A3, Stirling Agricultural Centre
Stirling FK9 4RN
Tel: 01786 478100
Categories of Work
Adjudication
Adoption
Advice the Elderly & Powers of Attorney
Agriculture and estates
Agriculture and Estates (for the individual)
Agriculture, crofting and fishing
Competition
Construction
Debt (for the individual)
Disability
Discrimination
Employment
Employment Law
Environment (property)
EU / International
Family and Divorce
Health and Safety
Housing
Insolvency & Corporate Recovery
Insurance
Insurance (finance)
IT and Intellectual Property
Landlord & Tenant
Liquor Licensing
Media and entertainment
Medical Negligence – Claimant
Medical Negligence – Defender
Mergers and Acquisitions
Mining
Oil & Gas
Pensions (finance)
Personal Injury

Personal Injury – Defender
Planning
Planning (property)
Power and utilities
Property Litigation
Public Sector (corporate & commercial)
Residential Property
Road Traffic
Shipping
SME Business Advice
Social Housing
Software Licensing
Wills, executries and trusts
Partners
James Cunison Drysdale
Associates
Diana Agnes Stewart Thurston Smith
Employees
Stephen Higgins
Linda Jane Aird Tinson